Germany since 1945

WHEN THE WALL CAME DOWN

REACTIONS TO GERMAN UNIFICATION

EDITED BY

HAROLD JAMES
AND
MARLA STONE

ROUTLEDGE NEW YORK / LONDON

Published in 1992 by

Routledge
An imprint of Routledge, Chapman and Hall, Inc.
29 West 35 Street
New York, NY 10001

Published in Great Britain by

Routledge
11 New Fetter Lane
London EC4P 4EE

Library of Congress Cataloging in Publication Data

When the Wall came down : reactions to German unification / edited by Harold James
and Marla Stone.
    p.   cm.
    Includes bibliographical references and index.
    ISBN 0-415-90589-3 — ISBN 0-415-90590-7 (pbk.)
    1. Germany—Politics and government—1945–1990. 2. German reunification
question (1945–1990). 3. Germany—Politics and government—1990–
I. James, Harold. II. Stone, Marla, 1960–
DD257.25.W46 1992
943.087—dc20   92-2393
                                                                                CIP

British Library Cataloguing in Publication also available.

Contents

West Germany

East Germany

United States

United Kingdom

France

Italy

Israel

Japan

Preface

This book originated in a course on recent German history taught in Princeton University. The aim was to provide a wide range of articles from differing perspectives that placed in a long-range historical context the dramatic events of 1989–90 in Germany, culminating in the unification of the country. Responses to German events were shaped to a great extent by historical memories of the political success of the Federal Republic, but also of the tragedies imposed on the world by some Germans in the past.

Many issues examined in this collection are controversial, and may well continue to be so: modern Germany's relationship with her past, the role of German intellectuals in public life, the prospects for peace and stability in Central Europe, the future of the nation-state, the road to European integration. One of the issues at stake—the existence, practicality, and desirability of alternatives to market societies—still seems contentious to the editors (who have differing views on the subject).

The editors would like to thank the following for assistance with the selection and translation of material: Eva Giloi, Stephen Kotkin, Marzenna Kowalik-James, Louis Miller, Gregory Murphy, Dror Wahrman, and the German Information Service, New York.

H.J. and M.S.
Princeton, N.J., November 1991

Chronology of Events

1989

February–April   In Poland, discussions take place between Solidarity leaders and the Communist government, leading to an agreement on free elections.

May   Fall of the "Iron Curtain" between Austria and Hungary, as Hungary begins to dismantle the fences along its border.

June 4   Solidarity wins in the Polish parliamentary elections.

August 24   Tadeusz Mazowiecki of Solidarity is elected prime minister of Poland.

August–September   East Germans start emigrating to West Germany through Hungary. Between August and early October 1989, thirty thousand East Germans leave the GDR. The flood of refugees grows toward the end of the summer, with many taking exile in the West German embassies in Prague and Warsaw.

September 4   Police in Leipzig, East Germany's second largest city, violently disperse several hundred church and civil rights activists. These events were repeated on September 11 and 18.

September 10   Hungary officially opens its frontier with Austria. It also announces the suspension of a 1969 bilateral agreement with East Germany under which citizens without valid travel documents were sent back.

September 10   Founding of the New Forum reform movement in East Germany. Soon after, New Forum applies for official permission to establish local organizations in eleven of East Germany's fifteen administrative districts, in the hopes of creating a national organization. Permission was refused on September 21.

September 19   In Hungary the ruling Communist party and the opposition agree on constitutional changes, the creation of a multiparty system, and free elections to be held in 1990.

September 30   West German Foreign Minister Hans-Dietrich Genscher allows East German citizens who have taken refuge in the West German embassy in Prague to enter West Germany.

October 7 Fortieth anniversary of the founding of the GDR. Soviet President Mikhail Gorbachev visits and asserts that "matters affecting the GDR are decided not in Moscow but in Berlin." Members of the opposition, in particular New Forum, organize mass demonstrations against the government that disrupt official celebrations. Demonstrations take place in East Berlin, Dresden, and Leipzig, in addition to other smaller cities. The East German police use violence to break up the demonstrations.

October 8 The East German Social Democratic party is founded, the first such party since 1946.

October 9 The "Monday Demonstrations" begin in Leipzig, with 100,000 people in attendance.

Similar marches with thousands participating were held in Dresden, Magdeburg, Plauen, Halle, and other towns.

October 18 In the face of a growing crisis both within the nation and the ruling SED (Socialist Unity Party), General Secretary Erich Honecker resigns from office after eighteen years. He is replaced by Egon Krenz who begins to introduce reforms, while asserting the inviolability of the GDR's socialism. In an address on national television, the new general secretary declares that "we have to recognize the sign of the times and react accordingly, otherwise life will punish us."

October 27 The government of the GDR announces an amnesty for those attempting to leave the country illegally and for those arrested during the demonstrations prior to October 27.

October 31–November 4 Mass demonstration in Dresden and Leipzig. In Leipzig, 300,000 people demonstrate, with 80,000 in Schwerin and 50,000 in Magdeburg. Participants call for economic reform, freedom of the press, and a multiparty system. Krenz announces the resignations of five members of the Politburo.

November 4 A demonstration in East Berlin draws one million people, the largest gathering in the history of the GDR. The crowd is addressed by the SED, as well as by opposition leaders.

November 7 Government of the GDR resigns. At the start of a special three-day session of the SED central committee, the standing Politburo resigns and a new one is elected.

November 8 The opposition group New Forum is made legal.

November 9 The Berlin Wall, which had divided the city since 1961, is opened. Krenz announces that in the future East Germans can travel freely abroad. East German frontiers are opened to the West and thousands of East Germans cross over. The SED central committee meeting's closing statement declares: "A revolutionary movement has set in motion a process of serious upheaval. . . . The aim is to imbue socialism in the GDR with new dynamism through more democracy." The meeting approved a series of reforms, in an effort to end the SED power monopoly.

November 10–11   More than 200,000 East Germans cross through the Berlin Wall to visit West Berlin. West German Chancellor Helmut Kohl addresses a large crowd at the Schoeneberg City Hall in West Berlin.

November 13   Hans Modrow (SED) is elected new president of the GDR. Honecker and twenty-six other discredited SED members are expelled from the East German *Volkskammer*, which holds its first extraordinary session and uses the secret ballot for the first time. West Berlin Mayor Walter Momper meets his East Berlin counterpart, Eduard Krack, at a break in the Wall on the Potsdamerplatz.

November 17–23   In Czechoslovakia, the democratic movement under the leadership of Vaclav Havel's Civic Forum removes the ruling Communist party from power.

November 23   By this date, the GDR has issued over eleven million visas for its citizens wishing to visit West Germany.

November 24   Green party and a liberal Free Democratic party are founded in the GDR.

November 28   West German Chancellor Helmut Kohl delivers his Ten-Point Program for the reunification of Germany. In his speech to the West German *Bundestag*, Kohl laid out a plan for a German confederation that would lead to eventual unification. On the same day, East German artists and intellectuals, including Krenz, sign a petition entitled "For Our Country," which declared: "We still have a chance . . . to develop a socialist alternative to the Federal Republic."

December 1   The East German People's Chamber removes the SED's power monopoly from the constitution. Investigations into the SED's abuses of power and corruption begin. At the still frequent protest demonstrations, banners calling for reunification are seen among those demanding political and economic reform.

December 6   SED General Secretary Egon Krenz resigns from government and party offices and is replaced by Gregor Gysi.

December 7   The Round Table talks between the East German government and opposition begin, and elections are announced.

December 8–9   At the European Council in Strasbourg, European representatives declare that German reunification must be within the context of European integration.

December 12   U.S. Secretary of State James Baker meets with Kohl and Genscher in West Berlin; Baker supports German unity, but stresses that it should be a gradual process.

December 17   The SED changes its name from Socialist Unity party to the Party of Democratic Socialism (PDS).

December 19–20   West German Chancellor Helmut Kohl meets with East German Prime Minister Hans Modrow in Dresden to discuss relations between the two states. In Brussels, Soviet Foreign Minister Eduard Shevardnadze poses seven questions about a future united Germany on issues from national security to military alliances.

December 20–25   Romanian revolution, with the execution of President Ceausescu on December 26.

December 21   President Mitterrand of France visits East Germany and declares that France will not stand in the way of a united Germany.

December 22   The Brandenburg Gate, the symbol of the division of the nation and the city, is officially opened in the presence of heads of both German states.

December 29   In Czechoslovakia, Vaclav Havel is elected president.

December 31   New Year's Eve celebrations in Berlin. In East Germany, crowds invade the State Security headquarters.

1990

January 31   Soviet President Gorbachev, meeting with Hans Modrow, acknowledges that pressure is building for German reunification.

February 1   East German Prime Minister Hans Modrow presents a plan for the reunification of Germany, which he says should be militarily neutral.

February 8   West German government establishes "German Unity" committee, charged with creating blueprint for monetary union to rescue East Germany from economic disaster.

February 10   West German Chancellor Kohl and Foreign Minister Genscher meet with President Gorbachev, who offers assurances on German reunification.

February 14   The foreign ministers of the four major World War II Allies— United States, Soviet Union, France, and Great Britain—and of the two German states agree to begin formal talks on German reunification (the Two Plus Four talks).

February 24–25 Chancellor Kohl meets with President Bush at Camp David to discuss the security alliance between Europe and North America and the centrality of this issue to German reunification.

March 5 The East German Round Table and *Volkskammer* approve a social charter for the GDR.

March 14 The first meeting of the Two Plus Four talks is held in Bonn, involving East and West German officials and representatives of the Soviet Union, France, Great Britain, and the United States.

March 18 Elections in the GDR. The "Alliance for Germany" coalition, formed by the East German Christian Democrats, wins with 48.12 percent of the vote. The Social Democratic party (SPD) polled 21.8 percent, and the former ruling party (PDS) polled 16.4 percent. The "Alliance for Germany" backed by West German Chancellor Kohl, advocated rapid monetary union, to be followed shortly by political reunification under Article 23 of the West German constitution. Sabine Bergmann-Pohl is elected speaker of the parliament and becomes acting head of state for the GDR.

March 25–April 8 In Hungary, national elections and runoff elections for parliament result in a victory for the United Democratic Front.

April 12 The "Grand Coalition" government takes office in the GDR, consisting of the "Alliance for Germany" parties (the CDU, the DSU, and Democratic Awakening), the SPD, and the League of Free Democrats. Lothar de Maiziere (CDU) is prime minister. This government agrees to a swift and responsible unification with the Federal Republic under Article 23 of the West German Basic Law.

April 24 Chancellor Kohl and Prime Minister Maiziere agree on the date of July 1, 1990, for merging the economies of the two German states. Formal negotiations on the terms of reunification are begun.

May 5 The foreign ministers of East and West Germany and of the four major victorious allied powers of World War II meet in Bonn for the first meeting at this level in the Two Plus Four discussions on the security implications of German reunification.

May 6 Local elections in the GDR; the CDU won 34.4 percent of the vote; the SPD 21.3 percent; the PDS 14.6 percent; the League of Free Democrats 6.7 percent.

May 14, 18, 28 Chancellor Kohl and Prime Minister de Maiziere hold official talks.

May 17 During Kohl's visit to the United States, President Bush gives unqualified support to a unified Germany.

May 18 The West and East German finance ministers sign a treaty on "the creation of a monetary, economic, and social union" between the two countries.

May 24   In Hungary, Josef Antall of the United Democratic Front becomes prime minister.

June 8–9   Elections in Czechoslovakia bring Civic Forum into power.

June 21   The West German *Bundestag* and the East German *Volkskammer* approve the state treaty on economic and monetary union.

June 22   The Two Plus Four talks hold a second round of ministerial-level discussions; the main topic was the status of a future united Germany, especially regarding defense alliances.

July 1   The West German mark becomes the legal currency for all of German territory.

August 23   After three weeks of heated debate, the East German parliament accepts October 3, 1990, as the date of reunification.

August 31   The two Germanys sign the unification treaty. The treaty is ratified on September 20 by the *Bundestag* with 442 votes in favor and 47 against and by the East German *Volkskammer* with 229 in favor and 101 against.

September 12   A treaty on the final settlement on Germany is signed by the foreign ministers of the Federal Republic of Germany and the German Democratic Republic and those of France, the Soviet Union, Great Britain, and the United States. The four Allies' "rights and responsibilities in relation to Berlin and Germany" were ended, giving Germany "full sovereignty over its internal and external affairs."

September 13   West Germany and the Soviet Union sign a bilateral treaty on "Good-Neighborliness, Partnership and Co-operation."

September 24   East Germany leaves the Warsaw Pact.

September 27   The SPD of East and West Germany merge into a single German Social Democratic party.

September 28   Hungary and the Soviet Union agree on the withdrawal of Soviet troops from Hungarian territory.

October 1   A four-power declaration signed in New York confers full sovereignty on the new unified Germany. The East and West German Christian Democratic parties merge at a party congress in Hamburg.

October 3   The two Germanys unite after forty-five years. The event is in Berlin, with an address by President Richard von Weizsäcker.

Introduction

by Harold James

On 3 October 1990, the division of Germany came to an end. It had effectively started forty-five years earlier, after the military defeat of the Nazi dictatorship, with the creation of zones of occupation at the Potsdam conference of July and August 1945. It had been made more enduring in 1949 with the creation of two separate states, the (western) Federal Republic (FRG) and the (eastern) Democratic Republic (GDR). The legacy as much of the cold war as of Hitler's war, division had come to represent an apparently permanent feature of Europe's political geography. It was not simply a German, but also a European partition, and its ending occurred as the direct result of a fundamental shift in the balance of power. The end on 9 November 1989 of the Berlin Wall as a barrier to the movement of people became a symbol, not just of a German liberation, but also of the removal of a political and artificial dissection of the continent into East and West. When the Wall disappeared, Germany could reappear, and so could Europe. Germans, Poles, Czechs, and Hungarians could become Europeans, not merely "East Europeans."

Clearly, 9 November 1989 and 3 October 1990 were not just isolated German events. They took place within the context of a complete reordering of Europe's political structures and ideological affinities. The obvious disintegration of the Soviet Union and its imperial power in Eastern Europe had started much earlier: in the early 1980s, with the rise of a mass working class opposition in Poland, at the same time as the military adventure of the invasion of Afghanistan ran into a blind end. After 1985, the new general secretary of the Communist Party of the Soviet Union attempted to draw the lessons from previous Soviet failures. His policies of openness (*glasnost*) and restructuring (*perestroika*) eventually contributed to economic chaos and political disintegration, and it became ever clearer that communism could not be reformed: only dismantled.

Initially, however, reform communism held out great hopes: more in the GDR than in Czechoslovakia, Poland, or Hungary, which had gone through their own disappointments as they encountered the limits of the reformability of what in the GDR was styled "real existing socialism." One of the traditional slogans of the GDR had been "learning from the Soviet Union means learning to be victorious"; but now some Soviet publications, and especially the dissident journal *Sputnik*, were banned in the GDR. The result was that Erich Honecker's regime looked ever more out of step with other Warsaw Pact states, and with the USSR.

The beginning of widespread discontent can be dated to protests against the manipulation of local elections in the GDR on 7 May 1989. The official results reported a turnout of 98.77 percent and a vote of 98.95 percent for the slate of the National Front, dominated by the Socialist Unity party (SED). In Berlin, opposition groups believed that the true turnout had been lower by some 12 percent, and the "yes" vote by 7 percent. But it took events outside the GDR to galvanize the small and heroic resistance into a mass movement. When Hungary dismantled the portion of the old East-West frontier with Austria (and the Hungarian leadership symbolically presented U.S. President George Bush with a strip of barbed wire), a new movement of people seemed possible. After early September, Hungary allowed GDR citizens to cross to Austria, from where they could travel to the Federal Republic. Thousands flowed across the frontier, and then—as the GDR leadership banned travel to Hungary—into the West German embassy compounds in Prague and Warsaw, and delivered a visible and embarrassing vote of no confidence in the GDR as a state. On 4–5 October, three days before the official fortieth anniversary celebrations of the GDR, eight to ten thousand demonstrators took to the streets in Dresden. In Berlin, President Gorbachev delivered a public rebuke to the GDR leadership, and the opposition accurately guessed that the Soviet army would not participate in the use of force against protestors. When the solution that had ended hopes of change on 17 June 1953 in East Berlin, in November 1956 in Budapest, and in August 1968 in Prague was ruled out, the path to a better future lay open. That many of the East German leadership favored a repression in the style of that imposed by the Chinese Communist party in Tiananmen Square ceased to matter. The East German party belatedly attempted to change in the direction required by Moscow. On 18 October, Honecker was replaced by Egon Krenz, previously considered a grey and bureaucratic hard-liner, the crown prince of the East German apparat. This administrative shake-up did not stop the protests or the Monday evening candlelight demonstrations, which now involved millions of citizens, and on 9 November the regime opened the frontier with the Federal Republic and with West Berlin. A member of the SED's Politburo, Harry Tisch, sent to Moscow to ask about the latest changes, reported that Gorbachev had said after he heard of the GDR leadership's plans to dismiss Honecker and grant freedom of travel: "Will that help at this stage? . . . "[1]

On 13 November a "reform communist", Hans Modrow, was appointed prime minister, and quickly produced a suggestion for a "Treaty Community" between the GDR and the FRG. On 28 November, West German Chancellor Helmut Kohl launched his own, slightly more adventurous, scheme for a linking of the two German states by means of a confederation, the whole

---

[1] Quoted in Melvin J. Lasky, *Wortmeldung zu einer Revolution* (Frankfurt 1991), p. 74.

process taking place within the context of a move towards closer political integration in Europe (by which he meant the European Community) [see text, pages 33–41].

Could the historical process have been stopped in November 1989, or with Modrow's or Kohl's plans of that month? Certainly the majority of the opposition in the GDR hoped so, and could not envisage their country being simply taken over by West Germany. Groups such as the citizens' movement New Forum appealed to GDR citizens not to continue to leave for the West. Many prominent GDR intellectuals, including some who had been victims of the GDR apparat, signed a declaration to this effect, entitled "For Our Country," but its moral effect was completely negated by the addition of the signature of Egon Krenz.

All through this period of attempted reform, the GDR moved closer to economic collapse as large numbers continued to move west, and shortages of labor developed in crucial sectors. But the political crisis came even more quickly than the economic one, as a result of Modrow's unwillingness or inability to deal decisively in ending the power of the state security police (*Staatssicherheit* or *Stasi*). Particularly after the activity of the Romanian *Securitate* in the fighting in Romania in December 1989—the only nonpeaceful revolution in Eastern Europe—the role of the *Stasi* became the subject of intense debate in the GDR. Through the first half of 1990, as revelations continued about the *Stasi* involvement of political figures associated with the transformation, the GDR's population increasingly took the view that the only way out lay in the adoption of the West German political system. The economic hopes associated with unification also helped this political reorientation.

The March 1990 GDR general election produced a surprisingly convincing victory for the "Alliance for Germany," a coalition constructed at the initiative of Chancellor Kohl from opposition groups around the citizens' movement Democratic Start, and from the old Christian Democratic Union (CDU), which had been a virtually silent puppet member of the old GDR National Front coalition. The victory came above all from the belief that the Alliance was the best placed political organization to bring about the speedy reunification of Germany, although by the last weeks of the election campaign the (eastern) Social Democratic Party of Germany (SPD), too, had argued for quick union. From 18 March, there could be no doubt at least of the East German will to unite, and on 22 June a State Treaty was ratified by the parliaments of the FRG and the GDR. On 1 July, an economic and currency union came into effect.

During and after the election campaign, the former SED, reconstructed as the party of Democratic Socialism (PDS) and led by Gregor Gysi, a lawyer who had previously defended East German dissidents, warned against a takeover by the parties of West Germany. The emotive term used, *Anschluss,* made the analogy with Hitler's seizure of Austria in 1938. In at least one sense, however, the PDS was correct about the West German takeover. Because of the legacy of nearly sixty years of dictatorship, it was almost impossible to find a new political elite. Even many of the most prominent leaders of the new political parties were obliged to resign in the wake of accusations of *Stasi* contacts. This fate overtook the SPD's Ibrahim Böhme, Democratic Start's Wolfgang Schnur, and later the CDU's Lothar de Maiziere. Only western parties, it was now believed, could be free from the stain of the totalitarian police state.

In the spring and summer of 1990, the most obviously difficult issues in the unification process concerned security issues, and the prerogatives of the former wartime Allies. There had been no peace treaty at the end of the Second World War, no equivalent of the 1919 Versailles Treaty. American, British, French, and Soviet troops remained on German territory, and later the two Germanys were integrated into rival military alliances: NATO and the Warsaw Pact. By 1990, after the installation of many noncommunist governments in Eastern Europe, the Warsaw Pact had little future (it was formally dissolved in June 1991). At the outset of negotiations between the two Germanys and the wartime coalition (the Two Plus Four talks), the USSR resolutely opposed NATO membership for the new Germany, and argued instead for options including demilitarization or neutrality. In the course of the talks, however, NATO membership looked increasingly attractive as a way of tying Germany down and stopping her becoming the proverbial "loose cannon." This position also was adopted by Germany's formerly communist eastern neighbors. At a meeting of Chancellor Kohl in the Caucasus at Stavropol with President Gorbachev (15–16 July 1990), the USSR conceded NATO membership for Germany, in return for substantial German financial help disguised as payments towards the expense of resettling the Red army in the USSR. On 12 September, the Two Plus Four talks came to an end [see text, pages 108–14].

German unification was made additionally secure in two ways: from the outset, Kohl had insisted that German unity should proceed simultaneously with European integration. This principle was accepted in December 1989 at the Strasbourg meeting of the European Community Council of Ministers, although at the time many commentators (including Rudolf Augstein in *Der Spiegel*: reprinted in this volume, pages 50–1) suspected that this compromise was merely a French plan to hold up German events, and that Kohl himself was skeptical about the political consequences of taking on board sixteen million former inhabitants of a communist state. Europe made Germany appear safer to other Europeans, and also to many Germans. It provided a political, economic, and institutional framework for the process of unification. Most Germans believed the intertwining of European and German integration to be a sign of a new political maturity that saw structures in a more global, cooperative, and universalistic fashion and less nationalist, idiosyncratic, and destructive. Later a senior German diplomat was quoted as saying: "Without the European Community, we might never have been able to get our reunification. Mr. Gorbachev might have been the only person prepared to agree."[2]

Secondly, the eastern frontier of Germany had historically been much more problematic than the boundary in the west. In the Second World War, Germans had systematically exploited Poland as part of the war economy and killed a large part of the Polish intelligentsia. After the war, expulsions and resettlements in the territories that had been included in Germany's 1937 frontiers but were transferred at the Potsdam conference "to Polish administration" meant that these areas had become effectively Polish. In 1970, Chancellor Willy Brandt initialed a treaty under which the FRG recognized the new frontier on the line of the rivers Oder and Neisse. Constitutionally, however, Kohl's government took the position that the FRG could not make international commitments that would bind a future united Germany (an argument originally used in 1955 to explain why NATO membership need not mean the end to hopes of unification). Only after weeks of bitter debate, in which Kohl unnecessarily complicated the issue by insisting that Poland formally renounce claims to reparation resulting from the Second World War, was an agreement reached under which both German parliaments committed themselves to the Oder-Neisse line, and promised a quick voting of a border treaty after unification. Such a treaty, accepting as final the boundaries of 3 October 1990, was indeed concluded on 14 November; and the Polish frontier, which had complicated the Two Plus Four negotiations, was finally removed from the realm of political debate. Responding to the unification on 3 October, the Polish Foreign Minister Krzystof Skubiszewski said: "The unification of Germany will become, we hope, a powerful factor of European stability and unification."

Reactions to the new Germany, and the process of unification, were in general more cautious—even if in general cautiously optimistic—than enthusiastic. With the reemergence of old concepts such as a single Germany and an undivided Europe, which seemed after 1945 to have been banished into a historical limbo, new fears as well as hopes gripped the political imagination. Supposing that with "Germany" and "Europe," all the old ills of the European continent, and particularly the German nation, should also return to haunt the world? Would there not be a new age of ultranationalism, destructive territorial conflicts, and murderous ethnic rivalries? Would not those clashes be fanned by economic collapse and disenchantment with the fruits of the newly obtained democracy? Would there not, in short, be a return to the

---

[2] *Financial Times*, October 28, 1991, III, p. 1.

interwar years (in which, as commentators loved to remind their nervous audience, Czechoslovakia was the only Central European state that succeeded in running a viable democratic system).

In addition, the transformation had not been calm or leisurely. In Central Europe and in Germany, events moved with a bewildering rapidity. Less than a year separated the abortive attempt of the Democratic Republic to celebrate its fortieth anniversary from the full political integration with the Federal Republic; and in practice the old GDR had stopped existing as a working political unit much earlier, between December 1989 and the March elections. The speed of the process meant that the new political world looked most unfamiliar. Germans, and foreign observers, often saw the worst memories of a brutal past: and the scenario of history flashed past as if the world were being taken on an uncontrollably wild roller coaster ride through the nightmares of the past century.

In particular, it was Germany whose aggression had imposed in this century two wars in Europe. During the Second World War, Germany had implemented a genocide directed against the Jewish, Slavic, and gypsy populations. These events had occurred less than fifty years ago: for a substantial number of people well within the time covered by memory. Most of the political elite in Germany, and other states, had at least some childhood memories of Hitler's war.

The reaction to a revived Germany came immediately. There were appeals for calm and assertions that the existing (but fast-vanishing system) had offered peace. Had not the post-1945 order been the guarantor of a peace and stability the like of which Europe had never previously known? Those who wanted calm certainly sometimes ignored the price paid for stability by the inhabitants of Eastern Europe; sometimes, more hypocritically, they attempted to present the outcome of Soviet political imposition as a partially successful experiment in a new kind of social engineering.

The responses—some positive, many critical—presented in the following pages document the memories and the nightmares of the immediate response to the new Germany. Some of them have subsequently been disavowed by their authors. Conor Cruise O'Brien rapidly regretted his apocalyptic vision in the London *Times*. Stefan Heym, one of the most articulate defenders of a separate socialist GDR (as "essential for those outside the Republic") in 1989 and 1990, by 1991 publicly thanked Chancellor Kohl for having acted so quickly, decisively—and correctly. The intellectual honesty of those who subsequently admitted that they were mistaken should not be an occasion for a false triumphalism.

These articles are all intelligent and sensitive readings of an entirely changed political situation. Studying them is in part, of course, an interesting way of seeing how the world reacted to Germany. But it is also in a more general sense an illuminating example of how analysts and politicians interpret events through a dense filter of hypotheses about the causes of events, previous experiences, and externalizations of their own pressing preoccupations.

Perceptions of causes crucially influence the reactions to outcomes. If the revolution in the GDR had been the product of some new German nationalism, of teenage skinhead groups calling for a new *Grossdeutschland,* or of a mass rising against the shackles of the Potsdam-Yalta settlement analogous to the protests in the 1920s against the Versailles settlement, the outcome would have been much more obviously threatening.

But none of this was the case. The Monday evening demonstrations in Leipzig began not with a demonstration of nationalism, but of the solidarity of the East German population in the face of a regime that pretended to a popular legitimacy: "We are the people" (*Wir sind das Volk*). Later the slogan "We are one people" (*Wir sind ein Volk*) was an inevitable outcome of the former statement, since with the end of socialism, the GDR's justification as a state had come to an end. The movement to integration was guided by the logic of the single labor market that developed after 9 November, when East Germans were free to move: the old GDR leadership had in practice by this concession created a single German economy. The subsequent step of currency and economic union (1 July 1990) was guided by the need to stop an emptying of the territory of the GDR and a wave of migration to the old Federal Republic as workers took advantage of the new possibilities for mobility. The final step of political union came only after a single economic area had been created (unlike the case of the Empire of 1871, where political union preceded economic union). This integration was frequently justified not so much by statements about national community, but rather by reference to the inexorability of economic events. Once there was a currency union, it made sense that the inhabitants of the GDR should be given some measure of democratic control over those institutions, the Bonn ministries and the Frankfurt *Bundesbank,* that now ran the collective economic destinies of Germans.

In all of this there was little display of aggressive nationalism, or even of euphoria. The opening of the Wall on 9 November was treated with more curiosity than with jubilation. Only on New Year's Eve 1990–91 did the whole of Berlin turn into a gigantic and good-humored street party. The operation was conducted more in the manner of a solid business transaction. After the event, many disenchanted East Germans saw dramatically risen unemployment levels, and disillusioned West Germans found their tax bills higher; many treated this as a business transaction turned sour. The hangover was much more substantial, and lasted longer, than any euphoria about unity. It was then that there were some terrifying outbreaks of violence in both the former east and the west, in which teenage hooligans attacked and even killed foreigners and asylum seekers in Germany.

However, there were causes of German unity other than the drive of economic forces that stood out so clearly in the early months of 1990. The German public and German intellectuals took longer to understand these causes, which lay in the character of the international system, and for a time treated German unity as primarily a German issue, an affair of the German spirit. They forgot that the context that made German developments possible was a Soviet and East European one. The Polish strike movement of 1980, and the launching of Solidarity, provided the example of the first long lasting working class mobilization against a state and against state power in European history. It was the Hungarian decision to open the Hungarian-Austrian frontier to GDR citizens that prompted the first great exodus of population and demonstrably undermined the GDR's legitimacy. Mikhail Gorbachev's public rebuke to Erich Honecker on the occasion of the GDR's fortieth anniversary celebration provided a final push: "History punishes the late-comer." During the Two Plus Four talks, Bonn officials only half concealed their belief that there was a need to hurry because the situation in the Soviet Union might change: they thought that a successful outcome to unification depended on the continued political fortunes of President Gorbachev.

The later interpretation that German unity was the direct outcome of Soviet weakness made most observers much more sympathetic to the German position. Disintegrating empires, such as the Soviet one, are likely to be dangerous. They may pose a threat to peace; their inhabitant's may fight each other in bloody civil wars. In such a context, there is a need for as much regional stability as possible, and that is precisely what German unity provided. Already in early 1990, some observers pointed out that the real danger in the future lay not in German strength but in Soviet disintegration: and the conclusion that the new Germany would be a force for stability in Central Europe reconciled, belatedly, many of the former skeptics to the new political map of the continent.

Among the arguments of the initial skeptics, two arguments featured prominently in formulating an intellectually acceptable version of the fundamental fear that German history might repeat itself. They concerned, first, the peculiarities of East German society and the virtues of a social order not built around the market economy, and, second, geopolitical risks of change. Some observers saw virtue in a socialist alternative to western-style social market capitalism. Others believed that the division of Europe had been beneficial in promoting world political stability. Both responses were in large part highly nervous responses to the global situation: the ideological and intellectual bankruptcy of communism, and the new power political weakness of the USSR.

The reactions need to be understood in terms of the intellectual situation of 1989–90 and in particular to the feeling that these months marked the end of a quite well-defined historical period. The course of the twentieth century had been molded by the Bolshevik Revolution in Russia and by the twelve-year dictatorship of Adolf Hitler in Germany. The success of both bolshevism and national socialism can only be understood as an outgrowth of the tumult in European society caused by the First World War.

The conclusion of the Two Plus Four talks marked the formal end of the postwar era: but it was not just the post-Second World War order that came to an end. The events of 1989–91 also marked the liquidation of the terrible legacy of the First World War, and a century of totalitarianism, in which, as Czechoslovakia's new President Vaclav Havel movingly described, the struggle against one totalitarianism reinforced different but also destructive ideologies. The turmoil of war after 1914 had produced the successful Bolshevik seizure of power in the Russian empire. After 1918, the aftermath of war appeared to discredit liberal democracy and market economics, and either fascism or communism came to be regarded, not merely in the countries in which they were essential, as the "modern" creed that would lead to a rationalized and planned future. After the First World War, Europe entered a period in which the "modern" was profoundly misdiagnosed. In 1945, the equation of fascism with modernity was discredited; and in 1989 that of communism with modernity. The communist promise to transform mankind simply crumbled. The upheaval produced a return to the older, liberal values of the early twentieth century. Timothy Garton Ash, one of the most subtle observers of the revolutions of 1989, accurately stated that: "The ideas whose time has come are old, familiar, well-tested ones. (It is the new ideas whose time has passed.)"[3]

One of the most tenacious beliefs about the "East" in western societies, and especially among intellectuals, had been that both styles of society had virtues and faults, and that there might be pluses and minuses in both camps. To many observers, the East European experiments had involved an attempt to create a more just and equal society. They saw at least a partial success. Though very few accepted the whole Soviet-style system uncritically, the predominant view was that if indeed there were to be reform, it should be a moderate and cautious revising of social structures. It should preserve the "achievements" (*Errungenschaften* was a favorite word of GDR political vocabulary that spilled into western usage).

Such observers were appalled at the evidence that accumulated during the course of the revolutions of 1989. Suddenly there became visible a population in the GDR completely different from that described in the majority of western accounts.

Socialists believed that there might be a middle way between the planned economies of the East and Western-style capitalism. Many of the early critics

---

[3] Timothy Garton Ash, *The Magic Lantern: The Revolution of '89 Witnessed in Warsaw, Budapest, Berlin and Prague* (New York 1990), p. 154. This passage is also quoted in Ralf Dahrendorf, *Reflections on the Revolution in Europe* (London 1990), p. 24.

of the Honecker regime in the GDR, especially those who later became active in the citizens' movement New Forum, appealed for what they called a "third way." By the spring of 1990, most East German voters found this prescription increasingly implausible, and not just because they were seduced by the lures of a materialist West. (Although such was the belief of many leftists, who ridiculed consumerism as what they called the "banana revolution." They stood at the Wall satirically tossing bananas at East Germans coming to look at the West. One, Otto Schily, took a banana out of his pocket in a television panel discussion in order to demonstrate why Chancellor Kohl had won the March 1990 elections.)

In practice, however, few eastern Germans wanted new experiments along "third way" lines. Yugoslavia, long held up as the model of successful experimentation in mixing socialist and capitalist elements, was descending into civil war and anarchy. Less apocalyptically, Sweden, which had also been depicted as a model for a mixed economy with strong welfare elements, entered into a fiscal crisis that required the dismantling of large elements of the Swedish compromise. The "third way," the eastern German witticism now went, could only be a way into the Third World. It became clear that there only could be a quite simple either-or choice: the market or the plan. Mixtures of the two, analysts discovered (after over sixty years' experience of planned economies) could not work. A mixture of incentives and compulsion would only lead to a move in one or another direction: if voluntary targeting did not produce the right result, there would be a need for compulsion, and the market elements would be suppressed.

In the area of the economy, these debates about the character of a future society (and the inappropriateness of old-style socialist ideology) could be carried out with the highest degree of rationality and the least emotional damage. But even here, the result was the loss of the idealistic and utopian beliefs of several generations of would-be reformers. The utopia of a rationally planned alternative to the operation of the market was the earliest victim of the revolutions of 1989.

In another area, that concerned with the shape of the state as a national community, much more difficult problems arose. Part of the appeal of the postwar Federal Republic, at least in retrospect, appeared to lie in its modesty and its non-national character, which came to be derided as provincialism by such cultural critics as Karl Heinz Bohrer (in an article in the *Frankfurter Allgemeine Zeitung,* reprinted here. It was criticized by Ulrich Greiner and Reinhard Merkel in *Die Zeit*). Had not the German nation-state brought terrible catastrophes to Europe? This was the view set out most explicitly and directly, and with the greatest moral authority, by the writer Günter Grass in an essay in *Die Zeit*. In his account, united Germany had produced Auschwitz, and the division of Germany was not just a penalty for German crimes but also a guarantee that they could not happen again.

Before 1989, many Germans had felt unhappy with this interpretation. Politicians (usually on the right, though on the fringe of the left there also developed a variant of pacifist-neutralist-ecological-nationalism) had called for an end to the postwar period, an "upright walk," emancipation from a position of "semi-colonial tutelage." Chancellor Kohl once reminded his audience of his relatively young age, which gave the "grace of late birth" (or nonaccountability for the sins of the Nazis). But this demand for greater self-assertion did not have any impact other than a rhetorical one, because Germany's options were limited by the form of the postwar settlement.

In practice, all West German politicians, even those such as the Bavarian leader of the conservative Christian Social Union (CSU), Franz Josef Strauss, who used the language of escaping from the shadow of the past most enthusiastically, were tied in by Germany's international position. A policy consensus emerged to justify compliance with this position, in which politicians, bureaucrats in the foreign policy-making machine, and academics reinforced the prevailing orthodoxy. Nothing, it was believed, could be done that might disturb the status quo in which the GDR was gradually, by small steps, becoming more humane. This constituted the intellectual climate in which it was possible for Chancellor Kohl to receive Erich Honecker (who is now accused as a criminal for his part in ordering the shooting of fugitives from East Germany) as a state visitor; or for Franz Josef Strauss to broker billion mark credits in return for only very limited humanitarian concessions from the GDR government.

After 1989–90, with a new openness in politics, the past and its legacy became, for the first time since the end of the war, immediately relevant for the formulation of policy. The new debates often cut across traditional political and party lines. Thus, for instance, initially the publisher of the left-liberal news weekly, *Der Spiegel,* Rudolf Augstein, welcomed the new opportunities for Germany, whereas most of his staff felt rather more apprehensive. The veteran SPD leader, Willy Brandt, made a powerful appeal for unity and for what he termed the "growing together of what belongs together." However, the SPD's candidate for the chancellorship in the 1990 German-wide *Bundestag* elections, the Saarland Minister-President Oskar Lafontaine, in late 1989 called for a legal recognition of GDR citizenship as a way of stopping the inflow of people from the East. This suggestion was in violation of the Federal Republic's Basic Law, which in its Preamble stated that the law was a provisional one until the German people could decide about their constitution in freedom. It also alienated Eastern voters, who never forgave Lafontaine.

The discussion about the new capital of Germany raised more discussion, again across party lines. Berlin or Bonn? Was Bonn too provincial, an expression of all that was limited about the Federal Republic? Was perhaps this modesty appropriate in the new Germany? Was Berlin discredited by its past as the capital of Imperial Germany, of Hitler's "Thousand Year Empire" and then of Ulbricht and Honecker's "Real Existing Socialism"? Or did Berlin give the opportunity to show that Germans had overcome their history?

In 1990, these debates were all fought out at a rather high level of abstraction. There were a number of acerbic "intellectuals' debates" (*Intellektuellenstreit*) fought out in the literary pages (*Feuilletons*) of Germany's leading newspapers and periodicals. In the former West, Joachim Fest, the editor of the *Frankfurter Allgemeine Zeitung,* and Karl Heinz Bohrer, editor of the literary periodical *Merkur,* accused German intellectuals of having destroyed the sense of nation essential to the moral order of a stable and confident society. The Eastern intellectuals were also attacked: in *Die Zeit* Ulrich Greiner and in the *Frankfurter Allgemeine Zeitung* Frank Schirrmacher accused the leading GDR novelist Christa Wolf of intellectual dishonesty in disguising her complicity with the SED regime by claiming, falsely, the status of semi-dissident.

All of these writers used the literary and intellectual debate as a way of reaching for a higher, more idealized vision of Germany. But they may be criticized for a certain lack of clarity, an intellectual imprecision, about how that new Germany should be defined, apart from as an appeal in the Feuilleton pages.

Lothar de Maiziere claimed that the new German would have to be more eastern and more Protestant. But what did "eastern" mean at the time when "Eastern" as a political description was losing its meaning? And what did "Protestant" mean in the context of a largely secularized society in both parts of Germany? Did de Maiziere mean that even secularized Protestantism would follow the stern moralism of the bearded pastors who had been so active in the opposition to Honecker in 1989, and that political Catholicism, secularized, was too corrupt? In September 1991, de Maiziere resigned as deputy chairman of the CDU after accusing the western CDU of enriching itself through incorporation of the eastern party that had once been a member of the "National Front." Opposition to the communist dictatorship gave the luxury of allowing a high degree of morality—as does opposition in any political system. Rapidly it emerged that politics requires quite practical choices, which to the austere moralist may appear as corrupt. This was the adjustment that was made and that had to be made in the course of the early months of a new German political life.

The reckoning in political terms with the new German situation came only in 1991, as the result of a series of international crises: first the Gulf War, then the civil war in Yugoslavia, and then the end of the Soviet Union. In all of these moments of international tension, new debates occurred, debates that often crossed traditional political divisions.

The Gulf War in January 1991 started with a condemnation by the SPD chairman Hans Jochen Vogel of the U.S. action in the enforcement of United Nations Resolution 678 (which authorized the use of "all necessary means" to ensure the complete withdrawal of Iraq from Kuwait), and a tepidly distanced response to Washington by Chancellor Helmut Kohl. Some so-called "critical" intellectuals talked about a special German duty to preserve peace, but then others—notably Wolf Biermann and Hans Magnus Enzensberger—instead argued that the German past led to a special obligation to defend the victims of aggression, and—in this case—especially a threatened Israel. Enzensberger made a detailed and explicit comparison of Adolf Hitler and Saddam Hussein. The ferocity of the debate, coupled with the perception that Germany had in some ways "failed" in the Gulf War, helped to lead to a reexamination of whether Germans should not use their new power: at least for constructive purposes.

The response to the Yugoslav crisis of summer 1991 demonstrated the extent to which German politics and German thought had successfully internalized the experience of the Gulf War. At first, but only for a brief initial period, the official German course, and that of the European Community, was that the status quo should not be touched, and that a precarious "peace" or "stability" should be preserved. An intense criticism, coming from the same sources that had deplored German inactivity and passivity in the Gulf crisis, pressed for a more active approach, and German policy swung to a support of greater concessions for Croatia and Slovenia.

By the time of the Soviet crisis of August 1991, the lesson had been fully learned: stability did not necessarily mean upholding the status quo. Despite all the German gratitude to the Soviet Union for the completion of unification in the previous year, German policy towards the Baltic republics took a very different line to the highly cautious approach of the old Germany. Germans, including Foreign Minister Hans-Dietrich Genscher, appeared in the forefront of the movement to grant the Baltic states diplomatic recognition. In December 1991, despite heavy criticism from France and the United States, Germany took the initiative in recognizing two former Yugoslav Republics, and then successfully pressed the European Community to follow Bonn's example. In the aftermath of 1989, Germany had become a state with interest and policies it was prepared to realize. By 1991 this new confidence held beneficial and stabilizing effects in the middle of a world increasingly dislocated by the rapidity of change.

The perceptions in other countries of the new German power drew from a mixture of the elements that, it was suggested earlier, make up a "view" as much as a "policy." There were intellectual and ideological responses to the end of socialism. There were deep historical memories, particularly of the terror imposed by Nazi Germany. In addition, there were realistic calculations about the likely effects of a newly powerful Germany coupled with *Realpolitik* assessments of the consequences of the new weakness of the Soviet Union. Finally, responses also included externalized versions of domestic obsessions.

Most obviously, Koreans treated the unification as a precedent for the overcoming of their own division. Many Japanese saw in the new order a greater role for strong economic powers, and an opportunity to press their own territorial claims against the Soviet Union. Israelis largely reacted to the historical threats implied by a new German state. Germany's eastern neighbors welcomed the ideological aspect of German unity as a power-political cementing of communism in its coffin, and welcomed what they believed to be the economic strength of the new country as a help in rebuilding their own traumatized infrastructures. At the same time, they could not help being worried about memories from the past and concerned that economic influence would change the regional balance of power.

In many countries, the new Germany and its altered role was regarded with a certain ambiguity, indeed almost schizophrenia. Rudolf Augstein was right in December 1989 to suspect in *Der Spiegel* that the German development was taking place out of the control of the "responsible politicians," and that the "responsible politicians" were in consequence worried.

The relatively hostile private and semi-official British response, as exposed in the Chequers memorandum drawn up by the Prime Minister (Margaret Thatcher's) foreign policy adviser Charles (later Sir Charles) Powell, or the interview given to the *Spectator* by her trade secretary Nicholas Ridley, contrasted bizarrely with the beamingly optimistic official response from the British Foreign Office, which welcomed unflinchingly every move towards German unity. Why the contrast and ambiguity? Was Donald Sassoon writing in *Marxism Today* (pages 240–1) altogether inaccurate in seeing the veiled British paranoia about the new Germany as an expression of envy: concern about an economy that even eleven years of Mrs. Thatcher's government had failed to put right?

The hesitancy of François Mitterrand was as obvious, and as embarrassing, as the conflicts within the British government about how to deal with Germany and Europe. Officially, there was little alternative but to welcome the new neighbor across the Rhine. Unofficially, there came the lament that the French position in Europe had been eroded. Again, the unease reflected the end of an era in French domestic politics. Mitterrand had always conducted a balancing trick in order to maintain his position both domestically and internationally. He needed socialist ideology as a real existing force in order to build a bridge to his vision of a technocratic modernized market-oriented consensual and distinctly nonsocialist France. At the same time, standing firmly in the Gaullist tradition of foreign policy, he needed a strong Soviet Union and a politically incapacitated but economically strong Germany in order to deal with the United States, and with the rest of the world. In the course of 1989–90, all of the fundaments of this balancing act disappeared. Socialism was dead. The USSR was crippled. Germany no longer corresponded to the cliche of a political dwarf and an economic giant.

The only possible response was to abandon many traditional French policies, and instead use Europe as the instrument for the containment of a new Germany. After the Strasbourg meeting of December 1989, President Mitterrand took this course and pressed further the cause of European integration.

Historically, the United States had prided itself on its stance as West Germany's firmest ally, had resolutely and heroically defended democracy in the West during the Berlin crises, and had at least in public maintained a firm commitment to the principle of eventual reunification. Under the surface, there may have been deep doubts about the potential role of a united Germany and fears that such a state would be forced to accept an imposed neutrality and would break away from a western community of values. But even in the 1980s the public language of unity was maintained, most dramatically by President Reagan who in 1987 during a visit to Berlin called for a dismantling of the Wall.

In the course of 1989–90, President Bush and the State Department followed an uncompromisingly supportive course towards Germany. Even after unification, and at the moment of the greatest congressional and public attack on Germany for alleged pusillanimity during the Gulf War, official Washington abstained. Secretary of State James Baker even went out of his way to praise the German foreign minister's ideas as a serious basis for the establishment of peace in the Middle East.

At the same time in the media, and particularly in the op-ed pages of newspapers, there were much darker tones. Some of the criticism depended on the historical memory of the Nazis; but some also (as in the case of "Japan-bashing") reflected uncertainty about the future of the world's single remaining superpower. By 1992 doubts about the new Germany and its place in a reordered Europe appeared even in official United States documents. The February draft of the Defense Planning Guidance for the Fiscal Years 1994–1999 stated, in the context of an overall policy objective of preventing "the reemergence of a new rival, either on the territory of the former Soviet Union or elsewhere," that: "While the United States supports the goal of European integration, we must seek to prevent the emergence of European-only security arrangements which would undermine NATO."[4]

Of the old wartime coalition, the USSR followed what was probably the most direct and straightforward approach. There was little criticism here, little regret, and little hypocrisy. Instead, there was only a sense that whatever turns might be taken by official policy, German unity was inevitable. The turns in Soviet policy in 1989–90 came not from any fundamental opposition or hostility to German unity, but out of the hope that the reordering of the political map could be used as an opportunity to destroy NATO and set up in the heart of Europe a Germany that could provide a counterweight polit-

---

[4] *New York Times*, 8 March 1992, p. 14.

ically and economically to the United States. It was this calculation that was frustrated, in the course of 1990, by the speed of German unity. But the Soviets never doubted that unification was a historical necessity.

Indeed this position had been spelled out privately by some Soviet party and military figures well before 1989. In the summer of 1988, for instance, a prominent Soviet general told the astonished British politician Enoch Powell in a television interview that there could be no doubt that German unity would come. Eduard Shevardnadze, Soviet foreign minister at the time of German unification, later said that in 1986 he already had begun to believe in the inevitability of a united Germany: "I said that in the near future the German question would define Europe."[5]

In the Soviet Union, more than anywhere else, and above all more than in Germany, German unity was recognized as being not a chance construction, or the outcome of political manipulations, or the expression of new national sentiment, but rather the inexorable product of a geopolitical and intellectual shift. Here in the birthplace and the graveyard of communism, the end of socialism (at least as understood in Eastern Europe) and the end of Soviet power were accurately interpreted, and the German problem seen most sharply within the contours of a global framework.

That framework will continue to be crucial in shaping German developments. Both the security concerns raised by a disintegrating superpower in the east, and the global economic environment for the integration of the Federal Republic's new territories and Germany's eastern neighbors into a globalized market, will in the future be essential determinants of the new Germany's success.

The events of 1989–90, however, leave Germany in a strategic position to influence developments in Europe and in Eastern Europe. The self-limiting description of Germany as "economic giant and political pygmy" is clearly no longer relevant or valid. Here a new history is being written. Germany's task, and her opportunity, is to participate in collective efforts to shape both the security and the economic settings so as to promote stability and openness. Their realization requires a more international, and less introspective, orientation on the part of Germans, but also of other states. An understanding of the great economic and international movements that led to 1989–90 will help to generate an outlook appropriate for a new Germany, a new Europe, and a new global order.

---

[5] Eduard Shevardnadze (transl. Catherine A. Fitzpatrick), *The Future Belongs to Freedom* (New York 1991), p. 131.

Introduction

by Marla Stone

Ours is an age of instant history; events have been adapted to a postmodern appetite for immediate action. On 9 November 1989, the evening news brought the fall of the Berlin Wall into the American living room. The revelry at the site of this most potent symbol of both the post-World War II order and the cold war produced a form of cognitive dissonance in many accustomed to a divided Germany and a bipolar world. By 1989, most Americans and Europeans took for granted the existence of two German states. A generation had grown up and lived its life with the Berlin Wall as a physical and psychological reminder of a state system constructed out of the ruins of the Second World War and the defeat of nazism.

While the East German people's rejection of the state communism of Erich Honecker met with international approval, the event, and its future implications, raised profound questions from actors and observers alike. What new boundaries would replace the Wall? How would the world order its political consciousness without inherited categories of West and East, capitalist and communist, good and evil? Excitement at watching East Germans take to the streets against an oppressive state was tinged with deep-seated ideas about the "German Question," which for many had been locked in cold storage thanks to the cold war. The two German states had become a central locale for understanding the world ideological conflict: the concrete, tangible manifestations of the cold war, from Checkpoint Charlie to the Glienecke Bridge, were familiar and grounding images to westerners fed on James Bond and George Smiley.

The emotional challenge of German reunification created more anxiety and possessed a different character than Eastern Europe's dismantling of the Yalta system. While Poland's Solidarity movement and Czechoslovakia's Civic Forum lent themselves to an easy reading as the victory of the people over a discredited political and economic order, German events carried a variety of mixed meanings. All developments in the German Democratic Republic (GDR), from the first demonstrations against the state in September 1989, had a reciprocal effect in the Federal Republic, and, therefore, in the European Community where West German economic strength makes it a dominating force. Everything that took place in either German state between September 1989 and October 1990 had international repercussions.

The pace of events, faster than any of the players imagined, exacerbated feelings of uncertainty. Transformations in the two German states, beginning with Hungary's opening of the frontier in the summer of 1989 and the flood of East German refugees and ending only a year later with the end of the GDR and the creation of a new united Germany, continually outstripped the prognostications of the pundits. When the mass exodus of citizens forced the East German government to grant travel rights on 9 November 1989, and, hence, open the Berlin Wall, very few Germans or others envisioned that this move could or would catalyze reunification at a breakneck speed. In the last months of 1989, both German states, the Soviet Union, the United States, France, and England maintained that German unity was not on the immediate agenda. A scenario that appeared increasingly unlikely in the mid-1980s, as the two Germanys regularized relations, with East German President Erich Honecker making an official state visit to Bonn in 1986, was a peacefully accomplished fact, less than a year after it was first seriously considered.

German reunification, the name given to the meetings, resolutions, and treaties that codified the renunciation of the post-World War II order in Germany and the dissolution of the East German state, was both the last act of the postwar system and the first episode in an, as of now unnamed, post-cold war and post-Communist international order. Seventeen million East Germans witnessed the end of their country and society, and sixty million West Germans suddenly faced the prospect of sharing the state (and standard of living) that they had constructed since 1947 with their now culturally and socially different compatriots. In the process, the defense alliances, NATO and the Warsaw Pact, were recast or dissolved and the upcoming, and much planned for, European unification had to be reconceived. At the opening of the Berlin Wall, a bipolar world existed; by the declaration of a unified Germany, the former Soviet Union and Eastern bloc were desperately gazing westward for help and guidance.

This collection seeks to decipher a process that combined apprehension with relief at the end of the cold war and with sincere hopes at welcoming a peaceful Germany into the community of nations. A quotation of Prime Minister Thatcher's Memo on Germany summarizes the dual reaction: "Even the Optimists Had Some Unease." "Even the optimists" had unease; the pessimists often expressed strong fears at the specter of a united Germany. The pieces included in this book reveal the varieties of ambiguity and tension produced by the collapse of the East German state and its merger with the Federal Republic. By recognizing the ways in which observers and participants interpreted these events, the reader can better understand the complexities, uncertainties, and subtleties of rapid historical change and the issues accompanying the birth of a post-cold war world.

The "uneasiness" expressed by writers, politicians, academics, and journalists in the course of German reunification falls into four categories. First, there was the historically based anxiety over the resurgence of a single German state at the center of Europe. This entails the fear of a German past colored by militarism, nazism, war, and genocide. Second was the nationalist issue, related to, but different from historically motivated discomfort. Here one finds references to reunification as potentially provoking a rise of nationalism, perhaps a nationalism catalyzed by dislocation and crisis. Third, anxiety arose over the process itself. The image of an economic superpower taking over a weak, disintegrating East Germany troubled many; there was concern about the implications of this form of reunification and fears about the loss of valuable aspects of the East German experience. And, finally, the problem of historical conflation: the tendency, in the context of the collapse of the Soviet Union, to equate all movements critical of capitalism with advocacy of Soviet communism.

A historically grounded unease with German reunification was, perhaps, the most common reason cited for containing or limiting the union. After all, claimed opponents abroad and in Germany, it had been the united German nation that nurtured nazism and unleashed it upon the world. The Berlin Wall and the division of Germany seemed to have quelled the German (and Prussian) military tradition. The Bismarckian unification of 1870 appeared to many observers to have been the spark igniting German militarism; how could the world guarantee that 1990 would not be Round Two?

In the first months after the fall of the Berlin Wall, international reaction focused on historically constructed fears of German reunification. In Britain, a political crisis erupted in July 1990 as a memorandum based on Prime Minister Margaret Thatcher's private meeting with academics and specialists on the "German Question" was leaked and revealed that constructs such as a German national proclivity for aggression still had cachet in British councils of state [see text, Charles Powell's Leaked Chequers Memorandum, pages 233–9]. Soon after, the British Trade and Industry Secretary Nicholas Ridley's interview in *The Spectator* revealed his anxiety over German economic domination; he termed the European monetary union a "German racket," called the Germans "uppity," and seemed uncertain whether Kohl was preferable to Hitler.[1] Both incidents showed conservative British misgivings to be largely based on the legacy of the Second World War and the fear that a united Germany would once again dominate European affairs.

French and Polish reactions drew, as well, on historical reflexes, expressing fears of a resurgent and expansionist Germany on their borders. In part, such fears went farther back than Hitler and his blitzkrieg: both France and Poland had seen their borders repeatedly threatened in the brief history of the unified

---

[1] "Mr. Ridley and the Germans," *Manchester Guardian Weekly*, July 22, 1990.

German state. Chancellor Helmut Kohl's reluctance in February 1990 to recognize the inviolability of the Polish border at the Oder-Neisse line did little to dampen such fears.

Other critics focused on the German historic experience of unstable state-building, the failure of peaceful social and political integration in both the Kaiserreich and the Weimar Republic. Did Germany have a "special path" [*Sonderweg*] as a nation-state that made its coexistence in the community of nations problematic?

Frequently, the historically based reactions to German unity cited the Holocaust and called the division of Germany a just, permanent punishment for the crime of genocide. Opponents, both inside and out of Germany, saw Auschwitz as the ultimate obstacle to German reunification. Günter Grass, West German's most powerful exponent of this position, claimed that reunification would imply an abandonment of the past and saw the one German nation best embodied in two separate states. Speaking as a representative of a segment of the American Jewish community, Michael Lerner [page 181] "resisted German reunification," finding incomplete the denazification of 1945 to 1989. According to Lerner, the West Germans had not sufficiently dealt with their past and had not solidly repudiated nationalism and anti-Semitism. If the West German state had systematically educated its citizens against the evils of racism and nationalism, he argued, then they would earn the right to national self-determination. He also asked whether West Germany had really denazified or had the social and psychological reconversion been halted as the cold war forced the West to look elsewhere? Again and again, the movement toward unity forced the world to ask if Germany had truly laid to rest the demons of the past.

During the West German historians debate [*Historikerstreit*] of the late 1980s, the German relationship to the past, and the issue of "putting it in historical perspective," had engendered a heated polemic in West Germany. A group of conservative historians, articulating issues that would reappear in the reunification debate, called for the normalization of German history and declared that the time had arrived to create a new national identity, one not shaped by the Holocaust and nazism.

The fear of a loss of historical memory encouraged others to call for a confederation of the two states or, at least, a slow and thoughtful reunification. If the West no longer has the physical division of Germany to remind it of the nightmare of total war and the Holocaust, the horrors could fade from collective memory. Such sentiments were particularly palpable among the victims of the Second World War. A united Germany would mean the end of a historical epoch, the end of World War II. Or, as Milovan Djilas noted, the end of both the First and Second World Wars. People and nations whose identities had been shaped by those conflicts feared renouncing the memories; the postwar boundaries offered comfort and perpetual reminder. Supporters of German unity also raised the issue of historical memory and the anxiety of changed historical signposts. For Simone Veil, who had herself survived Auschwitz, 3 October 1990 implied *"la guerre est finie."* But, she added, support for German reunification does not mitigate "that we must never forget . . . we must be very vigilant, very demanding that we never forget."

One response to this historical discomfort called for the pursuit of German unity within the context of European unity: if the birth of the new German state came hand in hand with a unified Europe, perhaps the excesses of the "blood and iron" unification of 1871 could be avoided. The call to tie German unity with European integration came from numerous corners: the Green party in West Germany and members of the European Community itself. President François Mitterrand, in December 1989, asked that West Germany should in the first instance work on strengthening the European Community, before rebuilding East Germany. If Germany could be "Europeanized" in the process of being unified, it would weaken the nationalist elements of reunification and offer a solid foundation for European integration. This position held particular resonance for those members of the European Community, such as France and Italy, worried as much about Germany's present as an economic superpower, as about its past as a military one.

The memory of a nationalist and militarist past shaped the debate in Germany as well. The Christian Democrats, in both East and West Germany, by February 1990, favored rapid reunification under Article 23 of the West German Basic Law and showed little anxiety about historical legacies. Without consulting his party or the NATO allies, Kohl had quickly announced his Ten-Point Plan in November 1989. Critics, in turn, accused Kohl of an insensitivity to history and of chauvinism in pushing so stridently for immediate reunification. The West German left became the locus of attention to the past and used it as a brake on events. The West German Green party called for slow movement toward unity, with reunification to occur simultaneous to or following European integration. At first, the Social Democratic party also took a cautious attitude, advocating a wait-and-see policy. In the first months after the fall of the Berlin Wall, a large portion of the West German opposition supported a confederation of the two states in which reunification would follow after a period of reacquaintance and coexistence.

Nationalism, bound up in historically driven anxieties over German reunification, emerged as a second source of unease. This form of discomfort asked to what extent was the drive for a single German state fueled by nationalism and, if so, was it a healthy nationalism or a variant of chauvinism? Was it the desire for a shared national community and culture or somehow connected to past glories? Should those nations that still had influence on German affairs unquestioningly support a movement for national union, merely because both states were German?

Much has been made of the shift in East German demonstration slogans from "We are the people" to "We are one people." The street rallies of September 1989 through January 1990 focused on calls for reform: freedom of the press, of movement, an end to the SED's power monopoly. By mid-winter of 1990, banners calling for reunification with West Germany appeared, as did the flag of the Federal Republic. Why did the East German revolution turn so quickly from internal reform to national/ethnic self-determination? What was it about the Federal Republic, the idea of a single German state, and the East German sense of "Germanness" that made reunification the almost immediate popular response to the crisis of East Germany?

Anxiety that rapid social and economic dislocation would encourage the rise of a destructive nationalism grew as the East German state disintegrated. How would the citizens of East Germany respond to the challenges of a new reality? As noted by several authors in this collection, among them Christa Wolf and Gregor Gysi, the radical right had some successes in the GDR in its final days. Would the deprivations that East Germans were sure to experience after unity—loss of jobs, the shock of the marketplace, the disappearance of the social safety net—lead to the dark underside of nationalism: the search for an "other" to blame for the failures of the national community.

The "intellectuals' debate" raised questions about the prospects for the triumph of a progressive nationalism over its more destructive variant. The united German state would have to build a fresh sense of national identity to bind together the two halves of the new nation. The East Germans had torn down the Lenin- and Marx-based national myths of their immediate past. Given the taint on those of prior period, what sources were there? In the years after reunification, during which Germany will have to reinvent itself, where will the integrating ideas and myths come from? As Saul Friedlander writes, [page 301], reunification will "reunite the Germans not only with the eastern parts of their country, but with their past, with their national myths." This time the Germans face the challenge finding viable aspects of the national myth as the basis of a progressive nationalism.

It was not only the fate of nationalism in the disintegrating GDR that worried intellectuals. Some, such as Jürgen Habermas, wondered how the Federal Republic would sustain the resurrection of the national question; "the citizens of the Federal Republic had developed a non-nationalist self-understanding," but what would happen to this restrained self-identity in the light of the all-German movement? [See text, pages 86–102] Would the Federal Republic's national self-image, based on constitutionalism and the "economic miracle," weather the strain of reconstructing the GDR and hosting new waves of immigrants?

Is the reconstruction of a pre-existing German state along national lines necessarily a good thing? At a time when the category of the nation was being challenged in the West, nationalism raised its destructive face in Eastern

Europe, and particularly Yugoslavia, the former Soviet republics, and Czechoslovakia. Despite talk in Western Europe about the obsolescence of nationalism in the face of economic superblocs and a world economy, nationalism remains a dangerous force. The lifting of the Soviet lid quickly brought ethnic conflict, irredentist claims, and religious tensions out into the open. Certainly, as Eric Hobsbawm writes, the politics of group identity and nationalism are "easier to understand than others, especially for peoples who, after decades of dictatorship, lack both political education and experience."[2] Given the violence wrought by nationalist passions in the early 1990s, might not the world's approval of German nationalism send the wrong message?

Despite the fact that the nationalist rhetoric of German unity was by and large moderate and self-conscious, incidents did occur, fueling fears of the rise of a "Fourth Reich." During the festivities surrounding reunification, reporters noted the singing of songs from the Nazi period in and around the Berlin Wall and skinheads assaulting foreigners and guest workers. Neo-Nazi groups have successfully recruited members in East Germany, since freedom of movement began in late 1989. West German Neo-Nazis groups, such as the Republicans, a conglomeration of revanchists, ultrarightists, and xenophobes, used the power vacuum and social disintegration in the GDR to spread their message of hate. By the fall of 1991, Neo-Nazi violence against immigrants and foreigners reached epidemic proportions, with attacks on foreigners' hostels leading to deaths in a number of eastern German towns and with the *New York Times* labeling the wave of violence "Germany's racial crisis."[3] Over nine hundred attacks on foreigners were reported in October 1991.[4] While many German citizens have rallied to the aid of embattled immigrants, Chancellor Kohl has remained eerily quiet on the issue.

Chancellor Kohl's initial reluctance to secure the Germany/Polish border in early 1990 unleashed another flurry of unease over German intentions. Kohl's answer that he could not make commitments for both German states did little to dampen Polish fears; the crisis did not end until the West German government issued an unequivocal commitment and the Poles were brought into those aspects of the Two Plus Four talks that touched on their national interest. Polish Prime Minister Tadeusz Mazowiecki went so far as to propose that Soviet troops remain longer in Poland as protection. Some commentators, such as the East German Party of Democratic Socialism (PDS) official Hans Willerding, attributed Kohl's foot-dragging on the border issue to the need

---

[2] Eric Hobsbawm, "The Perils of the New Nationalism," *The Nation*, November 4, 1991.
[3] Stephen Kinzer, "Seeking Peace in a German Hostel Faced by Hate," *The New York Times*, October 13, 1991.
[4] Stephen Kinzer, "The Neo-Nazis: How Quickly They Remember," *The New York Times*, November 17, 1991.

to shore up right-wing and nationalist support in the March 1990 election. Kohl's deference to the nationalist far right attests to its continued power.

The Federal Republic, despite its record of democracy and stability, has shown, in the course of its history, tendencies that have worried some observers. Many, such as William Safire, raised questions about West German arms sales—conventional and chemical—to Middle Eastern dictators, from Libya's Khaddafi to Iraq's Hussein [see text, pages 186–7]. West German citizenship laws also did little to quell accusations of Pan-German sentiments: the Federal Republic's Basic Law or constitution recognizes only a single German citizenship, available to *all* and *only* ethnic Germans. On the one hand, prior to reunification, East Germans were automatically issued West German papers in the Federal Republic or at a West German embassy. Ethnic Germans from Eastern Europe, searching for proof of "Germanness," have used family Nazi affiliation as evidence. On the other hand, the nearly five million Turks and other foreigners resident in Germany cannot even aspire to citizenship, since they are not ethnically German.

The character of the reunification itself proved to be a third important source of anxiety. The integration of East Germany by West Germany, in a moment of weakness and chaos, led critics to worry about the process. The fact that the reunification took place under Article 23 of the West German Basic Law, with the five East German states joining the Federal Republic, gave the procedure an unequal character that mirrored the disparate power relations of the two states: was West German economic might triumphing over East Germany in a moment of total political, social, and economic crisis? For many, the absorption seemed like the "buying out" of the GDR by the Federal Republic. Others, drawing on the emotionalized memory of Nazi expansionism, pushed the metaphor further, calling it a modern day *Anschluss*.

Suddenly, in the fall and winter of 1989, East Germany was up for grabs. Critics of West Germany's active intervention in the East German economy and society labeled the West's absorption of the GDR a type of "discount sale." Or, at least for the businessmen of the Federal Republic, who, wrote Michael Burda in the *New York Times,* came to the GDR "to take part in the greatest fire sale in history."[5] Günter Grass called the West German intervention "colonization." Today, one year after reunification, 85 percent of East German real estate has at least one western property claim pending. Many former East Germans face losing their homes, in addition to jobs and the security of forty years of social protections. Communal kindergartens are being transformed into private estates as fast as one can say "post-industrial capitalism."[5]

---

[5] For the tale of one such kindergarten soon to be a private estate, see Katie Hafner, "The House We Lived In," *The New York Times Magazine,* November 10, 1991.

Why did the November Revolution in the GDR, the first democratic revolution on German soil since 1918, fail? The fall of 1989 in East Germany was a period of hope, as citizens' groups, such as New Forum and Democracy Now, called for a radical renewal of socialism. The well-known Monday Demonstrations in Leipzig focused on democracy, free elections, and an end to the police state. A reading of the early manifestoes reveals a language of dissent and social democracy. The rallying cries envisioned returning the GDR to the origins of German social democracy or what Christoph Hein called "socialism that doesn't make a caricature of the word" [see text, page 127]. For example, the founding manifesto of Democracy Now declared:

> Socialism must now find its true, democratic form, if it is not to be lost to history. It must not be lost, for threatened humanity, in its search for survivable forms of human coexistence, needs alternatives to Western consumer society, the prosperity of which is paid for by the rest of the world.

East German reformers and intellectuals, both associated with and in opposition to the former ruling party (SED) and its successor (PDS), spoke emotionally about a "third way" between capitalism and communism, about a critique of what western capitalism and West German society had to offer. Prior to the 18 March 1990 elections, some East Germans envisioned the construction of a society that could avoid the cruel lessons of both dictatorship and unrestrained capitalism. Many dissidents felt that there were aspects of life in East Germany worth preserving. Some East Germans feared the loss of social protections, the brutality and costs of the open market. East Germans had been buffered from the Social Darwinism of the West. And, as Martin Ahrends writes, the limited opportunities for expression in the public sphere and the lack of a commodity culture and mass culture resulted in an intense commitment to personal and familial ties on the part of East Germans [see text, pages 157–64]. The East German opposition feared the extent to which consumerism lay behind the calls for German unity. This critique was reinforced by pictures of the frenzied shopping of the 200,000 East Germans who visited the Federal Republic on 10–12 November 1989.

In the first months of the East German revolution, the pressure of citizens groups produced reform: the SED gave up its constitutional power monopoly, free elections were planned, the *Stasi* was dissolved, and Round Table negotiations were held between the government and the opposition. By March 1989, the East German cabinet included a Ministry for Disarmament and Defense, headed by the pastor Rainer Eppelmann and also contained three other pastors and four women. The "Social Charter" drafted by the last preelection *Volkskammer* provided for a range of rights—more comprehensive than those of West Germany—including the right to work, the right to strike, the banning of lockouts by management, and education and housing guarantees.

Advocates of immediate reunification under West German hegemony argued that the collapse of the Wall and Stalinism removed all legitimacy from the East German state. According to this position, the GDR represented a nightmare best forgotten, to be replaced as fast as possible by an eastern Germany reconstructed in the image of the Federal Republic. Was there an East German identity beyond the Wall? Had there evolved something culturally and socially different in the eastern part of Germany between 1945 and 1990? While many saw the GDR as defined by its political and economic centralization, others saw a more complex vision. Christa Wolf saw the history of the GDR as one of forward and backward steps; she found value in the state's antifascist foundation and socialist aspirations. East German intellectuals, such as Wolf and Stefan Heym, believed that forty years of a separate history and social system had produced an authentic East German voice, worthy of continued existence. They rejected the use of the crisis of the state as an excuse to declare it illegitimate and to erase its past [see text: Schoefer, pages 205–6].

The GDR, while the loser in a material competition with the Federal Republic, had functioned for forty years. Its economy had been the shining star of the Eastern Bloc. A certain social equality, beyond the party elite, existed; the social net prevented the creation of an underclass. A noncompetitive culture of resignation and material limits, writes Martin Ahrends, produced a society focused on the intangibles of daily reality: home, people, "poetry and self-concentration." Peter Marcuse favorably compared the "self-awareness and skepticism of the citizens of the GDR" with the "self-assurance to the point of arrogance of many West Germans" [see text, page 203].

One suggestion for mitigating the "fire-sale" aspect of a reunification dominated by the Federal Republic was the creation of a confederation. East German reformers, such as Gregor Gysi and the West German opposition, including Grass and Habermas, envisioned this as a way to achieve a more equal coexistence, allowing East Germany to work out its fate and, perhaps, retain some elements of its forty-year experiment. When reunification seemed a foregone conclusion in the spring of 1990, critics raised an alternative to absorption, which might limit the extent to which the Federal Republic could set the terms: a constitutional debate under Article 146 of the West German Basic Law. According to this position, the East Germans would not be entering the compact as second class citizens, but could participate in the creation of a new political culture. Maybe, ran this argument, even some of the positive social aspects of the reformed East German constitution could be integrated into a new German governing law.

Chancellor Kohl read the collapse of the GDR and Soviet preoccupations as the green light to "make history." His moment had come to be the "Unification Chancellor." Or, as Flora Lewis described, Kohl seemed "to be trying to gobble up East Germany without even saying grace."[6] Those West Germans urging immediate reunification used the draining of people and resources from the GDR to delegitimize the state and push forward reunification under a conservative agenda.

The March 1990 elections in the GDR, in addition to being the first free East German elections, quickly became a West German orchestrated referendum on economic and political union. The election campaign was marked by "Social Democrats and Kohl's Christian Democrats, swarm[ing] over the border with copious quantities of bananas, beer, and bratwurst . . ."[7] Advisers and money accompanied the beer and bananas. Kohl's repeated appearances at East German CDU rallies encouraged the citizens of the GDR to see a Christian Democratic victory as the promise of a West German standard of living.

East Germans went to the polls under pressure and from a position of weakness. By the time of the election, the GDR had been drained of resources and people. East Germans anxiously watched the other former East Bloc nations in the throes of economic dislocation and saw the merger with West Germany as the only life preserver tossed to them in rocky seas. The East German opposition could not compete with the highly organized, high-technology campaigning of the Western parties. The Christian Democrats (CDU) polled 40 percent, the Social Democrats (SPD) 21 percent, and the PDS 16 percent. The groups that led the revolution of November 1989, allied together as Alliance '90, made an exceedingly poor showing, attracting only 5 percent of the electorate.

The West German pressure, and the receding of other alternatives, was ensured in July 1990 with the monetary union. The power of the deutsche mark or what Jurgen Habermas calls *Deutschemarknationalismus,* which made the March 1990 elections a foregone conclusion, was enshrined by the monetary union. As Hans Magnus Enzensberger notes, the arrival of the D mark in July made rapid unity under West German direction a *fait accompli.*

Uneasiness over various aspects of the reunification process, from the first GDR/Federal Republic negotiations to the monetary union and the final state treaties, emerges in this collection. This aspect of the debate asked important questions about how the reunification process itself would affect the new German state.

Concerns over the ramifications of rapid reunification under West German predominance have proven salient. In the first year of national unity, former East Germany has been destabilized by mass unemployment and widespread disillusionment at the costs of transformation. The rejection of all elements of the pre-reunification society, and the elevation of all things "Western" have

---

[6] Flora Lewis, "No Time for Politics," *The New York Times,* March 10, 1990.

[7] Peter Rossman, "Dashed Hopes for A New Socialism," *The Nation,* April 2, 1990.

caused diffused insecurity and an identity crisis among many East Germans. In the name of rapid "purification," there have been massive renamings of towns, streets, and schools; witch-hunts and crusades are leveled against former elites at all levels. The universities have been purged of "ideologically impure" faculty. The two million former East Germans whose life histories were intricately bound up in their SED membership, as well as all the others who had accommodated in varying degrees with the regime, now face ostracism and self-hatred.

The schizophrenia and self-hatred has and will continue to have serious implications for the new nation. There will be growing anger, inflicted within and without, at the costs of transforming state socialism into capitalism. Some of the discontent at the price of transformation has turned into social regression, in the shape of radical nationalist and xenophobic sentiments.

A discussion of the anxieties produced by German unity must acknowledge the historical oversimplification that took place in the course of the debate. This fourth source of discomfort involved the tendency to equate German events with those in Eastern Europe and the Soviet Union and to interpret the changes as a seamless capitalist victory in the cold war. The rapidity of events lent them to a facile interpretation. For many, the historical demise of state socialism became a vindication of capitalism and its excesses.

We must be careful, in the rush to celebrate the end of dictatorship, not to merge all ideologies into two. The differences between social democracy, and the reformation of communism in a socialist direction, and what existed in the SED-controlled East Germany were stressed again and again by the opposition in both East and West Germany. The communism of Erich Honecker was not the Social Democracy of Sweden. In the March 1990 East German elections, the Christian Democrats played the game of oversimplification to their own advantage, calling the SPD "socialist" (using the appellation "PDSPD" to make the point) and trying to force the electorate to connect it to the SED. By the beginning of 1990, solutions to the left of Helmut Kohl had fallen prey to an atmosphere of accusation and hysteria. The delimiting of choices negated the possibility of compromise and encouraged a climate of witch-hunting.

There remains a viable pantheon of socialist and social democratic ideas that still have resonance and value today as the West seeks to reconcile a market economy with social opportunity. Some observers have posed the choice as a simple one between the "plan" and the "market." The lessons about command economies to be drawn from the collapse of communism are more complex. The dichotomy between the market and the plan is a false one: no pure market economy exists. The most successful capitalist state, Japan, is based on extensive state direction.

The pressing search is, rather, as Peter Marcuse writes, for "alternatives that are neither real existing socialism nor real existing capitalism" [see text, page 204]. A working "third way," writes Robin Blackburn, would "respect the complex structures of self-determination which the market embodies, while vigorously resisting its propensity to promote social division and stimulate an oblivious and greedy consumerism."[8] Further, to some the casual calamities of a market economy are no less repugnant than the predictable ones of a planned economy. As noted by authors in this collection, the conditions of inequality that first produced communism and socialism remain profoundly real in the wake of its collapse.

As the debate over German reunification and the fate of the GDR demonstrated, the failure of the command economies of Eastern Europe and the Soviet Union implied more than a green light for the free market. In the heat of rapid historical change, simple black and white answers are the most comforting. A facile anti-Stalinism, which equates all movements concerned with social justice and reform with the failed communist regimes, offers easy answers: collapse of communist block equals a capitalist victory in the cold war. The lifting of the lid of Soviet domination from East Germany was positive and desirable. Yet, with the lid removed the citizens of East Germany were required to make decisions under duress. What choices did they really have? What real options existed beyond the West German model?

With the arrival of a new historical epoch, one must beware of shaping history too closely to the vision of the victors. The cold war will not be over until the problems and limits of postindustrial capitalism are addressed and until the emerging ones of postcommunist societies in the throes of dislocation are met without condescension and arrogance.

From the distance of only a single year, some of the issues that resided in the debate are surprisingly obsolete. The pages written in the spring of 1990 about which defense alliance Germany should join, or the suggestion that they join both, were printed in vain.[9] The discussions over what to do with the 380,000 Soviet troops on GDR territory appears equally dated, in the light of the collapse of the Soviet Union. As of November 1991, the Warsaw Pact is dead; President Bush, in Rome for a NATO meeting, even suggested that the United States seriously redefine its role in the defense of Europe, hinting that NATO may also have to reconsider its purpose.

German unification took place with such speed that it was difficult to hear all the discordant voices at the time. In this way, the collection is also about giving space to the many voices, dominant and minority, assenting and dissenting, of the process. We have included the reactions of those who made the decisions, the politicians, from Helmut Kohl to François Mitterrand to

[8] Robin Blackburn, ed., *After the Fall* Verso: London & New York, 1991, p. xiv.
[9] John Lewis Gaddis, "One Germany—in Both Alliances," *The New York Times*, March 21, 1990.

Vaclav Havel and the words of those whose contributions were less directly political. Many of the pieces come from observers and interpreters of political change: journalists, writers, and academics. This book contains the voices that, in the end, emerged triumphant, as well as those that the engine of history has pushed into the background.

West Germany

A Ten-Point Program for Overcoming the Division of Germany and Europe

presented by Chancellor Helmut Kohl

Helmut Kohl, born in 1930, has been chairman of the
CDU since 1973 and chancellor of the Federal Republic
since 1982. From 1969 to 1976 he was minister-president
of the Rhineland-Palatinate. This ten-point program, announced in a speech to the *Bundestag* on 28 November
1989, constituted his initial response to the constitutional
issues raised by the impending collapse of the GDR.

All speakers today have rightly stressed that current political debate quite
naturally focuses on intra-German relations.

Since the opening of the intra-German border and the sectoral boundary
in Berlin on November 9, relations between the two German states have
entered into a new phase which offers new opportunities and poses new
challenges. We are all overjoyed about the newly won freedom of movement
for those living in divided Germany. We, along with the Germans in the GDR,
are glad that the wall and the border fortifications have finally, after decades,
been overcome peacefully.

We are also proud that the Germans in the GDR have, with their peaceful
intervention for freedom, human rights and self-determination, demonstrated
their courage and love of freedom to the world, setting an example which has
evoked praise all over the world.

We are deeply impressed by the passionate and unbroken desire for freedom
shown by the people of Leipzig and many other cities. They know what they
want. They want to determine their own future, in the true sense of the word.

We will, of course, respect every free decision taken by the people in the
GDR. Particularly at this time, we in the Federal Republic of Germany stand
side by side with our fellow countrymen. At the beginning of last week, Federal
Minister Seiters spoke with the chairman of the Council of State, Mr. Krenz,
and Prime Minister Modrow about the new leadership's intentions. We wanted
to find out how the announced reform program is to be put into effect, and
the time-frame for concrete steps which will genuinely benefit the people.

It was agreed that the talks would be continued at the beginning of December. If, as we hope, they produce signs of initial practical results, I would
personally like to meet the responsible groups in the GDR before Christmas.

Mr. Seiters also spoke with representatives of the opposition and the church in East Berlin. In the last few weeks I myself, like many others here in the house, have met representatives of the opposition. We have to take account of the views, opinions and recommendations of the opposition groups in the GDR in everything we decide and do now. We continue to place great value on these contacts. We should all cultivate them carefully.

Opportunities are presenting themselves for overcoming the division of Europe and hence of our fatherland. The Germans, who are now coming together in the spirit of freedom, will never pose a threat. Rather will they, I am convinced, be an asset to a Europe which is growing more and more together.

The credit for the present transformation goes primarily to the people, who are so impressively demonstrating their will for freedom. But it is also the outcome of numerous political developments in the past. We in the Federal Republic have with our policy also contributed substantially to this process.

- First, it was crucial that we pursued that policy on the solid foundation of our integration within the community of free democracies. The alliance's cohesion and steadfastness during the difficult test in 1983 have paid off. By steering a clear course in the Atlantic alliance and the European Community we have strengthened the backbone of the reform movement in Central, Eastern and Southeastern Europe by pursuing our clear course within the Atlantic alliance and in the European Community.

- By progressing to new stages of economic and political integration within the European Community we have successfully developed the model of a free association of European nations whose attraction, as anyone can see, extends far beyond the community itself.

- On the other hand, a decisive prerequisite was General Secretary Gorbachev's reform policy in the Soviet Union and the "new thinking" in Soviet foreign policy. Without the recognition of the right of nations and states to determine their own course, the reform movements in other Warsaw Pact countries would not have been successful.

- If Poland and Hungary had not led the way with far-reaching political, economic and social reforms, the dramatic developments in the GDR would not have taken place. The success of the reform movements in those countries is a prerequisite for the success of the reform movement in the GDR. This also means that we must do all we can to ensure that these two countries achieve the goals they have set themselves.

We all welcome the signs of change in Bulgaria and Czechoslovakia as well. I am particularly gratified to note that this year's winner of the German Book Association's Peace Prize, Vaclav Havel, is now finally able to harvest the fruits of his long struggle for freedom. His outstanding, unforgettable acceptance speech in Frankfurt's Paulskirche, which he could not deliver himself, was an impressive final reckoning with the system of "practical socialism."

- The CSCE [Conference on Security and Cooperation in Europe] process has also played an important role. We, together with our partners, have always pressed for the elimination of sources of tension, for dialogue and cooperation, and most particularly for respect for human rights.
- Thanks not least to the continuous summit diplomacy of the major powers and the numerous meetings between Eastern and Western heads of state and government, a new trust was able to develop in East-West relations. The historic breakthrough in disarmament and arms control is a visible expression of this trust.
- The federal government's broadly based contractual policy towards the Soviet Union and all other Warsaw Pact countries has generated strong impulses for the development of East-West relations.
- But our policy to maintain national solidarity is also one of the reasons for the recent changes. If we had listened to those, some of them members of this house, who called upon us to accept the demands made by Mr. Honecker in Gera, we would not have achieved anything like the progress
  . . .

Since 1987 millions of fellow countrymen from the GDR have visited us, among them many young people. This policy of small steps has in difficult times kept us aware of our national unity and strengthened the feeling of German fellowship.

The developments of recent years, the well over ten million visitors between 1987 and the summer of this year, refute all the gloomy predictions made in 1983, and constantly since, that this coalition government would usher in a new "ice age" in East-West relations. I mention once more that outrageous insinuation that we are "incapable of fostering peace."

But precisely the opposite has happened. Today we have a greater sense of understanding and community in Germany and Europe than has ever been felt since the end of the Second World War, and we are grateful for it.

Today, as everyone can see, we have reached a new epoch in European and German history. This is an age which points beyond the status quo and the old political structures in Europe. This change is primarily the work of the people, who demand freedom, respect for their human rights and their right to be masters of their own future.

All who bear responsibility in and for Europe have to make allowances for the will of the people and nations. We are called upon to design a new architecture for the European home and for a permanent and just peaceful order on our continent—as both General Secretary Gorbachev and I already stressed in our joint declaration on June 13. In this process the legitimate interests of all concerned must be guaranteed. This, of course, includes German interests as well.

We are thus approaching the goal set by the Atlantic alliance in December 1987, and I quote:

"No final and stable settlement in Europe is possible without a solution of the German Question which lies at the heart of present tensions in Europe. Any settlement must end the unnatural barriers between Eastern and Western Europe, which are most clearly and cruelly manifested in the division of Germany."

If that is our common foundation then all members of the house will, I hope, be able to agree to the following. We all know that we cannot plan the way to German unity simply in theory or with our appointment calendars. Abstract models may be all right for polemical purposes but they help us no further. Today, however, we are in a position to prepare in advance the stages which lead to this goal. These I would like to elucidate with the following ten-point plan.

1. Immediate measures are called for as a result of events of recent weeks, particularly the flow of resettlers and the huge increase in the number of travellers. The Federal government will provide immediate aid where it is needed. We will assist in the humanitarian sector and provide medical aid if it is wanted and considered helpful.

We are also aware that the welcome money given once a year to every visitor from the GDR is no answer to the question of travel funds. The GDR must itself provide travellers with the necessary foreign exchange. We are, however, prepared to contribute to a currency fund for a transitional period, provided that persons entering the GDR no longer have to exchange a minimum amount of currency, that entry into the GDR is made considerably easier, and that the GDR itself contributes substantially to the fund.

Our aim is to facilitate traffic as much as possible in both directions.

2. The Federal government will continue its cooperation with the GDR in all areas where it is of direct benefit to the people on both sides, especially in the economic, scientific, technological and cultural fields. It is particularly important to intensify cooperation in the field of environmental protection. Here we will be able to take decisions on new projects shortly, irrespective of other developments.

We also want to extensively increase telephone links with the GDR and help expand the GDR's telephone network. The Federal minister of posts and telecommunications has begun talks on this subject.

Negotiations continue on the extension of the Hanover-Berlin Railway Line. This is not enough, however, and we need to take a thorough look at transport and rail systems in the GDR and the Federal Republic in light of the new situation. Forty years of separation also mean that traffic routes have in some cases developed quite differently. This applies not only to border crossing-points but to the traditional east-west lines of communication in Central

Europe. There seems to be no reason why the classic Moscow-Warsaw-Berlin-Paris route, which always included Cologne and was of great importance at all times, should not be brought into consideration in the age of high-speed trains and extended accordingly.

3. I have offered comprehensive aid and cooperation, should the GDR bindingly undertake to carry out a fundamental change in the political and economic system and put the necessary measures irreversibly into effect. By "irreversible" we mean that the GDR leadership must reach agreement with opposition groups on constitutional amendments and a new electoral law.

We support the demand for free, equal and secret elections in the GDR, in which, of course, independent, that is to say, non-socialist, parties would also participate. The SED's monopoly on power must be removed. The introduction of a democratic system means, above all, the abolition of laws on political crimes and the immediate release of all political prisoners.

Economic aid can only be effective if the economic system is radically reformed. This is obvious from the situation in all COMECON [a popular abbreviation for the Council for Mutual Economic Assistance] states and is not a question of our preaching to them. The centrally planned economy must be dismantled.

We do not want to stabilize conditions that have become indefensible. Economic improvement can only occur if the GDR opens its doors to Western investment, if conditions of free enterprise are created, and if private initiative becomes possible. I don't understand those who accuse us of tutelage in this respect. There are daily examples of this in Hungary and Poland which can surely be followed by the GDR, likewise a member of COMECON.

Our sincere hope is that the necessary legislation will be introduced quickly, because we would not be very happy if private capital were to be invested in Poland and—with developments progressing so well—even more so in Hungary, which I would also welcome, but not in the middle of Germany. We want as many companies as possible to invest as much as possible.

I wish to emphasize once again that these are not preconditions but simply the foundations needed for effective assistance. Nor can there be any doubt that the people in the GDR want this. They want economic freedom which will enable them at long last to reap the fruit of their labor and enjoy more prosperity.

When I consider how this matter of the GDR's future economic system is being discussed by the SED itself—it will all be heard publicly at its special convention in a few days' time—I cannot for the life of me see how anyone saying this can be accused of meddling in the GDR's internal affairs. I find that rather absurd.

4. Prime Minister Modrow spoke in his government policy statement of a "contractual community." We are prepared to adopt this idea. The proximity of our two states in Germany and the special nature of their relationship demand an increasingly close network of agreements in all sectors and at all levels.

This cooperation will also require more common institutions. The existing commissions could be given new tasks and new ones created, especially for industry, transport, environmental protection, science and technology, health and cultural affairs. It goes without saying that Berlin will be fully incorporated in these cooperative efforts. This has always been our policy.

5. We are also prepared to take a further decisive step, namely, to develop confederative structures between the two states in Germany with a view to creating a federation. But this presupposes the election of a democratic government in the GDR.

We can envisage the following institutions being created after early, free elections:

- an intergovernmental committee for continuous consultation and political coordination,
- joint technical committees,
- a joint parliamentary body,
- and many others in the light of new developments.

Previous policy towards the GDR had to be limited mainly to small steps by which we sought above all to alleviate the consequences of division and to keep alive and strengthen the people's awareness of unity of the nation. If, in the future, a democratically legitimized, that is, a freely elected government, becomes our partner, that will open up completely new perspectives.

Gradually, new forms of institutional cooperation can be created and further developed. Such coalescence is inherent in the continuity of German history. State organization in Germany has nearly always taken the form of a confederation or federation. We can fall back on this past experience. Nobody knows at the present time what a reunited Germany will look like. I am, however, sure that unity will come, if it is wanted by the German people.

6. The development of intra-German relations remains embedded in the pan-European process, that is to say in the framework of East-West relations. The future architecture of Germany must fit into the future architecture of Europe as a whole. Here the West has shown itself to be pacemaker with its concept of a lasting and equitable peaceful order in Europe.

In our joint declaration of June this year, which I have already quoted, General Secretary Gorbachev and I spoke of the structural elements of a "common European Home." There are, for example:

- unqualified respect for the integrity and security of each state. Each state has the right freely to choose its own political and social system.
- unqualified respect for the principles and rules of international law, especially respect for the people's right of self-determination.
- the realization of human rights.
- respect for and maintenance of the traditional cultures of the nations of Europe.

With all of these points, as Mr. Gorbachev and I laid down, we aim to follow Europe's long traditions and help overcome the division of Europe.

7.   The attraction and aura of the European Community are and remain a constant feature of pan-European development. We want to and must strengthen them further still.

The European Community must now approach the reformist countries of Central, Eastern and Southeastern Europe with openness and flexibility. This was also endorsed by the heads of state and government of the EC member states at their recent meeting in Paris.

This of course includes the GDR. The Federal government therefore approves the early conclusion of a trade and cooperation agreement with the GDR. This would give it a wider access to the Common Market, also in the perspective of 1992.

We can envisage specific forms of association which would lead the reformist countries of Central and Southeastern Europe to the European Community, thus helping to level the economic and social gradients on our continent. This is one of the crucial issues if tomorrow's Europe is to be a united Europe.

We have always regarded the process leading to the recovery of German unity to be a European concern as well. It must, therefore, also be seen in the context of European integration. To put it simply, the EC must not end at the Elbe but must remain open to the East.

Only in this way can the EC be the foundation for a truly comprehensive European union—after all, we have always regarded the Twelve as only a part, not as the whole, of the continent. Only in this way can it maintain, assert and develop the common European identity. That identity is not only based on the cultural diversity of Europe but also, and especially, on the fundamental values of freedom, democracy, human rights and self-determination.

If the countries of Central and Southeastern Europe meet the requirements, we would also welcome their membership in the Council of Europe, and especially in the Convention for the Protection of Human Rights and Fundamental Freedoms.

8. The CSCE process is a central element of the pan-European architecture and must be vigorously promoted in the following forums:
    - the human rights conferences in Copenhagen, in 1990, and in Moscow, in 1991;
    - the Conference on Economic Cooperation in Bonn, in 1990;
    - the Symposium on Cultural Heritage in Cracow, in 1991; and
    - last but not least the next follow-up meeting in Helsinki.

There we should also think about new institutional forms of pan-European cooperation. We can well imagine a common institution for the coordination of East-West economic cooperation, as well as the creation of a pan-European environmental council.

9. Overcoming the division of Europe and Germany presupposes far-reaching and rapid steps in the field of disarmament and arms control. Disarmament and arms control must keep pace with political developments and thus be accelerated where necessary.

This is particularly true of the Vienna negotiations on the reduction of conventional forces in Europe, and for the agreement on confidence-building measures and the global ban on chemical weapons, which we hope will materialize in 1990. It also requires that the nuclear potential of the superpowers be reduced to the strategically necessary minimum. The forthcoming meeting between President Bush and General Secretary Gorbachev offers a good opportunity to add new impetus to the current negotiations.

We are doing our best—also in bilateral discussions with the Warsaw Pact countries, including the GDR—to support this process.

10. With this comprehensive policy we are working for a state of peace in Europe in which the German nation can recover its unity in free self-determination. Reunification—that is regaining national unity—remains the political goal of the Federal government. We are grateful that once again we have received support in this matter from our allies in the declaration issued after the NATO summit meeting in Brussels in May.

We are conscious of the fact that many difficult problems will confront us on the road to German unity, problems for which no one has a definitive solution today. Above all, this includes the difficult and crucial question of overlapping security structures in Europe.

The linking of the German Question to pan-European developments and

East-West relations, as explained in these ten points, will allow a natural development which takes account of the interests of all concerned and paves the way for peaceful development in freedom, which is our objective.

Only together and in an atmosphere of mutual trust will we be able to peacefully overcome the division of Europe, which is also the division of Germany. This calls for prudence, understanding and sound judgement on all sides so that the current promising developments may continue steadily and peacefully. This process cannot be hampered by reforms, rather by their rejection. It is not freedom that creates instability but its suppression. Every successful step towards reform means more stability and more freedom and security for the whole of Europe.

In a few weeks' time we enter the final decade of this century, a century which has seen so much misery, bloodshed and suffering. There are today many promising signs that the nineties will bring more peace and freedom in Europe and in Germany. Much depends, and everyone senses this, on the German contribution. We should all face this challenge of history.

Berlin City Hall Speech

by *Willy Brandt*

Willy Brandt, born in 1913, was chancellor of the Federal
Republic from 1969 until 1974 when he resigned after
the discovery of an East German intelligence agent on his
personal staff. Since 1976 he has been president of the
Socialist International, and is honorary chairman of the
SPD. He gave this speech on 10 November 1989 outside
the Schöneberg City Hall in Berlin (West), immediately
after the ending of travel restrictions for GDR citizens.

This is a beautiful day after a long journey. But we are presently only at an
intermediate step. We have not arrived at the end of the road yet. There is
still a lot ahead of us.

The fact that Berliners, and Germans in general, belong together manifests
itself in a way that moves us and stirs us up. It is most poignant in the cases
where separated families finally are unexpectedly and tearfully reunited. I
was also touched by the image of a policeman on our side who crossed over
to his colleague on the other side and said: "We have seen each other from
a distance for so many weeks, maybe even months; I want to shake your hand
for once." That is the right way to approach what is facing us: to take each
others' hands, and only to continue to bear a grudge if it is absolutely necessary. And, whenever possible, to overcome any bitterness. I also sensed that
this afternoon at the Brandenburg Gate.

As mayor during the difficult years from 1957 to 1966, at the time when
the Wall was built, and as a person who did a lot in and for the Federal
Republic to reduce tensions in Europe and who fought for the greatest amount
of practical connections and human contacts attainable: I give my sincerest
greetings to the Berliners in all parts of the city and equally to my compatriots
everywhere in Germany.

A great deal will now depend on whether we—we Germans on both sides—
prove to be equal to this historical situation. The fact that the Germans are
moving closer together is what really matters. The fact that the Germans are
moving closer together is happening differently than most people expected.
And no one should now pretend as if he knew exactly what concrete form
the new relationship between the people in both states will take. What is
important is that they develop a different relationship to one another, that
they can meet in freedom and grow with one another.

And what is certain is that nothing in the other part of Germany will ever be the same as it was. The winds of change that have been sweeping across Europe for some time now have not been able to sweep by Germany. It has always been my conviction that the concrete partition and the division through barbed wire and death strip stood in opposition to the course of history. And I had put it to paper once again this summer: Berlin will live, and the Wall will fall. Incidentally, as far as I am concerned, at that point we can even let a piece of that dreadful construction stand as a reminder of a historical monster. Just as, at the time, after intense discussion, we consciously decided to let the ruins of the *Gedächtniskirche* stand in our city.

Those who are still quite young and those who come hereafter will not always find it easy to understand clearly the historical context in which we are situated. This is why I am not only saying that we have a lot ahead of us until the end of the division—I spoke out against it in August '61 with anger, but also with a feeling of powerlessness—but I also want to remind us that all of this did not start on August 13, 1961. The German misery started with the terrorist Nazi regime and the war that was unleashed by it. That terrible war, that reduced Berlin, like so many other German and non-German cities, into mountains of rubble. Out of that war and out of the rupture between the victorious powers grew the division of Europe. Germany and Berlin: What belongs together now grows together. Now we are experiencing, and I am grateful to God that I can live to see this, the parts of Europe growing together.

I am confident that the President of the United States and the first man of the Soviet Union will know to appreciate what is happening here when they meet on a ship in the Mediterranean in the near future. And I am confident that our French and British friends—along with the Americans they were reliable protectors [*Schutzmächte*] in difficult years—know to regard the process of change and the new awakening as important. I know that our neighbors in Eastern Europe understand what it is that moves us, and that it is part of the new ways of thinking and acting that the Central and Eastern Europeans are themselves involved in. The assurance that we can offer our neighbors and the great powers of this world as well is that we will not seek any solutions to our problems that are not in accordance with our responsibilities towards peace and towards Europe. We are led by the common conviction that the European Community must be developed further and that the parceling of our continent must gradually but definitely be overcome.

Back then, in August '61, we did not only demand out of a justifiable rage that the Wall must come down. We also had to say: Berlin must continue to live in spite of the Wall. We rebuilt the city—with the help of the Federal government, which we also do not want to forget. Others who came after us contributed many important things to the reconstruction. But here in Berlin, in addition to all of the inner city tasks, in addition to housing construction and to cultural and economic reconstruction, we were instructed to keep the path to Germany open. We deliberated intensely on how we could counteract the particularly brutal effects of the partition, even when these efforts seemed virtually hopeless, and how German and European cohesion could be maintained and cultivated in spite of the division. Naturally there was not always an immediate consensus on how this could be accomplished most effectively.

The date of December 18, 1963 has particularly imprinted itself upon my memory. Not just because it was my birthday, but because that was the day that, on the basis of passes—we could not get anything more than that— hundreds of thousands of people were on the other side, not only visiting relatives but also those who were from "the zone." All that was of course insufficient and remained terribly fragile. But we did not let ourselves be discouraged from making every possible effort to foster contacts between people and to keep the cohesion of the nation alive.

It took almost another decade until the changes that were possible at the time were actually achieved by means of a transit treaty [*Verkehrsvertrag*] and a Basic Treaty [*Grundlagenvertrag*]. A large number of agreements and arrangements followed. It is still right that we could not afford to allow a vacuum to develop even for national reasons.

It was also right for us to relieve and improve the external circumstances of the divided Germany and the people in it whenever the opportunity arose. That was the essence of our treaty policy. That was the essence of our efforts to organize an all-European conference in Helsinki, which had a difficult inception but was dedicated to human rights, to cooperation, and also to the dismantling of the excessive armaments in Europe. And this slow movement towards stability and towards dismantling rather than fostering the arms race is now paying off. This movement is underway; it has considerably contributed to the fact that we have a better framework of conditions to deal with today. And I add to this: if I know my compatriots in the other part of Germany well, then they will agree with me, and I think with all of us, on these matters. No one wants any difficulties with the Soviet soldiers that are still situated on German soil. They will not always remain there. Things will change concerning the military presence. We want to find peaceful solutions, particularly in regard to the superpower in the East.

I still want to add: in addition to the fact that the situation in the Soviet Union also looks rather promising and that there are democratic movements in Poland and Hungary—they will follow in other countries—a new factor of original quality has to be taken into account. This factor consists of the fact that our compatriots in the GDR and in East Berlin have taken their destiny into their own hands for all the world to see. The people themselves have spoken, have demanded changes, not least of all the right to accurate information, to free travel, and to assemble in organizations freely. I believe that the popular movement in the other part of Germany can only find its fulfillment in truly free elections. And I also believe that it can be a very rewarding experience to play a part in the work of renewal here and now, and not simply to leave that work to those who are left behind.

Once again: nothing will ever be the same as it was. That also means that we in the West will no longer be judged according to the more or less flattering slogans of the past, but rather according to what we are prepared and able to accomplish in intellectual and material terms in the present and the future. I hope that in regard to the intellectual aspect, the cupboards are not empty. I also hope that there will still be some cash flow. And I hope that the engagement calendars leave space open for the things that now must come. What will be put to the test now is not the readiness to lecture, but to show solidarity, balance, a new beginning. What matters now is that we try to move together anew. To keep a clear head and to do the things, as best as possible, that are in accordance with our German interests as well as with our responsibilities towards Europe.

Berlin City Hall Speech

by Walter Momper

Walter Momper, born in 1945, was mayor of West Berlin
in 1989–90, and is chairman of the SPD Berlin parliamentary party. He gave this speech in front of the City
Hall in Berlin on 10 November 1989.

Dear Berliners,

We welcome all those who have come into our midst as guests from East
Berlin and from the GDR. Welcome!

We also welcome all those who have come to us as guests from Bonn today,
Mr. Federal Chancellor, the Federal Foreign Minister.

We welcome Willy Brandt, and we welcome Hans-Jochen Vogel in our
midst.

Dear Berliners,

Today is a magnificent day. The Wall no longer separates us. I greet all of
those who have come to us; they are very welcome in our midst. Anyone who
was at the border crossings yesterday will never forget that day and that night.
In Berlin there was a carnival feeling in the air; on the *Kurfürstendamm* as
well as at *Alexanderplatz*. Our entire city and all of its citizens will never forget
this November 9, 1989. That was the moment that we had been awaiting for
so long. For 28 years, since the construction of the Wall on August 13, 1961,
we have longed and hoped for this day. We Germans are now the happiest
people in the world.

In this hour of joy we are also reminded, however, of the many people who
died and were wounded, of the sorrow and the misery that this Wall caused.
May this never, never happen again.

The border that tormented us for so long lost its divisive quality yesterday.
The freedom to travel is a human right. Yesterday, the citizens of the GDR
claimed this human right for themselves. Just as, in the past few weeks, they
have claimed the right to make up their minds for themselves and to organize
their country themselves. In the GDR, a fascinating chapter of German history
is now being written. This chapter of history is being written by the people
of the GDR themselves. We congratulate the citizens of the GDR for their
peaceful and democratic revolution.

Yesterday was not the day of reunification but of reunion [*Wiedersehen*] in
our city. Several thousand GDR citizens have come to West Berlin today and

will come in the upcoming days and weeks. They will travel from East Berlin, from Dresden, from Frankfurt/Oder and from Magdeburg. We Berliners welcome all these visitors to our city with open arms. We look forward to this reunion and to the opportunity of being together.

Some people here in our part of the city are afraid of the rapid changes, and they fear the problems and burdens that we will have to face. I beseech all Berliners to remember always the happy hours of this day, and I beseech all of us to ever be mindful of the grief that the Wall has symbolized for us. If we always remain conscious of these things, then together we will be able to master the problems that now confront us.

Berlin has overcome all sorts of other problems and circumstances. What is important is that we want it, that we do not lose our optimism, and that we look into and take hold of the future with courage and energy. It is not our business to give the citizens of the GDR any advice. The will—and I have to add, the courage—to live in the GDR has to grow in the GDR itself. The people there have to see prospects for their futures themselves. If they cannot do that, then it is the fault of the system, the fault of the state or of the previous leadership. Many people are considering leaving the GDR. I entreat these people to consider whether they cannot now, after all, have more faith in the process of renewal and the process of reform in the GDR, whether they are not needed in the democratic awakening of the GDR. I cannot give any advice, but I want to ask people to reflect on whether they are not needed for a better society in the GDR. In the GDR, nothing can be decided against the will of the people anymore. The past few days have shown that. And I would like to add, in the future only the people themselves will make decisions in the GDR.

We support the goals of the democratic movement in the GDR. We support the demands for democratic competition of all parties and groups in the GDR and for the holding of free elections.

The SED leadership created the crisis in the GDR. It wasted a lot of time in the last few weeks and has lost people's confidence in it. The introduction of the freedom of travel, the nomination of Hans Modrow as head [*Vorsitzender*] of the ministers' council [*Ministerrat*], and the radical changes and protests within the SED itself all show that the SED is now also willing to risk a fundamentally new beginning. A new day has dawned in the GDR. The SED must give up its claim to leadership because, in all reality, it lost that claim a long time ago.

Perhaps we will still be able to learn something from the democratic culture in the GDR. Our democracy was given to us as a gift by our liberators in 1945. The citizens of the GDR have fought for their democracy themselves. They know how highly to value democracy. The demonstration on November 4 in East Berlin was forged by an exemplary democratic culture. This is the first democratic revolution in Germany since the revolution of 1918, which also took place on November 9, 71 years ago. It is the first revolution that has succeeded with completely peaceful means, that is being implemented with peaceful means. Here in the West, we admire the courage and we admire the discipline of the democratic movement in the GDR. The democratic culture of the citizens of the GDR is inexhaustible. It testifies to social responsibility and to the aversion to a rat-race society. Some of us over here should take an example from them. We must not endanger this great process through rash actions—this is what I ask of you. This is why I implore all Berliners to maintain their levelheadedness and self-control. Our desire is for the democratic movement in the GDR to run its own country, the second German state, as it sees fit. We Berliners support the reform process in the GDR with a passion and with solidarity. We will stand by each other and we will help, so that the GDR will get ahead economically as well.

The common European house, of which Mikhail Gorbachev has spoken, is taking shape. We will all have to change our way of thinking in the upcoming weeks and months. We must tear down the walls in our minds. The East Bloc does not exist as a bloc anymore. Poland and Hungary are not Communist states any longer, and the GDR is essentially not one either anymore. And even the Soviet Union is casting off the bonds of dogmatism. The Europe of the future will not be composed of rigid nation-states and blocs. The future will be created by people. For us here in Berlin, this development is opening up tremendous perspectives. In the European house, we will furnish the Berlin room with doors open to all sides, and we can now say that the doors of the GDR are also wide open. And I would like to use this opportunity to announce that the government of the GDR has informed us that more border crossings will be opened in approximately one hour. That is, I believe, great news, although I would like to add that one can never have enough doors in a room, regardless of whether it is the Berlin room or the GDR room in the common European house.

Ladies and gentlemen, dear Berliners,

Berlin once again stands at the center of the world's interest. Berlin is the place where European history is made. Berlin is the place that can propel Europe forward. Where East and West shake hands, just as people shook hands last night and all day long today at the borders. Berlin will be the city of exchange and the city of cooperation, and in fifteen years we want, in full and equal cooperation with East Berlin, to be the city of the Olympic Games.

Berlin looks into the future with optimism. Along with all of the other people in Europe, we hope for a new time of peace and of good neighborliness on our continent. And the fact that this hope can be accomplished more quickly, and is indeed progressing more quickly, can perhaps be seen in a poster that I noticed here and that touched me. One or two of you will still be able to remember that in December 1988, the Social Democratic party had a poster in this city which depicted two children, one from the East and one from the West, as they were reaching for each others' hands across the top of the Wall. At that time, many people in this city did not consider that very realistic. I have to say, I also would not have thought that things could come this far so soon. Today we have seen the people on the top of the Wall at the Brandenburg Gate. Those were young people. It all happened faster than any of us thought, and I hope that other developments will come as quickly as all of us hope: the development of Berlin as freedom. Berlin is freedom!

Ignoring the Chancelleries

by Rudolf Augstein

Rudolf Augstein, born in 1923, has since 1946 been the
publisher of the news and opinion weekly *Der Spiegel.* This
essay was published as a leader in the edition of 4 December 1989.

According to the stereotype of the high and mighty in East and West, German
unity is "not on the order of the day." In this Gorbachev, Mitterrand, Thatcher,
yes even George Bush agree: and Krenz of course also.

But that process which we still call history has its own order of the day.
People say that man proposes and God disposes. At the moment, despite all
the summitry, men are thinking very differently. Mitterrand will use any
argument to refuse the help France promised by treaty in facilitating the
integration of the rump of Germany. Poland's wetern frontier will do as an
issue.

This rotten card has been pressed into his hand by Helmut Kohl, the
electoral opportunist, who still insists *de jure* on the German frontiers of 1937
even though *de facto* there is not the slightest intention or possibility of altering
Poland's western frontier, which might have been guaranteed by international
agreement long ago.

If we consider what is technically easier, German or European unification,
there can be no doubt about the answer. To give precedence at all costs to
European unity, as is currently fashionable, harms and delays both processes.
The new German state can be built solidly, but the "European house" will
take longer. The Lady from London has taken the most interesting position
for herself: she wants neither.

It is, however, no longer a question of the business of statesmen. It is a
question of processes which are difficult to calculate and predict. With his
federation and confederation plans Kohl has moved onto a slippery path, which
could lead to the breaking up of NATO. Already the "Republicans"* are
demanding a Germany free of the blocs, and are finding support for that
position. Why not, if this state can neither attack or be attacked.

In truth German reunification is not the most urgent problem on our world.
In the West we could continue to live without it. But there is a danger of
something else, and it is hard to be sure that the progressive forces in the

---

*Franz Schönhuber's party of the extreme right.

GDR understand the threat. There is the "horror vacui": nature deplores a vacuum. To be more precise: can the GDR Germans, sucked dry by Soviet communism, fill up their state again?

People who still speak of the Wall as an "unbelievable deed of shame" as does the *Frankfurter Allgemeine Zeitung* of course make themselves suspect. This "shame" was programmed in Teheran, Yalta and Potsdam, and in 1961 there was no longer any alternative. The Wall was the price for western prosperity.

The question should be dealt with without any moralizing undertone. Did common elements develop in GDR society, aside from Marxism and Leninism, because of or even precisely because of the sacrifices made by the population? That could be the case, but we, blinded by western capitalism, are probably blind to them.

How should the sought after "socialism with a human face" appear, if it still lacks half of its body? Those people who wonder why this efficient industrial state should be worse off than the CSSR [Czechoslovakia]—also an efficient industrial state—should think of the following points: war damages, exploitation by the Soviet victors, the maintenance of an occupation army of 380,000 soldiers, etc. etc. All that has a cumulative effect. In addition there was "Land Reform," the planned economy, and endless sloganeering produced by the party and the dictatorship. If all this could be removed on one day, there would be a chance of keeping people in the country, or winning them back again. But obviously this is not possible, even if we exhaust all the opportunities available to us. Because we are not going to do what [former Economics Minister Graf] Lambsdorff suggested in a freudian slip: bring the "miserable difference in the standard of living [between East and West] closer together."

So there is only the alternative of exodus, comparable to that of the flight of the Huguenots from France after the toleration edict [of Nantes] was repealed in 1685. And this has produced a general shortage of labor "in many essential occupations" (*FAZ*), and even a general state of emergency.

The Silence of the Clerks

by Joachim Fest

Joachim C. Fest, born in 1926, has since 1973 been editor
of the daily newspaper *Frankfurter Allgemeine Zeitung*. He
is the author of many books, including the biography of
Hitler (1973). This article appeared originally in the
Frankfurter Allgemeine Zeitung of 30 December 1989, under the title "*Schweigende Wortführer: Uberlegungen zu einer
Revolution ohne Vorbild.*"

There are times when silence is more articulate than any number of words.
One of the most striking things about 1989 was the silence with which the
intelligentsia of the Federal Republic and the GDR met the year's revolutionary events. This became a silence compounded by despondency when the
results of the first free election in East Germany were declared. There is a
somewhat ironic angle to this. The words that poured out *ad nauseam* on the
bicentennial of the French Revolution only made the silent response to the
current revolution all the more audible. Critical awareness had suddenly become speechless.

This astonishing reticence deserves some consideration. It can be interpreted as a mark of embarrassment in face of the failure of an idea, namely
socialism, which, more than any other, could rely on the sympathy of those
who love dreaming up plans for social happiness. Furthermore, as long as the
people stayed put, and the Wall stayed up, this silence could be justified as
concern for a status quo which secured peace (even though this ultimately
amounted to a justification of the existing repression). But the grounds for
that explanation have now been destroyed, and it is fair to ask whether there
are deeper reasons for this dumbness.

Leaving aside the tragic events in Rumania, what strikes one about the
revolutions of 1989 is not just their largely peaceful development, which has
undermined the classic concept of revolution involving insurrection, violence,
and civil war. In addition, they took on a confusing and poignant nature
precisely because they lacked that element of social revolutionary fervor which
has dominated almost every historical revolution of modern times. (The various attempts to interpret the current revolution as one of true socialism
against its deformation merely turn the truth upon its head.)

Revolution without Theorists

We are dealing in Germany for the first time with a revolution that has not been preceded by its theorists. That may help to explain something of the uneasiness which the intellectuals' silence expresses. It also reveals a deep break with the past. Ever since the Enlightenment, when the undermining of traditional power structures began and power had to justify itself to reason, all revolutions have been preceded by intellectual theorists, who devised, justified, yearned for, and in some cases even helped realize a radical change in the course of history. Even the National Socialist seizure of power had its own ancestry of remarkable names.

But current developments diverge from this tradition. The gulf between those who usually lay down the revolutionary law and the actual protagonists in the streets is reflected in two events: the loyal address proffered to Erich Honecker by the Students Committee of the Free University of West Berlin on the occasion of the fortieth anniversary of the GDR; and the failure of the proclamation "for our country" with which Christa Wolf and others tried to assert the autonomy of the GDR. This would have vanished without even an echo if Egon Krenz's support had not given it some unwelcome resonance.

The intellectuals, whether from East or West Germany, unlike those of Poland, Czechoslovakia, and Rumania, did not prepare the ground for the revolutionary nights of last November. There never was in Germany a movement like Charter 77, not even one directed from the safe terrain of the Federal Republic. One looks in vain for such outright champions of fundamental human rights as Vaclav Havel or Mircea Dinescu among German intellectuals. Most of them reserved their enthusiasm for imaginary paradises, untouched by the misery of the people next door.

Nowhere is this better revealed than in the attitude of the Greens. It is legitimate to have some reservations about the idea of a unitary German state; it is possible to see the so-called German question as demanding a greater peace order, for which an increasingly unified Europe provides the framework. On that assumption, it would certainly be necessary to insist that the unification of Europe and Germany proceed hand in hand.

But the indifference with which most speakers of the Green Party, even in the turbulence of those November days, denied their neighbors those rights that they are only too ready to press for in foreign lands, was something altogether different. It is probably wrong to think that this stance revealed a lack of national feeling. What emerged more forcefully was a lack of basic human compassion.

Continuing the German tradition of cultural pessimism and staring at holes in the ozone layer, the Greens adhere so rigidly to visions of apocalypse that better times anywhere in the world are a concept too subtle and imaginative for them. One is sometimes tempted to think that many who are molded by this most German of all German traditions are paralyzed by the discovery that history has, for once, not hatched a catastrophe.

It says something about his standing that Willy Brandt grasped the importance of these events at an early stage and, brushing aside all tactical considerations, found the right words not only to express the emotion of the moment but also to do justice to political reason. That is all the more impressive since, in saying these things, he had to abandon positions advanced by his own party.

On the other hand, the opinions of those who believe themselves free of the need to make political calculations seem, curiously, far more biased by rigid patterns of thought. The reflections of many in the intelligentsia have all too obviously been conditioned by ideological preoccupations as well as by estimates of who and what is likely to gain or lose politically. On top of these, there is a tendency to elevate theory high above life—an old German trait.

The discussion about whether the collapse of the East German Communist regime should be seen as a "triumph of capitalism" can be seen in this light. It reveals not only the fixation on ideology, rather than on people, but also the well-worn tracks of intellectual argument. For, of course, it is not capitalism that has triumphed—least of all that obsolete form of capitalism whose image is readily conjured up in this context. What has proved superior is rather the concept and (albeit inadequate) practice of an open society which is identified with capitalism only insofar as capitalism is the economic order with which it is affiliated. It is a misunderstanding of the revolutionary processes in Warsaw, Budapest, or East Berlin to judge them by such preconditioned patterns and ignore the demand for civil rights which so obviously spurs them on.

An open society consists of meaningful basic rights, a free vote, freedom of expression, constitutional safeguards including separation of powers, and control of an administration. What is coming to an end is the anachronistic class society under a socialist aegis—the neo-feudalism of the Honeckers, Husaks, and Ceausescus.

Increasingly, however, this silence of the intellectuals is superseded by a new utopianism—by dreams of a brave new world which apparently no debacle can put paid to. Amidst the ruins not only of the GDR but of all socialist systems in Europe, plans are already being devised for new orders where societies once again figure as experimental domains and the people are mere material. According to a literary wisdom which has again found followers, no thinking being can live without a utopia.

Speaking from an experience which excludes any suspicion of ideology, the writer Monika Maron has written: "Whenever I hear that somebody knows what will render other people happy, whenever I read that somebody commands the services of millions of people in the name of an idea, be it only in their imagination, whenever I see fresh make-up being applied to an old ideology in order to disguise its death, I am seized with horror."

Ultimately, the lesson of the epoch, painful to some, must probably be that utopia, the yearning for a world full of harmony, order, and justice heightened by spiritual luster, is an illusion. Perhaps one will have to make do without utopia. The irritation and even open derision with which neighboring Eastern countries greet attempts at salvaging the idea of socialism suggest that those people do not give it the slightest chance, that they do not grant socialism or any other "ism" the status even of a possible alternative. For utopias have always ended in a system of subjugation, which constitute not an aberration but the inevitable logic of all "isms" in practice.

Utopia Limited

By their nature it could not be otherwise. For utopian ideologies do not conceive of themselves as merely an idea coexisting with other competing ideas, but as the one true idea against the darkness of all others. As was stated last May in all presumptuous innocence in *Neues Deutschland*, the official organ of the East German Communists: "Anti-Communists are always in the wrong: despite some mistakes and defeats we, the Communists, are always right." That sentence describes with the utmost brevity why such systems of thought, of whatever provenance, are irreconcilable with the principle of an open society, and why the democratic socialism on which new expectations are staked either is a mistake or is the political and social order which, with all its weaknesses, already exists in the Federal Republic and elsewhere.

Suspicion of intellectuals as political spokesmen is making itself felt in the polarization now taking place in East Germany and reflected in the success of the Christian Democrats in the election there. Hardly any of these intellectuals had spoken up and demanded the obvious when it mattered. Rather, that was done by the people in the streets, moved not by any ideal vision but simply by the intolerable character of prevailing circumstances. Perhaps it was this that determined the level-headed course of this unprecedented revolution, this dispensing with radicalism which many have felt to be the real miracle. For the turn to inhumanity always springs from the dogmatism of a theory.

What comes through as the impulse behind all the uprisings from Warsaw to Bucharest is the people's demand to be spared those political systems of deliverance which have their roots in the nineteenth century and which have claimed millions of victims in our century. Vaclav Havel recently spoke up against the terror of ideologies and interpreted the revolutions of 1989 as an uprising of the right to modest happiness against the great political blueprints of salvation: "Who is proposing some 'radiant dawn' to us yet again?"

Should this be so, it would not only reveal to what extent those who are devising social plans yet again are dreaming the dreams of yesteryear. It would also help to explain how, in their fixation on systems and in their estrangement from the people, they have missed the revolution of the past year. For the nineteenth century—still the source for the polarizations and the ideal visions—is coming to an end. The pack has been shuffled. But many are still sitting at the table with the old cards, trying desperately and unsuccessfully to read the signs.

Don't Reunify Germany

by Günter Grass

Günter Grass, born in 1927 in Danzig, is Germany's best known novelist. His works include *The Tin Drum* (1959) and *Dog Years* (1963), and mark an important point in Germany's critical engagement with her past. This article appeared in *The New York Times* on 7 January 1990.

Twenty years ago, [President] Gustav Heinemann spoke of "difficult fatherlands," calling one by name: Germany. That astute appraisal is now being confirmed. Once again, it looks as if a reasonable sense of nationhood is being inundated by diffuse nationalist emotion. Our neighbors watch with anxiety, even with alarm, as Germans recklessly talk themselves into the will to unity.

Day by day, the people of the German Democratic Republic are struggling for greater freedom and razing the bastions of a hated system by nonviolent means. This is an event unique in German history—a successful revolutionary movement. What is actually happening, however, is in danger of receding into the background.

Other, secondary concerns are thrust to the fore. Numerous West German politicians demand the stage, and with it, of course, the spotlight. The West German Government, its Minister of Finance in the vanguard, drapes its cornucopia in glittering promises, then dangles it ever higher, demanding that the revolutionaries take ever riskier leaps to get it.

Meanwhile, the Chancellor attempts to direct the world's attention to himself and his 10 point program. And that patchwork program, wrapped in statesmanlike oratory, met with applause! A few reasonable rudimentary suggestions obscured its contradictions and the omissions made with an eye to re-election, including once again the refusal to recognize Poland's western borders with no qualifications.

Disenchantment came the very next day. The hoax lost its appeal. Reality—in the form of our neighbors' justifiable fears rooted in their own experience—caught up with the Bundestag. The "reunification" bubble burst because no one of sound mind and memory can ever again permit such a concentration of power in the heart of Europe. Certainly the great powers, with the accent now on victorious powers, cannot; nor can the Poles, the French, the Dutch, the Danes.

But neither can we Germans. Because there can be no demand for a new version of a unified nation that in the course of barely 75 years, though under several managements, filled the history books, ours and theirs, with suffering, rubble, defeat, millions of refugees, millions of dead, and the burden of crimes that can never be undone.

Such a nation—no matter how much good will we think we've come to show in the meantime—should never again ignite political resolve. Instead, we should learn from our compatriots in the G.D.R., for they were not given freedom as a gift, as were the citizens of the Federal Republic, but had to wrest their freedom from an all-embracing system. They have had to struggle to achieve it on their own, while here we stand amid our riches, poor by comparison.

So what is this arrogance, with its boasts of a favorable balance of trade and great glass houses? What is this "we know better" about democracy, when our grade on the first exam is "satisfactory" at best? What is this exultation at their scandals over there, when stench clings to our own?

And measured against the modest wishes of those we presume to call the have-nots on the other side, what is this imperiousness incarnate in the person of Helmut Kohl?

Have we forgotten? Do we want to repress now, too (being masters at repressing) how the smaller German state was weighed down, far more than is just, with the burden of a lost war?

Consider the possibilities open to the G.D.R. after 1945—and their present day effects. No sooner had greater Germany's systematic coercion lost its power than the Stalinist system took hold with new, though familiar forms of coercion.

Economically exploited by the Soviet Union (itself exploited and ravaged by the greater German Reich), confronted by Soviet tanks during the workers' uprising of June 1953 and then finally trapped inside walls—the citizens of the G.D.R. have had to pay, and as proxies for the citizens of the Federal Republic, to pay and pay again. It was not we who bore the chief burden for a world war that all Germans lost. No, they bore it, in unfair measure.

And so we owe them quite a lot. What is needed is not a patronizing "quick boost" or a brisk buyout of the "bankrupt G.D.R.," but rather a far-reaching equalization of burdens, payable at once and with no conditions. We can finance the debt we owe by cutting our military budget and imposing on every West German citizen a surtax commensurate with his or her income.

Only then, when our compatriots in the G.D.R.—exhausted, up to their necks in water and still fighting for freedom piece by piece—receive justice from our side, only then can we speak and negotiate as equals, they with us and we with them, about Germany and Germany, about two states with one history and one culture, about two confederated states in a European house. The precondition for self-determination is all-encompassing independence, and that includes economic independence.

The hocus-pocus of reunification rhetoric is seductive but gets us nowhere.

Once it is set aside, it becomes clear that the suggestion of Hans Modrow, the Prime Minister of the G.D.R., for a contractual community is well suited to the present situation and its eventual possibilities.

This would allow for a commission, with equal representation from both countries, to coordinate obvious matters such as transportation, energy and postal service—and to oversee the equalization payment that the Federal Republic owes the G.D.R. An additional task in the service of peace would be a step by step reduction of defense budgets, as well as coordination of joint German responsibility for development aid to the third world.

The commission could likewise enrich with new meaning Johann Gottfried Herder's concept of national culture. And, not the least of its tasks, it could put a halt to environmental pollution, which disregards all national boundaries.

All such efforts and more like them, if they are successful, will make room for further German-German advances, and so smooth the way for a confederation of the two states, if that is what is wished. But with one precondition: the renunciation of a single state on the basis of reunification.

Union with the G.D.R. in the form of annexation would involve losses that could never be made good. For the citizens of a subsumed state, there would be nothing left of their hard-earned identity—achieved at least at the cost of exemplary struggles. Their own history would sink beneath the dull weight of a standardized history. Nothing would be gained except an alarming excess of power, swollen with the lust for more and more power.

Despite all our protestations, even well-intentioned ones, we Germans would once again be feared. For our neighbors would gaze at us with justifiable mistrust and from ever-increasing distance, which would very quickly give rise to a renewed sense of isolation and with it the dangerous self-pitying mentality that sees itself as "surrounded by enemies." A reunited Germany would be a colossus, bedeviled by complexes and blocking its own path and the path to European unity.

On the other hand, a confederation of the two German states, and their declared renunciation of a unified state, would benefit European union, especially because, like the new German self-conception, it too will be a confederation.

Why We Are Not a Nation—And Why We Should Become One

by Karl Heinz Bohrer

Karl Heinz Bohrer was born in 1935, and is professor of literature in Bielefeld University. Since 1983 he has been editor of the literary and political-philosophical periodical *Merkur*. This article appeared under the title "*Warum wir keien Nation sind: Warum wir eine werden sollen*" in the *Frankfurter Allgemeine Zeitung* of 13 January 1990.

Why is it that so many East and West German intellectuals have been and continue to be so adamant in claiming that the future unification of West and East Germany is either impossible or, at any rate, undesirable? The suggestion that a national integration of the two Germanys is, in the long run, inevitable even if only for economic reasons, has taken on the character of an obscene act in large parts of the liberal to left intellectual milieu. In this respect the intellectuals are in agreement with the declaration of East German writers, inaugurated by Stefan Heym, whose ideology states that the GDR, as a truly "good" state, must not lose the character of a socialist experiment, and that it must continue on as a quasi-utopian regulative for the Federal Republic, which is truly "bad" because it is capitalist. To combine the GDR with the Federal Republic would, in that view, mean to lose for all time a leftist utopian point of view. Moreover—to put the thought into the appropriate moral, even religious categories—it would mean that the world would become merely worldly, it would literally lose the transcendence of a border—no matter how deformed—beyond which lies another possibility.

It is only the chiliasm slumbering away in the leftist intellectual consciousness, never renounced, that can explain why such intellectuals have lived so well for so many years with the East German defenders of a system that, until very recently, was well acquainted with political torture. It was the same lethal coziness, clinging to a "totally different" possibility, that allowed so many leftist intellectuals in the 1930s to ignore the Stalinist show trials. This sentimentality, tending towards permanent mendacity, may have been understandable for intellectuals; for decades they have been holding meetings with their East German counterparts who always tended to present themselves as "antifascists." However the revolt of the East German masses has brought such sentimentality under increasing pressure, because this revolt was led not by the East German intelligentsia; it was prompted by masses of refugees looking for capitalism and subsequently articulated by the white- and blue-collar workers of Leipzig and East Berlin.

In the wake of these events, intellectuals are clinging to a new illusion and bearing it before them like a monstrance. Not the East German masses but West German intellectual advocates acting as acolytes follow in the train of this monstrance: it is the illusion of a "third path." The illusion springs from the mentality of teachers, pedagogues, and pastors, whose competence still consists of a penetratingly paternalistic humanism, unencumbered by any knowledge of macroeconomics.

Such intellectuals do not want the heroism of so many Communists who died under Hitler and Stalin to have been in vain. That is understandable. But standing up for this tradition in spite of all obstacles is one thing; intellectual mendacity and blindness are something else. This false hope for a "third path" had already transformed the entirely unpolitical, expressionistic dreamer Bloch into a defender of repression; and he remained an apologist even long after he had been relieved of his duties as a philosopher of socialism by his own tyrants. In this respect Günter Grass's accusation against "national declarations," in which he says that they have "a great deal of emotion but little consciousness," can be thrown back at him and all the intellectuals who think like him; the self-interest of these older leftist writers is transparent. Overnight all their hopes have disappeared, in the East sometimes with serious social consequences, and in the West with (at the very least) consequences for their prestige.

Before I put forward a few arguments for the necessity of the category of nation, I must take into consideration several serious objections. I will exclude right away the objection that national unity between East and West Germany would never be allowed by the other powers, specifically by the Soviet Union. This may well be true. But I am speaking here of the desirability, not the possibility of unity. Obedience before the fact is no substitute for an internal clarification of what one really desires.

The Lost Concept

Resorting to this argument is the clearest expression of the fact that German intellectuals have lost the concept of nation and consider a kind of colonized consciousness to be advanced political rationality. Parallel to this is the objection that the population of the GDR wants neither this nor any other form of unity. This too may be true, even if it is not probable that the majority of East Germans have the same political consciousness as those still adhering to Marxism in the old parties, the opposition, and the intelligentsia. To base such groups by now highly diverse reasons for rejecting unification on the supposed opinion of the people is to run the danger of suppressing the voice of the majority yet again.

The objections which can be taken seriously have their origins in an old German story. When Heinrich von Kleist first came to postrevolutionary Paris in 1801, his head was full of utopias in which an enlightened, humanized world gradually marched towards its own perfection. The young poet, who until then had known only the narrow confines of his Prussian provincial town and the as yet idyllic Berlin, was horrified by the turbulence of the anonymous big-city crowds: the Parisians hurried by without demonstrating any obvious concern for each other. At one point Kleist saw a fireworks balloon, whose fall had been calculated, actually land in the middle of a festive crowd, killing several people. No one gave a second thought to the whole affair. This event became for Kleist a symbol of the human coldness in the glitzy European metropolis. The romantic small-town boy Kleist longed unconsciously to be back in the narrow confines of an inwardness protected by military power. This story is only the beginning of a history which—leaving out the case of the cosmopolitan Heinrich Heine, who fell in love with Paris—was played out later on by many German intellectuals and poets.

One is reminded of the end of this history when one reads the notes a French journalist wrote for the Parisian daily *Libération* about his meeting with a young East Berliner one day after the Wall came down. Even linguistically, this is a fascinating contemporary document. It shows the state of mind of an idyll sheltered by power almost psychotically afraid of infection by the moral and psychic extremities of the West: afraid that the little street behind the Wall, gray but inhabited by rare birds, will disappear; this place where a young East German can simply dream, far away from the world of profit, removed from AIDS and drugs, protected from the hectic pace of consumption-happy, loud masses. The young man is afraid that his little republic will be gobbled up by the Moloch of the Babylonian West: "Go away, go away, leave my Wall where it is. . . . My God, what will happen if the West Germans come here to renovate and beautify everything, to put geraniums in the windows? Where am I supposed to go then?" A chaste inwardness defends itself against the idea of a unified Berlin, of unified East and West German provinces, because these provinces have long since developed irreconcilably different feelings for life, complete with different existential contexts. "It is so ugly, our Alex . . , but it is our Berlin. . . . I hope that I will have the strength to go on living on *Oderbergerstraße*. It would be so beautiful, an East Germany independent and democratic."

Martin Ahrends has located this difference, which must be called existential, in the emotions of a deep, introverted, almost sleepy state of mind. He has analyzed this state of mind for its almost romantic intellectual attractions. Behind the political lack of freedom he has discovered the freedom of an infinite imagination of daydreams, the possibility of "not growing up entirely."

Ahrends ranges from the good-for-nothing charm that lies beyond West German business careers and their superficiality all the way to the objective cynicism of deriving the Gothic depths of Hoffmannesque fantasy worlds from the East German world of prisons and interrogations. This depth dimension of the one-time "Zone" has always appeared to West German visitors, too, as an exotic attraction in which a romantic Germany, long since lost in the West, resurfaces like a remembered dream in the cities and landscapes of Thuringa, Brandenburg and Saxony. All this unique, special quality should be destroyed? Because of the opening of the border or an economic osmosis or even a political unification it is supposed to be rendered impossible?

In this question, which immediately reveals the utopian character of a romantic, Rousseauian critique of civilization, there is an unconscious intention to preserve the GDR as a kind of anticapitalist utopia, to cause time to stand still; an intention not to breathe in the poisons of a modernity now accelerated into postmodernity, or alternatively—from a West German point of view—to preserve the GDR as a kind of nature sanctuary for socially and economically dreamed-of yesterdays, a sanctuary in which the Federal Republic can daily renew its necessarily guilty conscience. This intention, however, is not just politically and economically impossible; it is also morally indefensible. Inasmuch as the utopia of cultural criticism is combined with the political hope for a "third path," the entire explosive amalgam is only loaded with double intensity. It merely reproduces Kleist's misinterpretation of what he saw in Paris as amorality, and what was really the oncoming chaos of a nonregimented, non-patronized modern world.

This misinterpretation continues to propagate itself in West and East German cultural criticism of the West. What the East Germans still have ahead of them is the discovery of America: that unheard-of event when the American soldiers—to use a phrase by the Italian writer Malaparte—strode like Greek gods onto the shores of Europe and the twentieth century really got its start. But not in the East. This will be the real drama of the liberated GDR.

Politically more convincing is the argument that the Germans have lost for all time the right to unity, because the loss of unity was the result of a war which they forced upon the world not just with criminal intentions but with criminal results. To propose unity—thus runs the argument—is somewhat akin to an attempt to remove oneself from the consequences which must be morally borne, or even worse: with the restoration of the greater nation state, to renounce penitence and once more risk an aggressive exercise of power. One could add onto this explanation other variants, above all the suspicion that the one-time victorious powers, in spite of declarations to the contrary (which have been voiced less and less of late), view the possibility of a unification of the two Germanys with deep antipathy, an antipathy motivated not just by power politics but by concern for the structurability of a future Europe.

Not a Failure of Unity

Let us set aside that concern as rather ephemeral and concentrate instead on the stigmatization of the powerful and unified German state as the cause of political crimes between 1933 and 1945. To this consideration belongs as well the thesis that Germany owes the unity it finally achieved in 1870/71 solely to Bismarck's military-political craving for power. The idea of the criminality of the German power-state [*Machtstaat*] under Hitler is closely connected to the belief in the supposed moral-political birth defect of the unified German state, a defect which, so the theory goes, necessarily preprogrammed that state for war and military aggression.

Irrespective of the considerations of professional historians, let me counter this argument quite simply: Bismarck's Reich, called forth in the Hall of Mirrors at Versailles, was always conceived of by Bismarck as an entity that would defend Prussia, not as pan-German. Bismarck led the Reich as a self-satisfied entity for over two decades. The ultimate destruction of Bismarck's treaty policies had nothing at all to do with unity; rather, it had to do with national-psychological and economic developments specific to their historical epoch which can never be repeated. Even the fact that the post-Bismarck phase conceived of unity as demanding nationalist aggression does nothing to refute this consideration. Hence the argument that unity in and of itself must always from the outset be politically poisonous—that it will breed a dragon or a new murderous German eagle—does not follow logically. It is true that the victory of Prussian Germany over Bonapartist France brought forth not only the golden era of the early Third Republic in France, but also the final political defeat of the revolutionary liberals and the triumph of the nationalist mentality in Germany. But Bismarck's Reich shared such nationalism with all the other European states at the time, where this mentality, under the aegis of pan-Slavism, British imperialism and French colonial *gloire* plus irredentism, was to strike the decisive spark for the bourgeoisie.

Yet to view the nationalist German bourgeoisie alone as representative of German unity is to forget or deny the central motif of the entire nineteenth-century liberal parliamentary movement, which experienced a wonderful intellectual and artistic renaissance in the Weimar Republic. The model of the Weimar Republic, in its turn, failed as a result not of "unity," but rather of the aggravation of the same nationalist syndrome which came into being after Bismarck's unity. These considerations should suffice to show the following: the nationalist syndrome was a result of the "delayed nation" [*verspätete Nation*] and came into being parallel with the process of unity. Its ideological, political and historical causes have become obsolete, just as the idea of unity has survived. While the German syndrome may be historically derived from the idea of unity, it is nevertheless not identical with it.

The Tradition of the Police State

One supporting motif of the anti-Bismarck argument is the concept of a supposedly golden era during the decades-long loose federation of many small German states, the structural condition, so to speak, for a "cultural nation" of the Germans. What this kind of argument tends to neglect, however, is the fact that this paradigm was only able to function for so long because there was once something like a constitution for the Reich which served to bind these tiny states together. This constitution was entirely conscious in ideology and mentality, as one can see, for instance, in the "Frederician Legend." Above and beyond this, there existed a German teleology, born at the latest during the period of baroque patriotism and its literary leitmotifs, such as the Arminius myth. This teleology reached its first high point around 1800: the feeling of a spiritual, even cultural-missionary creative community shaped the German intelligentsia from early idealism onward, and it was still being formulated emphatically by the left-Hegelians, including Heine.

Thus the existing federalist structure was transcended by the concept of a future political unity. The absolute ease with which leading luminaries and intellectuals of the nation saw themselves and dealt with each other as "Germans," not just as inhabitants of their respective provinces, tends to render unconvincing the thesis that a separate GDR and Federal Republic are only repeating a structure long since happily established.

Moreover, the small-state concept is burdened with an even more decisive political problem: the police structure of the German small state of the eighteenth century was able to develop into the very essence of German state rationality as a result of the grotesque minimalism of the population and territory to be kept under surveillance. This fact ought to choke off every radical federationist or even cultural-national argument. Ludwig Tieck and Georg Büchner have enough to say about the German small state of the nineteenth century; one can read the same thing as an ideology of confinement in E. T. A. Hoffmann and Richard Wagner, if one is willing to overlook the brilliance of their writing. All these examples provide an understanding sufficiently horrible to contradict the bloated, spoiled utopia, and the supposed civilization, of a Weimar removed from power. Goethe's infinitely complex selfhood which did not come to full realization until his trip to Italy, was a cosmopolitan accident in the midst of Weimar; one can draw from this accident no law to support the idea of the supposedly happy, sunny, spiritual German small state. The misery of the GDR milieu, which has struck anyone willing to look at it without blinders, was derived to a large extent from the tradition of the small German police state, and the "authoritarian character" which was born there. If the possibility of unification is indeed inauspicious, then this is because of the idea of a unification of this "authoritarian character" on both sides.

In the end, then, what is left of all the arguments meant to destroy the idea of unity? Only the moral argument: that the Germans have given up their right to unity. This argument remains even after one has disproved the theory of historical deduction, as I have tried to do here. In principle, there are two punishments: the death penalty for capital crimes and the chronologically limited loss of liberty for lesser crimes. If an entire nation is to be treated like one person—a proposition against which, precisely in the debate over the collective guilt, much has been brought forth, but which I am willing to allow in the special case of a German nation that had become National Socialist—then the disappearance of that state's territory, as originally planned by the Allies, would have been the appropriate version of the death penalty: the annihilation of Germany forever. What happened when, instead, the former Reich was divided into two parts, plus the final removal of several of its once Prussian territories?

The loss of the two provinces East Prussia and Silesia, which once undoubtedly played a role of central importance for German national identity, has paid a debt and enacted a restitution that is overlooked by the "moral" argumentation. The seriousness of this loss is not appreciated precisely because the political power center of the remaining Rhenish state has been pushed to the West by five hundred kilometers, and its leading politicians and parties, for good reasons, can no longer connect this loss to any kind of memory. But to overlook this loss is the height of thoughtlessness, because the "moral" argumentation makes the accusation that the unification of the remaining parts of Germany, separated for forty years, is equivalent to the recreation of a Bismarckian or even Fourth Reich, invoking this as a deterrent trope. Yet the substantive parts of Bismarck's nation lay precisely in East Prussia and Silesia. A fusion of East and West Berlin, the Federal Republic and the GDR, hence, would by no means imply the supposed renaissance of earlier historical structures; it would, on the contrary, mean something entirely new. The renunciation of substantial parts of the defeated nation, which has become necessary, is thus not the death penalty, not annihilation, but nevertheless a radical structural change in Germany, whether one speaks of the political nation of the nineteenth or the cultural nation of the eighteenth, seventeenth and sixteenth centuries. The crime, then, has been punished.

But the moral argument demands even more: it demands division into two states. To demand this division seems yet one more of many indications of the highly neurotic self-destruction of the Germans as a nation. A secret, unspoken thought plays a decisive role here: by attempting to erase the unbearable—the crimes of the father—one believes oneself capable of a saving transformation. One simply separates oneself from the physical circumstance of the father—the land mass—in order to live on psychologically in a new identity. One would like to cease to exist entirely as a "political" nation. Hence the annihilation of the nation via division into two parts, and hence the understandable "hysterical" reaction now that this transformation into the non-political may be reversed. The fear of politics and the annihilation of Germany as a whole belong closely together. Such fear, however, is anything but a promising point of departure for a theory of eternal division which claims to be political.

My contrary view assumes that the division brought about in 1945 between West and East Germany was an annihilation of the nation, and that the demand for a continuation of this state of affairs is morally, but not politically founded.

Far more important is a current diagnosis according to which the last forty years have proved that not only the GDR but also the Federal Republic has not survived the amputation well, and that a truly national identity was unable to develop, in spite of the fact that state thinkers and politicians here and there worked intensively to achieve such a goal. National identity is not the same as a sense of well-being in the midst of provincial attractions, attractions which—and this I do not deny—are by no means lacking in the Federal Republic and the GDR. On the contrary: in contrast to the GDR, we have, so to speak, transformed the provincial gesture into the very style of the state at the highest symbolic level. I developed this concept some time ago as part of the category "aesthetic of the state," and as a result of the political and spiritual stupidities in Bonn this deficit has propagated itself into the farthest reaches of the Republic.

Yet those who by their very nature ought to champion this theme, the West German conservatives, stand helpless in the face of Central European erosion and the chances for a unified Germany. This can be seen in their positively vacuous thick-headedness vis-à-vis the problem of Poland's Western border. If any first step is necessary before the second, then this first step is certainly a final and permanent recognition of the Western border of Poland, without any constitutional reservations: this means the final renunciation of the former Prussian provinces. Such an acknowledgement is precisely the security decision in favor of the remaining half of Germany, which can potentially still be salvaged. Even the slightest lack of clarity in this question would doom any active unification policy to failure in the wake of (not just) political suspicions.

These days have shown more clearly what was less evident at the beginning of the 1970s: the objective and subjective reasons for our no longer being a nation. Since the moment of the Eastern treaties, the very conclusion of which once more brought to life something akin to pan-German fantasies (the northern German Social Democrat Brandt in Erfurt), the Federal Republic has succumbed increasingly to the illusion that economic prosperity and pedestrian malls, the superiority of the D-Mark and a house to the north of Rome could serve as symbols of identity for an internationally oriented, happy economic bourgeoisie without political ambitions. The category of the nation—I mean the symbolic and reflexive constants of a collective historical and cultural ability to remember—appeared, hence, to have become outdated.

Particularly illustrative of this nexus of symptoms is an essay that the French writer Daniele Sallenave published under the title "My Dream of Germany" in a transnational supplement to *Die Zeit* and *Le Monde* before the recent events in Eastern Europe. The essence of this dark dream is the idea of a kind of spiritual suicide of the Germans, or rather, to say the same thing in a metaphor perhaps more effective right now, a kind of higher *Waldsterben*. It is not just the trees that are dying in Germany; almost the entirety of the cultural tradition of what was once called Germany has been attacked by a notorious plague called loss of memory:

> Germany has become for me nothing more than a kind of ecological Sweden, a general pedestrian mall through which, in the winter, a cold wind blows torn posters against nuclear energy, and where, in the summer, colorfully-clad babies are carried for walks on the backs of young men with beards in alternative city suburbs.

It is quite obvious—thus the impression of the French woman looking for Germany so late in the game—that those young men no longer know the names of great poets.

With this I have touched on a problem I worked on ten years ago under the heading of the polemical question "Germany—still a spiritual possibility?" At the time I was immediately criticized by Jürgen Habermas, the most influential philosophical representative of an expressly Federal-German republicanism, although our difference of opinion never developed into an extensive public controversy. Now the not entirely clear question as to a "spiritual possibility" should be replaced by the question as to the "spiritual nation," a concept one can develop by following the example of the European fatherlands. In the meantime Habermas has transformed his mild skepticism with respect to this question into the rigid demand for a Federal-Republican constitutional patriotism, a concept originally developed by Dolf Sternberger. I do not question the rational foundation of this concept, but I do question its historico-political durability and hence, logically, also its desirability.

If I have understood Habermas's concept correctly, it does not, of course, simply mean the anemic presence of democratic loyalty, drummed in with pedagogical rigor, to the "free state of German soil." Far more than this, Habermas's concept includes a specific awareness of Germany's recent history, which, above all, makes the remembrance of the fascist period into a moral-political law for any German national consciousness. When I look more closely into Habermas's Protestant argument, I find hidden within it a kind of negative chiliasm, the idea of the one overriding event of our history: it is called the Holocaust. The Holocaust is the great, unavoidable fact of our modern history, and any hermeneutic of a new German self-understanding has to be developed from it. In this respect the demand for a Federal-German constitutional patriotism gains, in fact, a kind of emphatic power which—should it indeed succeed as a national project—ought, in a hundred years, to be seen as the spiritual turning point of the modern nation: as a successful spiritual-political innovation after the catastrophe, as an enlightened myth of the victory of reason against nationalism. In contrast to run-of-the-mill departures from national categories, Habermas's concept is the most sublime variation of the tabooization of the nation, and it possesses a remarkable depth of historical reflexivity.

But to use a constitutional utopia as a substitute for the nation has one disadvantage which is becoming increasingly clear: it cannot avoid repressing entire categories of the psychic and cultural tradition which used to form part of German identity, because their categories supposedly helped prepare the consciousness that ultimately made the Holocaust possible. With respect to a thesis by Carl Friedrich von Weizsäcker, which states that "Germany as a spiritual possibility" has been destroyed for all time, since this spirit let loose a titanism which became criminal, I must ask: what is to follow the necessary decay of our elite cultural system? That this academically articulated elite system, remembered by Weizsäcker, was unsalvageable should be clear from the fact that it was precisely this system that Martin Heidegger tried so emphatically to identify with National Socialism.

But does this necessarily mean that our specific "irrational" tradition of Romanticism had to be so thoroughly destroyed by the bulldozers of a new sociology? Since the 1970s, Italian, French, and American philosophers, aestheticians, linguists, and psychoanalysts have developed an entirely new system of (postmodern) value perspectives from the realizations of precisely that German "irrational heritage" (Friedrich Schlegel, Novalis, Nietzsche), paying no attention to the West German reaction to this development. Hence, it is high time for us to look again at the tabooization of this tradition—in our own heads. If one is willing to overlook a few eccentricities, thinkers in France, Italy, and the United States have made entirely original and important contributions using this "irrational" heritage, while here in the Federal Republic, with few exceptions, a new historicism and the old critique of ideology have remained predominant. The spiritual provincialization of the "FRG," whose characteristic symptom has been the moralization of literature and literary theory, is indirectly connected to the annihilation of national unity and the atomization of what remained into political and intellectual regionalism. The guiding principle has been pacification through innocuousness.

Of course my plea for the concept of the nation demands a spiritual-symbolic criterion. For one thing it assumes that the nation has not, in fact, been superseded by the idea of cross-cultural, different, new identities in Europe, as has frequently been suggested in West Germany. But even those with a very minimal knowledge of the European nations know that such a supposed European identity is nowhere to be found, if one excludes the technical-economic sector. Nowhere does the encounter of French, English, Spanish, and Dutch mentalities show up more obvious differences than at the very center of their respective psychological-intellectual structures. The privileging of the technical-economic argument and the failure to see the deeper spiritual dimensions of national identity are themselves part of the West German loss of identity. Moreover, the attempt to write off the category of the nation in favor of a category of political belief, or even to combine the two, had already failed with Cromwell and the Jacobins; it has now also failed with the SED and its concepts of the "socialist nation."

The other criterion for my plea, of course, is that the self-understanding of Germans in the GDR has not been so influenced by the SED and Marxist intellectuals as to render the concept of the nation which I have recalled here a hopeless bourgeois phantom. In the next few months we will experience what renowned East German intellectuals, unified in their vulgar Marxism and dishonest utopianism, will once again try to do to demonstrate the hopelessness of unification. But at least this decision against the nation, if made, will be real. It will probably also be final.

The West Is Getting Wilder
Intellectuals and the German Question: The Claims Are Being Staked Out

by Friedrich Christian Delius

Friedrich Christian Delius was born in 1943 and is a novelist and poet. He is a regular contributor to *Die Zeit*. This essay appeared in the 2 February 1990 issue.

Someday, perhaps, one will be able to explain this phase of German history by pointing to the substitution of the definite article by a numeral. Ever since the phrase "We are the people" turned into "We are one people," the path into the future seems clear. The departure from the definite article, dictated by the desperation of many GDR inhabitants as well, is one thing. The linguistic usage in this country, intoxicated with new interests, is an entirely different thing.

Not to say anything against openness, contacts, cooperation, and relief. But the Federal Republic has barely fallen in love, and already the new arrogance that comes from power is blossoming "in the glory of this bliss." The bigger the "unified Fatherland" figures in the imagination, the deeper the inner divisions become—today in the GDR, tomorrow here in us.

Already one needs to be reminded that there was and is something besides the national euphoria: the excitement about the sudden realization of the dream of freedom. When "the state ownership of the living person is abolished" (Uwe Kolbe), when systems of force and incarceration collapse, when morality, temporarily awkward and clownish, returns to politics, when borders are razed and people find new paths—the nation in which these things occur has little to do with them at first. The excitement about these occurrences has a different quality than the euphoria over the usurpation of a nation; namely, it consists of an empathy that respects the other in its new freedom and dignity.

Many victors surface at such a colossal defeat of an entire system. The triumphant feelings of those who have always found their salvation in sheer anticommunism are understandable. Only the leftists (I mean the great majority of the independent leftists, and must continue to use this shorthand phrase, despite all possible confusion, for the sake of conciseness) still hesitate to show their feelings, let alone "peddle them." They seem hardly to have grasped it yet: the crisis that has followed the long overdue capitulation does

71

not consist of the fact that feudalistic socialism lies in ruins. Rather, it is caused by the fact that now everything must be thought through anew. The mortgage is on the past—and on the future as well. That takes a lot of effort.

The opinion brokers and strategists of the other faction use this to their advantage. In the whirlwind of events it is necessary to occupy new positions quickly. The West is becoming wilder. The opportunity for a spring cleaning in domestic affairs will not return very soon. In the process of general land acquisition, new claims are being staked out.

In one of the side arenas a debate about the mining rights of intellectuals has now broken out. A guild, which had formerly been declared nonexistent, is suddenly being rediscovered. The discoverers are intellectuals who reproach other intellectuals of failure. At first glance, it is a variation on the old "Italian game."

This debate is not being conducted in the relaxed or humorous spirit that is normally inherent in such debates, since they inevitably deal with overrated opinions. What is surprising about this debate is the great degree of emotion. Rage, scorn, and threats accompany the reproaches that are being strewn about the country, particularly from the pages of the *Frankfurter Allgemeine.* "The intellectual class of the Federal Republic," Joachim Fest writes, for example, had reacted to the revolutionary events in the eastward neighboring countries with "silence," and had always been silent and had played down the situation.

Suddenly one hears the same accusations from all corners and newspapers, as if the decade-long criticism of what had been established as "really existing" had never been. Aside from the false crocodile tears, such reproaches are never totally wrong. Even among the colorful mass of people who are categorized as being left, a great deal of foolishness is written and said. Not everyone said it all about everything, or loudly enough at that. Even the left has a history of mistakes and embarrassments—but it is aware of this history. "Left" cannot be defined without the elements of dispute, doubt, and contradiction. I am not going to give a lecture here, only a few reminders.

At least since the crushing of the Prague Spring in 1968 (and for the younger generation since Solzhenitsyn, the expatriation of Biermann, martial law in Poland), the "demystification of socialism" has progressed in the Federal Republic as a broad process. This socialism has long since ceased to be a utopia. Instead, it rather aided the rediscovery of fundamental democratic rights. For more than twenty years the discussions of the increasingly undogmatic leftists centered around these questions. It is possible to look them up in *Kursbuch, Freibeuter, taz,* and other periodicals, not to mention in books.

Although I do not tend to idealize the writers of the Federal Republic, it must be said that they made their greatest sacrifice for the Solidarity Movement: their previously powerful Writers' Association. The conflict over martial law in Poland and the disbandment of the Polish Writers' Association became the central moral question in 1983–84, in which one side pleaded for accommodation, the other for openness. The fact that these debates broke up the Association may be a German problem with the usual punch line: the Poles did not gain anything from the fight.

More importantly, dissidents and the opposition from Eastern European countries often found a forum in leftist publishing houses. Not without reason did the opposition in the GDR primarily use *taz* as its mouthpiece. In order to interpret the recent, diverse (intellectual) commentaries as silence, regardless of the fact that they have produced thousands of contacts and conversations across the borders for years, one has to be pretty hard of hearing— or be harboring ulterior motives.

These motives are illuminated when the revolution in Eastern Europe and the GDR are interpreted as being "without intellectual predecessors, without any intellectual engagement at all." Trotsky, Semprun, Bahro, Sakharov, and so on, apparently never existed. Nor, supposedly, were there any artists in the GDR who for years more or less courageously prepared the way for the abolition of fear through books, speeches, and oppositional endeavors. The intention here is to destroy the historical awareness of a long, intense, sacrificial criticism of Stalinism. The contribution of the left, of intellectuals to the developments in Eastern Europe may have been slight (provided that, next to the pressure that people felt, ideas were important at all); to deny it corresponds conspicuously to the Stalinist tradition.

"The cards have been reshuffled," according to Fest's conclusions, and "the leftists," "the intellectuals" have the "old cards." In other words, they no longer have any right to play, to enter the discussion.

The suspense in these efforts lies in their strategy, a sort of continuation of the *Historikerstreit* with different methods. That controversy was also a debate in which the cards were to have been reshuffled. With Fest's participation, the attempts to redefine German history were aimed at the creation of a good conscience. Now, since that cleansing is bearing fruit, apparently the second prank is supposed to follow: to steal from leftist intellectuals their history and to shut them out from the discourse on human dignity.

Amazingly, several authors are drawing the greatest amount of rage upon themselves. Untiring critics of Stalinism are alleged to be its open or silent sympathizers. Those who have conceded some noncriminal energies to the comparatively young socialism are regarded as potential criminals. Those who distinguish the national question from its utilization by the right are called ideologues, while those who on the other hand are in favor of a fast unification are not.

Thus, under the counter, a new criterion for intellectual credibility has surfaced: the declared belief in German unity. As ideological companion to the entrepreneurs, Joachim Fest still veils his use of this concept. Karl Heinz Bohrer, on the other hand, has been developing it with all intelligence.

Whereas Fest can only arrive at his goal through a demagogical sleight of hand, Bohrer, like Dieter Wellershoff in the *Merkur* before him, hits the nail on the head in his criticism of intellectuals who plead for two separate states as a result of their socialist leanings.

He suspects that they "unconsciously have the intention of preserving the GDR as a kind of anti-capitalistic utopia, of letting time stand still and not having to breathe the poisons of post-modern society; that is to say—from the West German perspective—to protect the GDR as a kind of national park from a distant, socially and economically illusionary past, in the face of which the Federal Republic can daily renew its requisite bad conscience." That hits the spot, but really only of one of several psychological aspects.

These other aspects can be enhanced. Let us just take one thesis: unification would be a national disaster. Why? Because it would foster aggression, narcissism, and feelings of superiority to such a great degree that our compatriots, cast in an authoritarian mould, would not be able to cope with it, and so on. Or: one has to wonder about the fact that the national question is being discussed almost exclusively by men, and so on.

However much we may speculate, some sort of unification will take place. But should the slogan "no experiments" therefore determine not only reality but also thought? Everyone should speak out about their failures and their illusions, but isn't there by now a general opportunism behind the calls for an "end to socialism"? Are there not, after all, a few differences between the worker in Leipzig, whose stairwell collapses, who does not want any guardianship and as a result calls for unification, and his ideological fellow traveller, sitting at his fine western desk, who for years has regarded the GDR as a garbage dump, and who has been more concerned with Sanssouci than with the living conditions of workers here, there, and everywhere?

Psychographies do not explain everything. The embarrassing thing for all intellectuals is that the economy, and not ideas, dictates the future (even the German one). Marx had already said that, but the east-west-left-right thinkers do not want to come to terms with this thought. This is understandable, since no one wants to become the fool of capital and politics. Therefore, in short, there are two natural reactions: on the one hand, those who rush ahead of capital in their thoughts, and on the other hand those who, although not able to put on the brakes, seek resistance in art, opinion, or practice.

The latter (skeptics; dreamers; broad, cross, and solidarity thinkers) do not have to strive for an idyll as a result—at least not more than those who are comfortable in the thought of unification. One consideration, for example, is that "capitalism" and "socialism" need each other as correctives. When either of these collapses without a substitute, what then happens to its corrective action? Or should we completely rely on the market economy's "ability to heal itself"? And should we praise the constructive sides of the capitalistic economic system, but dismiss the destructive aspects as propaganda?

The shouts of those who see these things differently can be heard. They issue forth, not only from Latin America and Africa, and pass over the deadly ravines of the "terms of trade" and cash flow, right up to our German-German table. The whispers of growing human misery and brutalization in the cracks of our fabulous growth are near. Eastern Europe, caught outside of the DMark barricade and running on empty, is asking these questions of the West's excessive piousness with increasing intensity.

These arguments are not aimed against GDR inhabitants who call for unification out of need. But must one therefore constrict rather than expand the horizons of thought nationally? Is the song in praise of the prevailing economic order unanimous? Has the opportunity to at least acknowledge the experiences and questions from without Europe been wasted?

When advantages come about with fewer disadvantages for many people, "socialist ideas" cease then and there. And, if the new trend had its way, these ideas should from this moment on no longer be tolerated. As always, philistine commandments follow prohibitions of thought.

Bohrer fears the Federal Republic's "vacuum . . . , in which any psychological or spiritual center is missing," and seeks "categories for a politically articulate nation." In light of the decentralizing tendencies of industry, bureaucracies, and machinery, one can only wish him good luck.

Whether they are overtaken by the processes of unification or not, intellectuals whose Latin is nowadays restricted to Martin Walser's feelings and Bohrer's categories will soon perhaps stand in the limelight, but even so will look rather ugly—in the sense of Konrad's motto. On the other hand, it would be advisable to explore other alternatives, designate other correctives, "keep conflicts alive" (Nossack), and disrupt the utopia of a final victory of the western paradigm through references to the flip sides and costs of that paradigm. To remind people that the revolution in the GDR was a civil revolution, yet one with the rules and goals of the Greens—that is, of protestantism—in other words with consequences. (Sarah Kirsch in November: "the revolution must be one by the Greens, for otherwise all thought and action are in vain").

Yes, must. Yes, if. If only some of the newly acquired virtues and practices in the GDR would be common in this country, perhaps it would become clear who really has something to hide. The moralistic rigor, expanded westward, would not support the system particularly well. It was therefore muffled nationwide.

The liberation of the peoples of Eastern Europe and the GDR also means liberation for leftists in this country. Relieved of the pressure of the reality of a fraudulent socialism, they can heave a sigh of relief. The end of the having their minds made up for them, of false authorities and fronts, the demystification of concepts, what an opportunity!

The liberation of our neighboring countries has brightened the ordinarily pessimistic picture of humanity (even if one must fear that it will soon be darkened again through nationalism, church, and permanent poverty). This still needs to be grasped, through openness, respect and a willingness to listen. This openness must not be buried under new patterns of thought either by the right or left. But it is being buried, at the moment diligently by the right. Leftists might for the time being be satisfied if a strong, historical, ethical, and ecological consciousness remains effective and reaches beyond the German European church spires and bank towers. Only one thing seems clear: the more the dissidents in the East are successful, the more important the dissidents in the West become.

The Phantom of the Nation
Why We Are Not a Nation Anymore and Why We Do Not Have to Become One—A Futile Interruption in the Intellectuals' Debate About German Unity

by Ulrich Greiner

Ulrich Greiner was born in 1945, and has worked at *Die Zeit* since 1980. This essay appeared in *Die Zeit* on 16 March 1990.

"The term 'nation,' if at all unambiguous, cannot be defined by the empirical common qualities of those who compose it. For those who respectively use the term, it undoubtedly mainly implies that certain groups of people can be expected to exhibit a specific feeling of solidarity, excluding others from the group, and that the term therefore belongs to the sphere of values. There is no consensus, however, as to how those groups are to be delimited, nor as to what collective action should result from this solidarity."

Max Weber, *Economy and Society*

Have we debated enough now? Has the last word about German unity finally been spoken? Apparently so. Thus: end of the debate. The last one out turns off the lights. A few dogs still bark.

There is no shortage of this kind of sarcastic metaphor. During a recent televised discussion with Günter Grass, Rudolf Augstein droned repeatedly that "the show is over." He had taken the risk of promoting the model of a confederation in spite of the general cry for the unification of the nation-state.

Could be: the show is over. Could be: the deal is done, as according to Willy Brandt in his short and unsophisticated summary of his view of the situation after Helmut Kohl's talks with Gorbachev in Moscow. But intellectual battles cannot be judged solely on their ability to stop the material course of things. I do not want to disturb Hegel's famous owl of Minerva to make it clear to myself that the recent intellectual discussions, whether they concern the end of socialism or the future of Germany, are defeated by futility and retrospection. But should we stop arguing because of that?

Obviously, the thousands of people who cross the border to the west on a daily basis are a silent argument. Obviously, the black, red, and gold banners in Leipzig are an eloquent testimony. But I suspect and hope that the DMark lies closer than the nation does to the hearts of those who call for unity in the GDR. That they do not long for the German fatherland as much as for a BMW. And I, who have the luck to possess DMarks and had the luck to drive a BMW, will refrain from discouraging others from such good luck. But all of this doesn't have the slightest to do with the intellectual uproar around the German nation. Or have I misunderstood everything?

Whether over or a done deal, it does not matter. I am interested in the question: what, after all, speaks in favor of German unity? And since I am taking the floor unasked and admit that I am less convinced by Karl Heinz Bohrer, the advocate for unity, than by Günter Grass, the opponent of unity, I want to know first of all who actually has the burden of proof? Who is the defendant here? Quite obviously, it is the German intellectuals, be they Günter Grass (FRG) or Stefan Heym (GDR), who do not want reunification or unity or integration, but rather something else—two separate states, or the confederation, or a "third way." If I see it correctly, then there is currently a preliminary trial against these intellectuals because of insufficient love for the Fatherland, because of apolitical day-dreaming, because of willful desertion from the troops.

If we take this quarrel between intellectuals seriously just this once, despite the increasing amount of Trabis [a cheap two-stroke automobile produced in the GDR] on the precious parking lots in West German cities, then what follows is: the burden of proof lies on those who sing the song of the German nation. Let us look, then, at their arguments.

Martin Walser spoke out in favor of reunification in his essay "Talking about Germany" in the 4 November 1989 issue of the *Zeit* at a time when there was no discussion about the subject. He wrote: "if the story had turned out well, I would go to a theater in Leipzig tonight, and tomorrow I would be in Dresden, and the fact that I would be in Germany would be most insignificant." The story has turned out well now in the sense that the trip to the theater in Leipzig and the journey to Dresden are by now as simple as a trip to the theater in Vienna or a journey to Zurich, and the fact that Vienna and Zurich are not Germany is most insignificant.

But this is apparently not enough for Walser. For he says: "in the human measure of things, the nation is the mightiest historical occurrence until now. Mighty in a geological, not in a political sense." That is a difficult sentence. It seems clear, but is completely unclear. It is evidently meant to imply that the historical experience and the identity of a people have most often found their expression through the creation of nations. That may be so. But first of all, this will not continue to be so (as Walser himself admits by adding "until now"). Secondly, we thereby start to enter into the peculiar field of mystical and generally hollow concepts like People, Nation, State. These are dream-concepts for collective emotions.

Now, the opponents of unity are readily regarded as cold rationalists, as human beings who cannot afford to "take a look into the imponderability of the people's soul [*Volksseele*]," to use Brigitte Seebacher-Brandt's accusation against the Greens (*FAZ* of November 21, 1989). Here we have a concept that is even foggier than the others. Apparently they cannot do without fog. But I must admit that emotions of this kind are not unknown to me; that I have nostalgic feelings after returning from foreign travels; that since my ten-year-long residence in Hamburg, I sometimes become homesick for the Mittelgebirge, the Taunus where I grew up; that I felt touched when, many years ago, I went to Naumburg, Weimar, and Eisenach for the first time. But what I nevertheless do not understand is: why do we need a German nation for that? Why does Fritz J. Raddatz, who longs in the September 1, 1989 issue of the *Zeit* for the "dry creak of the pine trees in the Mark Brandenburg," need a united Fatherland? He can drive there if he wants to. I'll come along.

To continue the quarrel with Walser does not seem very promising, since he refers to a "feeling of history" and states: "one either has it or does not have it." Sorry, I do not have it. Let us therefore look for another opponent: Karl Heinz Bohrer, who published the essay "Why We Are Not a Nation and Why We Should Become One" in the January 13, 1990 issue of the *Zeit*. Here we also find the warning not to "suppress the voice of the people yet again." It surprises me to find the esoteric and elitist Bohrer on the side of "the people," listening to its voice. But let us listen to his arguments. As in his earlier essays, he finds fault with the provincialism of the Federal Republic, "the continuing political and mental clumsiness in Bonn." The preference of the technical-economic argument and the underestimation of the deep spiritual dimensions of national identity is part of the West German loss of identity. Bohrer sees herein the unfortunate tradition of a "colonized consciousness," the reservations of a "chaste inwardness" against civilization. His evaluation: "national identity is something else than the feeling of comfort experienced in provincial situations. The category of the nation—those are the symbolic and reflexive constants of a collective historical and cultural ability to remember."

Bohrer's criticism of German provincialism is right, but his conclusion is wrong. The increase of the German mark, and therefore also the increase of power and the consequently logical reinstatement of Berlin as the capital, is by no means a guaranty against provincialism and clumsiness of any sort. On the contrary: it is downright absurd to think that the Wartburg drivers with their crocheted toilet paper covers in their rear windows, the touchingly unsophisticated and ascetic ministers from Dresden, the well-coiffed policewomen and *Stasi* officers from East Berlin could clear the stale German air. The teutonic furor, which the consumerism of the West with Lacoste and

Benetton and the cultural admixture of Pizza, Paella, and Mallorca have been able to neutralize, will reappear with a vengeance in Bohrer's desired nation.

The mistake lies in making a connection between a state's territorial size and its mental and cultural size. Are the small European states, are the Netherlands or Portugal provincial? And why should the "collective historical and cultural ability to remember" be tied to having the same sales tax or passport?

The "psychological and cultural tradition that constructs identity," which Bohrer sees as repressed and because of which he wants German unity, is not tied to the concept of nationhood, however. For me this tradition undoubtedly includes—since I love him so much—Franz Kafka, the German Jew from Prague. It includes Joseph Roth, the Austrian Jew from Galicia. The history of Austria and the history of the European Jews, as well as the history of Silesia and Lithuania, are part of German history and culture. The reason that all of these regions and all of these histories have been repressed is surely not because they do not constitute a nation anymore; rather, it is because an ideological, cultural, and economic rupture has split Europe. And this rupture is the consequence of the German war against the rest of the world.

Now that one can once again enter the intellectual and geographical sphere of what belongs to the German tradition, the creation of a German nation—be it in the framework of 1990—is the best way to aggravate or even to hinder the recapturing of a cultural identity. For that would mean waking sleeping dogs: not the European neighbors, but the old geopolitical misunderstandings.

Bohrer's "German nation" is nothing else than the entrance requirements of those traditions which can now be realigned from pragmatic power politics to national territory. This national territory, however, would not be identical with the "German nation."

To mention Auschwitz is inevitable in this debate. The history of the Germans is irrevocably determined by it. But what does this mean? Bohrer finds a "negative chiliasm" in this argument, namely a permanent expectancy of disaster. In the same sense, Günter Grass has most recently pleaded against unification in the February 9 issue of the *Zeit*. Only the powerful, large, megalomaniacal German nation could have created the organizational and ideological conditions for the Holocaust. Therefore the return to the failed project of the German nation as an all-German state becomes impossible.

So much for Grass. Ulrich Oevermann, the sociologist from Frankfurt, provides a counter-argument to this in his essay "Two States or Unity," published in the February issue of the *Merkur*. He takes up the concept of the "delayed nation," which Helmuth Plessner had already coined in 1935 and which Christian Graf von Krockow has continued to expound (for example in his 1970 book, *Nationalism as a German Problem*). Oevermann shows, as did Krockow, that the "linkage of the political nation-state and democratic rule," accomplished by the French Revolution, has never worked in Germany, and that this has led to the pernicious "German Peculiar Path [*Sonderweg*]." But now this linkage is all the more necessary, especially since it has taken so long to leave this peculiar path and not to look for a third one, but to take the step towards the unity of democracy and nationhood.

This sounds logical. And how does it sound when Oevermann says: the moral-political liability for Auschwitz can only be responsibly assumed by a unified German nation-state? For the division of the "national people [*Nationalvolkes*]" (Oevermann) into a morally impeccable anti-fascist part (the GDR) and a morally contestable part that relied on economic efficiency (the FRG) had missed the political dimensions of responsibility for Auschwitz.

It sounds good, but it is wrong (see also Reinhard Merkel's essay "The Illusion of the Nation" in the March 9 issue of the *Zeit*). Auschwitz—and this applies to Günter Grass as well—is no argument and should not be made one. This becomes completely clear if we reduce the arguments to their essential components. Because Auschwitz was, we must have German unity (Oevermann). Because Auschwitz was, German unity is impossible (Grass). Because Auschwitz was, we must not throw Auschwitz into the balance in the quarrel over German unity; we must not call up the murdered millions as witnesses in a trial that has nothing to do with them.

In order to resolve the dilemma, let us try a mind-game. Let us assume that National Socialism had existed without a Holocaust: what would remain is a German nation that is seized by the fantasies of world power, that misconstrues itself as a people without space because of its precarious geographical position in the center of Europe, and that asserts the myths of its nationhood imperially and with inner and outer violence. Is this nightmare so far from reality that we can afford to forget it? Have we not already seen all sorts of political clumsiness and diplomatic awkwardness, instigated by people who are presently aware of their economic power, but have no understanding for anything else, either historically or politically? And isn't the personnel responsible for political tasks already hopelessly overwhelmed? How much more would they be overwhelmed (up to unthinkably catastrophic levels) if they were confronted with a real political and historical task of global dimensions, namely the role of the honest broker between East and West, between ruined socialism and ruinous capitalism?

But by talking like this, we are again starting to defend our reservations towards unity, while the real task at hand is to question the reasons of the advocates of unity. And here something strange appears: namely that all of the most recent pleas rely on seemingly rational and reasonable arguments, while in reality, at their most crucial moments, they are completely unclear and irrational. Suddenly there is talk of the "voice of the people," of the "imponderability of the soul of the people," of the "German nation," of the "national people" [*Nationalvolk*], of the "nation-state," of "political nation-statehood." Those are words whose conceptual vagueness is as big as their emotional circle of haze [*emotionaler Dunstkreis*]. It is enough to take a look at Max Weber and Chapter VIII ("Political Community") in *Economy and Society* in order to be sure that this suggested demarcation of the nation concept is not sufficient, in terms of language or culture or people or race. "Nation," according to Weber, "belongs to the sphere of values." This means that the idea of the nation is not a descriptive or analytical concept, but one that is loaded with emotional and political purpose. Weber says: "the naked prestige of 'power' transforms itself into other specific forms, namely into the idea of the 'nation.'"

From this follows: in this case, we would do well to not only pay attention to what the advocates of the German nation say, but also to how they say it and with what interests in mind. These interests cannot be economically based, since the currency-union will come about even without the consent of the intellectuals; and BMW's plans to invest in Eisenach are quite independent from the debate about unity. The desired freedoms, from the freedom to travel to the freedom to invest, would exist just as well in a confederation. Even the moral and social problems cannot be dealt with more easily in a unified state. What remains? Only political interests, that is: the power-political interest in a bigger, more powerful German state.

Why do intellectuals, intentionally or unwittingly, act as the mouthpieces for power-political interests? One can guess at their motives. The economic annexation of the Central German provinces is followed by the mental annexation of the educational and leftist tradition that has become easy prey with the end of socialism. The vacated intellectual space is now being filled with argumentative campaigns that march under the banner of rationality and modernity, but in reality reproduce the same old misery of German irrationality.

"The unification will come if the people in Germany want it." Helmut Kohl said this, as the Federal Press Agency informed us on countless posters. So be it. In this respect, this debate is only the enchanting backdrop of a process which intellectuals have no part in determining. But intellectuals do have to determine their own role in this debate: if they want to be accomplices in a power-political and economic land grab—or if they want to be the sand in the gears of something that is already rolling.

Rigmarole

by Hans Magnus Enzensberger

Hans Magnus Enzensberger was born in 1929 and lives in Munich. He is a poet, novelist, and essayist and has been a leader of the West German and European left. He has directed the journals *Kursbuch* and *TransAtlantik* and, along with Günter Grass and Heinrich Böll, participated in the "Group 47" movement. This article first appeared in *Time* magazine on 9 July 1990.

The world at large is not in the habit of regarding the German question as a laughing matter. The pundits view it, with the utmost gravity; they can, of course, draw on abundant evidence from the past to justify their alarm. It is not for me to quarrel with their pronouncements, but what they fail to see, is the ludicrous side of German events. I should like to redress the balance. Granted that the opening of the Berlin Wall was a moment of high drama, but the consequences turned into low comedy almost overnight.

In itself, absurdity is hardly a newcomer on the German political scene. For the better part of 30 years, unification had been an article not of faith but of cant. Nobody took it seriously, nobody believed in it, and in the West at least, there was hardly anyone who really wanted it. One Chancellor after another talked about it absentmindedly, rather like an old lady reciting her Rosary, a performance that became even more embarrassing when the red carpet rolled out during Erich Honecker's state visit in Bonn in 1987.

As soon as ordinary people from Dresden and Potsdam, wearing tennis shoes and loaded with plastic bags and perambulators, were seen hobbling through the underbrush across the Hungarian border in the fall of 1989, crowding embassies in Warsaw and trains in Prague, there were raised eyebrows and mixed feelings in Bonn and elsewhere. For there is nothing dearer to the heart of responsible statesmen than stability. Yalta may have had certain drawbacks, but it was an arrangement one had learned to live with—and in the end any situation seemed acceptable as long as it was "under control." Was it not a bit inconsiderate on the part of all those Poles, Hungarians and Czechs, of Charter 77 and all, to rock the boat? And now even the placid, nondescript East Germans were taking to the streets, without giving a thought to the delicate balance of power prevailing in the Old World, to the problems of NATO, to the risk involved in any sort of change.

The nervous fiddling in Bonn was nothing compared with the havoc wrought in East Berlin. In hindsight it is clear that the fall of the Berlin Wall was due not to strategic planning, but to a sudden loss of nerve. A single ambiguous sentence uttered at a press conference, a mere slip of the tongue, was enough to start an avalanche. The unification of Germany was set off not by grand design but by a blunder.

The political leaders on both sides were caught off guard. While the "masses" did not lose a moment, organizing a sort of national jumble sale, changing money, swapping rumors, pulling down fences and repairing bridges, the statesmen scurried from summit to summit, looking more and more nonplussed as they poured forth a torrent of declarations, cautionary tales and contingency plans.

When they finally came round to understand that they were faced with a fait accompli, they swallowed their misgivings and tried to regain control. This turned out to be rather difficult, for by now not only East Germany but half a continent was out of hand. It would have taken a nimble man indeed to handle a problem of such dimensions. Whatever else may be said about Helmut Kohl, he is not known to have a light foot.

When he saw the night of revelry round the Brandenburg Gate and the flag-waving crowds in Dresden, he decided that the time was ripe for him to make History. Blinded by the vision of enthusiastic voters carrying him on their shoulders, he decided to forge ahead—never mind the bickering of the Poles, the reluctance of the Soviets and the suspicions of the rest of the world. Kohl was not to be ruffled by the specter of a Fourth Reich evoked by foreign or domestic critics who accused him of jingoism, and for a few weeks he enjoyed one historic moment after another and put on more and more weight.

But very soon the euphoria subsided and the outlook palled. From the very start there had been portents that had escaped the West German government's notice: a conspicuous absence of rousing meetings in the streets of Frankfurt and Cologne, a strange lack of passion, a suspicion of second thoughts. No amount of force-feeding on the part of the media had managed to intoxicate the West German populace. Faced with a flood of newcomers from the East, it began to worry about the cost of unity, about jobs, housing problems and rising interest rates. In the opinion polls, more than two-thirds complained about the excessive haste of unification.

And such pedestrian sentiments were fully reciprocated by a growing part of opinion in East Germany. Citizens there, used to safe and easy jobs, subsidized rents, and cheap food, began to panic about the pitfalls of capitalism. They also resented the idea that the fruits of 40 years' labor had proved to be rotten and that East Germans would continue to be for years to come, the poor relatives of their Western counterparts.

Irritation on both sides erupted in a bout of frenzied haggling about the rate at which the flimsy East German currency, popularly known as aluminum chips, would be exchanged against the bullish DMark. In the event, both sides felt vaguely cheated. The day after an agreement was finally signed, a Munich paper ran the headline, A NICE START: EAST GERMAN GOVERNMENT SWINDLING US FOR 7.5 BILLION!

It looks as if Kohl's Great Historic Moment has been rather brief. A bit of schadenfreude may be in order, though the entertainment value of our family squabble is in rapid decline. The truth of the matter is that the Germans have acquired a normality bordering on the tedious. They have become a nation of successful shopkeepers, incapable of a greatness that the world, in any case, is better off without.

Yet Again: German Identity—A Unified Nation of Angry DM-Burghers?

by Jürgen Habermas

Jürgen Habermas, born in 1929, is professor of philosophy at Frankfurt University. He was a leading figure in the *Historikerstreit* of 1986–87, in which he criticized revisionist historians for relativizing and minimizing Nazi crimes. This essay was published in *Die Zeit* on 30 March 1990 under the title *"Der DM-Nationalismus,"* and a full and annotated version appeared in the *New German Critique*, winter 1991.

Three months after the democratic revolution "over there," they are shaking each others' hands "over here"—the politicians have become businessmen, the intellectuals have metamorphosed into bards of German unity. Günter Grass is castigated in the literary supplements, and in the talk shows the very sight of a leftist economics professor is enough to transform friendly ladies and gentlemen of the middle class into a mob. Today the self-torturing, superfluous question is finally justified: What will become of the identity of the Germans? Will economic problems guide the process of unification onto sober pathways? Or will the D-Mark become the object of libido, emotionally revalued so that a kind of economic-nationalism will overwhelm republican consciousness? The question is open, but it demands to be answered in view of the psychic damage already caused by the conquests of western political parties in the East.

It is difficult not to write a satire about the first flowerings of chubby-faced DM-nationalism. The triumphant Chancellor let the thin but honest Prime Minister[1] know the conditions under which he was willing to buy up the GDR; in terms of monetary policy he pumped up the voters of an "Alliance for Germany" blackmailed into existence by himself;[2] in terms of constitutional

---

[1] At the time, Hans Modrow, whose February 1990 trip to Bonn had been spectacularly unsuccessful.—Ed. [Footnotes by Jürgen Habermas unless otherwise noted.]

[2] The Alliance for Germany was a coalition put together by Kohl for the March 1990 elections in the GDR. It consisted of the CDU, which had, for the forty years of the GDR's existence, been one of the parties supporting the Communists in the National Front, thus providing a fig leaf of pluralism; Democratic Awakening (Demokratischer Aufbruch), one of the original citizens movements of the October Revolution, many of whose more left-leaning members resigned on hearing of the coalition; and the DSU (Deutsche Soziale Union, or German Social Union), a right-wing party controlled by the CSU, the CDU's Bavarian sister party.—Ed.

policy he set the course for annexation via article 23 of the Basic Law; and in terms of foreign policy he protested against the phrase "victorious powers" and left open the question of Poland's western border. When it finally dawned on him that Mr. Schönhuber[3] would be able to hold high the long-since collapsed legal fictions far longer than he would, he wanted at the very least to take away from Schönhuber an issue that could prove powerful among radical rightwingers: the "reparations," whatever that might mean. The shamelessness of his nationalism, supported by the stock market trends, set up a coldblooded comparison between, on the one hand, the historically justified moral rights of Polish forced laborers to compensation (and the rights of neighboring countries to a guarantee of the existing borders) and on the other the fiscal-political "wiggle room" and the liquidity of the third great industrial power, which found itself in the process of swallowing up the leading industrial power of Comecon and wanted to keep itself fit for this transaction. Only *one* unit of currency for *all* transactions. German interests are weighed and forced through in German marks. True, the language of the Stukas was even worse. But the sight of this German muscle game is obscene nevertheless.

I

To understand how it could come to this, one must remember the inner situation of the Federal Republic at the moment when—and let us admit it in the jargon of youth—it was caught with its pants down by the stream of refugees over the Hungarian border and by the subsequent reaction to that stream: the opening of the Wall. All rhetoric aside, who had really still counted on anything like reunification—and who had even really still wanted it at all? Willy Brandt, at any rate, had declared at the Munich Chamber Theater in 1984 that the German Question was no longer open; and the audience had applauded. Outside the theater, in the country at large, the mood can not have been very different.

In 1960 Karl Jaspers had spoken clearly: "The history of the German nation-state is at an end. What we . . . can achieve as a great nation is insight into the world's situation: that today the idea of the nation-state is a calamity for Europe and all the continents."[4] This credo was shared at the time not only by the liberals and the leftist intellectuals. In a study published in 1983, Wolfgang Mommsen paints a complex picture of the "transformations of na-

---

[3] The head of the radical right-wing Republican party; he took the position that Poland's western territories legally belonged to Germany. During the controversy on this issue, Kohl suggested that Germany might be willing to renounce its claims on Poland in return for reparations made by Poland to refugees.—Ed.

[4] K. Jaspers, *Freiheit und Wiedervereinigung* (Munich: Piper, 1960) 53.

tional identity of the Germans" in the Federal Republic. While the politicians of the first generation, the "fathers of the Basic Law," still believed that they would be able to continue the nation-state tradition of the Weimar Republic and thus also of the "small-German" Bismarck Reich without a thoroughgoing process of questioning and reform, the general public in the fifties and sixties had developed a more pragmatic self-understanding which put the question of national identity on the back burner. According to Mommsen, this consciousness is characterized by four elements: the dethematization of Germany's most recent past and a rather ahistorical definition of the current situation; furthermore an aggressive separation from the systems of Eastern Europe, particularly the GDR, i.e., a continuation of the historically rooted anti-Communist syndrome; an orientation toward the values and behavior patterns of Western civilization, especially the "protective power" U.S.A.; and, last but not least, pride in West Germany's own economic accomplishments. Mommsen is probably correct in suspecting that this last element, the self-confidence of a successful economic nation, forms the core of the political self-understanding of the population of the Federal Republic—and a substitute for a national pride that is widely lacking. This also explains why the high level of acceptance for the constitution and the institutions of democratic rule of law are not really anchored in normative convictions:

> Among the citizens of the Federal Republic there is a very strong tendency
> . . . to view the parliamentary system not first and foremost as a democratic
> framework for the continuous development of social relations, but rather to
> confound the constitutional system with the social order and view them as
> one thing.[5]

Although Mommsen still touches on discussions that had begun in the 1970s about the alternative between a Federal-Republican national consciousness on the one hand and an all-German national-consciousness on the other hand, he comes to a surprisingly clear conclusion:

> If I am not completely mistaken, then the history of the German Question
> has today returned to its normal state . . . that is, the existence of a German
> cultural nation in the center of Europe which is divided into several German
> state-nations. Everything suggests that the phase of consolidated nation-state-
> hood from 1871 to 1933 was merely an episode in German history, and that
> we have once again, though at a higher level, reached the state of affairs that
> existed in Germany after 1815: a plurality of German states with mutual
> cultural-national identity.[6]

---

[5] W. Mommsen, "Wandlungen der nationalen Identität der Deutschen" (1983), *Nation und Geschichte* (Munich: Piper, 1990) 62.

[6] Mommsen 76; cf. Siegred Meuschel, "Kulturnation oder Staatsnation," *Leviathan* 3 (1988) 406–35.

This argument from 1983 puts Wolfgang Mommsen, in hindsight, into the group of those fighting for a constitutional patriotism oriented toward the civic state-nation of the Federal Republic. Since the end of the 1960s, all the elements of self-understanding for the citizens of the Federal Republic have been put into question except one: the self-confidence of the economic nation. The student protest movement put an end to the shoving aside of a Nazi past that was sweepingly condemned but generally bracketed out. The Eastern treaties (with the recognition of the GDR) and the initial successes of detente at the very least destabilized the anti-Communism so typical of Germany. The Vietnam War, the growing strength of the European Community, and the recognition of diverging interests between Europe and the U.S.A. all increased the distance between the Federal Republic and the United States. Since then "national identity" has become the topic of public discussions. The liberal consensus, characterized by the slogan "two states—one nation" now had to be spelled out explicitly and defended not only against leftist nationalists on the margins of the Green spectrum but also, and above all, against the neoconservatives.

In a climate of economic crises and debates on security policy, these neo-conservatives suspected legitimational weaknesses in the political system, as-cribing them to a "loss of history" and inadequate national self-confidence. Such neoconservative attempts at compensatory creation of meaning had dif-ferent accents, however, depending on whether the longed-for "return to the nation" was tailored to a Federal-Republican or an all-German identity; the "fatherland Federal Republic" was the position of a minority.

The new conceptions would have been capable of finding support solely from the still unquestioned element of pride in the rebuilding achievements and economic power of the Federal Republic. The "Model Germany," brought into play for a while by the Social Democrats, contained traces of such pride, but it never had any significance beyond the realm of campaign strategy. However, the attempts to renew a traditional patriotism necessarily had to seek a connection with the identity of the entire nation, on the left and on the right; for this reason they were unable to use a value ascribed only to the Federal Republic as the basis for an economic-nationalist-based self-under-standing. And the proponents of a Federal-Republican constitutional patri-otism, of course, had to pursue a strategy of strengthening the normative value of identification with the civic state-nation founded in 1949 in order to dif-ferentiate that value from *prepolitical* values: the *Volk* as a historic community of fate, the nation as a linguistic and cultural community, or, now, the social and economic system as a performance community.

On the basis of the statistical data available in 1987, H. Honolka showed that the transformations in mentality of the citizens of the Federal Republic were, in fact, moving in this direction. While opinion polls up into the 1970s had shown a rising curve for economic pride, the most recent polls have shown that pride in democracy is now more important:

> In the well-known international study of political culture done in 1959 by American political scientists Gabriel A. Almond and Sidney Verba, national pride still rested chiefly on *volk* characteristics and the economic system, while the political identity of other western nations like the U.S.A. and Great Britain was based above all on political institutions. By now the citizens of the Federal Republic have also come closer to the normal kind of Western national identity. Pride in aspects of the political system has pushed far ahead.[7]

The data which show that the national pride of the Germans is comparatively weak do not contradict this. It was precisely in the course of the 1980s that evidence was growing for the position announced by M.R. Lepsius at the twenty-fourth conference of sociologists:

> An essential transformation in the political culture of the Federal Republic lies precisely in the acceptance of a political order which determines and legitimates itself in constitutionally concrete forms through rights of individual participation. In contrast to this, the idea that political order is bound to the collective values of a nation separated from other nations as a "community of fate" via ethnic, historic, and cultural categories has faded. The crystallization of "constitutional patriotism," the acceptance of a political order constituted by rights of self-determination, and the separation of such an order from the idea of an ethnic, cultural, collective "community of fate" are the central result of the delegitimization of German nationalism.[8]

These thoughts give voice to the pride of an entire generation of postwar West German intellectuals. They are only a year older than the opening of the Wall, with which, suddenly, the unification of two of the three successor states to the "Greater German Reich" has come into view. Will this unification throw the Federal Republic, which Lepsius and many others of us believed only a short while ago to be a "post-nation-state political commonwealth," back into a nationalist past that its own citizens had believed was over?

How this question will be decided depends to some extent on the way in which the process of political unification is presented and invoked—i.e. on the mobilization of emotions "back here" and "over there." Now, from an

---

[7] H. Honolka, *Die Bundesrepublik auf der Suche nach ihrer Identität*, (Munich: C.H. Beck, 1987) 104. Compare also D.P. Conradt, "Changing German Political Culture," in eds. G.A. Almond, S. Verba, *The Civic Culture Revisited* (Boston: Little, Brown, 1980) 212–72.

[8] M. R. Lepsius, "Das Erbe des Nationalsozialismus und die politische Kultur der Nachfolgestaaten des 'Großdeutschen Reiches,' " in M. Haller, ed., *Kultur und Nation*, (Frankfurt/Main, 1989) 254ff.

all-German perspective, the resistance which previously prevented the inclusion of the repressed components of Federal Republican economic pride into national identity as a whole has disappeared. With a view toward the German-German currency union, all Germans might now be able to identify themselves with the potency of an expanded empire of the D-Mark. The "Alliance for Germany" already seems to have opened up this fallow emotional field, and already the arrogance of economic power has caused nationalist weeds to sprout.

Classical imperialism had channeled similar emotions in a different way. Back then territorial conquest and military protection of domestic industries were supposed to open up markets. In the sensitive web of an interdependent world economy which knows no national boundaries, market power itself becomes the national clarion. A new economic nationalism would trade in its militarist face for the philistine attitudes of the friendly, supercilious development helper. Thus even the compensatory ideas of the neoconservatives would be outdated. The renewed national consciousness would no longer make up for the burdens of a capitalist modernization that is nevertheless also cushioned by social-welfare measures; a national consciousness that found its symbolic expression in the strength of the D-Mark would, on the contrary, be forced to ignore the voice of enlightened self-interest, pushing the skeptical economic Burgher to collective efforts and sacrifices *in his own language*.

II

These are reflections on a transformation in the identity of the reunified Germans that has become *possible* in the current constellation. I am not asserting that anyone is actually *working for* an economic nationalism of this sort. Nevertheless, the German policies which the Chancellor's Office has been following in a very goal-oriented way after its initial hesitations pave the way for such a transformation in mentality.

As early as his ten-point declaration, the Federal Chancellor showed a certain impatience to push forward on the path to nation-state unity—less in the contents of the plan itself than in the fact that stages were operationalized at all on the way to the goal. But the rhetoric of these first weeks after November Ninth left open the alternative between a seriously European solution to the German Question and a German solo effort. Viewed more closely, the alternative remained unclear. The invocation of a European solution offered an empty formula which anyone could fill up as he wished. In those first weeks it was not just the European neighbors and the two superpowers but also spokespeople for the GDR opposition and the majority of the West German population who viewed the process of unification in a chronological framework which seemed of necessity to give European unification a certain procedural priority. At any rate there seemed to exist an option to plan operative steps for a period in which the independence of the GDR would be guaranteed—even after the process of confederation—so that the difficult process of economic equalization would take place in a European framework.

What interests me above all in this scenario, which reserves an important role for the European Community, is the unencumbered role that the Federal Republic could have taken on as the proponent of coordinated European economic assistance *for all* the countries of Central and Eastern Europe currently undergoing a process of transormation. Far from the heave-ho tactic of dragging their German fellow-countrymen onto their own ship via constitutional law and an over-hasty German-German currency union, the Federal Republic, as the strongest power within the European Community, could have appealed to the solidarity of *all* Europeans and to the historical indebtedness of Western Europe vis-à-vis *all* its Central and Eastern European neighbors. In spite of this, the Federal Republic could have carried out its specific German-German duties via a transfer of capital (to date rejected) for building up the infrastructure of the GDR. This reflection is written in the historical subjunctive and is intended merely to recall an option which would have been immune to normative objections. Such a policy would certainly have privileged our fellow countrymen with respect to the citizens of other Eastern neighbors who found themselves in the same situation—but only to the obvious extent normal for states belonging to the same nation; and it would have been understood by others. The most basic political wisdom teaches us that simply shoving the living standard gap from the Elbe to the Oder and Neisse rivers is bound to arouse nationalist distrust vis-à-vis the reunited Germany among the neighboring states unfortunate enough to wind up on the wrong side of the gap. Above all, however, the European alternative recommended itself by taking the rhetoric of non-paternalism and non-interference seriously. Without a breathing spell and without freedom to maneuver and for an independent political public sphere to crystallize, however, the first free election degenerated into a "battle of the parties of the Federal Republic for the GDR" (H. Rudolph in the *Süddeutsche Zeitung* of 8 March 1990).

After his visit to Dresden,[9] the Chancellor quickly decided on a double strategy of undisguised destabilization and quick annexation of the GDR, in order to make the Federal Republic master of the situation and at the same time preempt international friction. Evidently, the Federal government wants to enter into the difficult negotiations about distributing the burdens among the EC partners, about a transformed security system, and about decisions on a peace treaty from a position of strength provided by an economic and

---

[9] In December, 1989.—Ed.

political annexation that is already a *fait accompli*. Hence, on the one hand, the Federal government stepped on the gas pedal; it effectively dramatized the number of refugees, even though no one knew how to influence their motives. On the other hand, it could reach the goal of annexation—i.e., unification according to the Federal Republic's terms—only by breaking down the GDR's resistance and creating the necessary majority for unification via Article 23 of the Basic Law.

The destabilization, which took on a macabre twist in Teltschik's[10] rumors, was directed not just at the remnants of the old regime, but also at the very opposition that had toppled the regime and was now primarily interested in changing structures from within—i.e. in self-stabilization and self-reflection. Only this fact can explain the silent delegitimization of the Round Table[11] and the rudeness to Modrow's government, which, as two Federal constitutional judges determined, had gained a certain legitimacy even according to our own standards to the extent

> ... that is is supported by the Round Table and the oppositional groups represented in the government. This means: the old system is already liquidated—in fact, only the execution of liquidation still remains to be accomplished. It is no longer necessary to withhold "success" from this government, if time is of the essence. (*Der Spiegel* 10[1990])

But "withhold success" is precisely what the federal government did. It opposed the very financial assistance for the infrastructure that it will have to put forward anyway to improve investment conditions for private capital now pushing into the GDR.

The CDU/CSU campaigned for the support of GDR voters with its wonted charm. If it had simply been a question of disempowering the old regime, the Chancellor would certainly not personally have taken the trouble to force an oppositional group like Democratic Awakening into an alliance with a discredited block party, only to turn around and lead an election campaign which flew in the face of historical truth by putting the newly founded SPD into the same boat with the successors to the SED.[12] In this way it mobilized the masses, who (according to a report in the *Süddeutsche Zeitung* of 7 March

---

[10] Horst Teltschik was one of the Chancellor's most intimate advisers; throughout early 1990, he spread word that the GDR was on the brink of collapse. In the fall of 1990 he left public office, rumored to be upset at not having been offered an important government post.—Ed.

[11] Created after the fall of SED as an open forum between Hans Modrow's government and the oppositional groups. While it had no executive authority, it had considerable moral weight.—Ed.

[12] The campaign rhetoric accused the SPD of being socialist, thus linking it in the public's mind with the SED. Unlike the CDU, the SPD had not existed in the GDR prior to the October Revolution. It had, in fact, been forced to join the KPD in a forced union ("*Zwangsvereinigung*") to form the Socialist Unity Party in 1946.—Ed.

1990) beat up student counterdemonstrators at a DSU rally in front of the Leipzig Opera House, shouting slogans like "red fascists—leftist terrorists," "red pack" and "reds go home." Whatever else was necessary was accomplished by people like Schnur and Ebeling, and by the promise of an economic miracle attested to with refrains from Ludwig Erhard, a miracle which was supposed to be inaugurated by the currency union dangled all-powerfully in front of the people's eyes. For forty long years the population of the GDR had been forced to vote for the ruling elite. Kohl made it clear that this time it was also wiser to do the same thing.

The role of the SPD was hardly any more honorable. If things should go badly, the SPD will have to ask itself if it did not make a historic mistake at its convention in Berlin out of fear of a replay of the role of "unpatriotic so-and-so's." I will not say anything about Willy Brandt; it was the party, after all, which sent him to the marketplaces of the GDR. It is understandable that the SPD did not want to hand over their most famous name to the young founders of the SDP, whose mentality recalls precisely the all-German party of Heinemann in the early 1950s, without taking a hand in molding the new party. And the emotions which overcame old comrades in the historic triangle of Gotha, Erfurt and Leipzig are certainly understandable. Moreover, it is naive to accuse a political party that wants to win a majority of opportunism. Nevertheless, these honorable motivations do not suffice to justify ignoring other considerations—or refusing to make any decisions at all and singing hymns of praise to both Willy Brandt and Oskar Lafontaine at the same volume.[13] When the SPD decided to fight with the CDU/CSU for the laurels of the first all-German party and to fill its sails with national emotions, it was not just betraying its better traditions; it was also helping to create the very smokescreen behind which any alternative to the German policies of the federal government disappeared. The SPD, too, ignored the recommendation of the Round Table to restrict election campaign imports from the West. Even worse, it advised its comrades to reject electoral alliances which were the only chance for leftist opposition groups to establish themselves throughout the country. It is true that this, too, conforms to the ordinary rules of party power politics. But these ordinary rules assume an ordinary situation in which the rules do not have to be dictated from the outside and do not discriminate against the very same people who created the revolution in the first place.

The policies of *faits accomplis* have not yet reached their goal; the mentality they count upon, and which they reward, has not yet triumphed; the election campaign in the Federal Republic has not yet begun.

As far as we citizens of the Federal Republic are concerned, it seems that

---

[13] Willy Brandt staunchly supported national unity; Oskar Lafontaine seemed at the very least skeptical on the subject. Throughout 1990 the SPD did not seem to be able to make up its mind as to which of its leaders represented the real views of the party.—Ed.

we can still count on that mixture of enlightened egotism of economic Burghers and *gratis* altruism of *citoyens*, which gives Ralf Dahrendorf cause to rejoice:

> The self-satisfied think it's very good that things are getting better in the East, but those folks ought really to stay where they are. And if there really isn't a Wall any more, then we'll just have to reunify. Perhaps then even a few of those people will go back to where they came from, the ones who got an inspection sticker for their Trabis without being punished and who, to make matters worse, are filling up the local youth hostel during school vacations. . . . Under these conditions nationalism is entirely the wrong word. Whatever has become of the Germans?[14]

I do not want to pour water into the wine with references to a climate that has, in the meantime, become noticeably more severe, especially in and around the "local youth hostels." But the economic Burgher's premise that the citizen's altruism can be had for nothing is true only in times of calm. In times of uproar, what will become of a mentality which the citizens of the Federal republic had actually gained after forty years? It is usually the others who are concerned with ordinary citizens' identity problems: the politicians on Sunday and the intellectuals even during the week. The citizens of the Federal Republic *had developed* a non-nationalist self-understanding, as well as a sober view of what the political process produces for every individual in terms of cash and useful things. What will become of these attitudes under the pressure of a policy which hides its own insecurity under arrogance, and which is steering directly toward an all-German nation-state?

This policy has already achieved one thing: the national question has once again been opposed to questions of republican equality and social justice. If prepolitical values like nationality are not kept in strict convergence with the universalist spirit of civil fights, dangerous collisions can ensue. Now, before the local elections in Bavaria, the CSU has to cut back on social programs for refugees with its left hand at the same time that, with its right hand, it continues to denounce the unpatriotic Lafontaine, who has long since been suggesting the very same thing, but for different reasons. Lafontaine had shown an early sensitivity to normative confusion when he warned of German jingoism and demanded equal treatment for non-German asylum-seekers and German immigrants from the GDR and other countries. The policy of the German one-man show threatens to throw citizens into a value dilemma which has a sad prehistory in Germany. Once the economic Burgher's premise of cost neutrality can no longer be adhered to, the very large "Alliance for Germany" might well look for the wrong way out of the dilemma. With easy variations, it could continue its election campaign within the Federal Republic

---

[14] *Merkur* (Mar. 1990): 231.

and demand of citizens here collective efforts in the spirit of nationalist identification with the expansion of the DM empire from which they have lived
very well up to now.

III

The alternative to this version of economic nationalism is the strengthening
of those components of our self-understanding with which, in the 1980s, "the
citizens of the Federal Republic have also come closer to the normal kind of
western national identity." Identification with the principles and the institutions of our constitution demands, however, an agenda for reunification
which gives priority to the freely exercised right of the citizens to determine
their own future by direct vote, within the framework of a non-occupied public
sphere that has not already been willed away. This means, concretely, that
the will of the voting public is given precedence over an annexation cleverly
initiated but in the final analysis carried through only at the administrative
level—an annexation which dishonestly evades one of the essential conditions
for the founding of any nation of state-citizens: the public act of a carefully
considered democratic decision taken in both parts of Germany. This act of
foundation can only be carried out consciously and intentionally if we agree
not to accomplish unification via Article 23 of our Basic Law (which governs
the accession "of other parts of Germany").

I do not ignore the weight of the arguments in favor of conserving a proven
constitution. But reflections on stability cannot replace normative considerations. It is strange to see how those who base their arguments on Article 23
are the very same people who insisted for decades on the call for reunification
in the preamble of the Basic Law. The preamble makes it unmistakably clear
why the Basic Law is called a "Basic Law" and not a "constitution": it is
intended to give the political life of the federal states "a new order for a
transitional period", i.e. until the time comes "to perfect the unity and freedom of Germany in free self-determination." If, now, the GDR, like the
Saarland, accedes according to Article 23, without any further changes in the
Basic Law, the chosen method of unification will implicitly underline what
the irredentists have always affirmed: that the conditions for Article 146 have
not yet been fulfilled. That article states: "This Basic Law loses its validity
on the day that a new constitution takes effect, chosen by the German people
in free determination." And it is quite true: an "accession" of the GDR could
not be the same thing as a free decision of the *entire* German people; because
the citizens of the Federal Republic would have to leave the decision to the
representatives of the GDR. When, then, if not now, will that day foreseen
in Article 146 ever come? Are we still waiting for East Prussia and Silesia?
If one wants to exclude this misinterpretation—as I do, after the Bundestag's

decision on Poland's western border—the last article and the preamble of the Basic Law would have to be cut, and the Basic Law itself would have to be stripped of its temporary nature. Such changes, however, would simply prove that the "accession" of the GDR cannot fulfill what it is supposed to fulfill: the unification of two parts to one *whole*. An accession via Article 23 would let Article 146 "run itself empty," and that would run counter to the methodological premise of interpreting every single rule with a view to the unity of the constitution.

Manipulations ahead and behind and a problematic interpretation of Article 23 of the Basic Law would simply be the juridical price for a policy of speed. The political price would be even greater; we might wind up paying it for several generations. We would not just lose the chance of improving a good constitution—which, at the time, of course, was not legitimized by a popular referendum—we would also lose the historic chance of carrying out the process of state unification with the clear political understanding of constituting a nation of state-citizens.

If we do not free ourselves from the diffuse notions about the nation-state, if we do not rid ourselves of the prepolitical crutches of nationality and community of fate, we will be unable to continue unburdened on the very path that we have long since chosen: the path to a multicultural society, the path to a federal state with wide regional differences and strong federal power, and above all the path to a unified European state of many nationalities. A national identity which is not based predominantly on republican self-understanding and constitutional patriotism necessarily collides with the universalist rules of mutual coexistence for human beings; it collides with the fact that state integration is now happening simultaneously on three levels—the state, the federation, and the European Community. Via Article 23, citizens can merely *suffer* the process of unification. The path via a constitutional convention, on the other hand, prevents a policy of *faits accomplis* and might wind up giving the citizens of the GDR room to breathe after all, allowing time for a discussion about the priority of European viewpoints.

Only a popular referendum on the constitution—i.e. on the alternative between an all-German federal state and a federation that would allow the Federal Republic to keep the Basic Law—gives *all* citizens the chance to say no. It makes possible a quantified minority vote; it is only then that the decision of the majority becomes an act consciously carried out, around which the republican self-understanding of future generations can crystallize. It is only in view of freedom to choose between alternatives that the consciousness that is already widespread among the younger generation can be made clear to all: that the founding of a single nation of state-citizens on the territories of what, until now, were the Federal Republic and the GDR, is not already a foregone conclusion because of prepolitical imponderables like linguistic community, culture, or history. For that reason one would at least like to be asked.

My friend Ulrich Oevermann argues that "with the revolutionary events in the GDR the *unaccomplished* task of constituting a political nation-state has once again posed itself practically."[15] I consider this argument entirely false. It is supposed to be a revolution "to make up for lost time," but not with respect to society or the democratic state of law; rather, with respect to a nation that arrived too late, which is finally coming to self-realization in the nation-state. If, as Oevermann does, one decisively rejects the "transposition of the political onto the level of culture and spirit," it is inconsistent to blur the distinction between a nation of state-citizens and a nation of *Volk* developed by M.R. Lepsius. In contrast to the classical nation-states of the West, the successor states to the old German Reich and the small-German Reich of Bismarck never succeeded in intertwining the political incorporation of state-citizens with the prepolitical conditions of the "historically and materially given unitary nation" to which Oevermann refers. In Germany, as Lepsius notes, there were strong tensions between the "political level of the people as bearers of political sovereignty" and the prepolitical "level of the *Volk* as an ethnic, cultural, socioeconomic unity":

> The recognition of these tensions is the basis for a civil society of democratic self-legitimation. Any confusion between the "demos" as bearer of political sovereignty with a specific "ethnos" leads ultimately to the repression or forced assimilation of other ethnic, cultural, religious, and socioeconomic groups of the population within a political union. Thus an effort was made in the German Reich after 1871 to Germanize the Poles in Germany's eastern provinces, as well as the citizens of Alsace and Lorraine; and Catholics and Social Democrats were discriminated against as unpatriotic and unreliable—ultramontane or internationalist. . . . Depending on the characteristics that are chosen to fill up the nominal category of the state-citizen, a whole range of highly differentiated possibilities for discrimination emerges, because the law of equality among state-citizens can be vitiated via additional categories: ethnic sameness, religious sameness, cultural sameness, or racial sameness. The most extreme example of such vitiation of the norm of equality for state-citizens via the addition of a further criterion to ensure political sameness were the National Socialist laws concerning the Jews, according to which German state-citizens of Jewish origin were deprived of their rights to equality.[16]

It is only in this connection that the subject Auschwitz gains its relevance for the consciousness in which the process of political unification is being

---

[15] U. Oevermann, "Zwei Staaten oder Einheit?" *Merkur* (Feb. 1990): 92.

[16] M. R. Lepsius, "Ethnos und Demos," *Kölner Zeitschrift für Soziologie und Sozialpsychologie* 4 (1986): 753; for a critique of the concept of a nation of state-citizens, see B. Estel, "Gesellschaft ohne Nation?" *Sociologia Internationalis* 2 (1988): 197 ff.

carried out. It is entirely erroneous to bring Auschwitz to play as a metaphysical guilt which is concretely paid off by the loss of East Prussia and Silesia, as Karl Heinz Bohrer suggests. It is just as false to use Auschwitz as the axis for the negative nationalism of a community of fate, which Oevermann would like to make the basis of a nation-state subject which can (now for the first time?) be held responsible. Auschwitz can and should remind the Germans, no matter in what state territories they may find themselves, of something else: that they cannot count on the continuities of their history. Because of that horrible break in continuity the Germans have given up the possibility of constituting their identity on something other than universalist principles of state citizenship, in the light of which national traditions can no longer remain unexamined, but can only be critically and self-critically appropriated. Post-traditional identity loses its substantial, its unproblematic character; it *exists* only in the method of the public, discursive battle around the interpretation of a constitutional patriotism made concrete under particular historical circumstances.[17]

In an essay on "The Insanity of the Nation," Reinhard Merkel hits the nail on the head:

> German nationalist intellectuals still reject the lessons of the Enlightenment, the French Revolution and Ernest Renan: that the "nation" in democratic states—if it is anything at all—cannot be the protection of the particularity of the *Volk* against outside forces. It must, rather, be the symbol of a "daily plebiscite" within society itself on democratic participation in political in political self-organization. (*Die Zeit*, 9 May 1990: 52.)

IV

Karl Heinz Bohrer may well suspect that the self-understanding of constitutional patriotism is guided by a moralism which robs artworks of their uncanniness, and which brings us to the point of "repressing entire categories of the psychic and cultural tradition which used to form part of German identity, because these categories supposedly helped prepare the consciousness that ultimately made the Holocaust possible." Here he may have been thinking of the sources of new French inspirations: Carl Schmitt, Martin Heidegger, or Ernst Jünger. But the very prestige of the newspaper in which Bohrer gives voice to his concerns gives the lie to his fears. It is news to me, at any rate, that the critical investigation of our young-conservative tradition

---

[17] J. Habermas "Geschichtsbewußstein und posttraditionale Identität," *Eine Art Schadensabwicklung* (Frankfurt/Main: Suhrkamp, 1987) 159–79.

has led to a taboo or even to a marginalization of the tradition. Bohrer himself mentions the " 'irrational' tradition" of Friedrich Schlegel, Novalis, and Nietzsche. I have to wonder who on earth might come up with the daring idea of *not* hooking up with the tradition of *early* Romanticism and the criticism of the Enlightenment carried out by our greatest Enlightener. This is a fight against paper tigers. At most what has been forgotten is the tradition of anti-Enlightenment and German nationalist intellectuals who, starting with Franz Baader and Adam Müller, Ernst Moritz Arndt and J.F. Fries, were able to mould the German bourgeoisie politically. This tradition, which was mocked so brilliantly by Hegel and Heine, Engels and Marx,[18] is a constant in German intellectual life right up through Werner Sombart's *Merchants and Heroes*. During every national wave—after 1813, 1848, 1871 and 1914, not to mention other dates—there were always new generations of intellectuals who joined this tradition, moved by the storms of German fate. This stream of energy, which was crystallized in the "ideas of 1914," ought not to be regenerated in the new national wave. This is a matter of intellectual hygiene, not repression. Bohrer complains about the colonization of our consciousness, the epidemic of a notorious loss of memory, spiritual provincialization. But is it not in the Federal Republic that, for the first time, we have brought our spiritual traditions to play *in all their forms*, including Heine and Marx, Freud and Mach, Bloch and Benjamin, Lukács and Wittgenstein? Is it not here that, for the first time, this tradition has operated in its more radical dimensions? The spiritual sparks of a German-Jewish culture that was preserved in the emigration are responsible for the fact that the Federal Republic "has become connected not just economically, but also culturally with the West. In other words, its strength lies precisely in the fact that here a culture characterized by international thought was able to develop, nevertheless structured by Germans."[19]

We ought not to establish any short-circuited connections between large-scale national growth and intellectual productivity. Karl Heinz Bohrer is a brilliant essayist and an excellent literary critic. With remarkable intransigence, he likes to follow the traces of the ecstatic abysses of aesthetic experience. He is fascinated by the grand gestures of the amoral. These gestures signal the autonomy of an art which has broken off communication with the good and the true. But Bohrer also knows that this transgression can only be born "in the head." Why should a cerebralized art—it can be studied via Gottfried Benn—dive into the belly of the nation? The aestheticization of the political is one of the worst arguments for us "becoming a nation again." And intellectuals will be among the first to suffer if they once again get a national podium from the top of which they can hold their speeches.

---

[18] D. Losurdo, *Hegel und das deutsche Erbe* (Cologne: Pahl-Rugenstein, 1989).
[19] Mommsen 83.

Inasmuch as German intellectuals have become spiritually provincial, they ought to blame themselves first and foremost; they certainly ought not to hope that the longed-for symbolism of a resurrected Reich will make them more productive. The "aesthetics of the state"—which have been a thing of the past since Louis Philippe, and for good reasons—will not experience a renaissance simply because Kohl and Waigel will soon be joined by Thuringians and Saxons in raising the flag of a new economic nationalism above the ruins of the Reichstag.

Fear of making what is most particular in our national cultural tradition taboo takes on another meaning with certain other intellectuals. Such intellectuals first equate the Stasi past with the Nazi past, and then they throw both onto the trash heap of a covered-up, silent history. "Without Trial Courts" is the title of one lead article in which retroactive melancholy reveals an unsuspected generosity:

> This time we ought not to speak of "coming to terms" with the past. Even the semantic cudgel "repression" . . . ought not to be used. And especially the shabby assertion of an "inability to mourn" as the supposed spiritually constitutive cause for obduracy and repression . . . The insistence on that kind of "coming to terms" transformed a moral intention into immorality. It became clearer and clearer that such terms were essentially being used in order to produce a political submissiveness intended to further claims to power. (*Frankfurter Allgemeine Zeitung*, 6 February 1990)

What that meant was explained earlier by the *Rheinische Merkur* (in a guest column of 24 November 1989). With the help of bankrupt state socialism, it was finally time to draw a line under the past: "Is the emotion of antifascism ('antifa'), this brooding on coming to terms with the past, losing its privileged position, shoved aside by the power of the present?" Antifascism, the spirit which alone gave birth to the democratic state of law in Germany after 1945, is now supposed to belong finally to the past, along with the hollowly propagandistic antifa organizations of state socialism.

It is not a coincidence that this obscene debate is being revived at a moment when Gorbachev is robbing anticommunism of its *raison d'être*. The facade of that antitotalitarian consensus, always strangely asymmetrical, which seemed to unite the population of the Federal Republic, has been broken irreversibly. Under these circumstances the bankruptcy lawyers of anticommunism are making one last effort and offering a deal: discretion is supposed to reign "back here" and "over there." As if the non-Communist left in the Federal Republic could have any interest in spreading the cover of communicative silence over the part of Stalinism which has, via the GDR, become an element of German history!

In his speech on his own country Peter Sloterdijk looks at "German silence" as well as the great Silent Ones, the "former bearers of the Reich's word," the "powerful speech makers of yesterday, now relieved of their positions." Then he turns to his own generation: "Those born in Germany after 1945 ought to realize clearly that the later-born, in order to come into the world, will have to break the silence of their ancestors after the fact at the decisive points."[20]

---

[20] P. Sloterdijk, *Versprechen auf Deutsch* (Frankfurt/Main: Suhrkamp, 1990) 52.

Reunification II: This Time, No Hobnail Boots

by Josef Joffe

Josef Joffe is a columnist for and foreign editor of *Suddeutsche Zeitung* in Munich. His most recent book is *The Limited Partnership: Europe, the U.S. and the Burdens of Alliance*. The piece was first published in the *New York Times* on 30 September 1990.

In 1871, Germany was unified, and a few years later, the *Times* of London editorialized darkly: "We feel that an enormous power for good or evil has risen up somewhat suddenly in the midst of us, and we watch with interested attention for signs of its character and intention."

On Wednesday, the world will watch "Reunification II"—and as anxiously as 120 years ago. Will the sequel be a repeat performance, starring a restless giant who has become too big for his turf? Will Germany '90 move from strength to arrogance, again bringing grief to Europe and the rest of the world?

The Bismarck-to-Hitler analogy is tempting but misleading. Just compare the opening scenes. In 1871, Germany was unified by "blood and iron"—in a war of aggression launched against France. Today, Germans and French are no longer archenemies but the best of friends. On Wednesday, the loudest sounds to be heard in Berlin will be the whistling of fireworks not the rumble of artillery. Reunification will be a thoroughly peaceful affair.

Not only is the overture different this time; the stage, script and actors have also changed beyond recognition. Take the lead player. In the Bismarckian Reich, democracy was shouldered aside by a Prussian-dominated state that unleashed an economic revolution while chaining down liberty and dissent. The Kaiser's message to the rising middle classes was: Go ahead and enrich yourselves, but leave the driving to us.

In the Weimar Republic, born in defeat and disgrace after World War I, democracy never had a chance. Yes, there was a parliamentary regime, but it was ground down in a two-pronged attack by Communists and Nazis who flourished because millions were caught in the maw of the Great Depression. And in 1933, when Hitler came to power, democracy was simply torn to shreds.

After 1945 democracy could at last sink its roots into fertile soil, and in many ways the postwar political miracle in Germany even dwarfed its vaunted economic twin. This time, thanks to generous American help, democracy was not associated with economic misery and humiliation. Instead of reparations, there was Marshall Plan aid; instead of towering tariffs, there was free trade, instead of encirclement, there was NATO and the European Community, extending to the Germans a shelter and a role.

At last, then, German democracy was off to a good start, and today the Cassandras of 1945 have fallen silent. The parties of the extreme right and left have all but vanished, leaving in place a sluggishly centrist regime that is almost boring in its normalcy. The democratic system has weathered every political crisis: neo-Nazis and terrorists, insubordinate generals and rebellious students, large-scale unemployment and mass protests.

In many respects, the political system looks like America writ small. Federalism works, and so does the separation of powers. Compared with the "republican monarchy" that is France, the Federal Republic is a political free-for-all. Nor is there an Official Secrets Act that so hampers the freedom of the press in Britain. State secrets in Bonn last about as long as in Washington— until tomorrow's edition.

The point is not that today's Germans are "good" whereas their grandfathers were thoroughbred authoritarians. The point is that after World War II the stage changed. Flawed as it was in the past, the drama of German history at last could unfold before a benign backdrop. Consider the ugly brew of paranoia and chauvinism that had poisoned the body politic before. The Bismarck Reich, a late arrival in the great power club, was bound to threaten all of its neighbors—and in turn to be threatened by them. The Weimar Republic was a pariah among nations and a target of endless distrust—a perfect breeding ground for the enemies of peace and democracy. It was "us against them" and "Deutschland Uber Alles."

Reunified Germany, by contrast, will be embedded in a larger community, surrounded by friends and not by resentful neighbors. The Federal Republic grew up in security, provided courtesy of the United States, and this cut down the business opportunities of the Pied Pipers. Try as they may, right-wing parties, hawking their message of hate, have never established a foothold in the Federal Parliament.

But, so the skeptics will demur, that wonderful edifice is collapsing before our own eyes. With the Soviet surrender in the Cold War, the Atlantic alliance is fading and the Americans are going home. Won't Germany, finally un-shackled from its postwar fetters, again be tempted by sheer strength and the heady lure of aggrandizement?

True, waning dependence equals less deference. Absent the Soviet threat, Bonn-Berlin might be less hesitant to convert economic muscle into political clout, But to argue that Reunification II will turn into a remake of the 1871 original is to ignore how much the script itself has changed.

The rivalry of nations in the democratic-industrial world has moved from the battlefield into the economic arena, and it promises to stay there as long as the marvelous economic community Europeans have built persists. Nobody expects the Germans to invade Alsace again; now they pay for the pleasure of owning the choice plots there, just as the Japanese are buying, not bombing, Pearl Harbor.

Power in Europe (as opposed to Saddam Hussein's neighborhood) is measured not by conquest but by capital surpluses. Not booty and glory define the stakes, but questions such as: "Who determines currency parities?" It so happens that the *Bundesbank* calls the shots, which understandably grates hard on the French. But worlds separate this contest from the game played out with the German jackboots in Paris 50 years ago. The battle lines are drawn in the balance-of-payments ledgers, and the accounts are settled with dollars and Deutsche marks, not blood and iron. The rivalry is about joint welfare, not this or that province; both sides lose or win together (American victims of Sony resent cheap VCRs made in Japan, but who would go to war over the privilege of buying worse-quality goods at higher prices?)

Still, might not Bonn-Berlin hanker after nuclear weapons and push for revision of its eastern borders? What for? The new, more civilized and civilianized game of nations offers the largest payoffs to nations such as German and Japan. The game has devalued the military chips, delivering power and prestige to those who can back up their bets with investments and loans. Why, then, should they forego their advantage by changing the rules? In the attempt, they would certainly revive the hostile coalitions that proved their undoing in 1945. Also, well-settled democracies are more sensible about such risks than were the Hohenzollerns and Hitlerites.

On Wednesday, Bonn Inc. will take over bankrupt Prusso-Marx, a k a East Germany. But the remake of 1871 will not be shot with a cast of latter-day Erich von Stroheims. The soundtrack will not be *"Deutschland Uber Alles,"* but Beethoven's "Ode to Joy," Europe's unofficial anthem. Walking alone in the distant past, Germans easily fell for the mesmerizing music of the Pied Pipers. But in the meantime Europe has changed, and so has Germany. Hamburg and Rome, Munich and Marseilles have been listening to the same tune for a long time; adding Dresden and Leipzig should not ruin that score.

Uncomfortable Questions

by Rainer Zitelmann

Rainer Zitelmann, born in 1957, is a historian and author of a biography of *Hitler* (1989). This article appeared in *Die Welt* on 13 October 1990.

"But a reunification in which the two German states, as they are and as they have become, are fused into an operating state is not conceivable, even theoretically." This sentence appears in a book published in 1987 by a highly esteemed historian and publicist—who incidentally was once a vigorous proponent of German unity.

One might object that no one could foresee the current development. Of course that is true. One might also say that the sentence expresses only what the majority of intellectuals in the Federal Republic thought. That too is—unfortunately—true.

On the other side: is it not remarkable that a historian announces that history has reached a point at which a change of the status quo is unthinkable? Exactly the opposite is inconceivable: the assumption of the continuing maintenance of a condition that is in addition artificial and depends on the denial of the right to self-determination.

If there is a law in history, it is of the continual change—of state systems, values, and social systems. And yet every system tends to except itself from this analysis. Scientists attempt to justify the beliefs of those held in constrained circumstances: that the present condition will last forever.

That was also true in the case of the division of Germany, which was understood by the majority of intellectuals in this country not at all as a burden but rather as an opportunity. Two attitudes must be distinguished. Some people did not believe in the restoration of German unity because of a lack of optimism, or of historical and political imagination. That can be forgiven at once. But it is quite a different matter in the case of those who also believed the two-state Germany to be desirable.

The historian and publicist Jochen Thies rightly spoke about a "group of 50 to 60 year old opinion makers, who can on account of their age be described as the last burnt children of National Socialism." Their credo ran as follows: the German nation-state destroyed itself in 1945, and as a consequence Germans in East and West must renounce a restoration of the nation-state. Modifying the concept of an alleged "peculiar German path [*Sonderweg*]," they preached the peculiar path of the two states. They were proud that they had drawn the right lesson from the terrible history of the German Empire.

This is more a question of generations than of political positions. In 1988 Martin Walser remarked bitterly: "Left and right intellectuals here agree about nothing so much as about the acceptability of division."

Should we name names? It would not be worth it. It would be easy to fill a whole page of newsprint with the names of intellectuals who in the last years and decades had expressly opposed the restoration of German unity. Those who still clung to the goal were at best pitifully dismissed as abstracted illusionists, but more often defamed as nationalists of the eternal yesterday.

In the meantime we know: it was rather those who held the division of Germany to be the "inexorable result of history" who were the illusionists. Many of them have in the meantime altered their views. They place themselves on the new "factual basis," some hesitantly, others aggressively.

Certainly a belated insight is better than none at all. But it is only then a genuine insight when it is linked with self-critical reflection on the standpoint defended earlier. Otherwise a generation of German intellectuals will have to deal with the uncomfortable questions of a younger generation. These will demand of their (intellectual) fathers why they participated so enthusiastically in the "rationalization of division" (Martin Walser).

The Two Plus Four Settlement

In contrast to the international settlement after the First
World War, in which the German government accepted
the Treaty of Versailles (1919), there was no peace treaty
after the Second World War, and German affairs were
settled by decisions of the major Allied powers (USA,
USSR, UK, and France, although France was represented
neither at the wartime summits nor at the 1945 Potsdam
conference). The treaty of 12 September 1990 between
the two German states, the FRG and the GDR (the Two),
and the wartime allies (the Four), both formally ended
the Second World War, and gave the necessary consent
of the Allies to the merging of the two German states in
accordance with the expressed wishes and intentions of
the parliaments of those states. The name given to the
negotiations preparing this treaty implied that the prime
mover in the process of unification was the German people: the talks were called "Two Plus Four" rather than
"Four Plus Two," as some of the Allies looking at the
texts of international agreements initially suggested. In
international politics, unlike in mathematics, Four Plus
Two is not necessarily the same as Two Plus Four.

Treaty of 12 September 1990 on the Final Settlement with Respect to Germany

The Federal Republic of Germany, the German Democratic Republic, the
French Republic, the Union of Soviet Socialist Republics, the United Kingdom
of Great Britain and Northern Ireland and the United States of America.

Conscious of the fact that their peoples have been living together in peace
since 1945;

Mindful of the recent historic changes in Europe which make it possible
to overcome the division of the continent;

Having regard to the rights and responsibilities of the Four Powers relating
to Berlin and to Germany as a whole, and the corresponding wartime and
post-war agreements and decisions of the Four Powers;

Resolved in accordance with their obligations under the Charter of the United Nations to develop friendly relations among nations based on respect for the principle of equal rights and self-determination of peoples, and to take other appropriate measures to strengthen universal peace;

Recalling the principles of the Final Act of the Conference on Security and Cooperation in Europe, signed in Helsinki;

Recognizing that those principles have laid firm foundations for the establishment of a just and lasting peaceful order in Europe;

Determined to take account of everyone's security interests;

Convinced of the need finally to overcome antagonism and to develop cooperation in Europe;

Confirming their readiness to reinforce security, in particular by adopting effective arms control, disarmament and confidence-building measures; their willingness not to regard each other as adversaries but to work for a relationship of trust and cooperation and accordingly their readiness to consider positively setting up appropriate institutional arrangements within the framework of the Conference on Security and Cooperation in Europe;

Welcoming the fact that the German people, freely exercising their right of self-determination, have expressed their will to bring about the unity of Germany as a state so that they will be able to serve the peace of the world as an equal and sovereign partner in a united Europe;

Convinced that the unification of Germany as a state with definitive borders is a significant contribution to peace and stability in Europe;

Intending to conclude the final settlement with respect to Germany;

Recognizing that thereby, and with the unification of Germany as a democratic and peaceful state, the rights and responsibilities of the Four Powers relating to Berlin and to Germany as a whole lose their function;

Represented by their Ministers for Foreign Affairs who, in accordance with the Ottawa Declaration of 13 February 1990, met in Bonn on 5 May 1990, in Berlin on 22 June 1990, in Paris on 17 July 1990 with the participation of the Minister for Foreign Affairs of the Republic of Poland, and in Moscow on 12 September 1990;

Have agreed as follows:

Article 1

1. The united Germany shall comprise the territory of the Federal Republic of Germany, the German Democratic Republic and the whole of Berlin. Its external borders shall be the borders of the Federal Republic of Germany and the German Democratic Republic and shall be definitive from the date on which the present Treaty comes into force. The confirmation of the definitive nature of the borders of the united Germany is an essential element of the peaceful order in Europe.

2. The united Germany and the Republic of Poland shall confirm the ex-

isting border between them in a treaty that is binding under international law.

3. The united Germany has no territorial claims whatsoever against other states and shall not assert any in the future.

4. The Governments of the Federal Republic of Germany and the German Democratic Republic shall ensure that the constitution of the united Germany does not contain any provision incompatible with these principles. This applies accordingly to the provisions laid down in the preamble, the second sentence of Article 23, and Article 146 of the Basic Law for the Federal Republic of Germany.[1]

5. The Governments of the French Republic, the Union of Soviet Socialist Republics, the United Kingdom of Great Britain and Northern Ireland and the United States of America take formal note of the corresponding commitments and declarations by the Governments of the Federal Republic of Germany and the German Democratic Republic and declare that their implementation will confirm the definitive nature of the united Germany's borders.

Article 2

The Governments of the Federal Republic of Germany and the German Democratic Republic reaffirm their declarations that only peace will emanate from German soil. According to the constitution of the united Germany, acts tending to and undertaken with the intent to disturb the peaceful relations between nations, especially to prepare for aggressive war, are unconstitutional and a punishable offence.[2] The Governments of the Federal Republic of Germany and the German Democratic Republic declare that the united Germany will never employ any of its weapons except in accordance with its constitution and the Charter of the United Nations.

Article 3

1. The Governments of the Federal Republic of Germany and the German Democratic Republic reaffirm their renunciation of the manufacture and possession of and control over nuclear, biological and chemical weapons. They declare that the united Germany, too, will abide by these commitments. In particular, rights and obligations arising from the Treaty on the Non-Proliferation of Nuclear Weapons of 1 July 1968 will continue to apply to the united Germany.

---

[1] This requirement was fulfilled by the provisions of article 4 amending the Basic Law.
[2] Article 26 of the Basic Law reads: "Acts tending to and undertaken with the intent to disturb the peaceful relations between nations, especially to prepare for aggressive war, shall be unconstitutional. They shall be made a punishable offence."

2. The Government of the Federal Republic of Germany, acting in full agreement with the Government of the German Democratic Republic, made the following statement on 30 August 1990 in Vienna at the Negotiations on Conventional Armed Forces in Europe:

   "The Government of the Federal Republic of Germany undertakes to reduce the personnel strength of the armed forces of the united Germany to 370,000 (ground, air and naval forces) within three to four years. This reduction will commence on the entry into force of the first CFE agreement. Within the scope of this overall ceiling no more than 345,000 will belong to the ground and air forces which, pursuant to the agreed mandate, alone are the subject of the Negotiations on Conventional Armed Forces in Europe. The Federal Government regards its commitment to reduce ground and air forces as a significant German contribution to the reduction of conventional armed forces in Europe. It assumes that in follow-on negotiations the other participants in the negotiations, too, will render their contribution to enhancing security and stability in Europe, including measures to limit personnel strengths."

   The Government of the German Democratic Republic has expressly associated itself with this statement.

3. The Governments of the French Republic, the Union of Soviet Socialist Republics, the United Kingdom of Great Britain and Northern Ireland and the United States of America take note of these statements by the Governments of the Federal Republic of Germany and the German Democratic Republic.

Article 4

1. The Governments of the Federal Republic of Germany, the German Democratic Republic and the Union of Soviet Socialist Republics state that the united Germany and the Union of Soviet Socialist Republics will settle by treaty the conditions for and the duration of the presence of Soviet armed forces on the territory of the present German Democratic Republic and of Berlin, as well as the conduct of the withdrawal of these armed forces which will be completed by the end of 1994, in connection with the implementation of the undertaking of the Federal Republic of Germany and the German Democratic Republic referred to in paragraph 2 of Article 3 of the present Treaty.

2. The Governments of the French Republic, the United Kingdom of Great Britain and Northern Ireland and the United States of America take note of this statement.

Article 5

1. Until the completion of the withdrawal of the Soviet armed forces from

the territory of the present German Democratic Republic and of Berlin in accordance with Article 4 of the present Treaty, only German territorial defence units which are not integrated into the alliance structures to which German armed forces in the rest of German territory are assigned will be stationed in that territory as armed forces of the united Germany. During that period and subject to the provisions of paragraph 2 of this Article, armed forces of other states will not be stationed in that territory or carry out any other military activity there.

2. For the duration of the presence of Soviet armed forces in the territory of the present German Democratic Republic and of Berlin, armed forces of the French Republic, the United Kingdom of Great Britain and Northern Ireland and the United States of America will, upon German request, remain stationed in Berlin by agreement to this effect between the Government of the unified Germany and the Governments of the states concerned. The number of troops and the amount of equipment of all non-German armed forces stationed in Berlin will not be greater than at the time of signature of the present Treaty. New categories of weapons will not be introduced there by non-German armed forces. The Government of the united Germany will conclude with the Governments of those states which have armed forces stationed in Berlin treaties with conditions which are fair taking account of the relations existing with the states concerned.

3. Following the completion of the withdrawal of the Soviet armed forces from the territory of the present German Democratic Republic and of Berlin, units of German armed forces assigned to military alliance structures in the same way as those in the rest of German territory may also be stationed in that part of Germany, but without nuclear weapon carriers. This does not apply to conventional weapon systems which may have other capabilities in addition to conventional ones but which in that part of Germany are equipped for a conventional role and designated only for such. Foreign armed forces and nuclear weapons or their carriers will not be stationed in that part of Germany or deployed there.

Article 6

The right of the united Germany to belong to alliances, with all the rights and responsibilities arising therefrom, shall not be affected by the present Treaty.

Article 7

1. The French Republic, the Union of Soviet Socialist Republics, the United Kingdom of Great Britain and Northern Ireland and the United States of America hereby terminate their rights and responsibilities relating to

Berlin and to Germany as a whole. As a result, the corresponding, related quadripartite agreements, decisions and practices are terminated and all related Four Power institutions are dissolved.

2. The united Germany shall have accordingly full sovereignty over its internal and external affairs.

Article 8

1. The present Treaty is subject to ratification or acceptance as soon as possible. On the German side it will be ratified by the united Germany. The Treaty will therefore apply to the united Germany.

2. The instruments of ratification or acceptance shall be deposited with the Government of the united Germany. That Government shall inform the Governments of the other Contracting Parties of the deposit of each instrument of ratification or acceptance.

Article 9

The present Treaty shall enter into force for the united Germany, the French Republic, the Union of Soviet Socialist Republics, the United Kingdom of Great Britain and Northern Ireland and the United States of America on the date of deposit of the last instrument of ratification or acceptance by these states.

Article 10

The original of the present treaty, of which the English, French, German and Russian texts are equally authentic, shall be deposited with the Government of the Federal Republic of Germany, which shall transmit certified true copies to the Governments of the other Contracting Parties.

Done at Moscow on 12 September 1990.

For the Federal Republic of Germany
Hans-Dietrich Genscher

For the German Democratic Republic
Lothar de Maizière

For the French Republic
Roland Dumas

For the United Kingdom of Great Britain and Northern Ireland
Douglas Hurd

For the United States of America
James Baker

For the Union of Soviet Socialist Republics
Eduard Shevardnadze

Agreed Minute

to the Treaty on the Final Settlement with respect to Germany of 12 September 1990.

Any questions with respect to the application of the word "deployed" as used in the last sentence of paragraph 3 of Article 5 will be decided by the Government of the united Germany in a reasonable and responsible way taking into account the security interests of each Contracting Party as set forth in the preamble.

East Germany

"Awakening 89—New Forum"
Call for the Founding of New Forum

10 September 1989

New Forum and *Democracy Now* were the citizens' movements founded in the fall of 1989. The groups led the protests against the East German Communist government that catalyzed the East German revolution.

In our country the communication between state and society is obviously troubled. Evidence for this is the widespread dissatisfaction that has led people to withdraw into their private niches or, in large numbers, to emigrate. Such a degree of flight is caused elsewhere by deprivation, hunger, or violence. This is not at all the case with us.

The disturbed connection between state and society paralyzes the creative energies of our society and hinders the solution of the local and general tasks that face us. We are dissipating our strength in dourful passivity while we have more important things to do for our life, our country, and humanity.

In the state and economy, the balancing of the interests of various groups and sectors is not functioning properly. Communication about our situation and between competing interests in our society is blocked. Everyone easily speaks his mind in private about his diagnosis and the measures that he deems most important. But people's wishes and strivings are very different and are not being rationally weighed against each other, nor is their practicability being examined. On the one hand, we would like an expansion of the range of available consumer goods and better distribution, on the other hand we see the social and economic costs of these things and ask for a rejection of unlimited growth. We want to give room to economic initiative, but don't want this to degenerate into the "elbow society." We want to retain the tried and true and yet create space for renewal, in order to live more economically and ecologically. We want order but no paternalism. We want free, independent individuals, who yet act with regard for society as a whole. We want to be protected from violence without having to tolerate a state of spies and thugs. Loafers and loudmouths are to be driven from their sinecures, but we don't want to disadvantage the socially weak and defenseless. We want health care for everyone, but no one should be able to play sick at the expense of others.

In order to recognize all of these contradictions, to hear and evaluate opinions and arguments concerning them, we need a democratic dialogue regarding the tasks of the state, of the economy, and of culture. We must think about and discuss these questions publicly, together, and in the entire country. Whether we will find ways out of the present crisis in the foreseeable future will depend upon our readiness and our will to do this. In the present social development it is crucial that:

- a greater number of people take part in the process of social reform, and
- the various individual and group activities find a way to act in concert.

For this reason we are forming a political platform for the entire GDR that will make it possible for people from all professions, walks of life, parties, and groups to take part in the discussion and consideration of crucial social problems in this country. For this comprehensive initiative we choose the name:

New Forum

We will place the activity of New Forum on a legal basis. In doing this we refer to Article 29 of the constitution of the GDR, which specifies the right to realize our political interest through common action in an association. We will register the founding of this association with the responsible agencies of the GDR in accordance with the Decree of November 11, 1975 on the "Founding and Activity of Associations".

Beneath all of the strivings to which New Forum wants to give a voice lies the wish for justice, democracy, and peace as well as for the protection and preservation of nature. This is the impulse that we want to see brought to life in all realms in the coming reconstruction of society.

We appeal to all citizens of the GDR who want to take part in the reconstruction of our society to become members of New Forum.

The time is ripe.

A Plea to Get Involved in Our Own Cause
Flier of the Citizens' Movement
"Democracy Now"

of September 12, 1989

New Forum and *Democracy Now* were the citizens' movements founded in the fall of 1989. These groups led the protests against the East German Communist government which catalyzed the East German revolution.

Dear friends, fellow citizens and all concerned!

Our land lives in inner disquiet. People are chafing under the present conditions, some resign themselves. A great loss of confidence in that which has historically grown up in the GDR is going through the country. Many hardly can give any justification for still being here. Many are leaving the country, because accommodation has its limits.

Only a few years ago "real existing socialism" was thought to be the only socialism possible. Its characteristics are the monopoly of a centralized state party, state control of the means of production, the permeation of society and imposition of uniformity upon it by the state, and the incapacitation of the citizenry. Despite its indisputable achievements for social security and justice, it is today evident that the era of state socialism is coming to a close. It requires a peaceful, democratic renewal.

Introduced and furthered by Gorbachev's initiative, the path of democratic reconstruction is being pursued in the Soviet Union, Hungary, and Poland. Enormous economic, social, ecological, and also ethnic problems stand in the way and could cause this reconstruction to fail, with disastrous consequences for the entire world. Everything that the socialist workers' movement has strived for in the way of social justice and solidarity is at stake. Socialism must now find its true, democratic form, if it is not to be lost to history. It must not be lost, for threatened humanity, in its search for survivable forms of human coexistence, needs alternatives to Western consumer society, the prosperity of which is paid for by the rest of the world.

Despite all attempts to whitewash matters, the signs of the political, economic and ecological crisis of state socialism are unmistakable even in "the colors of the GDR." But there are no indications that the SED leadership is ready to reorient its thinking. It seems as though they are speculating on the failure of reforms in the Soviet Union. But the GDR also must undertake this democratic reconstruction.

The political crisis of the GDR became especially clear in the local elections of May 5, 1989. The doctrine of the "moral-political unity of party, state, and people," which is supposed to justify a monopoly of power independent of elections, could only be protected from refutation by falsifying the election results. Between 10 and 20 percent of the populace of the big cities openly denied their vote to the candidates of the National Front. Doubtless this figure would have been considerably higher in secret elections.

Many people are no longer represented by the National Front. They have no political representation in society. The wish of many citizens for a democratization of the relationship between state and society cannot be publicly expressed in the GDR. For this reason we call for a

Citizens' Movement "Democracy Now"

We appeal to all those who are affected by the crisis of our country. We invite all initiative groups with similar concerns to join with us. We particularly hope for an alliance with Christians and critical Marxists. Let us reflect together on our future, on a society of solidarity, in which:

- social justice, freedom, and the value of the human individual are guaranteed,
- social consensus is sought in public dialogue and is realized through the just balancing of various interests,
- the responsible and creative work of our citizenry creates a lively pluralism within our community,
- a just political order secures domestic peace,
- economy and ecology are brought into harmony,
- prosperity is no longer increased at the expense of poor countries,
- life fulfillment in commonality and creative activity for the common good can be sought and found more than hitherto.

We invite all who are interested to take part in a dialogue on the principles of and plans for a democratic reconstruction of our country. In January or February of 1990 we want to hold a meeting of the representatives of those who want to take part. A program of principles shall be decided upon and speakers shall be elected who can bring this program into the urgently necessary dialogue between all social forces.

We also hope to assemble a list of candidates for the approaching People's Assembly elections.

As a first unfinished, incomplete, and provisional contribution to discussion we attach "Theses for a Democratic Transformation in the GDR." Write us your opinion and your criticism. We ask for suggestions for changes. Write to us also if you want to support this initiative, and let us know if you want to support our organization. Please write to one of the following addresses.

Let us join together and together raise up hope again in our country! Please copy and circulate [this flier].

Theses for a Democratic Transformation in the GDR

The goal of our suggestions is to secure the domestic peace of our country and thereby serve external peace as well. We want to help form a society of solidarity and democratize all spheres of life. At the same time we must find a new relation of partnership with our natural environment.

We want to see the socialist revolution that has stagnated in state socialism carried further and thereby given a lease on the future. Instead of a paternalistic state dominated by the party, a state that without the sanction of society has presumed to be the director and schoolmaster of the people, we want a state founded upon the fundamental consensus of society, a state that is accountable to the people and thereby becomes a public matter (*res publica*) of autonomous citizens. Successful social accomplishments must not be placed at risk through any program of reform.

As Germans we have a special responsibility. This responsibility requires that the relationship of the [two] German states be freed on both sides from ideological prejudices and be shaped in the spirit and practice of neighborliness on equal terms. We invite the Germans in the Federal Republic to work toward a reconstruction of their society that could make possible a new unity of the German people under the common roof of the European peoples. Each German state should for the sake of unity undertake reforms in the direction of the other.

History imposes on us Germans a special obligation of peace. We should meet this obligation by reducing the defensive capabilities of the National People's Army and through the introduction of alternative service.

1. From Authoritarian State to Republic

The subordination of the state to the bureaucracy of the party and its institutionalized system of office patronage must end.

The strict separation of the legislative and executive branches is necessary, so that the organs of popular representation have effective oversight over the executive.

The election laws must be reformed so as to guarantee free and secret elections. A choice must be possible between different political programs and representatives. We suggest inviting UNO observers to the next People's Assembly elections.

The state should withdraw from functions that are a matter for society:

- The media belong in the hands of noncommercial public bodies so that they can become instruments of the free expression of opinion. All social groups must have access to the press, radio, and television.

- Schools and institutions of higher education may no longer remain an instrument of ideological training and indoctrination for a party, even when this party is in power. The schools and previously existing youth organizations must be disassociated from each other. New child and youth organizations must be permitted. Parents should receive the right to help determine curriculum and teaching methods.

- Parties and organizations should be released from state supervision and direction. The full freedom of association must be guaranteed.

- The unions must become independent representative organs of workers' interests and receive the right to strike.

- Art, science and culture must be free from the imposition of ideology by the state, and the right to self-administration of their institutions must be constitutionally guaranteed. Legal prescriptions and provisions to the contrary must be revoked.

A reform of the justice system should eliminate offenses that are subject to arbitrary interpretation and guarantee the independence of judges and defense counsel. The penal system must be reformed so as to guarantee public oversight and an effective right of appeal.

A constitutional court should be introduced, and an administrative court fully realized.

Freedom of travel and emigration should be enacted in accordance with the Vienna resolutions of the Committee for Security and Cooperation in Europe (CSCE).

2. From State to Societal Control of the Means of Production

We are in favor of an end to the politbureaucratic command economy: the existing state planning/*dirigisme* should give way to a state skeletal planning. Only such state organs for the supervision and direction of the economy as are required for tying any economic activity to the common good (compatibility with social and economic interests) should continue to exist.

Businesses and conglomerates should become economically independent and orient their prices by the market, so that a competition of supply replaces the existing competition of demand.

We are in favor of a degree of union control in the business place, election of management, a true obligation of accountability toward the employees, and employee profit sharing.

We are in favor of a strengthening and independence of the existing agricultural, craft and trade organizations as well as the formation of new production and trade associations.

We are in favor of allowing private cooperatives as well as private economic and property forms, providing that an appropriate degree of employee control is guaranteed.

3. From the Exploitation and Pollution of the Environment to a Lasting Coexistence with Nature

The relevant environmental data and the pollution and resource problems of our country must first of all be determined and made public.

We need comprehensive nationwide monitoring of pollutant concentrations in our air, water and soil.

The practice of "costfree" treatment of pollutants must be ended as quickly as possible. All pollutant treatment costs must be assumed by the business concerns.

A requirement of responsibility toward the environment should be introduced. The burden of proof for the environmental safety of production should lie with the producing concerns.

A rigorous energy conservation program must have precedence. An effective participation of all consumers must be brought about through a corresponding price and taxation policy.

Strict state environmental safety requirements and state oversight of production and products are necessary.

The use, development, and study of renewable energy sources should be encouraged in every regard.

A public discussion of environmental problems, especially of the energy problem, the risks of nuclear energy, the greenhouse effect and growth is necessary.

A change in our societal goals and in our guiding values is necessary so that we can achieve a change in lifestyle, a greater sense of community, and a higher quality of life.

Declaration of New Forum on the Fortieth Anniversary of the GDR
Appeal to All Members of the SED

The activity of New Forum is as new for our society as it is crucial. Ten thousand signatures from all parts of the populace already prove that communal action and a sense of responsibility have not been lost in the stagnation of our societal life. Not only has our society's condition of crisis become intolerable, but the prohibition upon public discussion of the societal conditions of our life has become indefensible.

These ten thousand signatures are far from being a treasonous action: they are an act of civic responsibility.

We protest against the attempts of the government to depict us as enemies of socialism. The New Forum is a place for new thinking, which is no more hostile to socialism here than it is in the Soviet Union. New Forum may one day be unnecessary—now it is indispensable. We employ our democratic initiative to oppose all attempts to evade social dialogue through criminalization, exclusion, or intimidation.

Socialism, which the government so sanctimoniously sees as being endangered, cannot be threatened by a popular movement. Citizens' initiatives do not threaten, but rather develop new social life.

It is rather the inactivity of the SED itself that is endangering socialism on German soil. We appeal expressly to the two million members of the SED: you form the largest and most important political body in our country. You possess an enormous reserve of expertise and leadership experience that is urgently needed for the renewal of our society. You claim the role of leadership—exercise it! Lead the discussion in your ranks, lead the whole of the party to a constructive course! In the last weeks many resolutions have been sent from subsidiary organizations to the Central Committee. Do the members of the Central Committee at least know the number and content of these resolutions? Were they discussed? Will they be enacted? If in a socialist society internal discussion and cooperation is denied even to the leadership party of two million people, then agonizing and unbearable tensions must arise. The discussion that the SED itself must hold is an important part of the total societal discussion that our country needs.

We call for an active and responsible stance from all citizens of the GDR. Precisely the resignation that has spread so deeply into all realms of society and the mistrustful helplessness of the political leadership demand the revitalization of the democratic activity of all citizens in all existing structures over the next months.

Protest Demonstration at Berlin-Alexanderplatz:
Texts of recorded speeches by Stefan Heym, Christoph Hein, and Christa Wolf

4 November 1989

Stefan Heym

Stefan Heym, born 1913, was one of East Germany's most prominent writers. His works include *Collin* and *Five Days in June*. He was an active participant in the East German citizens' movements of 1989–90.

Friends and fellow citizens!

It is as though someone had thrown open a window, after all the years of intellectual, economic, and political stagnation; the years of torpor and staleness, of phrasemongering and bureaucratic arbitrariness, of official blindness and deafness—what a transformation. Not four weeks ago, a nicely constructed reviewing stand stood just around the corner from here. With the parade, as ordered. Before our illustrious leaders. And today: today you, you are gathered here by your own free will for freedom and democracy and for a socialism that is worthy of the name.

In the time that is now, I hope, at an end, people often came to me with their complaints: this one had suffered an injustice, that one was oppressed and harassed, and they were all frustrated. And I said: so do something. And they said resignedly: we can't do anything. And that was the way it went in this republic, until it couldn't go on that way any longer. Until so much indignation had built up in the state, and so much discontent in the life of the people, that a part of them ran away. But the others, the majority, declared, in the streets, publicly, "No more! Change! We are the people!" One man wrote to me: in these last weeks we have overcome our speechlessness and learned to walk erect.—He was right. And that, my friends, in Germany, where until now all revolutions have gone awry. And where the people have always bowed and scraped, under the Kaiser, under the Nazis, and later as well. But speaking, speaking freely and walking erect, that isn't enough. Let us also learn to govern. Power doesn't belong in the hands of an individual, or of the few, or of an apparatus, or of a party. All must have a share in this power. And whoever exercises it and wherever must be subject to the oversight of the citizens. For power corrupts, and absolute power—we can still see this today—corrupts absolutely. Socialism, not the Stalinist kind, the true socialism that we finally want to build for our benefit and the benefit of all Germany: this socialism is not possible without democracy. But democracy—a Greek word—means: "the rule of the people." Friends, fellow citizens: let us exercise it, this rule!

Christoph Hein

Christoph Hein, born in 1944, is a poet, playwright, and novelist. In 1982 he won the Heinrich Mann Prize and in 1983 the West German Critics Prize. His novel, *The Distant Lover,* was published in the United States in 1989.

Dear liberated fellow citizens!

There is much for all of us to do, and little time in which to do it. The structures of this society must be changed, if it is to become democratic and socialist. And there is no alternative to this.

We must also speak of the dirty hands, the dirty vests. Here, too, society and the media still have much to do. Decay, corruption, abuse of office, theft of public property: this has to be cleared up, and the clearing up must take place even in the highest places of government. It must begin there.

Let us beware of confusing the euphoria of these days with the changes we have yet to achieve. The enthusiasm and the demonstrations were and are beneficial and necessary, but they are no substitute for work. Let us not be deceived by our own enthusiasm: we haven't made it yet. We aren't out of the tunnel yet. And there are still sufficient forces that wish no changes, that fear a new society and indeed have reason to fear it.

I would like to remind all of us about an old man, an old and now probably very lonely man. I'm speaking of Erich Honecker. This man had a dream, and he was ready to go to prison for this dream. Then he had the chance to realize this dream. It wasn't a good chance, because a defeated fascism and an overpowerful Stalinism attended the birth. A society came into being that had little to do with socialism. This society was and is characterized by bureaucracy, demagogy, surveillance, abuse of power, paternalism and also criminality. A structure came into being to which many good, intelligent and honest people had to subjugate themselves if they didn't want to leave the country. And no one knew anymore how to take action against this structure, how it might be broken up.

And I believe that even for this old man our society is not the fulfillment of his dreams. Even he, standing at the top of this state and especially responsible for it, for its successes but also for its mistakes, failings and crimes, even he was almost powerless over these moribund structures.

I remind us about this old man only in order to warn us against now creating structures of which we will one day be the helpless victims. Let us create a democratic society on a legal basis that is subject to challenge. A socialism that doesn't make a caricature of the word. A society that is commensurate with humanity instead of subjugating humanity to its structures. That will provide a lot of work for us all, including a lot of painstaking work. Worse than knitting.

Another word. Success, we know, has many fathers. Apparently, many believe that the changes in the GDR are successful, for now many are claiming the paternity of this success. Curious fathers have come forward even out of the highest reaches of the government. But I think that our memory isn't so bad that we don't know who began the dissolution of these overpowerful structures; who dealt the blow of reason. It was the reason of the street, the demonstrations of the people. Without these demonstrations the government would never have been changed, without them the work that is just beginning would not be possible.

Leipzig above all deserves mention. I think that the mayor of our town should propose in the name of the citizens of Berlin—since we all happen to be standing here together—to the state council and the Chamber of Deputies that Leipzig be christened the "City of Heroes of the GDR."

We've had to accustom ourselves to the long name, "Berlin, Capital of the GDR." I think that it will be easier to get used to the street sign, "Leipzig, City of Heroes of the GDR."

The title will manifest our thanks. It will help us to make reform irreversible. It will remind us of our failings and mistakes in the past. And it will remind the government of the reason of the streets, which always remained alert and will, if it is necessary, be heard from again.

Christa Wolf

Christa Wolf was born in 1929. She is one of the most respected and controversial contemporary German writers. Her novels include A *Model Childhood* (1980) and *Cassandra* (1984).

Every revolutionary movement also liberates language. What was before so difficult to pronounce all at once comes freely over our lips and we are amazed to hear what we've apparently been thinking for a long time, to hear what we now call out to each other: Democracy—now or never! And saying it we mean the rule of the people, and we remember the approaches to democracy in our history that ran aground or were bloodily put down and we don't want to again sleep through the opportunity that lies in this crisis, because it awakens all of our productive power. But we also don't want to squander this opportunity through imprudence or through a mere transposition of the old adversarial way of thinking.

I have my difficulties with the word "Turn [*Wende*]." It makes me think of a sailboat with the captain calling out "Prepare to jibe!" because the wind has turned, and the crew ducks as the boom sweeps across the deck. Is this image true? Is it still true in this situation that is moving forward with every passing day?

I would speak of a "revolutionary renewal." Revolutions come from below. "Above" and "below" exchange places in the system of values, and this change turns the socialist system from its head back on its feet. Great social movements are underway; never have we talked so much as in these weeks, talked with each other, and never with this passion, with so much rage and grief, and with so much hope. We want to use every day, we sleep not at all or only little, we make friends with many new people, and we have painful fallings out with others. That is called "dialogue," we demanded it, now we can hardly bear to hear the word and yet haven't really learned what it means. We stare distrustfully at many a suddenly outstretched hand, into many a previously so unexpressive face. We turn old slogans around and return them to their sender. We are afraid of being exploited, "used," and we are afraid of declining an honestly meant offer—the entire country now faces this dilemma. We know that we must exercise the art of not letting conflict degenerate into confrontation. These weeks, these possibilities are given us only once, by ourselves.

With astonishment, we observe the chameleons, what the vernacular now calls "*Wendehälse*" who, according to the dictionary, "quickly and easily adapt themselves to a given new situation, move skillfully in it, know how to make use of it." They more than anyone undermine the credibility of the new political course. We haven't yet come far enough to be able to take them humorously—although we don't lack a sense of humour in other situations. "Hangers on—Resign!" I read on banners. And a chant from demonstrators directed at the police: "Take Off Your Uniforms and Join Us!"—a generous offer. We can also think in the language of economics: "*Rechtssicherheit spart Staatssicherheit!* [Constitutional government saves on internal security expenses]," and we are ready for existential sacrifices: "*Bürger, stell die Glotze ab, setz dich mit uns jetzt in Trab!* [Citizen, stop gaping at television and join us!]." Today I saw, incredibly: "No Privileges For Us Berliners!"

Yes: language is jumping out of the bureaucratese and newspaper German in which it was wrapped, and is remembering its emotional words. One of them is "dream"; so let us dream, with our reason wide awake.

"Imagine there was socialism and nobody ran away!" But we see the pictures of those who are still leaving and ask ourselves: what to do? and hear as an echo the answer: what to do! Our task is just now beginning, if demands become rights, and therefore obligations: investigative commissions, constitutional court, administrative reform. Much to do, and our jobs besides. And still find time to read the paper!

We won't have any more time for ceremonial parades and prescribed demonstrations. This is a demonstration, officially approved, peaceful. If it remains so until the end, then we'll know still more about what we're capable of, and then we'll insist on it.

"Suggestion for the First of May—The Leadership Hold a Parade for the People!" All this popular literary talent! Unbelievable changes. The "*Staatsvolk der DDR*" must go onto the streets in order to recognize itself—a people. And this is for me the most important sentence of these last weeks—the thousandfold refrain: We – are – the – people!

A simple statement of fact. We won't forget it.

Notes on the Reactions of Progressive Forces to the Current Domestic Political Situation in the GDR

The Ministry for State Security (*Ministerium für Staats-sicherheit* or MfS) was created immediately after the foundation of the GDR. By the end of the 1980s, it employed 85,000 full-time employees and around 120,000 "IMs" (Unofficial Employees) or informers. Reports of the informers were collected by the Central Group for Evaluation and Information (ZAIG). In the course of 1989, the ZAIG reported extensively on the increasingly hostile public opinion in the GDR. On the basis of its reports, it made proposals for Soviet-style reform (as in this document, which sets out the demands of so-called "progressive forces": in other words, the MfS's own staff). There is a considerable irony that at many times the secret police seemed to be the official institution in the GDR that produced the boldest reform suggestions. This report intended for the Minister of State Security, Erich Mielke, follows the abortive fortieth anniversary celebrations.

According to available information from the capital and all districts of the GDR many progressive forces, and in particular members of the SED, believe that the socialist order of state and society in the GDR is seriously endangered. At the same time, they announce their readiness to support the party and defend the power of workers and peasants against all attacks by internal and external enemies. They observe that the mood of the population in the GDR has become rapidly worse. According to their accounts, many statements of opinion and submissions of workers claim that the system and leadership of political, ideological and economic processes in the GDR have become inflexible. The noticeable intensification of internal political problems and difficulties and the mass flights of population indicate a general social crisis in the GDR. The result is an increasing number of signs of uncertainty, helplessness and resignation among party members, members of the state apparatus and other socially active persons.

Among workers doubts about the perspective of socialism in the GDR increase. Many progressive forces, including above all older workers, fear that there will be major disruptions in society which cannot be controlled by the party. Already now they argue that GDR is in a situation similar to that before the counterrevolutionary events of 17 June 1953. They are above all worried about the increasing loss of confidence of workers in the party and state leadership. Many workers, including numerous members and functionaries of the party, say quite openly that the party and state leadership is no longer capable of assessing the situation realistically and taking appropriate measures for change. It can no longer react flexibly because of its age. The fact that leading representatives of the GDR have not so far personally and directly made contact with workers, in order to present the standpoint of the party and give orientations for political-ideological work, is considered to be particularly disappointing and is occasionally viewed with great bitterness. The previously employed method of interpreting processes which interest the whole of the GDR's population exclusively through the ADN [Official News Agency] and selected commentators is seen as an expression of a lack of confidence in the people on the part of the political leadership of the GDR. This is also clear in the opportunity lost by leading representatives of the party and state to use the fortieth anniversary of the GDR in order to describe clearly and openly the current situation in the GDR and indicate appropriate solutions.

Repeatedly this way of proceeding is linked with the information policy of the party, which according to many party members no longer is based on Leninist information policy. Many persons active in journalism argue in the light of the concrete situation that the GDR mass media no longer reach the people. Progressive forces completely fail to understand the failure to engage in a political offensive against hostile oppositional forces and with the anti-socialist pamphlets prepared and disseminated by these circles. Such a passive and defensive position opens the door for an ideological offensive by the enemy.

As a result the situation has arisen that many citizens, including in particular persons employed in higher education, art and culture, as well as students, identify positively with the aims and contents of the oppositional move-ment"New Forum," and accept the political contents and demands in the foundation appeal of this group and spread them further.

With reference to these problems, progressive forces are ever more uncertain and claim to have no arguments to convince the workers. As a result they are ever more frightened of conducting discussion in the factories. In addition it is still the practice of full-time party functionaries to give no answers to questions from party members or to rescue themselves by citations from party documents. In some cases, party members who ask awkward questions are threatened with party disciplinary measures, and as a result discussion is stifled. In an attempt nevertheless to continue political dialogue with workers, party members attempt to use their own information and solutions: but these unauthorized attempts have little power to convince and occasionally deviate from the party line as a result of ignorance of the concrete situation. In ideological dialogues in the work collectives, many progressive forces are confronted to a large extent with discussions about the existence of a so-called privileged class (by this is meant the functionaries of the party and leaders of state and economic organs from the central to the district level), and with reference to widespread corruption and speculation. The aggressive discussion contains the arguments that these aforementioned persons are the true beneficiaries of socialism. Honestly earned money no longer plays a role in our social system.

Many workers, especially class conscious workers from industry and agriculture, members of the intelligentsia, and employees of state and economic organs are motivated by concern about the political stability of the GDR. They expect and demand an immediate open discussion of the party leadership with the workers about current problems. Members and functionaries of the SED, the friendly parties [the National Bloc], and social organizations and collectives from all social areas demand, in part very forcibly and emotionally, that the party and state leadership conduct an immediate discussion about solutions to the problems and about strategic development, and a political offensive against enemy opposition forces in the GDR.

The most urgent changes named are the following.

1. The Economy:
   - the depiction of a clear perspective on economic development in a form intelligible to all citizens of the GDR
   - the implementation of modern and effective methods of economic management in particular in planning and accounting, while reducing the administrative cost of the planning process
   - an increase in the responsibility and independence of factories
   - the elimination of the misproportion between the size of the productive apparatus and that of the administrative superstructure
   - changes in the policy of subsidies
   - a consequent application of the principle of rewarding performance

2. The further development of socialist democracy:
   - the development of new ways of integrating workers in the preparation of all social decisions
   - the consequent implementation of the principle of co-determination and co-responsibility
   - making decisions by central party and state organs more "transparent" to the people

- the responsibility of party and state functionaries on the central level to the people

3. Information policy:
    - a removal of the discrepancy between social claim and reality
    - an open and honest depiction of all problems and difficulties as a way of mobilizing the whole of society
    - a current and offensive reaction to attacks of the opponents and of internal enemies
    - the ending of "court reporting" and one-sided depictions of successes

4. Internal party life:
    - develop criticism as a law of development in the party
    - the guarantee of an open atmosphere, in which all party members have the opportunity to discuss problems and difficulties and questions that concern them
    - the guarantee that leading party functionaries will meet active party members
    - the full guarantee of internal party democracy.

Pious Wishes, Open Questions

by Günter de Bruyn

Günter de Bruyn was born in Berlin in 1926. He is a
prominent East German writer and the author of numerous novels, short stories, and essays. This essay is reprinted from Michael Naumann, *Die Geschichte ist offen:
DDR 1990 Hoffnung auf eine neue Republik*, Rowohlt, 1990.

Pious wishes, *Pia desideria*, were, when people were still pious, actually just
that and therefore not without effect, at least upon the wishers themselves;
only later, in impious times, in which people no longer believed in their power,
did "pious" wishes come to be "unfulfillable" ones. Even political wishes in
times of upheaval have their value, independently of their practicability, in
and of themselves. They are reality, even if they can be realized only partly
or not at all. They can give courage and elan to the oppressed and a fright
to the rulers. Such wishes breed prophecies of salvation and party programs,
all of which (including the party of conservatism, which wants the absolutely
impossible: historical standstill) have goals that lie in the realm of the un-
attainable, but are nevertheless useful.

When Egon Krenz assumed his high office as a consequence of the double
protest movement of emigration and revolt, it became clear from his first
utterances that he meant to appear as the personification of a turn, but a turn
that belonged to a GDR-conservatism. All the changes that he permitted
served the preservation of the status quo, and were therefore not fundamental
changes but only modifications. He sought to rescue the theory [of socialism]
by describing the upheavals that had proceeded out of crisis in the socialist
countries as lawful and he declared the practice "socialism under the leadership of its party" to be sacrosanct. All liberties that were demanded from
below and granted from above could not in Krenz's opinion be allowed to
alter this practice; "socialist pluralism" was to become a playground of future
creativity, in which the party would also play, but which it could also close
at any time.

Because of the protest movement, Krenz soon distanced himself from this
initial idea. For him, insight came too late. And the party? Now the Party's
leadership role is not to be relinquished entirely, but it is no longer fixed in
the constitution; rather it is to be won in daily battle. With that the SED has
abandoned the presumption of power without yet giving up power itself. For
a time at least, it can accommodate the people's wishes and play the game

of party equality without any loss of power, because it still for now has the state firmly in its grasp. For "the" party, as it was commonly and rightly called for decades, turned the state into an administrative and executive organ of its own will and is doubly present at every level, both through those of its people whom it has integrated into the state and through the functionaries of its own hierarchy. The replacement of a few men who have unpleasantly distinguished themselves ought not to deceive us into forgetting that the actual centers of power in Berlin and in the regional and state capitals still lie not in the buildings of public offices, but in the equally large buildings of the party authorities.

The previous block parties, who in the past could only say "yes" or in the best event keep silent, if they wanted to make something serious out of the game, have means and possibilities at their disposal which, while modest in comparison to those of the ruling party, are nevertheless considerable. They possess not only a seasoned party apparatus and the corresponding facilities, but also printing plants, publishing firms and several newspapers with which they could dare not only as before to play their role in the prescribed game, but to strive for participation in government or enter into opposition. The opportunity to act here with a good conscience would consist in the fact that "socialism" can be defined in different ways. Since their role provides for them to deviate from the worldview of the ruling party, there are not bound to the politico-economic doctrines of the SED and therefore can take that which is sacrosanct, Socialism, to be synonymous with social justice. Article 1 of the constitution was another obstacle in their path, since it would not have been credible to offer themselves as an alternative to the party in power while simultaneously accepting this party's absolute claim to leadership. But to have success, these block parties require both a program that distinguishes itself from that of the SED by more than just adjectives such as "Christian" or "liberal," and a membership that wants not just, as until now, to be taken care of and tolerated, but to be politically successful.

The established parties share the lack of a distinct program with a new group of parties. These have no history and no property; they lack political experience, organizational structures, meeting places, publication resources and even official sanction. They are not the carriers, but the products of the democratic popular movement, whose demands they partly formulate, and their strength rests for now above all in the freshness and ingenuousness of their engagement. That their programs seem so indistinct is due on the one hand to established parties' tactic of writing the demands for civil liberties and ecological improvements into the catalog of their promises, and on the other hand to the common democratic point of departure of the new move-ments and to their shared goal, a goal that is decisive for all future political work. They all want to move from one-party to democratic rule, without touching the existing socialist foundations, and only then do they want to set priorities—out of caution and uncertainty. They don't yet have any prescriptions for the crisis of the economy, and it is difficult for them to gauge which of their demands can be fulfilled through SED reforms before the elections, and where the holes and shortcomings will then be. Since they all share the opinion that not socialism but only its Stalinist variant has failed, and since they have therefore set themselves the bold and honorable, but uncertain and never before realized goal of a democratic socialism, it is conceivable that the wind of renewal will not blow in their sails, but in those of a reformed SED.

It would be presumptuous in this early stage of rapid development to venture more prognoses than this one: that the pious wishes will lose their driving force and only be partly realized, because they obstruct each other (as for example the resuscitation of industry with the flood of cars and—in contradiction to this—an end to the poisoning of the environment). The free elections, if they are held, will offer surprises, and not only because one doesn't know the extent of the economic distress that will influence them, but also because for the first time those people will be heard who belong neither to the old nor to the new parties and who also don't go out into the streets. Without drawing premature conclusions from this, one ought to keep in mind that while hundreds or thousands of people forced reforms either by flight or by protest, millions used the opening of the borders to head immediately for the display windows of the west, no matter how trying the journey, in an impressive state of euphoria. The question, whether the new and previously inaccessible attracted them, or a prosperity that they wish for themselves, or whether also (or primarily) feelings of national solidarity came into play: this question cannot be answered today, but will be decisive for the future. At the protest demonstrations, which distinguished themselves not only by discipline and peacefulness, but also by political moderation, demands for Germany unity were initially not to be heard at all, and later were not predominant; but this ought not to mislead us into thinking that they don't exist.

It seems that the activists of the opposition have developed a GDR patriotism that is stronger than the one hitherto prescribed from above. It is composed of pride in that which has been achieved through democratic protest of insight into what is attainable in the Europe of today, of a vision of social justice and of defiance of the rich, paternalistically inclined relative in the West (to which one also owes thanks), and it doesn't take national feelings seriously, but frequently suspects them of serving as a cover either for chauvinism or for the yearning for prosperity. It can be assumed that the new parties do not in this respect represent a broad spectrum of the voters. Most of these will perhaps bet rather on the "safety and security" of the SED, which has proven itself in this regard, or on German unity, which promises them less certain but tangible prosperity. If the emotional plea "For Our Country" means something other than the reasonable declaration that for the sake of peace the sensitive stability of Europe ought not to be disturbed by a German unity *before* European unity; if instead of this the old adversarial slogans by which we set ourselves apart from the West are served up in new clothing and, in the manner of the old block parties, uniformly approved by the independent organizations: then the unrealistic taboo upon the German question that has been enforced for two decades now will remain even longer in force. But to push all national concerns over to the right could soon prove to be dangerous. For the alternative dream of true, but this time truly perfect socialism (no longer encumbered by the hunting lodges of a few villains) has for many already been dreamed too long.

The Forty Year Itch

by Stefan Heym

Stefan Heym, born in 1913, was one of East Germany's most prominent writers. His works include *Collin* and *5 Days in June*. He was an active participant in the East German citizens' movements of 1989–90. This interview and essay appeared in *Marxism Today* in November 1989.

Gorbachev's reforms in the Soviet Union have unleashed forces for change throughout Eastern Europe, but the leadership of the GDR's ruling Socialist Unity Party (SED) tried to continue business as usual. "You don't redecorate your living room just because your neighbours start to do theirs," explained SED minister, Kurt Hager, in 1986. Three years later, SED leader Eric Honecker has resigned and the future of the SED looks uncertain.

Until September the SED's bunker mentality had hardly been challenged by opposition in the GDR. Only in a crisis caused by the mass exodus of its population via neighbouring Poland and Hungary where reforms are already underway, did significant opposition groups form to challenge the SED's inertia. After years of political stagnation, the GDR now finds itself at the centre of the changes that are sweeping through Eastern Europe.

The political crisis in the GDR is more complex than those in other Eastern European countries. The GDR and the Federal Republic of Germany have forty years of separate experience and development behind them. They are two states but one nation, with one past and a shared National Socialist legacy. The sense of national cohesion in the GDR is complicated by the existence of the other Germany which also offers automatic citizenship to those who arrive from the East. The crisis in the GDR is not simply one of democracy, but one of national legitimacy.

The following interview with Stefan Heym reflects the importance of Germany's socialist traditions to many in the GDR who are critical of the SED, but who are determined to stay. His essay, an account of the GDR's history by someone who was fighting for socialism long before the GDR came into existence, gives an insight into the ways in which the crisis of legitimacy of the GDR's ruling elite is interpreted by those who hold on to the dream of a different kind of socialist future.

Exciting times.
Yes. An exciting moment.

How will the Socialist Unity Party (SED) face up to these developments?
I don't know what they're going to do; that will probably be decided in the next few hours.

Given that the two German states emerged out of the cold war and that the situation has now changed, it might be argued that the conditions for the existence of the GDR no longer exist.
That is not true. As you will find in my article, I am saying that a socialist state in Germany is absolutely necessary for socialist development in the whole world.

Will that socialism be along the lines of current developments in the Soviet Union?
I don't know. I think German socialism has a different tradition and it might not have to go through all the contortions that the Russians do because we have all the functioning industry. We have excellent workers, trained workers, while in the Soviet Union they still have trouble with their workforce. People here would be able to get up tomorrow morning and take over the factories. They have marvelous managers too, you know, and technicians and engineers. The trouble is that the apparatus does not allow them to work properly.

Which of the opposition groups provides most hope for change in the GDR?
I don't think it matters which group, as you can see from the Leipzig events. I think that something is happening that Rosa Luxemburg dreamed of. The spontaneity that she was waiting for, and which never came, is happening now. The people are going on to the streets . . . and in the factories something must be happening too, I am sure.

How do you think that can be articulated politically?
I don't know, the people will do that themselves. It might be that within the SED there are enough progressive forces to take over. I feel that this is the case, I know some of them, and even an absolute apparatchik like Hermann Kant[1] has jumped on the bandwagon with his statement. Only a few weeks ago he was still fighting tooth and nail against a resolution in the Writers' Union which called for reform and demanded dialogue—he voted against that. And now he himself is saying that reform must come. He is an opportunist from way back and so he knows what's coming.

---

[1] Hermann Kant was the chairman of the GDR Writers' Union. On Monday October 9, he published an open letter in *Junge Welt*, the Free German Youth newspaper, in which he called for dialogue between the SED and the people.

So do you think, as a result of such statements and the mass demonstrations in Leipzig, that more and more members of the SED will move quickly towards reform?

If the top boys, the gerontocrats, still insist on their old ways and they call out the armed forces, then it will be very tough. But I don't think people are going to take it. They've tasted freedom . . . and it tastes *damned* good.

Do you think that the changing relations between the Soviet Union and the GDR . . . ?

Well, of course, that is the whole reason why it could happen. You see, if Brezhnev had still been there you would still have the ice age. Gorbachev's position will be strengthened enormously if they succeed in bringing in reforms in the GDR. It would be strengthened enormously because events like those in Poland would not happen here.

This country has a socialist tradition, a democratic-socialist tradition, socialism was started here. Marx was a German, Engels was a German, Lassalle was a German. This is the tradition here, not this Catholic position that you have in Poland.

Recent events have started speculations, particularly in the West, about reunification. The word is increasingly being used publicly again.

That is Western propaganda. If there is unification, it certainly won't happen in the way that they think—that the *Bundesrepublik* is going to swallow the German Democratic Republic—that is out. Reunification is possible only if the two big blocs are dissolved, and then it will come in an entirely new and different way that neither side can now predict.

Do you consider yourself to be a marxist or a social democrat? How would you describe yourself?

I would say you should read my books and then you will know.

You are published widely in the West because you have difficulty getting published in the GDR. You appear frequently on television but only in West German programmes that are also broadcast throughout the GDR. Given the fact that the culture of the GDR has had to develop under such conditions, would you describe it as a national culture?

There is no national culture of the GDR, there is no GDR *nation*. These are Germans in a *socialist* state, or in a 'socialist' state, a still-Stalinist state. But things are changing and they will probably be citizens of a truly socialist state if things go well.

What kind of allegiance do you feel towards the country that you are living in now?
That's a big word, allegiance. You see I have been staying here all the while, even though the leadership here has been kicking me in the pants fairly regularly, so that's a kind of allegiance, isn't it?

And is there an emotional commitment there?
Oh, I'm not that kind of person. My emotions run along entirely different lines.

Why are you still there? A lot of people wonder why you have stayed.
For moments like this one. And do you think that socialism would get better in this country if I left?

No.
Well, that's why I'm staying.

Is that your role as a writer in the GDR?
It's part of my business, it's not the entire business. I'm a storyteller, but that's part of the business.

And what do you make of the narrative that's unfolding now?
It's most dramatic, on both sides. These old boys are not evil-intentioned men, by any means, they are tragic characters. This is a time for Shakespeare.

Never before in the history of mankind has a state been plunged into crisis in such a ridiculous fashion as the GDR. No reformer proclaiming new theses here, no general riding into the capital city at the head of his tanks. No, this acute crisis has arisen as a result of the population running away; instead of barricades, a mass exodus; instead of strikes and demonstrations, the occupation of embassies; instead of clashes with the police, trips to Hungary. What remains is a party without direction, a multitude of gluttonous authorities, a mass media which stalwartly promulgates official claptrap, and at the head of all this is a government which is no longer capable of losing face for the simple reason that it no longer has face to lose.

And the enemy scoffs: 'Marx is dead,' and points, quite rightly of course, to antiquation and decay within the country and to intellectual desolation, to the filth in the towns and rivers, to the scarcity of virtually everything, except schnapps, which makes life bright and entertaining, to the daily injustices, the nepotism and economic privilege, and to the despotism with which those who wield power dictate to the people what *they* are to do and think and where they may go and when.

Then, into the bargain, the vision on their screens evening after evening of a richer world, a world without boundaries and which is said to belong to the industrious; and, as if comrades in high places actually wished to bear witness to the image personally, their Intershops, where the superiority of western goods and eastern currency is paraded with official blessing before the poor inhabitants of the GDR, for them to see, touch, taste. No wonder that the people of the country run off at the first available opportunity.

In reality, however, it is not Marx who is dead, but Stalin, and it is not socialism which has fallen flat on its face, but only the particular form which is in operation here. The other, better form, in whose name so many courageous people have set down their ideas and laid down their lives, is still to come. And we are beginning to think, now that change is at hand in the countries which surround the GDR, that we should also help propagate real socialism, under which all people shape their own lives, hand in hand, in freedom and justice, and in doing so should give the GDR new meaning.

Why is it, then, that something which began so optimistically has proved so unsuccessful? It all began with the world war, the first, followed by the Revolution in Russia.

It was then that Rosa Luxemburg warned that the Revolution could only succeed in the long run if it were both socialist and democratic, and Lenin and his comrades believed that the success of their revolution depended on a second: one which would be forced to come to the aid of the first—the German Revolution. The German Revolution, however, petered out soon after it had erupted, and the Russian Revolution remained isolated in its backward country and turned into a dictatorship, not of the proletariat, but of the state and party apparatus: into Stalinism.

In the eastern third of Germany, the second world war, which ended with the disintegration of the Reich and its occupation by the Allies, brought an order which, in terms of its structure and its relationship between those at the top and those at the bottom, was an imitation of that which had developed in the Soviet Union.

And what else could it have been? What other working model was there, from which the German comrades could have taken their bearings? And since they had, after all, not seized their power themselves, but had received it as a gift from their Soviet patrons, they were unable, even if they had wanted to, to lay claim to their own brand of socialism, a brand of their own design and moulded to suit their own country.

A history inlaid with tragedy from the outset—the explosion of June 1953 and the mass exodus of the summer of 1961 attest to that. The wall which brought the exodus to an end was an act of desperation. It had only one advantage: in future the people would no longer be able to avoid being courted by party and government. That would have been the time and opportunity for change. Enough time and opportunity to make the form of socialism which was in operation in the GDR into a form of socialism to which the people would devote themselves, instead of one from which they would flee: 28 years of time.

But the years slipped by without improvement. In the shadow of the anti-fascist protection wall it was possible to believe that socialist life in the GDR was safe and sound and really rather good. Those who led the Party and the nation closed their eyes and their ears to the views and feelings of the people in the country and clung to their bankrupt methods and slogans—until comrade Gorbachev's *perestroika* also began to win hearts in the eastern part of Germany and Hungary even punched holes in the border fence, an extension of the GDR's wall, and the holes became an escape route, and elsewhere West German embassies transformed themselves into refuges for the thousands who preferred to hold out in their filth rather than to return for even a few weeks under the wing of their government.

It is important to realize that the temptation to leave the GDR cannot be put down merely to the bigger blobs of fat in the western saucepan. For the people who are turning their backs on the Republic, whether by submitting applications for exit permits or by illegal means, were raised there and grew up there, and they have been told often enough of the ideals of socialism, of solidarity and common ownership, of a just wage and fair treatment.

The church too has done its bit, and in the light of all this it would be reasonable to assume that some of that might have stuck in their minds, and that at least some of those who have left were motivated not only by the thought of gorging themselves, but also by more noble considerations.

Either way, the bloodletting will continue unless the government modifies its attitudes—or until it seals the borders completely and hermetically. No more trips abroad for anyone, no visits anywhere, nothing more. Although wholly conceivable, this drastic solution would generate opposition of an equally drastic nature, and then God help us all.

The state is suffering from mental exhaustion. It was already suffering from this by the time that the wall, a kind of corset for a disintegrating body, was built. But unfortunately no doctor ever turned up, who might have been able, with sensible methods, wisdom and tolerance, to treat the disease.

But what are we to do today, and how, in the face of catastrophe and the obvious inability of those in high places to contemplate change and reform? Cross ourselves three times and hand over the GDR, or that part of it which has not already run away, to West Germany for safe keeping? What European nation and what non-European nation wishes, after the historical experiences of the last 100 years, to see a new united Germany? And I ask, from the bottom of my heart: is the noble experiment of socialism here in the heart of Europe to be abandoned altogether simply because it has been run for so long with poor equipment and the wrong ingredients? There are, of this there is no doubt, enough people in the country who would stay in order to attempt the experiment again under new, democratic conditions. And there have long been individuals and institutions, even within and around the Socialist Unity Party (SED), who have developed models for a workable form of socialism and who are ready to put their new programme into effect jointly with all of the citizens.

A German Democratic Republic, but a better one than that which now exists, is vital, if only as a counterbalance to the *Daimler-Messerschmitt-Bölkow-Blohm-BASF-Höchst-Deutsche-Bank Republic* on the opposite side of the Elbe. What is needed is a socialist state on German soil which will grant its citizens genuine freedom and all of the rights to which free citizens are entitled. And not only for the sake of the people who live in the GDR and who would like to remain there. A sensibly functioning form of GDR socialism is surely also essential for those outside the Republic, for all over the world the Left is suffering as a result of the complete failure of the SED state. All over the world the reactionaries are scoffing: "Call that socialism! Take a look at it, this socialist state whose own people are fleeing in droves!"

When all that is said, it is high time for us to extricate ourselves from the old scheme of things and to transform the variety of socialism in operation here into a genuinely socialist system.

In almost every sphere of human life, whether economic and administrative, whether cultural, whether in the field of the media, education, health, transport, environment protection, or, last but not least, in the military and the police, we need to evolve new ideas, new attitudes, new methods, new values and words. Moreover, we need to create new—democratic—ways for people to relate to each other, a new rapport based on criticism and debate between those at the top and those at the bottom, every one responsible for the other, elected and capable of being voted out.

All citizens must contribute their portion to these attempts at change and must be able to rely on the fact that their views too will be heard and their suggestions taken seriously. If the years since the GDR's founding have given us anything, then it is maturity. In their internal opposition to the official line, a surprising number of people have learned how to think and act independently. All that is now necessary is for us to exhort them to participate in the process of reform.

The process of change must surely begin in the field of practical politics. It is here that the first corrections must be made, and they must be fundamental in nature; the monopoly of the one and only apparatus of power, the major feature of the Stalinist system, has demonstrated its sterility. The diversity of opinion and the forthcoming important dialogue, must be given the scope to fling open the door to democratisation, openness and guaranteed rights for all which comrade Gorbachev demanded of the government of the GDR on the eve of the Republic's 40th anniversary.

Elections to the People's Chamber of the GDR would then be part of this process. Free, secret, democratic elections, not the shadow-boxing which has been the order of the day until now, with more than one candidate, chosen by the people themselves, for each seat and with several parties—which already exist in the GDR and would only need to free themselves from the chains with which they have tied themselves to the senior party, the Socialist Unity Party. And of course care must be taken that the counting of votes takes place under the supervision of electors themselves or of people in whom they have confidence.

A government named and confirmed by a Peoples' Chamber elected in this way would possess a legitimacy which the present one does not have and would set any new chapter in the history of the GDR on a safe course: a GDR which would also one day have to build temporary accommodation in order to be able to offer a first home to those migrating to its new form of socialism.

But Gysi Does Not Despair

by Hans J. Willerding

Hans J. Willerding was a member of the Direction Committee and head of the Office for International Affairs for the East German PDS, the successor party of the SED. This interview was first published in *Rinascita* on 18 March 1990, under the title, "*Ma Gysi non dispera.*"

The leaders of the ex-SED are not pessimistic about the election results. "Our past is not to be totally thrown away," says Hans J. Willerding.

The fear of annexation was rejected as false and instrumental, or evoked as a disturbing possibility (even by New Forum, the most important of the movements which emerged prior to the opening of the Wall). These positions, nonetheless, have characterized the electoral campaign in the first free elections in the history of the GDR, scheduled for March 18. The new leaders of the PDS (the ex-SED, now renamed the Party of Democratic Socialism) have focused their election initiatives on just this fear of *Anschluss,* in an attempt to regain the credibility and popular consensus dissipated after forty years of a monopoly of power. This new group of leaders, headed by the 42-year-old lawyer, Gregor Gysi, is separate from the old leaders of the Party-State, but, nonetheless, they are forced to come to terms with the unforgettable legacy left by them. Hans Joachim Willerding, member of the Direction Committee and head of the Office for International Affairs, is one of the PDS's most representative figures.

Your party has strong reservations about the speed of the process of unification between the two Germanys? What are the reasons?
We are not opposed to the unification of the two Germanys, but we do not want it to take the shape of an *Anschluss* of the GDR by the Federal Republic, as it seems to be in Chancellor Kohl's plan; his idea of an annexation via Article 23 of the West German Constitution represents the reduction of my country into a group of regions which flow "naturally" into West Germany. One fact is certain: if this destabilizing offensive continues, the GDR will quickly become a type of "colonized Third World" and the immigrants to the West will be the "new Turks," looked at with growing hostility by the weakest elements of West German society. Today and for the near future we believe that the best thing—also to avoid a war between the poor and socially devastated—is a close cooperation between two distinct states. Unification should take place gradually, within the context of a pan-European solution

and the two blocs will have to be dissolved. The new Germany will have to be a nonaligned and demilitarized state; this position is diametrically opposed to the one followed by those who intend to integrate the future state, totally or partially, into NATO.

In the course of the election campaign, you have persistently spoken about the threat to the process of democratization represented by the growth of an extreme right position . . .
Certainly, I am very worried about this tendency which finds its source in the myth of the Great German nation, in the yearning for a "Fourth Reich." The "deference" which Helmut Kohl shows towards these views is even more disturbing to observe. It is a deference dictated by electoral calculations. These calculations are also at the base of the Federal Chancellor's recent declarations on the new Germany's position on the Helsinki Accords, regarding the inviolability of existing European borders and the recognition of the untouchable nature of the current border with Poland. These willfully ambiguous attitudes risk corroborating the ex-director of the CIA, Richard Helms, when he called German reunification, "a train which is beyond the control of the engineer and which is no longer capable of being driven." If this were the case, the very stability of the old continent, and not only the destiny of the German people, will be at stake. Certainly, Kohl's recent back-peddling on the question of the Polish frontier is a very important political fact. But his recent commitments could be thrown away, if the political line-up of the center-right, heavily supported by the Federal Chancellor, prevails in the March 18 elections.

In your party's recent congress, there was much talk about a third way to be followed by the GDR. What does this involve?
Look, we have acted upon the incontestable and total failure of bureaucratic and Stalinist "state socialism"; but socialism can also represent a progressive alternative to a totally deregulated capitalism devoid of any and all social and environmental obligations. In our opinion, this perspective remains completely valid and viable. We support a socialism in solidarity with pluralism and the market; one which knows how to look with critical intelligence at the evolution/differentiation of capitalist systems, without falling into the error of seeing as the panacea of all our evils the application of the neoliberal recipe in this part of Germany. In the search for a practical and democratic alternative to "real socialism" and neoliberalism without rules or values, we feel in profound agreement with Gorbachev's *perestroika*.

Your adversaries accuse you of not facing your past.
A ruthless self-critical review of the past, such as that which we have conducted in these months, cannot signify a total negation of forty years of history, as though it was only one long, uninterrupted sequence of horrors and depri-

vations. The decisive question to which "real socialism" failed to offer any sufficient solution was how to wed economic efficiency and social justice, political liberty and material well-being. Above all, this was the cause of the extreme rigidity of a system based on the guiding role of the "Party-Leviathan." But, "state socialism" also represented, at least in my country, the creation of a diffused system of social security and assistance, and the maintenance, although precarious, of full employment. People do not seem willing to give this up light-heartedly in the name of free private initiative, as, for one, demonstrated by the "Social Charter" drawn up by the parties and civic associations which gathered in the Round Table.

I do not want to offer a "nostalgic" discourse, but simply to underline a particular given that cannot be replaced: the necessity to think of the state which we intend to build on the ashes of "real communism" as a modern welfare state, subjecting the market to strict social regulations. We want to work towards this project, even in the role of the opposition, if this is to be the result of the March 18 elections.

Germany United and Divided
Interview with Gregor Gysi

by Stefano Vastano

Gregor Gysi was a lawyer who made his reputation through the defense of East German dissidents. In December 1989, he succeeded Egon Krenz as General Secretary of the SED, which under his leadership transformed itself into the PDS. He now serves in the German Bundestag. This interview was first published in *Rinascita* on 23 September 1990 under the title, *"Germania unita e divisa."*

Gregor Gysi, the young secretary of the PDS (the party formed following the dissolution of Honecker's SED) was aware from the beginning of the enormous responsibility he was assuming: forty years of "real socialism" and the bankrupt economy of the GDR seemed to weigh on his shoulders. Yet, he was able to shake off the role of scapegoat which was put on him; he created a system of alliances with various groups within the West German alternative parties. His program has some guiding ideas, such as the search for a "third way," the limits of the market economy, and the place for social protections.

You have said that forty years of SED-State should not be judged as a block. What do you see as positive in this experience?
I believe that the positive element was the attempt to follow a noncapitalist path. Positive, as well, was an antifascist state which developed something which I still today maintain as important: one thinks of the minimal social differences, of the fact that the line between rich and poor was very small compared to that which occurs in all capitalist states. In social relations, for example, state services worked to reduce differences. Many of these institutions could have been maintained; if a more cautious road to unification had been taken, we could have held onto these experiences, rather than uncritically adapting everything that is done in the Federal Republic.

What are the real prospects for the PDS?
I believe that there is a need for a new type of order which aspires to the concrete and free development of the individual, guaranteeing dignity and ability, in the sense that the freedom, dignity and possibility for growth of the individual must be contingent on the freedom, dignity and possibility for growth of others. For this reason I assert that one must begin to work con-

cretely on four main themes: ecology, social justice, peace and disarmament, and sexual equality. Given that the capitalist world produces false concerns, we must address them ourselves; and, we will need to continue to do so I believe, for some time to come. But, be attentive, because if we do not succeed in finding a solution soon, it could already be too late.

Regarding unification, do you believe that it would have been possible to maintain double sovereignty, aiming at a confederation of the two Germanys, rather than resorting to Article 23 of the West German constitution?
Maybe in November of last year, if it had been pursued in a consistent manner.

What do you mean by "consistent"?
It would have required agreements on the conditions for opening the borders, for example by stopping the draining of subsidized goods from East German economy, but this did not happen. We were taken by panic and forced to reject any idea of a confederation—to the point where events took on such speed that such a question has been put aside since January [1990].

What effects has this kind of unification had on the consciousness of East German citizens?
Catastrophic. After the fall of 1989, the people had already lost faith in themselves, and they have already come to reject the possibility of approaching unification in an impartial fashion. The East German population has been "immersed" in unity. In short, it has been treated like a unilateral act. For this reason, I am afraid of a rise of the extreme right, since the construction of self-gratification through nationalism has always been a psychologically effective way.

What do you think are the specific causes of the new nationalism in the GDR?
East Germany has always had a difficult relationship with the national question, particularly since the 1960s. At that time there was an attempt to spread a state consciousness, rather than a feeling for the nation. For this our educational system was too authoritarian and totally insufficient; it did not teach tolerance—the issue of homosexuality was never touched, nor those of ethnic and religious differences. It was believed that something not spoken about automatically did not exist, while the exact opposite is true. From here began the destruction of the self-awareness of the people, and thus, after the fall of 1989, the population no longer wanted to be citizens of the GDR. But, they had to be something! And therefore, they must be Germans! On the other hand, a European consciousness could not have been formed after 28 years of seclusion; and the only possibility was to tighten bonds with West Berlin and the Federal Republic, in the hopes of becoming like them and attaining

their status . . . with the desire even to become the soccer champions of the world.

What do you think of Berlin as the capital of a united Germany?
I am decidedly in favor of it. I don't see how Bonn could be the capital, given that it has always been considered a temporary solution. And anyway Bonn is too small. The capital must be a great city, and Berlin was the German capital during that brief period in which there was a united Germany. But there is a more serious reason: if the capital is located in the eastern part of the state, this could result in initiatives to develop this part of Germany. If, instead, the capital remains in Bonn, the eastern zone could remain too distant, and therefore all questions relating to the development of its infrastructure would take on a secondary importance. Thus, there would not be pressure to build economic and social equality between the two areas.

Why We Hoped
Interview with Christa Wolf

by Aafke Steenhuis

Christa Wolf was born in 1929. She is one of the most
respected and controversial contemporary German writers. Her novels include *A Model Childhood* (1980) and
Cassandra (1984). This interview originally appeared in
Rinascita on 14 October 1990 under the title, *"Perche ab-
biamo sperato."*

(This interview with the East German author was given in December 1989
and also appeared in *Reden im Herbst*).

**In *Kindheitsmuster*, there is a key phrase spoken (a Communist reveals
to Nelly, the protagonist, that during the long years under Hitler she
never realized the evil transpiring around her): "But where have you
all been living?" After the war, the people of the GDR supported for
forty years the authoritarian Communist system, from which they
are now liberating themselves. But where have you been living for
all this time? Did you imagine that the situation would take this turn?**
I don't believe that anyone envisioned the speed and also the means of change
begun by the people in the streets. At any rate, I did not. In the last few
years, we were continually more oppressed and desperate because we realized
the blind alleys that the system was getting into, as a result of irremediable
rigidity of the leadership, incapable of appreciating the signs. Meanwhile, the
warning signs were accumulating. The situation was becoming worse in every
respect. Culture is always a good indicator of this. From another side, both
inside and outside the Party, the criticisms were becoming stronger and more
explicit. It was clear that sooner or later this would necessarily produce change.
But how the change would come, no one truly imagined.

The question cited by you: "But where have you all been living?" is in
effect, applicable to many situations. Yesterday I received a letter from a
woman, a worker who was in the Party and who is now totally desperate and
confused. She writes that she knew nothing of all this, that she always did
her best, that she worked honestly. I believe her. She lives in a small town
in the south of the GDR. I could not but then ask myself if the warnings that
literature, for example, had been sending for some time, simply did not arrive.
Your question can be posited in different ways: the answer will vary according
to the diverse social strata and regions of the GDR.

How do you experience these sudden changes? The exodus from the country, the collapse of state institutions, the call for reunification with the GDR?

I find it difficult to speak of this because things are continually changing, even in the course of a single day. The revolutionary movement is still evolving. It is no longer the same one as that of October 7 or 8, when here in Berlin young people went peacefully down into the streets and were beaten and 'taken in,' that is, arrested, by the police and the *Stasi*. That was the beginning of what the Party called the 'turning point'—one which they intended to control, without realizing that there was no longer any room for maneuver regarding what the populace wanted and how it would react. In the course of a demonstration called by artists on November 4 [1989] we experienced, we hope, a moment of joy. In the streets were a great number of people acting in autonomous and critical ways, but, at the same time, very serenely. Even, if at first one was afraid that the demonstration would get out of hand as a result of provocateurs, such as the *Stasi*. But the people were so committed to not letting themselves be ruined that the danger was never realized. This was also a positive encounter between the intelligentsia and other sections of the populace.

But the evolution of the movement went further. Soon after, there emerged weighty revelations about the abuses of power and the personal wealth of many top Party members. This, together with the hesitant and dilatory reaction of the provisional heads of the Party under Egon Krenz, transformed the movement and the popular masses in the street. The situation in Leipzig was a good indication of this. Many people, who in the first weeks constituted the backbone of the demonstrations, no longer took part. Others now shaped the scene. In the last few weeks, reunification has been demanded in a noisy and aggressive manner. Even in Berlin. This tendency is very powerful, though I think it will be different later on. The leaders of the new parties and movements such as New Forum and Democracy Now are putting the requests for reunification into perspective and asserting instead the possibility of a gradual process, even towards a form of confederation. To them, and myself, it does not seem positive that things continue to evolve at the same pace and that a reunification should take place in a moment of economic and political weakness. This would represent an absorption of the GDR by the most economically strong forces within the FRG. But, from the inside of our businesses one hears it said that the economic situation is considered by many so desperate that people ask themselves—or rather have already ceased to ask themselves—if they want to or can support another socialist experience.

Was it a consequence of the war that in the GDR Stalinism was tolerated for forty years?

In differing ways, the two German states have not overcome their fascist pasts. My generation quickly identified with the society which was being born, because during the 1940s we were forced to face our fascist past in an intense and drastic manner, more drastically than in the FRG. Thus, there was constructed a strong tie with this society, founded by anti-fascists. This situation has lasted so long because we saw no alternatives. It seems to me impossible to want to live in the Federal Republic of Adenauer, Globke, Lübke. Naturally, in the meantime, the Federal Republic changed, as well as my relationship with it and the people who live there. But, we continued to hope that here forces about to save a core of socialism would prove themselves and would find allies in pursuit of this goal. Now I am expressing myself very cautiously. In the first years, of course, we had greater hopes. In 1968, with the entrance of the tanks into Czechoslovakia, they diminished. We experienced an existential shock. In the following twenty years, things became better and then worse, but at the end the old institutions and the Stalinist mentalities reinforced themselves. But, at the same time, it is strange to say there developed in the GDR many people able to think honestly and openly. Still, I am convinced that all these political movements are shaped by the war, fascism and unresolved generational conflicts. The emergence of nationalist and xenophobic undertones brings me almost to desperation: we know these tones well. It is simply terrible that they continued to reappear.

Why did the formation of a widespread democratic movement take so long?

This has certainly something to do with the fascist past and the division of Germany. Recently, one of our film directors, Frank Beyer, whose best films of the 1970s were banned, has analyzed why our generation has such ties to this State. Because we, who grew up during fascism, have felt very guilty and we are grateful to those who could bring these feelings forward. They were anti-fascist and communist veterans from concentration camps, from jail, from exile and they shaped political life in the GDR much more than in the Federal Republic. We were very reluctant to oppose people who during Nazism had been in the lager.

It is true that we raised intellectual resistance—in my case this has been clear since the early 1960s—but no mass political opposition, or only one of a limited importance. People left, or were arrested, and then expelled or deprived of citizenship. The division of Germany made it so that the critical minds—and here I use a neutral term—were driven away. The nucleus of the opposition, through protests or criticisms, ended up dissolving itself each time. A vast movement of opposition is possible today because of the birth of a mass movement and because of the involvement of young people less affected by senses of guilt in the church and minority groups—and above all because of Gorbachev.

Among our friends we always repeated that something must change, that it must come from the Soviet Union. But, it would not definitely happen there. I recounted recent events to my Soviet friends and they laughed because they never imagined that these changes would come from themselves. In the Soviet Union there has been a revolution from above. For some time many people thought this would also happen to us; that in the high levels of the Party would be formed a group of reformers able to introduce changes against the immobility of the old guard. In effect this group never formed and this is the reason for the collapse of the Party. It failed to use the potential opposition present within its own ranks. I am certain it existed; but this opposition was blocked and unable to reach levels within the Party that would have allowed it to reform itself and the entire country. They were too afraid, and now here are the results.

Did one notice great tensions in the GDR in the last few years? Did the people feel locked in?
In the worlds of culture and literature—where they still continued to monitor bureaucratic intervention—certain liberties were gained, but in the economy and administration this was not even thinkable. The people had the sensation of being shut in, even if in the last few years many more people could travel to the West. The Party leadership saw this as a type of safety valve. But the people did not want a 'little finger,' they wanted an entire arm. This feeling poured forth as soon as they opened the borders and is a sign that people felt like they were in a covered pot. Many wanted to experiment with liberation in a concrete way, by changing locations. In the first few weeks they needed to do this. Now there is much depression and uneasiness. While not being served by those in power in a strict sense, the old structures offered forms of maintenance. As they disappeared, jobs also often disappeared. What could they do? For example, someone who worked at the Ministry of State Security is not going to be welcomed with great enthusiasm by other enterprises. Many people collapsed. The psychiatric institutes are overflowing.

But, nonetheless, the revolution removed power from a class and rank, and many injustices, false accusations and offenses towards those who do not merit them are inevitable. On the other hand, it is quite admirable that all this unfolded with moderation and without violence. The *Stasi* buildings were not attacked, but occupied, which is a moderate action. We also ask ourselves: "Why am I alive?" And then we realized: to love, to have friends, to feel alive. Because this, to have friends, a family, children is terribly important. Daily life is much more important than twenty years ago, when one still believed in ideologies. There were many people here who clung to ideology up until the last minute, in large part to justify the things they had done. Now they find themselves facing an abyss. Those who had already recognized that this could not be a life are now being shaken by details of which they are now becoming conscious. But they are not fundamentally shaken, and they look instead to connect themselves with the positive things. All the same, these are dangerous times: the things which flourish immediately to fill the void are hatred, revenge and violence.

You asked me what literature must do now. It can do nothing other than honestly support this process. But many years will pass before literature can achieve this task. Looking at the hundreds of letters that I have received in the past weeks, I can identify the characteristic voices of this country in its period of fundamental change. Through these collages, one could contribute in a rapid and direct way by clarifying what is going on here.

How do you pass your time during this period?
For a while, I have been very busy writing about principle problems. For example, I wrote articles about why so many members of the young generation were able to leave with such ease, from the moment when they could no longer identify with this country, not even in opposing it, or resisting it from the opposition. For this is also a form of identification. I asked how they experienced childhood and adolescence. For this article I received almost three hundred reaction letters. Many teachers felt attacked, even if that had not been my intention. It is a symptom of our unusual state of mind that no one read that which was actually written; everyone read only the phrases and lines which made them angry and they reacted accordingly. On the other side, there were also disturbing confessions by teachers who lived a double morality and in this sense influenced their students. A portion of the letters testified to a growing hostility towards the intelligentsia.

As well, I am part of a commission dealing with the *Stasi* violence against demonstrators on October 7 and 8 [1989]. People are continually coming to me with requests, otherwise I participate in meetings. I haven't had a free minute in many weeks, above all in the evenings, but we do now watch the evening news. I never see films, only documentaries. It has been weeks since I read a book. It is totally impossible to read anything literary; it is too painful and of little interest. I can't remember a period in my life in which this happened before. We find ourselves truly in an emergency situation: all our thoughts and feelings are totally absorbed in social issues.

The Great Waiting, or
The Freedom of the East:
An Obituary for Life in
Sleeping Beauty's Castle

by Martin Ahrends

Martin Ahrends is a writer from the former East Germany.
This essay is reprinted from the *New German Critique,*
Winter 1991.

Our friend Hercules had a better idea. He was able to take care of fifty
girls, heroic girls, in one night, for the good of humanity. He also worked
hard and strangled many horrible monsters, but the goal of his life was always noble leisure, and that's why he got into Olympus. He wasn't at all
like Prometheus, that inventer of education and enlightenment. It's Prometheus you have to thank for never being able to sit still and being constantly
driven . . .

— Friedrich Schlegel, "In Praise of Leisure," from *Lucinde*

There they lay in the dust of the border, in the spotlights of the public access
institutions. In front of the humming cameras they hit upon the grand gestures
they had learned from television, because now they were going to be on
television too. Then we saw how they kissed the ground, the poor, traumatized
grass. Freedom! Freedom!

Freedom is always somewhere else. It is always the freedom one would
like to have and never the freedom that one has. It may be that after a couple
of years they will be remembering something like a freedom of the East, the
counterpart to Western freedom. It may bloom for them in the soft light of
memory.

Sleeping for a hundred years in the enchanted castle, the sweet and dreadful
dreams of those who lie there in "necessary" slumber, a slumber for which
not they themselves are to blame but, rather, a general law of their existence,
the magic spell, the system. They are allowed to slumber because they are
forced to slumber, undisturbed by a guilty conscience or lost opportunities.
They are allowed to dream about the handsome prince promised to them,
while all around them the world continues to grow. A hedge of thorns covers

with graceful twilight everything that has remained undone for decades. To wait, to dream, to be allowed to daydream time away. That is, that was, the freedom of the East.

It has only been twenty-eight years, and already it is coming to an end. Instead of the prince, some unauthorized person has turned on the light and started making nasty remarks about the slum in which one has been living. One wakes up blinking one's eyes and becomes aware of all the spider webs, the inch-thick dust, the worn-out carpets, the flaking paint.

The era of expectations now appears to have been nothing but couch-potato laziness. One has to make up for and catch up to what the West has accomplished in the intervening years. In the sober light shining into one's little nook, one is ashamed to face the West. One drives a shabby jalopy, walks around in simple clothes, eats gray bread and artificial honey. That did not use to be so important, but now it is shameful, now that there is no pride left in sacrifice, no dignity in poverty. It now seems that the long journey had no destination other than the return to the starting point. All right then, wake up, Mr. King and Mrs. Queen, servants and kitchen maids! Hit hard, Cook, so that the lazy good-for-nothing servant boy finally feels it!

But it is not just the East, it is also the West that has been deprived of its dream: that there, in a dilapidated and not entirely couth castle the most beautiful of princesses is sleeping and waiting for the day of her liberation. Any real transfiguration of the East is possible only from the West; and it becomes even more powerful when it is assigned the role of an obituary. All right then, invest your capital and send in your construction crews, but think about what you are losing in the freedom of the East.

Not to have to walk the treadmill of capital, not to have to produce, sell, consume, take care of things ASAP: that, too, is the freedom of the East. Armies of hard-working entrepreneurs, trade representatives, advertising experts were not needed here behind the hedge of thorns. Their entrepreneurship, their imagination, their fighting spirit, everything having to do with the macho ambition that lies sleeping in the primeval brain—all of that lay fallow. It was an untilled field, covered over with the most beautiful weeds, which bloomed impressively, able to reproduce themselves without interruption. Weeds that were not needed and which, if they did not suffer too much from their existence as weeds, lived happily, spreading wildly, self-satisfied, useful to no one.

Do-it-your-men, improvisationalists who invest weeks and months in confusing and adventuresome, truly romantic journeys, journeys that lead them in a circle on the search for some construction material or spare part. (A small city in the Harz Mountains, spring 1989: a Trabant is driving along behind a Simson Moped. A paper bag on its luggage rack gradually reveals its contents: the individual parts for the pipes leading out of a sink. The Trabant driver has been looking for them for quite some time. Gradually he has been gathering the parts, and now he believes himself to be a child of fortune, blessed by the hand of Lady Luck.)

The freedom of the East is the freedom to be a dilettante. One man spends his life fixing up a 1958 Renault Dauphine, and his yard is decorated with no less than six naked frames for this model; if the automobile ever works, it will be a joy to sit inside it, it is such a charming, feminine, French car, and such charm is as invaluable as France is unreachable. The fix-it man, by the way, earns his money working as a coal shoveler at a fully automated industrial furnace. Another man is head janitor at a school, but he really earns his money by working on his hobby: in ignorant Thuringia he buys old farmers' chests and drawers, carries them in a Wartburg trailer back to his garage, fixes them up, and sells them to the nouveau riche in Berlin. This business is not without its dangers, since there is a state monopoly on trade, and antiques bring in hard currency. A third man sits in an office at the waterworks and plays guitar regularly on children's TV. They are all dilettantes, not only in their jobs but also in their real, their private activities.

To be able to do a passable job as a mason, a carpenter, a wall-paperer, a locksmith—those are the virtues of the GDR-Man. Good-for-nothing men ready to do anything, sweet and lazy, boyish, talented, and never truly challenged. Love adventurers of the most innocent sort. (They make the best lovers, but they would blush with shame if you told them about any of their "sex techniques." They are not, after all, technicians; they are dreamers. They worship their women as princesses or sprites or priestesses of the temple, and they know nothing of G-spots and other apparatuses.)

They are not challenged by their work life, but they are also not obsessed with it like their brothers in the West. This workaday commitment, if commitment is what it is, is what distinguishes the West-Man from the East-Man. East-Men make their commitments in other ways. They are all alternative entrepreneurs: without certificates, without capital, without shops, without tools, etc. But they are driven forward by an inexhaustible demand. Their commitment is to be responsible for what is desperately needed, but what the state cannot provide: beautiful things.

And this different quality of time, this half-sleep time, practically undisturbed by occasional campaigns to raise workers' productivity, this East-Time, according to the current exchange rate, is worth only an eighth of West-Time. Because it is worth less, it can pass by unused, unobserved, unnoticed, just like children's time, which is not yet measured in hours and minutes, but rather by what chances and moods happen to produce in the way of experience. (For instance, spring has suddenly come, the first day of spring, and you are sitting around uselessly in some office. In the West, work is always the most important thing, even if it is only work-time that has to be strictly observed— the beautiful day has exerted itself in vain. The truly important event of the day is hidden behind various self-important events of the bureaucratic sort.

Things are different in the East, where perhaps you may decide to take the day off to go to the barber, to sniff at the wind. Or perhaps, instead of going to the barber, you will go to the doctor and have yourself withdrawn from circulation for fourteen days because of strong stomach cramps. Office work in the East is inefficient enough to be able to do without almost anyone any time. Not really to be needed in this imitation of industrial society—it has its liberating aspects as well.)

The East exists in a nature preserve for scientific and technical backwardness, and no economic mechanism forces anyone to stay outside its borders. People are needed, instead, to drive away the boredom which, in the absence of bright ideas, naturally arises in this twilight waking-time. People are needed to tell stories, to spread rumors, to nourish illusions; people are needed to help weave the artful net of the counter-public sphere, to make toys, minor art, poetry, and music that are not available in the big department stores. People are needed to comfort each other about the miserable waiting-time, and they are always waiting for something. People are needed to help each other pass the time enjoyably, because there is no commercialized leisure-time industry as in the West. People are needed to give each other meaning, a meaning which often consists of resisting the mass of non-meaning, of making the best of a bad situation, or of making from it something that differs from official plans. This measured resistance, possible any day, provides all kinds of meaning—and the unique freedom of the East: the freedom not to go along, a freedom Westerners have much less of when they have to make themselves slippery to pave paths through a constipated job market.

Men do not take themselves as seriously in the East as they do in the West. They do not have to put on such manly airs, they can let the women do things once in a while, and they are free of all the silly struggles demanded of the West-Man by his prestige.

The West—that is the freedom of activity; in the East one is free to let events take their course. The freedom of the East is the leisure one can gain by the measured passage of time, far removed from the ever-changing media fads of the West. It is the freedom to digest things thoroughly. It is the freedom to chew over the same thing again and again and to realize how this changes the thing and oneself. To work on something with one's thoughts far longer than is necessary or feasible: one discovers how suffering from the circumstances tends to condense itself, to become a reason in and of itself, to become humorous, holy, the goal of one's life, and to collapse in on itself as a laughable fetish. And in these discursive wanderings people get to know each other well, so amazingly and horribly well: as well as they can probably never know each other in the West, the busy West. (But it must be admitted that the existential intensity of people thrown back upon themselves is also hard to take. It has masochistic elements. And you can hardly blame anyone for not enjoying it.)

Capital sucks people empty, it removes from them not just productive power but their own wishes, desires, and longings. It buys these from them. The East leaves people alone with themselves, it does not pump them dry, draw them out of themselves. There is nothing there, after all, that could tempt them to suck themselves dry: money is worth nothing. The East is a simple society. People are less extroverted, they do not know how to talk in front of TV cameras, and they find it difficult to talk about themselves. They are not hunted down by the newspapers, forced again and again to become self-conscious. Life in the East is not so bright, so shiny, so awake, so flat; the East is visually undernourished. Inner pictures bloom instead.

In the East people are free of the digestive juices of capital, the sweet ones and the aggressive ones. The sweet: free from the confusing attacks of an ever-present advertising industry. (Even sprouting, immature desires are attacked before their unfulfilled promises have time to make life hard and sweet. Pleasure: now. To long and dream for nothing; neither to hope nor to wait. Immediacy. Immediate credit. Immediate pictures. Immediate potency.) The aggressive: free from the struggles and fears for survival, free from worry about losing one's home or one's job. Freedom from the real winds of existence.

In the East people may be dependent on institutions that have no genuine authority; but they are also free from the real, active, and functioning authority of Western social institutions. They are responsible themselves for everything that has to do with human contact; above all, they have a responsibility for each other.

The freedom of the East is the freedom not to have to grow up entirely, to be allowed to keep one foot in the unself-consciousness of childhood. To remain in the Not-Yet, the temporary. One does not have to test one's limits, one doesn't even get to know them. All possible limitations and shortcomings can simply be labeled "The Wall." One remains in the innocent condition of those who are not allowed to do what they might be capable of doing. One is free to overestimate oneself as much as one wants, because life as an adult in the East can be handled in neutral; no one "works himself to death," and "privacy takes precedence over catastrophe." There is no need to spend an entire decade building up a "livelihood," because one has it from the state anyway.

This kind of state-run adult life quickly runs its course, plays itself out, especially since one cannot expect much from one's career. So what does one do? One opens oneself up completely to the family, cultivates family life, has a bunch of children. The children provide meaning, entertainment, sympathy. Apartments are cheap, child care is certain, and so is one's job when one takes one's year off for the baby. No one stands to lose anything because of the children, no surfing vacation in the Caribbean, no sizzling night life, no steep career rises. Nothing important is missed by sacrificing oneself for the next generation. (But the crunch comes when the children grow older and one begins to ask oneself troublesome questions about "self-realization.")

The Easterner has children before he has "lived"—that is what it may look like in the West. But in fact the family is already his entire adult life. There is nothing else. The cheap apartment as a reward for a pregnant belly, the cheap loan that one can work off with children, the guaranteed baby year—that is freedom, the first freedom for a young adult who has known nothing but patronization all his life. And it is already all the freedom he will ever be offered, the freedom, finally, to be the boss—of a family. It is true: this freedom seems like coercion. Perhaps this will only make the East-Man a bad father; perhaps he will see himself once again as having been forced into being a supporter of the state. But if this is not the case, it might well be that he will have more time, more patience, and more leisure for his family than stressed-out West-Dads. East-Dads will shower their loved ones with all their unfulfilled lust for life, they will maltreat them and swallow them up, they will worship and hate them—they will release all their energies on them. Children will be the challenge that is denied to them elsewhere.

That is the nature of boredom. One escapes it by moving inward, into the infinite freedoms of the labyrinth, which one can never escape, but which one can forget, if one manages to lose oneself in twists and turns that are constantly getting smaller. There are two kinds of infinity, the big one and the little one. And there are two kinds of human freedom, the one lying outside and the other within. The first kind of freedom has to do with travel and excess, the other with poetry and self-concentration. The two freedoms really belong together, but in Germany they are separated, one on this side and one on the other side.

The freedom of the interior, labyrinthine forms and motifs can be found particularly often in recent East German prose. But the muse of boredom does not kiss poets alone: the union vacation slot on the Baltic, where one is trapped in the rhythms of meals, in the uneventfulness of days spent in canopied wicker beach chairs, where one starts dreaming about co-worker X because she sits across from one every day. The final party is lady's choice—eternal school days—no champagne, just soda on tap, and a sky full of unfilled, no, unfulfillable desires. Boredom that does not make one nervous; it makes one "deep." Hans Castorp does not discover his "weak spot," his religious devotion to vinyl tenors, until 800 pages into *The Magic Mountain*. The flowers of stasis and the creepy horror that is always present, ghost stories that are only half imaginary. (The big-busted fellow worker introduced to me one day at the office really does have a secret mission. All of it, even this woman, are inescapable. In the East is always an afterwards, because it is so hard to run away from home.)

Stagnation blows romantic bubbles. This has been the case before, too. The rediscovery of E. T. A. Hoffmann, Carl Maria von Weber, Caspar David

Friedrich, the thorough and entirely contemporary interest for German Romanticism in the GDR all represent this parallel, which is of course officially denied. The GDR is a Romantic country, dark, musty, and full of chaotic dreams, dreams of escape, dreams of fear. The Ministry of State Security provides the gruesome Romanticism. Every person who leaves the country is told not to tell any "gruesome fairy tales" about Security; but the security officers themselves behave so much like wicked uncles in a gruesome fairy tale that it is—almost—funny. It is precisely the demonic nature of their appearances that makes their otherwise completely silly activities so fascinating. (I can easily imagine the goose pimples of horror that must have run down my interrogator when he informed me, after the door had slammed shut behind us, that I had no legal recourse against his Institution, and that he alone would decide when I was released from his custody—"there's not a cock crowing for you outside, I can promise you that, and we have the authority to keep you in custody as long as we want . . .") Endless, unmeasured East-Time becomes a nightmare when the minions of the Stasi put it to their uses. But these "dark powers" are a part of the fairy-tale game that makes East-Life so seductive in the first place.

And at some point, maybe one is even prepared to play along with the minions whose existence seems most fascinating and certainly most lucrative. Moral barriers have themselves become a toy. Playing with evil, with one's own seduction, can drive away boredom once again and squeeze a last drop of subtle masochism from the game. It is surrender to the hated, unavoidable dragon. The duty to resist has made one exhausted for life. One escapes to the interior, into the labyrinth of secret services. The Stasi can help its employees get everything that socialism in the GDR has to offer, even an extended stay in the West without financial worries. Yet this freedom to take part in an infamy under the protection of the authorities also brings into play a special temptation to do good.

It is hard to escape the East—the heavy, unchangeable, muzzled conditions that reign there. Thrown back again and again onto oneself, one has to learn to get along with oneself and others. Those who do not escape into alcohol, insanity, bureaucracy, or the West have to learn to be patient, as they wait day-in and day-out. They have to learn to do without the very values which enlightened Europeans see as the core of life: productivity and pleasure. The Easterner has achieved the pedagogical goal when he lags behind this human ideal or when he by-passes it. When he arrives at a monkish existence.

At an existence justified and fulfilled solely by its moral standards. A fulfillment which consists of resisting the forces of moral decay emanating from the great and the powerful. Unnoticed and, hence, unassailable, to think thoughts different from official expectations—that is the virtue of the East (it is what finally pulled the rug out from under the rulers' feet).

To know that one has many allies in this resistance, the massive solidarity directed against the dragon of the state, spiritual homogeneity as resistance to totalitarian "consciousness"—these are the fruits of patience that are now becoming visible in the solemn mass demonstrations.

It is, perhaps, here, where the industrial system is at its weakest, where it has shown practically nothing but its bad sides—here that its transcendence is most imminent. Those who consciously decided to remain here have no intention to catch up with the West; perhaps they are proud of having arrived at virtues that will be desperately needed in a postindustrial society, ascetic virtues which bloom only on the margins of Western civilization. Perhaps this period of waiting has resulted in a headstart in postindustrial thinking. "To pass by without catching up"—maybe this old SED slogan from the 1960s, which was abandoned as laughable under Honecker (under whom official policy was to run along behind the West) has found a kind of truth that was not originally intended.

The pressures specific to the GDR have encouraged the emergence of counter-pressures specific to the GDR. Resistance that found no place to go solidified inside itself, it learned to give up on short-term political goals and to comprehend itself as a way of life. To be alone within a spiritual community—to discuss, to research, to uncover the points where this GDR society had grown beyond itself, where it had come up against limitations that were not just its own limitations, ecological limitations which revealed themselves with particular speed and intensity precisely here. All the discussion groups inside the churches, which discovered that the true historical meaning of the East lay in the radicality of its ecological disaster. A breakout from the provinciality typical to the country, and a retreat into intensified reflection, into shock and dismay, in order to escape, in spiritual perspective, the narrowness of the GDR.

Awakened from Sleeping Beauty's slumber, the last here may really be the first.

United States

Hidden Words

by A.M. Rosenthal

A.M. Rosenthal, born in 1922, is a regular columnist to
the *New York Times* on foreign affairs. A *New York Times*
correspondent since 1946, Mr. Rosenthal was United Nations correspondent (1946–54), executive editor (1977–
86), and associate editor and columnist (1986–87). He
won a Pulitzer Prize for international reporting in 1960.
This column originally appeared in the *New York Times*
on 4 February 1990.

I search through the endless newspaper columns about the German wave
rolling toward unification, but I cannot find any of the words I am looking
for.

I cannot hear them in the drone of experts mustered up for TV nor in the
Sunday talk shows about how unification is all just a matter of time, now very
little time.

And when leaders of so many nations issue their carefully crafted statements
about how the will of the German people must be honored, the words are
not there either.

These are some of the words: Jew, Auschwitz, Rotterdam, Polish unter-
menschen, Leningrad, slave labor, crematorium, Holocaust, Nazi.

Strange how even speaking the words, which after all are at least as much
a part of German history as of Jewish, Polish, Dutch or Soviet, is already
considered inappropriate, vulgar, emotional, not really fit for decent political
discussion about Germany.

Why not? Are they not still part of every European, American and Soviet
mind and memory? Did not the two earlier German unifications lead to war?
Is there not a terror in millions of human minds and hearts that the nightmare
visage of the past may be the face of the future?

Do not the very leaders who speak with such warmth about today's two
Germanys talk sometimes in private of their apprehension about tomorrow's
one Germany?

On Friday, Foreign Minister Eduard Shevardnadze of the Soviet Union at
last brought forward the fears of the German past. He called for world discussion of unification—an idea that Chancellor Helmut Kohl of West Germany
immediately, rejected. Soviet policy on Germany is still murky and undecided,
but Mr. Shevardnadze did himself honor.

No, no apologies are necessary for bringing up the hidden words—no apologies for insisting that they bear on discussion of Germany's future.

To keep the words hidden is to kill the murdered twice, this time with the forgetting mind. And it is a serious disservice to those younger Germans, who will lead the new Germany, to delude them into thinking that either they or the rest of the world should or can forget those hidden words.

Let us not be frightened off by the whiny argument that to remember the truth of the past is to blame the sins of German fathers and mothers on German sons and daughters.

To equate this with Nazi racism is sickening. For one thing, lots of the fathers are still around. Personally I would much rather wait for unification another 20 or 30 years until God receives them, or for whatever awaits them.

But most of the world speaks as if the German desire for reunification is so strong and morally powerful that it would be positively sinful to try to delay it until the whole Nazi generation has come to Judgment Day. So in time, a new generation of Germans may indeed rule over what will probably be the most powerful nation on earth.

Young Germans can only be helped by understanding that the fears are as real as torn flesh still bleeding. Their task should be to remove those fears if they can, not to pretend they do not exist or are unworthy.

They cannot simply say, trust us. Nazi Germany has imposed upon them the responsibility of showing a total emotional separation from that past, vicious beyond human ken. A burden perhaps, but much lighter than that carried by the children of the victims of Germany's yesterday.

These things must be said. And it is time we all stopped allowing only our political "leaders" to speak for us. By nature and position they are people who often feel it is in their national or personal interests to hide emotions and reality.

Do we really want to leave it to the State Department, for heaven's sake, to decide and say what we dread or hope about Germany?

I would much rather hear from writers who were brave enough to write about the German yesterday, among them, in this country, John Hersey, I. B. Singer, Cynthia Ozick, Lucy Davidowicz, Elie Wiesel, Saul Bellow, William Styron. I would like to hear from others of talent and respect—Mailer, Wolfe, Talese, Heller, Miller, Roth, Doctorow, McMurtry—make your own list. And from priests and ministers, scientists, students, black leaders, conservatives, feminists.

Are they going to be silent at one of the most important junctures in our history—the point where a new and unknown Germany is growing out of some reasonable hope for the future and a great deal of reasonable fear of the past? Is there anything more worthwhile writing about, talking about and thinking about?

It's Already Happening

by Norman Birnbaum

Norman Birnbaum is University professor at the George-
town University Law Center. He is author, most recently,
of *The Radical Renewal: The Politics of Ideas in Modern America.* This article is reprinted from *The Nation,* 5 February
1990.

The world asks if the two German states should be joined and, if so, how and
when. The Germans, in both the Democratic Republic and the Federal Republic, are themselves debating the question. But unification from above and
below has already begun. It cannot be stopped, or even much delayed.

A torrent of visitors is flooding across the border between the two states in
both directions. The largest West German banks and firms are planning investment and joint ventures in East Germany. (Lufthansa and Volkswagen
have just announced large projects there.) The West German government is
providing financial guarantees for private sector investment, and is itself about
to spend heavily on East Germany's telecommunications, railways and roads.
West German magazines and newspapers not only circulate in the Democratic
Republic; some plan to publish there. Churches and organizations of every
kind, local governments in the border areas and universities and research
institutes have begun to work together. Supposedly under the authority of
the three Western powers, Mayor Walter Momper of West Berlin has initiated
a metropolitan commission for the two Berlins and their hinterland without
asking leave to do so.

An unlikely couple is presiding over this frenetic activity, or, more precisely,
trying to keep up with it. The systematically unsubtle West German Chancellor, Helmut Kohl, has joined the ascetic and cautious Communist reformer,
Prime Minister Hans Modrow of the Democratic Republic, in what is vaguely
termed a "contractual community." Kohl seeks unification, and, with an eye
to West German elections in December, the faster the better. Modrow wants
the Democratic Republic to remain an independent and socialist republic.
They have found common ground, however, in seeking to avert the chaos of
a collapse of the Democratic Republic. Each, moreover, is aware that Germany
has neighbors who are already disturbed by the scale and rate of change in,
and between, the two Germanys.

The situation within the Democratic Republic is paradoxical. The revolution
was initiated and led by dissident Communists and Socialists, who sought,

and seek, an independent state with democratic socialist institutions. Now that the citizenry can express itself, it is entirely unclear that it wants either independence or socialism. A large part of the sentiment for unification in the Democratic Republic has nothing to do with nationalist fervor or demands for geopolitical aggrandizement. It may reflect the desire to live as the West Germans do, as consumers with a high standard of living. These people are convinced that unification is the speediest and surest route to modernizing the economy.

As for socialism, forty years of Stalinist and neo-Stalinist oppression have done their work. One slogan heard frequently in the Democratic Republic is, "No More Experiments." Since none of those advocating democratic socialism can explain how a small socialist state could prosper in the midst of capitalist Europe, the West German model seems compelling to the East Germans. It is also true, however, that millions of citizens of the Democratic Republic are wary of the harsh, competitive aspects of the other German society. That society, though, is very unlike the United States. It provides a dense network of social benefits, and there is a large public investment in social infrastructure, especially education. The groups in the Democratic Republic demanding unification are therefore careful to announce their adherence to the capitalist welfare state of the Federal Republic, which is what a substantial segment of the political right in the Federal Republic also endorses. The least that can be said is that should unification occur, millions of citizens of the Democratic Republic will carry into the new state a large sense of social solidarity and a revulsion for social Darwinism.

For the moment, everything is in flux. The government of the Democratic Republic is made up of reformist Communists, representatives of the former satellite parties of the Socialist Unity Party, and technocrats. The satellite parties include one connected to Hans-Dietrich Genscher's Free Democrats in West Germany and a Christian Democratic Party connected to Kohl's party. The composition of the Parliament is the same as the prerevolutionary one and has little or no authority. The government's policies are scrutinized by an ad hoc round table made up of churches, old and new dissident groups and parties, academics, environmentalists and feminists. Some of the one-time dissident groups draw their inspiration from the West German Greens, and they have recently displayed that party's most self-destructive traits: moral absolutism and political impracticality. An attempted electoral alliance of the newer movements and parties promptly fell apart.

The situation in the Democratic Republic is volatile. There is a good deal of social pressure, and sometimes violence, against Communists and ex-Communists. A Protestant pastor whose resistance to the fallen regime began years ago said, "Those who were the most cowardly are now the most aggressive." There are older (and younger) nationalists in the Democratic Republic, and neo-Nazis and skinheads, too. The West German Republicans, a chaotic if energetic assemblage of revanchists, ultrarightists and xenophobes, have been organizing in East Germany. At the demonstrations that are now features of the Democratic Republic's political life, antagonisms between advocates of unification and those backing autonomy threaten to degenerate into serious street clashes. A chasm of distrust divides the round table from Modrow's government. Indeed, the non-Communist parties in the government and the opposition forced Modrow to withdraw a plan to develop a new internal security agency. The working effectiveness of the government remains fragile, as conflicts old and new threaten its ability to last until the May elections. The danger of chaos, then, is acute.

No one can say what will happen between now and the elections scheduled for May 6. The public opinion polls give widely fluctuating predictions. The reformed Communist Party might do rather well, the more so as it has just advanced a reasonable plan for gradual disarmament of the two Germanys and the withdrawal of Western and Soviet troops by the end of the decade. The West German government denounces the Communists for monopolizing the news media and political resources. However, the West German parties and, let it be said, the unions are prodigal with advisers, money and resources for their allies in the Democratic Republic. One important question is how well a newly revived Social Democratic Party will do. The territory of the Democratic Republic is the traditional heartland of German social democracy, and the party should profit from the demise of Stalinism. So far, however, the industrial working class has not come forward to support it.

There will be a national election in the Federal Republic in December, and politics in the two Germanys are, in fact, merging. These days, politicians from the Federal Republic appear in the Democratic Republic more often than in their own constituencies. West German television is an indispensable medium for East German debate.

Is the Federal Republic in the throes, meanwhile, of a nationalist seizure? Kohl seems to think so. In November he promulgated his ten-point plan for unification without consulting either his own coalition partners or the opposition—or the Western allies and the Soviet Union. Criticized and even repudiated for his haste (and for failing to guarantee Germany's acceptance of Poland's western border with Germany), he has since executed an elephantine retreat. His plan, he now says, is only a set of guidelines, not a timetable. While visiting Prime Minister Modrow in Dresden, Kohl did warn the citizenry of the Democratic Republic that unification had to be taken step by step, and he backed Modrow's call for stability. (Some politicians in the Federal Republic, however, appear to be speculating on, if not actually inciting, chaos in the Democratic Republic.) Meanwhile, Kohl has assured the West Europeans that, on his side of the Rhine, there are only good Europeans. In Dresden, he went out of his way to thank Soviet President Mikhail Gorbachev for making change in the Democratic Republic possible.

Kohl's primary concern remains keeping the Republican Party out of the next West German Parliament—that is, to under 5 percent of the vote. To accomplish this, he has voiced the accents of an assertive nationalism. His party's General Secretary, Volker Ruehe, once tireless in denouncing the Social Democrats and the peace movement for "neutralist nationalism," now says that unification is no one's business but the Germans'. There is no doubt that the revolution in the Democratic Republic, and the breaching of the wall, have evoked profound emotions in the Federal Republic. It would be absurd to suppose, however, that the majority of West Germans will now abandon parliamentary democracy or integration with Western Europe in the European Community, much less ready themselves for new wars of conquest.

More than a thousand citizens of the Democratic Republic are still settling daily in the Federal Republic. If these numbers do not diminish, the welfare-state economy of West Germany will be undermined, and the West Germans know this. That is why the probable Social Democratic candidate for Chancellor, Oskar Lafontaine, the Minister President of the Saarland, has chosen to open his campaign on an insistent socioeconomic note. Unification, he says, can come only after social equality and prosperity are guaranteed for both German states.

That much said, Kohl dominates the political scene at the moment. The Federal Republic is prospering. The Social Democrats are in an unenviable starting position. They have no alternative economic policy. They have been unable to exploit their just share of credit for the revolution in the Democratic Republic. Their policy of dialogue with the Communists was seized upon by the East German opposition to demand that the regime begin talks with its own citizens. The Social Democrats, now under attack from the West German right, have put themselves in the impossible position of declaring that they were willing to talk to Erich Honecker but that they abjure contact with his reformist Communist successors. Some Social Democrats were ready to join the Greens, the only West German party favoring the permanence of two states on German soil. A rejuvenated Willy Brandt, at the height of his prestige in both Germanys, has called for the party to return to its traditions. It originally opposed German rearmament and membership in NATO because such actions would make irreparable the division of Germany. Now both NATO and the Warsaw Pact strike most Germans as increasingly anachronistic. Brandt has declared that, on the road to association and confederation, the two Germanys must contribute to a demilitarized, democratic and socially equitable future for Europe's once divided halves. He has also warned both the Soviet Union and the West that the most certain way to evoke German nationalism is to block the legitimate aspirations of the Germans for self-determination. The election, then, will pit Kohl not only against Lafontaine but against Brandt. The Social Democrats in the Democratic Republic, moreover, have just declared strongly for reunification—making it impossible for the West

German right to monopolize national themes. Again, exact predictions are impossible, but the Social Democrats cannot be counted out, the more so as their skepticism about NATO is now shared by Kohl's party. Indeed, if there is a consensus in the Federal Republic, it is that NATO and the Warsaw Pact should be converted into arms-control agencies as soon as possible.

Meanwhile, countless smaller steps toward some form of unification are being taken. Imprecations about "stability" from President Bush and French President François Mitterrand do not fall on deaf German ears, but they are taken with large doses of political salt. The Germans sense that their erstwhile friends care little about German interests—belated confirmation of what the peace movement was saying all along. For the moment, there is a curious international alignment. The Communists in the Democratic Republic insist on the maintenance of two German states, although Modrow has said that unification is a possibility if the people wish it. As mentioned, the Greens in the Federal Republic oppose unification. They are in singular agreement with Bush, Mitterrand, British Prime Minister Margaret Thatcher and (with rather more openness about the future) Gorbachev. The debate within the two Germanys, however, is less about unification than about the kind of society and state that will come at the end of the process. In that debate, ideas of a democratic and social democratic, if not socialist, Germany have appreciably more chances of eventually triumphing than does an aggressive and chauvinistic nationalism.

The German Revival

by *Charles Krauthammer*

Charles Krauthammer, born in 1950, is a contributing editor of *The New Republic* and a nationally syndicated columnist. He was awarded a Pulitzer Prize for Distinguished
Commentary in 1987. This essay was published in *The
New Republic* on 26 March, 1990.

The great intervening parties of modern history, although by no means the
only ones, have been the great powers, and a great power is, among other
things, a power that cannot be intervened against. . . .

—Hedley Bull

Overnight and once again Germany has become a great power. Not for long
will it continue to be intervened against. All that is left to negotiate at the coming "two plus four" talks on reunification is the mode of liquidating the Big
Four's half-century intervention in Germany. Beyond those negotiations lies
the other half of the great power equation: In what ways and to what extent will
Germany once again become an intervening power?

German intervention, or, shall we say, German external intentions, are now
the major item on the European agenda. Because these intentions are as yet in-
determinate, the fear of Germany, once the great subtext of European politics,
is now the text. German reunification changes all geopolitical calculations of
only a few months ago. It colors plans for the single European market of 1992.
It infuses dead organisms, like the Warsaw Pact, with new life. (The Solidarity
prime minister of Poland has now asked Soviet troops to stay in his country until the "German problem" is solved.) Most chillingly, it evokes old memories.
Who would have thought that we would live to see, again, a headline reading:
"POLISH OFFICIAL VOWS TO DEFEND [German] BORDER" (*The New
York Times*, February 21)?

Anxiety about Germany is so pervasive and seems so self-explanatory that it
often escapes analysis. What exactly is the nature of the German danger? The
answer presents itself in three distinct parts: military, economic, and political.
The first two have been widely advertised and widely exaggerated. The third,
the subtle effect German reunification will have in the realm of geopolitical
ideas and institutions, is apt to prove the most serious.

I. Military

At the most concrete level, the fear of Germany has to do with borders. Much territory was stripped from Germany to punish it for starting World War II, and to diminish it as a hedge against World War III. With a reunified Germany dominating the continent, with Russia and America having gone home, who will stop Germany when it invokes a statute of limitations on World War II and demands restoration to its former, pre-Hitler self?

(That demand would not be without logic. The Arabs lost the West Bank in a war of aggression in 1967, yet the world seems unanimous in believing they have a right to get it back. If the "inadmissibility of the acquisition of territory by force" applies to the West Bank, a territory lost in a war of aggression and now kept as a buffer zone by the aggressors' would-be victim, why should Germans be denied the same right to their lost provinces of Silesia, Pomerania, and East Prussia? These, too, were lost in a war of aggression. These, too, the would-be victims, Poland and Russia, want to keep as buffer zones. By what right?)

Europeans, with memories of the Wehrmacht criss-crossing the continent, fear for their borders. If that fear is paranoia, then we must count Lech Walesa, Mikhail Gorbachev, most people in between, and much of Western Europe, too, as paranoid. Political philosopher Johnny Carson put it best. "The Berlin Wall is down," he noted the day after the event. "That means that all Germans are now free to go wherever they want in Europe. Hey, wasn't that the problem back in 1939?"

When the "two plus four" process is over and ratified by the thirty-five Helsinki countries at the end of this year, Germany will no doubt be required as the price for reunification to pledge adherence in perpetuity to its current borders. Yet no one can be absolutely sure that Germany ten or twenty years from now will not dismiss this agreement as the relic of a weakness long passed, as it did the Versailles agreements in the 1930s.

At the root of this fear of German revanchism lies the German national character, or more precisely, the belief in a German national character. The fear is that left to themselves Germans will revert to Teutonic barbarism, that German romanticism—the peculiarly fevered romanticism of the worker bee—will again seek fateful expression in politics and history. Beside this fear, forty years of democracy, forty years of peaceful accommodation to neighbors—in short, forty years of history—count for little.

One cannot definitively disprove this fear. How does one prove the negative proposition that Germans do not suffer from some peculiar character defect that inclines them toward expansion and aggression? One can only say that invoking national character as an explanatory principle or predictive device should always be cause for skepticism. The psychological interpretation of nations is even more unreliable than the psychological interpretation of individuals, itself a notoriously unreliable enterprise. By this reckoning, how do we account for the fact that the French disposition toward romantic expansionism, which took them all the way to Moscow in 1812, was abruptly banished in 1815?

We account for it as the triumph of history over "character." As Daniel Pipes says, there is no cure for total ambition quite like total defeat. Before there was a German problem, there was the French problem. Waterloo was its solution. Who worries about French national character now? There is no certainty, of course, that the German problem was solved in 1945 as surely as the French problem was solved in 1815. But the last forty years of German history cannot be so easily dismissed. (And security guarantees, such as a continued American presence on the continent, should provide sufficient reassurance until the new Germany has the time to demonstrate that it is indeed heir to the Federal Republic and not to more archaic German forms.)

II. Economic

The more realistic fear of the new Germany is economic and, as a result, cultural. As Rita Klimová, the new Czech ambassador to the United States, said recently, "The German-speaking world"—by which she meant the two Germanys and Austria—"will now achieve what the Hapsburgs, Bismarck, and Hitler failed to achieve: the Germanization of Central Europe." She added, "Through peaceful and laudable means, of course. And by the logic of commerce rather than conquest." Her point was clear. The dynamism of German commerce is already being felt in the weak economies of Eastern Europe. Czech schools, she explained, had just abolished Russian as the second language. The only question now was whether the new second language would be English or German. She urged the United States to send English teachers.

Eastern Europe fears outright domination by the German dynamo. Western Europe—Britain and France in particular—fear eclipse. This will be an economy of 80 million people producing fully forty percent of the European Community's gross domestic product. As the economic powerhouse of the continent, it will dictate policy to its neighbors even more powerfully than it does today.

One can understand the origin of these fears without granting them undue respect. The fear of being outcompeted by a peaceful commercial republic operating on fairly equal terms is a fear of which a nation ought not be proud. It characterizes, for example, the rather hysterical and occasionally racist American hostility toward Japan. German economic domination of the continent may be an injury to the pride of the British and the French. And the spread of German automobile manuals may be unwelcome to Czechs and Poles. But neither development constitutes a menace to anyone's standard of living (in market systems, prosperity is not a zero-sum game), or a threat to anyone's national existence, or an argument against German reunification.

III. Political

What then is the real problem with German reunification? It will reverse one of the most salutary European developments of the last fifty years: the decline of sovereignty. German reunification will constitute the most dramatic rebirth of sovereignty in the postwar era. In this era, Europe has enjoyed a historically unprecedented period of peace largely because the sovereignty of its warring nations was suppressed, brutally in the East and benignly in the West, by the advent of two great empires. Whatever else it did, the cold war division of Europe into a pax Sovietica and pax Americana did have the virtue of suppressing internecine European conflict.

But the imperial suppression of sovereignty must be temporary. Empire is not forever. Hence the post-cold war question: How to remove the artificial suppression of soverieignty by the superpowers, without then risking the national explosions that follow almost universally—in our time, in Asia and Africa—whenever the imperial power withdraws? Western Europe thought it had found the answer. Over the last forty years it has gradually built up transnational institutions, most notably the European Community. The great project accelerating toward completion was the formation of the single European market by 1992 that would transform the economies of the Twelve into an economic unit almost as free of legal barriers as that of the United States. Ireland and Greece would trade as freely as Maine and Texas.

But the importance of Europe '92 is not just economic. It involves one of history's greatest peacetime transfers of sovereignty. By giving up enormous economic, social, and regulatory power to a central European authority, the countries of Western Europe are consciously giving up much of their political autonomy. That is precisely why Margaret Thatcher so resists the process. She knows the EC monetary union, for example, may soon lead to a common currency, which will lead further to a common economic policy, which will lead inexorably toward political confederation. Talk of a United States of Europe is premature. But it is not farfetched. That is the trajectory that Western Europe is following.

Or was until November 9, the day the Berlin Wall fell. Europe '92 was to substitute the diminished sovereignty imposed by European integration for the diminished sovereignty once imposed by American domination. It was to be a transition from imperially- to self-imposed community. The great hope was that an integrated Europe would begin to acquire some of the internal stability of a federal country such as the United States. By diminishing the sovereignty of each country and centralizing more and more authority in

"Europe," the national rivalries that led to centuries of European wars would become obsolete. It would be as if Texas went to war with Maine.

German reunification challenges the idea and derails the process. West Germany, pledged to diminsh its sovereignty by joining this single European market, is now about to swallow the East, an incorporation that will augment its population, territory, economy, military strength, political centrality, and diplomatic clout. It is about to become the new giant on the continent. Leave aside potential territorial claims against its neighbors. Leave aside the possibility of Germany acquiring nuclear weapons. The simple fact of the explosive birth of a new and huge Germany in the center of the continent immediately undercuts the entire movement toward European confederation.

Such a Germany is its own confederation. Absent any malice, ill will, or "romanticism" on the part of its leadership, it will necessarily begin to act in accord with its new power—independently and with the kind of assertiveness and regard for distant interests that characterizes the other great powers, notably the United States and the Soviet Union.

The real danger posed by a reunified Germany is not that a new Bismarck or Hitler will arise. It is that the birth of a new giant in the middle of the continent will arrest Europe's great confederational project and produce in its place, as *The Economist* put it, a "revised version of a previously destructive balance-of-power system," a recapitulation of the kind of international system of the late nineteenth and early twentieth centuries that ended in catastrophe.

We can see the new balance-of-power system taking shape already. The shape is disturbingly familiar. The Western European powers are maneuvering to reestablish pre-war links with the ex-Soviet colonies of Eastern Europe, not just in pursuit of economic opportunity, but quite consciously to prevent Germany from dominating the region. Take the Polish question. Britain and France have forcefully supported Poland's demand for German acceptance of the current Polish frontier. Chancellor Helmut Kohl demurs and rejects out of hand Poland's demand for a presence at the coming "two plus four" deliberations. The Poles then seek Soviet assistance on the issue. They now wave the Soviet card—keeping Soviet troops in Poland, on Germany's border—as a warning to Germany to be more accommodating. This pattern is now new.

As the Europeans begin to maneuver to find partners to balance and contain Germany, each country is forced into a kind of reactive nationalism. Margaret Thatcher "is practicing a very narrow brand of nineteenth-century nationalism," complained a West German diplomat to *The Washington Post*. "The danger is that when one country does this, others may be forced to follow." She might reply, We didn't start this. But no matter. Wherever one chooses to place the blame; the result is the same: the movement toward integration, federalization, and dilution of sovereignty is halted. Europe invented the idea of sovereignty, suffered its consequences, and was about to demonstrate how to transcend it. Now Europe is heading back the other way. For a continent consisting of twenty-nine sovereignties speaking forty-five languages, that way is not just an anachronism, it is a prescription for instability.

To be sure, this revival of sovereignty had already begun elsewhere. In Eastern Europe the erosion of Soviet power is already giving rise to reassertions of contentious and conflicting nationalisms. The withdrawing Communists leave behind a myriad of territorial and other grievances and no structure to moderate these conflicts. Not surprisingly, the most advanced case of malignant nationalism can be seen in the place from which Soviet influence was first expelled. Yugoslavia, Eastern Europe's oldest Moscow-free zone, is home to ethnic strife of truly heroic depth and irrationality.

Everyone is aware of the dangers of these revived Eastern and Central European nationalisms. But there was a hope: that a powerfully united Western Europe would draw the Eastern countries into its orbit and that, as they attached themselves individually to this new stable center, their intramural conflicts would be tempered. The key to a pax Europa was to be a deeply integrated European Community: a core confederated Western Europe attracting and taming the newly freed sovereignties of the East.

That was the vision of the new Europe. In fact, it became the very definition of the word. When Vaclav Havel says that he wants Czechoslovakia to "rejoin Europe," he means not just a reunion with Western culture and political tradition, but something very concrete as well. He means joining the enterprise launched by the European Twelve and institutionalized in the framework of the European Community. He means the Council of Ministers in Brussels, the Parliament in Strasbourg, the Court of Justice in Luxembourg.

This institutional expression of the new Europe is often derided as the bureaucratic invention of an underemployed technocratic class, an invention that will, moreover, create yet another layer of European government and saddle brave new privatizing Europeans (e.g., Thatcher) with bad old social-democratic statism.

Hamilton would have had little difficulty with this familiar anti-federalist refrain. In purely economic terms, the economies of scale gained by confederation far outweigh the costs. Replacing a patchwork of contradictory national regulation with uniform Euroregulation will so significantly reduce costs and encourage economic rationalization that European GNP will enjoy a windfall growth estimated between 4.5 percent and seven percent over the next six years.

But as Jean Monnet would have told the antifederalists, the benefits are not just economic. Even if Brussels did cost European consumers a centime or two to cover new welfare-state, labor-driven Euroregulations, that would be a small price to pay for a Europe integrated beyond the possibility of ruinous civil war. When Tory MP Ian Gow moved last year's speech from the throne, he spoke ominously of "the vaulting ambitions of the supernationalists" in Brussels. If little England does so fear vaulting ambition, is it not better that such ambition emanate from Brussels rather than Berlin?

Last October, when writing about a post-cold war world, I ventured that among the great powers of the new multipolar order would be "Europe." It was possible then to imagine a confederated Europe emerging from the structure of the EC. It is harder to imagine that now. Not because Germany is by policy its enemy, but because the rebirth of a great German nation within Europe is provoking a rebirth of national self-assertion throughout Europe. In this climate, it is impossible to think of a "Europe" emerging. As we head toward multipolarity, the pole that was to be "Europe" will instead be greater Germany. It is possible that Germany might still choose to subsume itself in Europe, but in the first flush of post-(cold)-war independence, that is hardly likely.

The Berlin Wall came down too soon. Had East Germany been the last Soviet province to fall, as we thought the Kremlin would insist, it might have been but a small piece digestible by a new and stable Europe. Having come so quickly, German unification threatens to disrupt the whole by creating in the heart of Europe a greater Germany that Europe cannot contain.

The danger is not that greater Germany will march across Europe but that its birth turns the twilight of sovereignty into a new dawn. It derails a process by which Europe was hoping to make itself safe from itself. We return instead to the old Europe, balance of power Europe, the Europe that produces more history than it can consume.

"NO" to German Reunification

by Michael Lerner

Michael Lerner is the editor of *Tikkun*. This article is reprinted from *Tikkun* March/April 1990.

Had the German people, East and West, really engaged in a serious process of denazification, had each German child been required to study the history of anti-Semitism and come to understand how this perverse racism influenced people to vote for Hitler in 1933, and had there been a systematic attempt to uproot the rigid character structures that were encouraged by German cultural and educational norms, I might feel very different as I watch the two Germanies celebrate potential reunification. But when I hear talk of a resurgent German nationalism, when I read about Germans singing World War II songs as they dance on the ruins of the Berlin Wall, I have to question why the American occupiers of Germany seemed to think that fascism (and anti-Semitism) was suddenly not a problem, that the struggle was solely against communism. The sad truth is that in the name of enlisting Germans on our side of the cold war, we in the U.S. never insisted on a serious denazification in West Germany. Conversely, Jews in the Communist Party in Eastern Europe were so anxious to prove their internationalist credentials, and so afraid of appearing self-interested and sectarian, that they never insisted that the East Germans wage a serious campaign against anti-Semitism. No wonder, then, that neo-Nazis are once again popping out of the woodwork in Germany.

It's not that I'm so worried about a new wave of anti-Semitism in Germany—the dangers for that are much greater in Eastern Europe, and anyway the Germans killed so many of us that there just aren't enough remaining alive in that part of Europe for them to get worked up about. Rather, I resist the idea that Germans deserve reunification, that they've served their time and now can forget the past (something that most of them managed to do almost instantaneously in 1945). Judging from the ceremonies at Bitburg honoring the SS dead, and judging from the attempts by German historians to reconceptualize their role in World War II as part of a legitimate struggle to stop Soviet communism, they have a long way to go before the society can or should be treated as though it has the same rights as any other group. It's not a question of how much time has been served, but of how deeply Germans have grappled with their past and how much real change has occurred.

It is Germany's historical amnesia that worries me. The ability to massively repress awareness of a traumatic event, particularly when one is the perpetrator of the trauma, may provide momentary comfort, both for the perpetrator and for observers. "That was just a momentary aberration. We were taken over by some demonic spirit. We weren't really ourselves, it was someone else who was doing all that." But if the source of this behavior is ignored, it will continue to live in the collective unconscious of a people, and once they are no longer under close scrutiny (in this case, once the Soviet Union and the U.S. remove their hundreds of thousands of troops that still occupy Germany), the same problems may pop up again. Already we see neo-Nazi groups from West Germany organizing supporters in a newly liberalized East Germany. And we will see worse unless the Germans are forced to confront and work through their past.

The occasion of reunification could have arrived in a very different spirit. Had they not repressed their past (a repression, we must add, that was encouraged by both the U.S. and the Soviet Union in order to mobilize their respective sides of Germany into being more efficient allies in the cold war), both states might have developed a deep awareness of the dangers of nationalism and solidly repudiated anti-Semitism. The respective populations would have approached the issue of reunification with humility and a vision of a new nation that accepted the burden of rectifying wrongs that had been committed in the name of German nationalism. This never took place at all in East Germany; it happened symbolically in West Germany through payment of war reparations to Israel, but not substantively in the consciousness or education of the West German people. Had it happened, we would not see the German Right nostalgically yearning for the good old days of the last Reich. And we would not hear German leftists equating Israeli policy toward the Palestinians (a policy *Tikkun* has consistently opposed) with the Nazis' systematic gassing and cremation of a civilian population. That intelligent and morally sensitive young leftists could make this equation demonstrates how little they have been taught about the Nazis.

But doesn't every group have the right to national self-determination? If the German people want to reunite, what right does anyone have to stop them? Our answer: national self-determination is not an absolute right, but conditional on how it is used. There are some moments when a national group must limit its right, and other moments when it may temporarily lose its rights altogether. For example, we believe that Israel is a legitimate expression of the national self-determination of the Jewish people. But we put limits on that right, insisting that it does not include the rights to expropriate the land of Palestinians or to prevent Palestinians from exercising their own right to national self-determination in the occupied territories.

In the case of Germany, restrictions on national self-determination must go much further. The virulent form of nationalism that thrived in that society some forty-five years ago brought the world one of its greatest catastrophes, World War II. Tens of millions of people lost their lives in a senseless struggle, and millions of our own people were systematically brutalized, dehumanized, and then annihilated. It is now in the name of this very same German nationalism that we are asked to recognize the right of East and West Germany to reunite. (And possibly next we will be told about Germany's desire to absorb other areas where ethnic Germans live, precisely the pretext that led to German expansionism in the 1930s.) This is preposterous. German nationalism has no legitimate claim on us and will not until either the entire generation that grew up in Nazi Germany no longer plays any role in German life or until the German people, both in East and West Germany, engage in some set of public service activities aimed at uprooting and recompensing the evils that they let loose on this world. (I'm thinking here of a German peace corps dedicated to fighting racism and anti-Semitism all over the world, a German effort to provide direct economic aid to societies—including the Soviet Union and Israel—in which displaced Jews were resettled, a German educational system that trains its citizens in the skills of combating all forms of totalitarianism and prejudice, a German Church that teaches its members exactly how the Church had collaborated with evil; the list could go on.) A German reunification that comes to us in the name of repairing the damage Germany did would be worthy of consideration. But a German reunification suffused with historical amnesia and fueled by a desire for economic growth and power is a mortal danger to the world.

In short, while recognizing the prima facie claims of any nationalism, we need to distinguish between progressive and destructive nationalism. When national identity is used to satisfy the fundamental needs of a people for community, shared culture, shared ideas, and a shared history, we applaud it. But some nationalisms then become an instrument for the oppression of others. At this point we need to question the validity of that nationalism more closely.

There is a progressive nationalism that emerges from the shared struggle of a people against oppression. The kind of nationalism developed by African-Americans to counter the oppression of a white society embodies elements of humanity that can provide a meaningful and ethical framework for many who remain oppressed. Similarly, there are progressive elements of Jewish nationalism—exemplified in the insistence of Jews to root their history *not* in some glorious superhero founders but in a history of a people that is liberated from slavery (see the Haggadah supplement that is inserted in this issue of *Tikkun*)—that provide a liberatory framework. To the extent that nationalisms are progressive they enable people to identify with others who are oppressed (as the Torah puts it so clearly, "Do not oppress the stranger; remember that you were strangers in the land of Egypt"). But many nationalisms are not progressive, and as the Israeli experience is beginning to show, even progressive nationalisms can be transformed into mechanisms of oppression.

In the modern world, nationalism is too often an ideology used to allow people to repress awareness of their own pain and alienation in daily life. The need for connectedness and recognition by others is systematically frustrated in the contemporary world. From the moments in early life when alienated parents misrecognize their own children, deny their subjectivity and spontaneity, and project onto them fantasies of who they are (to which the child must conform in order to receive some degree of pseudo-recognition), to an adult life in which human relations are increasingly shaped by the competitive and dominating modes of the marketplace, our human community is increasingly fragmented and emptied of deep connections and ethical wholeness. "The nation" becomes a substitute gratification for the wholeness lacking in one's own immediate life; and instead of struggling to change daily life to make it less fragmented and alienated, people are encouraged to identify with this fantasized national community. Through identification with this larger reality one imagines oneself made whole, fully recognized (as citizen), and accepted into a community whose destiny will provide meaning to one's own fragmented life. But the community exists only in songs, movies, television images, and speeches of politicians—not in how people treat each other or lead their daily lives. So the pain of alienated lives is only momentarily assuaged by the moments of nationalist fantasy, and eventually people suspect that something is still wrong. The solution: to find some "other" (the Jew, the Communist, the Black, the homosexual, the Arab, the Japanese, the Chinese, the capitalist) who is the reason why the nation is not delivering the emotional goodies it was supposed to have in store. The rage that one feels at one's own alienated life can now get externalized in aggression against the other who is allegedly undermining the fantasized community that would otherwise be working well to make life fulfilling and meaningful.

This is the most prevalent way that nationalism functions in the modern world, and I see little reason to encourage it.

Nor is this a moment when we should look favorably on the reemergence of nationalisms throughout Europe. The U.S. helped foster these nationalisms as a way to counter Soviet influence. Yet all too often European nationalisms flourished—even while officially suppressed by the Communists—precisely because they embodied all the vitality of older reactionary fantasies, including anti-Semitism, xenophobia, and religious fundamentalism. These diseases may once again spring to life in a Central and Eastern Europe no longer governed by the Soviet Union. Giving the nod to a reunited Germany, the country that most embodied these tendencies in the recent past, can only encourage the plethora of national groupings that may recreate a Europe so similar to the pre-World War I picture that it dissolves into endless battling between ethnic and religious rivals.

Our point here is not to be unforgiving toward the enemies of the Jews. I would hold any country responsible to the same standard for a similar level of historical outrage in the recent past. For this same reason, I don't recognize any fundamental right for national self-determination of Cambodians under the Khmer Rouge. And I still hope that someday Kissinger and Nixon and others will stand trial for their war crimes against the people of Vietnam, and that they will be sentenced to spend years of their life working to repair the country they did so much to destroy.

I shared the great joy of seeing the Berlin Wall come down—because it symbolized an end to decades of Communist oppression in Eastern Europe—and I rejoice at the surge of democracy that has swept through Europe. There's a new spirit of openness that is shaking even the Soviet Union. South Africa, too, has recognized the African National Congress, leaving Israel as the one Western-style state unwilling to talk to her enemies (a position that was recently bolstered by the work of Arab terrorists, whose murder of Israeli civilians on a tour bus in Cairo gave aid and comfort to Israeli right-wingers). But much as I welcome the democratization of the world, I also remember that many of the peoples involved were in fact once racists and anti-Semites. The regimes that they are likely to democratically establish may well reflect those sentiments. Sounding the alarm now about German reunification is one way to introduce into the current discussion the notion that all of these resurgent nationalisms have our support only to the extent that they explicitly condemn and struggle against the legacies of anti-Semitism and racism with which they have been identified.

If Germany is allowed to reunite without simultaneously dealing with its past, we will be passing on to history a very unfortunate lesson that will soon come back to haunt us: a people can participate in the worst and most unspeakable crimes, and in a reasonable period of time our collective historical amnesia can be such that this people can return to the collective family of humanity acting as though nothing serious has really happened. If that is the lesson the world learns from Germany, we may see more terrible crimes in the name of nationalism in the years ahead. If it is too late to stop reunification, let it be remembered that liberal Jews sounded the warning.

Kohl at Camp David

by *William Safire*

William Safire, born in 1929, has been a *New York Times* columnist since 1973 and in 1978 he was awarded the Pulitzer Prize for Distinguished Commentary. He wrote this piece for the *New York Times* on 1 April 1990.

What worries the rest of the world most about a unified Germany?

Not the competition; if based on free markets, that should be healthy. Not a new demand for "a place in the sun"; Prussian or Nazi militarism seems not to be in the present generation's psyche.

What's troubling people around the world is an apparent cultural character flaw: the tendency of too many personally upright Germans to look the other way when moral values are threatened.

Germans usually get huffy when this perception is voiced. They say that talk of a national "trait" is bigoted and obsessed with the aberrations of 1870–1945; many angrily impugn the motives of the worriers, or suggest that a tendency of good people to turn one's back on bad happenings is not peculiar to German culture but is universal.

That response is what is known as "fighting the problem." It fails to deal with a real problem in a way that would both correct the historic tendency and allay the justifiable suspicion.

Example: When Chancellor Kohl came to the U.S. a couple of years ago, he was briefed for a solid hour on the evidence of West German nationals' help in building a huge poison gas facility in Libya. He professed ignorance, though his briefers knew that West German intelligence was fully apprised of the details of the moral outrage.

The reaction of this good German was to turn away and to want to hear no more about it. Not until The New York Times and later a newsmagazine in his own country, Der Stern, exposed the dealings and the official coverup—and not until he was reminded of the special sensitivity of the world to German association with poison gas—did an investigation begin.

It's been over a year, and the one man taken into custody on suspicion of exporting the machinery of mass murder has yet to be indicted, much less tried. Export of dual-use chemicals to Libya has been stopped, but the Bundestag has yet to pass a strong export control law.

While the Germans are taking so long to prohibit the sale of the means of mass murder, another potential scandal looms: Iraq, which has long been trying

186

to build an atomic bomb to put atop its advanced rocketry, may have been buying technological know-how from West Germans.

According to Der Spiegel, which was beaten by its rival to the previous export scandal, a German company delivered a machine to Iraq's Tuweitha atomic site that makes possible the enrichment of U-235. West Germany Embassy spokesmen here assure me that the story is complete "speculation," has been checked out and found wanting. That's what officials said last time; we'll see.

The point is that the German reaction to the possibility of something really wrong is first to deny it, then await proof from elsewhere, finally to delay prosecution for a few years until interest dies.

America's reaction to such charges is the opposite: where there's smoke, there's fire. For that reason, Senator Pat Leahy and Representative Charles Schumer are trying to find out if our multibillion loan guarantees to Iraq for commodity purchases (a) are affected by the Lavoro bank scandal, and (b) help that murderous regime by freeing funds to finance its rocketry and nuclear weaponry.

It is safer for a culture to be self-suspicious to a fault than self-deluding to a fault. On matters that affect civilization's core values, better to nose around too much than resolutely to see no evil.

At Camp David this weekend, President Bush and Chancellor Kohl should address the underlying question: What can a united Germany do to break the habit of turning away? What "confidence-building measures," in arms-control lingo, can it undertake to remove its neighbors' suspicion?

The answer is in another disarmament term: transparency. Unified Germany would do well to strengthen its federal structure, stressing checks and balances between branches and levels; openness is best guarded by insuring the highest standard of press freedom in Europe.

Germany's allies, rather than station troops forever on its soil, should establish the ties of multinational universities, agree on business disclosure standards, and start joint journalistic satellite ventures.

Such a new, open Germany would want to offer a Berlin site to the 35-nation European Security Conference, not to dominate this halfway house between the U.N. and NATO, but to have a vast bureaucracy of the Continent's politicians and reporters continually poking around.

Tomorrow's Germany will be happier place for embracing transparency. And the rest of the world will feel safer.

Ten for Germany

by Denis MacShane

Denis MacShane works for the Geneva-based International Metalworkers Federation. He has written extensively on labor topics, and his book *International Labour and the Origins of the Cold War* was published by Oxford University Press in 1991. This article was originally published in *The Nation* on 2 April 1990.

The reunification of Germany means a new Europe, but the left is absent from the discussion of its contours. Muted voices are heard on the German left—from Günter Grass, the I.G. Metall metalworkers' union, or the Social Democratic leader Hans-Jochen Vogel—about the exact form of the *Anschluss*, but these are like corks bobbing on a tidal wave. Here are ten conditions that the new Germany could fulfill to contribute to the security, well-being, progress and political pluralism of the rest of Europe, and the world.

One. Germany should follow Japan's example and insert into a new Constitution a clause renouncing forever the use of war as a means of settling disputes. In addition, the Constitution should state that Germany would never make or possess nuclear weapons, or station armed forces outside its borders.

Two. Bonn should remain as the capital of the new Germany. Berlin may become New York to Bonn's Washington, but Berlin symbolized the old Prussian, centralized system of power.

Three. German politicians should be unequivocal in renouncing any claim on prewar German territory. Germany's borders should be those of 1945. Until Chancellor Helmut Kohl gives this pledge, Polish suspicions about long-term German designs on Silesia, Gdansk and what was East Prussia will remain.

Four. The question of NATO or neutrality avoids the real issue—the size and capability of a unified German army. A Costa Rica solution—no army at all—is unlikely. No matter how democratically constituted, a German army whose size is proportionate to the country's population would frighten its neighbors and could start a new conventional arms race. Therefore, and although this means breaking with a cherished principle of post-1945 left thinking, NATO and Warsaw Pact troops, severely reduced in numbers and without nuclear weapons, should remain on German territory.

Five. A reunited Germany should be urged to outlaw industrial production of offensive weapons and especially chemical warfare capability. The merger last year between Daimler-Benz and the aerospace company M.B.B. gave rise to fears that another giant arms-producing monster was being conceived. (Warplanes, tanks and U-boats are now produced by the same company.)

Six. Germany should support the pressure from the French government and from Jacques Delors, president of the European Community Commission, for greater European unity and a transfer of some sovereignty from national governments to a more democratic European structure. In particular, the directly elected European Parliament needs more power. A federal Europe will lessen the dominance of any giant nation-state, including a reunited Germany.

Seven. A new Schuman plan is needed to integrate German industry with its European partners. The postwar Schuman plan, named after the French Foreign Minister, placed the German and French steel and coal industries under a common high authority. A modern version might link parts of the automobile or electronics industries.

Eight. A reunited Germany should take the lead in key social areas such as extending citizenship rights to immigrant workers. There are 4 million non-German workers—*Gastarbeiter*—in West Germany, most of them Turks. A reunited Germany cannot afford to have such an underclass of noncitizens.

Nine. Germany should also open up its labor market to Eastern European, especially Polish, workers. All demographic pointers suggest a labor shortage in Germany in the next few years. To overcome this and to contribute to the consolidation of democratic market economies in Eastern Europe, workers from the former Communist satellites should be allowed to earn money west of the Oder-Neisse Line.

Ten. Finally, German companies installing themselves in Eastern Europe should follow the same rules in the treatment of their new employees as they do under present West German law. The codetermination system that put workers on the boards of major German companies has been the key contributing factor to workplace stability and performance in postwar West Germany. Workplace rights and industrial democracy could show Eastern Europeans that Communist authoritarianism does not need to be replaced by a Latin American-style cauldron of repression of basic labor and human rights.

Uneasy About the Germans

by Arthur Miller

Arthur Miller, born in 1915, is one of America's most renowned writers and playwrights. His prominent works include *Death of a Salesman* (1949) and *The Crucible* (1953). His essay is reprinted from the *New York Times Sunday Magazine* of 6 May 1990.

Do Germans accept responsibility for the crimes of the Nazi era? Is their repentance such that they can be trusted never to repeat the past? When people worry about the unification of Germany, these are the usual questions. But for me there is a deeper mystery, and it concerns the idea of nationhood itself in the German mind.

Three attempts to create a successful state have been smashed to bits in the mere 72 years since Germany's defeat in 1918. And although we are now in the presence of a great victory of a democratic system over a one-party dictatorship, it is not a democratic system of German invention. The nation about to be born is one that never before existed. And in the apprehension over what this may mean, the Jews are by no means alone. The British are concerned and so are the French, not to speak of the Russians and numerous others whose lives were ruined by German aggression.

I have more than the usual contact with Germans and German-speaking people. My wife, Austrian by birth, spent the war years in Germany, and her family is involved in German industry; I have German journalist friends, as well as colleagues in the German theater and the film and publishing industries. If I were to announce that I am not too worried about unification and have confidence in the democratic commitments of the younger generation, my friends would doubtless be happy to hear it—and proceed to worry privately on their own.

No one can hope to predict what course any country will take. I believe that for Germans, including those who are eager for unification, the future of German democracy is as much of an enigma as it is for the rest of us. They simply don't know. More precisely, they are almost sure it will turn out all right. But that's a big almost.

Several weeks ago in West Berlin, one of my wife's high school friends, a woman in her late 60's who never left Germany through the rise of Nazism, the war and reconstruction, had some conflicted, if not dark, things to say about the question. "In Germany it will always be the same," she said. "We go up very high, but in the end we come down. We are winning and winning and winning, and then we lose. And when we are in trouble we turn to authority; orders and work make us the happiest."

She is using a cane these days, after a fall on the ice. She has a broad-beamed peasant air, thinning hennaed hair, ruddy cheeks. A survivor of a battered generation, she seems to refer to her own observations rather than to things she has read. "We must go slowly with unification," she said. "It is all darkness in front of us." And if the future is murky to West Germans, she wondered: "What is in the mind of the East Germans? We don't know. For us it was bad enough. We had 12 years of dictatorship, but after that we had nearly 50 years of democracy. They have had nothing but dictatorship since 1933. To become democratic, is it enough to want a good job and a car and to hate the left?"

She has come to visit, despite her injury, because in her circle it is hard to find an open-minded conversation. "I fear it is all very artificial," she said. "It is the same old story, in one sense. We are not like the French, the British, the Americans. We never created our own democracy, or even our own regime, like the Russians; ours was handed to us by the Allies, and we are handing it to the G.D.R. people. But we had a memory of democracy before Hitler. Even their fathers have no such memory now. Who will influence whom—we over them or they over us?"

She talks about the Republicans, a far-right extremist party that won 90,000 votes in the last West Berlin election after only a few months of existence. "People say they are non-sensical, a tiny minority," she said. "I remember the other tiny nonsensical minority and how fast it took over. And mind you, we are prosperous now. What happens if we run into hard times and un-employment?"

That conversation could be repeated as many times as you like in Germany. But it is entirely possible that two thirds of the Germans—those under 50, who can barely recollect Nazism—have only the remotest connection with the woman's sentiments and underlying worry. So hostile are they to any gov-ernment intrusion into their lives that some of them made it nearly impossible to conduct a national census a few years ago because the questions being asked seemed to threaten them with regimentation from on high. Questions had to be altered, and some census takers were even accompanied by in-spectors to make sure more personal questions than those prescribed were not asked.

Nevertheless, the Berlin woman's apprehensions do leave a nagging sus-picion. Does the Federal Republic of Germany arouse lofty democratic feelings in its citizens' minds, or is it simply a matter of historical convenience invented by foreigners? To be sure, this system has helped the nation to prosper as never before, but the issue is how deep the commitment is to its democratic precepts, how sacred they are, and if they will hold in hard times.

I have often sensed something factitious about German society in the minds of Germans, regardless of viewpoint. Discounting the zephyrs—or clouds—of guilt and resentment that obscure conversations with foreigners, especially Jewish liberals like me, it seems that the very reality of the German state is still not quite settled in their minds. I have never, for example, felt that Germans have very transcendent feelings toward the Federal Republic; it does not seem to have imbued them with sublime sensations, even among those who regard it as a triumph of German civic consciousness risen from the ruins of war.

Nothing, at least in my experience, approaches the French emotions toward their Republic, the British toward their confusing monarchy, the Swiss toward their multilingual democracy, or Americans' feelings toward their country (which at least once every quarter century is pronounced imminently dead from depression, war, racial conflict or corruption, and therefore requires the loudest avowals of patriotic fervor on the face of the earth).

In a word, the German ship, in the German mind, increasingly powerful and promising though it may be, seems to float slightly above the surface without displacing water. Again, I may get this impression because of the tendency of Germans to apologize for themselves implicitly, which in some is a form of secret boasting, given the incredible success of the German economy.

The Berlin woman's sense of the system as having been conferred on Germans, rather than created by them—a routine enough idea in Germany—nevertheless expresses the insubstantiality or, as she puts it, the artificiality of the society that is now being merely multiplied by unification. It has sometimes seemed to me in Germany that there is a feeling of walking on Astroturf rather than natural sod. Or maybe it is simply a feeling that the other shoe has not yet dropped.

But when one recalls the polities that they did unquestionably create on their own—Frederick the Great's Prussia, Bismarck's state and Hitler's—they were all dictatorial or at least heavily authoritarian and in their time remarkably successful. This is also what my wife's Berlin friend was trying to say to me, namely that as a German she does not quite trust her compatriots' civic instinct when it comes to constructing a free society. And I wonder whether, unspoken, this is the source of the distrust a great many people feel in and out of West Germany, especially now that its territory is to be reunited with the East.

Of course, for the foreigner, Germany's civic failure is most perfectly expressed by the Holocaust and the military aggressions of Hitler. But I have wondered whether foreigners and their accusing attitudes on these counts apart, a different and less obvious historical experience is not more active in creating an uneasiness in them, an experience uniquely German.

It has often been said that the Germans alone among the major peoples have never won a major revolution. Instead, Germany's intense integration of social services, economy and culture was conceived and handed down by kings, princes, and great chancellors like Count Bismarck (who though elected was kingly and sternly paternalistic), then a ferocious dictator and, since 1945, by her wartime victors. It is as though George Washington had accepted the widespread demand that he be crowned a king, and proceeded to carve out a new society with little or no contribution or interference by elected legislatures. America might well have emerged a well-ordered society in which the rules were very clear and life deeply organized from cradle to grave.

Instead, the state's decisions became the American citizens' rightful business, a conception that destroyed the time-honored relationship in which he was merely the subject of the state's attentions and efforts. The image of himself as citizen was thus vastly different from that in other post-feudal societies of the time—and from that of most people of our time.

Besides a lack of revolutionary past, the Federal Republic is unique among the great powers in another way: it came to life without a drop of blood being shed at its birth. No Germany soldier can say, "I fought for democracy." It was not given him by history to do so. West Germany is the creation of not arms, but work. The Japanese system, also practically America's creation, is a quite different case, in that the monarchy and the government were never destroyed as such; indeed, MacArthur took great pains to make its continuity with the past obvious to all.

The German break with Hitlerism, the last German-made system, had to be total and condign. And German society had to be started almost literally from a pile of bricks under which the shameful past was to be buried, put out of mind, deeply discredited.

If these observations are in fact operative, and I cannot imagine how they can be proved or disproved as such, then what Germans lack now is the consecration by blood of their democratic state. The torrent of German blood that has flowed in this era in the Hitler-launched wars was, in fact, to prevent any such state from coming into existence.

For me, this is what keeps sucking the life out of German protestations of a democratic faith and casts suspicion on the country's reassurances that its economic power is no menace to the world. The fact is, West German civic practice has been as democratic as any other society's for more than 40 years and is less repressive and all-controlling than, for example, that of France, whose bureaucracy is positively strangulating by comparison.

I know Germans who are as certain as it is possible to be about anything that democracy will hold; I know other Germans who do not believe that at all. The world, it seems to me, has no choice but to support the positive side of the split and to extend its hand to a democratic Germany. By giving it the recognition it deserves, German democracy can only be strengthened, but meeting it with endless suspicion may finally wither its hopes. A recent New York Times/CBS News poll shows a large majority of Americans in favor of reunification, a vote of confidence with which I agree. At the same time, no German should take umbrage at the reminder that his nation is a previous incarnation showed that it had aggressive impulses that brought death to 40 million people. This memory should not vanish: it is part of democratic Germany's defense against the temptation to gather around some new extreme nationalism in the future.

It does not really do any good to remind Germans of those horrendous statistics if the purpose is simply to gratify an impulse to punish. But it is necessary never to forget what nationalistic blood lust can come to, so that it will never happen again.

Likewise, German resentment at such reminders has to be understood. No one can live in a perpetual state of repentance without resentment. In the scale and the profundity of its degradation Nazism has no equal in modern time, but each country has had some level of experience with contrition, some taste of it, as a repayment for the oppression of other people. What if every nation guilty of persecution were to own up? Are we really prepared to believe in their remorse? And while penitence in the persecutors may be a moral necessity for those who survived the victimization, it will not bring back the dead. So is it not infinitely more important that the descendants of the persecutors demonstrate something more than contrition, namely political responsibility?

What do I care if a Nazi says he's sorry? I want to know what the Constitution and educational system of Germany are doing to defend democracy under possibly future difficult circumstances. That is important to me and to my children. It is equally important that democracy live not only in institutions but in the German heart. But in all candor how are we ever to know that it does, except as crises are faced in a democratic spirit?

The world has a right—its World War II dead have earned it—to reproach and criticize and make demands of Germans, if and when they seem to revert to bad habits. For a long time to come, the Germans are going to have to face the legacy of their last attempt to dominate other nations.

But there is another Germany—the Germany of high aspirations. It does truly exist, and it must be welcomed wholeheartedly in the hope that one day its permanent dominion over the country will be unquestioned by any fair-minded person. In short, the time has come to look the worst in the eye but to hope for the best.

A German journalist in her mid-40's, typical of many of her generation despite an upper-class Black Forest origin, has struggled with her country's past all her life and by turns is in despair and hopeful. "The problem," she says, "or part of it, is that the world is still thinking of Germany as it was in the Nazi time or shortly after. But a lot has happened in Germany in the last 40 years!" As her voice rises, I am struck by an odd resemblance to the Berlin woman. They both seem to doubt that they are registering; it is as if events were wild horses flying past with no one really pondering how to tame them.

"For example," she goes on, "the impact of the 1968 French students' rebellion. It overturned Germany's educational system and for the first time made it possible for German workers to go to universities, the way it happens in America. Until then, we had a very narrow elite system. In fact, ours is now far more democratic than the French or the English, and we are now paying people to go to university, 800 marks a month if their parents together earn less than 1,500 a month. University education is free. This has had good and bad results—a lowering of standards, actually—but socially it has broken the class system."

Slim, elegantly dressed and a stubbornly heavy smoker, she is unable to come psychologically to rest. "This generation cannot be confused with the stupid, lumpen people who flocked to Hitler," she said. "Moreover, there is an immense amount of travel by this generation. They are not the parochial, isolated mass that Hitler poisoned so easily with anti-foreign propaganda. This is not in any sense the pre-Hitler German people."

Then, hardly a moment later: "The problem with the German, the one great weakness of his character, is his worship of loyalty. Loyalty! Loyalty! It's the supreme virtue, the chain around his heart . . ." And she is quite suddenly angry, and, for a few minutes, blue and uncertain and perhaps fearful.

In short, the uneasiness about national character is subjective, difficult to catch in the nets of rationality, but it may turn out to be more decisive than any other.

The anxiety shown by the journalist and my wife's Berlin friend transcends political viewpoints, I believe. Nor is it purely a product of the catastrophic last war and the Holocaust. I know some liberal Germans, a couple of radicals and some very conservative business types, and from all of them I have felt a similar emanation of uncertainty as to what, in effect, the Germany is—and consequently what kind of society fits him, expresses his so contradictory nature. And this is what I think the perplexity comes down to.

The Federal Republic is not a nation like others, born of self-determining revolution. Paradoxically, perhaps, West Germany is the first great society born of peace; if it is to achieve a deep sense of identity it will have to be real, not slyly apologetic, an identity reflecting the evil past and the present resurrection together.

If Germany remains implicitly on trial for a long time to come, release must come through good works and a demonstrated devotion to democratic ideals and practice. The past cannot be changed, but the future of democracy is in the nation's hands. Perhaps Germany can one day even stand as an example to other new societies of how to win a place in the world by work and the intelligent use of science rather than arms.

There is now a generation that cannot remember the war or Nazism, and in fact finds it difficult to understand them, especially what to it is the incredible degree of Nazi regimentation to which Germans submitted. Maybe it is time for Germans to take a look at how and why their society began, not for the sake of cosmetizing an image, but to make themselves more real in their own eyes. If I may quote "Incident at Vichy," when the Jewish psychoanalyst confronts the self-blaming Austrian prince, "It's not your guilt I want, it's your responsibility." That is to say, to relinquish denial and take to heart the donations of history to one's character and the character of one's people, the most painful but rewarding job a people can undertake.

A Plan for Europe

by Henry A. Kissinger

Henry Kissinger, born in 1923, was assistant to the president for national security from 1969 to 1975 and secretary of state from 1973 to 1975. This essay is reprinted from *Newsweek*, 18 June 1990.

At his meeting with so-called intellectuals in Washington, Gorbachev took me aside to say that a road map for the future was his most important concern. He was right. The upheavals of the past year make the creation of a new structure for European security essential. It must take into account the imminent unification of Germany as well as the de facto collapse of the Warsaw Pact. It has to define America's new relationship with Europe while granting the Soviet Union a serious role in Europe.

Above all, such a design must transcend the euphoria based on personal relationships that surrounded the summit. With all respect for the subtlety of President Bush's conduct, it is important to recall that we have been there before. In 1955, the first postwar summit between Eisenhower and Khrushchev was lauded by The New York Times as follows: "Other men might have played strength against strength. It was Mr. Eisenhower's gift to draw others into the circle of his good will and to modify the attitudes if not the policies of the little band of visitors from the other side of the Elbe." One year later ensued the concurrent crises of Suez and Hungary, and two years after that the Soviet ultimatum over Berlin.

The world has changed dramatically since 1955. The United States has achieved most of the objectives it set for itself then; the Soviet Union is in deep crisis. For opposite reasons, both need a design for a journey from where they are to where they have never been. At the same time, this is likely to be the last summit at which it was possible to discuss the future of Europe without European participation. As Europe becomes politically unified and security concerns less dominant, the special advantage of the superpowers—their nuclear supremacy—will become less and less relevant to the political issues.

This may explain why the discussion on Germany at the summit was so inconclusive. The Soviets, shackled by the categories of the past, advanced a plethora of ideas that have been staples of Soviet foreign policy since the days of Stalin: that Germany join both NATO and the Warsaw Pact; that Germany become neutral; that it remain under the political umbrella of NATO but leave the military organization; that the Soviet Union join NATO; that an all-European security system replace existing alliances. The staleness of these proposals suggests that the Soviets find it hard to abandon their old dream of separating the United States from Western Europe; their number implies that the Soviets are groping for a way out.

The American response has been based on the assumption that in the end the Soviet Union will prefer to preserve NATO because Moscow looks to Washington to act as a restraint on a unified Germany. This is why, together with its allies, the United States has proposed a number of concessions to make the idea of German NATO membership more palatable. Among them: changing the emphasis of NATO to make it a more political institution; imposing a variety of arms limitations on Germany; asking a reunified Germany to provide economic assistance to the Soviet Union; having Germany pay for Soviet troops to remain in present-day East Germany for a specified period; and reducing the number of nuclear forces on German soil.

The loud Soviet expressions of fear, however well founded in the psyche of the Soviet people, are surely not without some design. It is difficult to believe that Soviet leaders in possession of well over 10,000 nuclear warheads and the largest tank force in the world genuinely fear another German attack. And if they do, they would be better off with German forces as a part of NATO, which would surely veto any such preposterous enterprise.

The Bush administration has rightly resisted the effort to organize Europe around the fear of Germany. A policy of isolation would throw Germany back on its own resources. It would repeat its historic tragedy of wandering between two worlds and disquieting both.

Those in the West who fall in with the Soviet definition of the German problem prevent Soviet consideration of realistic alternatives. While in the end the Soviet Union may well settle for a continuation of NATO in its present form, this is clearly not the Soviets' first choice. However remarkable Gorbachev's personality, he is a product of Russian history. And Russian foreign policy, at least since Peter the Great, has been a tale of expansion not only in Europe but to the gates of India and into northern China. Whenever a limit was reached, the Russian empire—under tsar or commissar—relentlessly sought to undermine whatever it had defined as the competing power center: Sweden; the Austro-Hungarian Empire; China; Britain in the Middle East; or the United States after World War II.

Since the days of Stalin, the various Soviet proposals regarding Germany have had one common characteristic: they have sought to sever the organic security link between Europe and the United States and undercut the American military presence. And as soon as the U.S. military presence is removed, the Soviet Union's huge nuclear arsenal and vast remaining tank armies would become strategically dominant. Then a partially recovered Soviet Union could attempt a deal that would keep Germany in check with Soviet nuclear strength while turning Germany into the chief engine of Soviet economic recovery. In this manner, the Soviet Union would have used its weakness to achieve the hegemony over Europe that eluded it when it seemed strong. And America would have acceded to the domination of Eurasia against which it fought two world wars.

Multiple concessions: Accepting the Soviet premise that Germany is the major threat to European security is likely to tempt the Soviets into seeking more ambitious goals than stability. And it would encourage a "compromise" whereby Germany would remain in NATO but NATO would be emasculated through multiple concessions to the Soviet Union. The reluctance to classify the Soviet Union as a potential military threat accentuates that danger. After the summit, the absurd Soviet proposal to join NATO was rejected far too gently with the extraordinary argument that the Soviet Union is not yet a democracy.

In their heart of hearts, Gorbachev and his advisors surely realize that they cannot stop German NATO membership and that their threat to keep troops in East Germany unilaterally is empty. Unification will occur because the so-called German Democratic Republic will dissolve itself into the five states ("Länder") out of which it was formed. Each of them would then seek admission to the Federal Republic under Article 23 of that country's constitution. All existing laws and treaties would apply automatically, including German membership in NATO. A neutral status could come about only through the deliberate destruction of the Atlantic alliance.

Nor does the Soviet Union have a realistic option to keep its troops in East Germany, as Gorbachev has hinted. For one thing, the Warsaw Pact provides that the GDR's obligations to it lapse after Germany is unified. At that point, Soviet forces in East Germany would no longer have any local counterpart to facilitate maneuvers, troop movements and other routine measures. Besides, reverting to the status of conqueror would mortgage Moscow's long-term relationship with a unified Germany.

The most realistic security system therefore would have the following components:

(a) the creation of a neutral belt composed of Poland, Czechoslovakia and Hungary—on the Austrian model;

(b) the creation on both sides of this zone—that is, in the Soviet Union and in Germany—of an area with strict limitations on types of weapons and numbers of men;

(c) special restrictions on the territory of present-day East Germany to ensure that NATO forces are not stationed there. (If Poland preferred to remain in the Warsaw Pact, symmetry could be maintained by prohibiting the stationing of Warsaw Pact forces on its soil.)

In such a scheme, neither side could launch an attack without extensive arms-control violations and military operations across several hundred miles of neutral territory, which would require months of preparation and give ample warning.

Such an approach would be both realistic and comprehensive. It would break the pattern of searching among the various Soviet schemes for the ones that do the least damage—an essentially negative enterprise. Though the Soviet Union is too traumatized by recent events to deviate from the familiar, it may in the end be relieved by an approach that changes the question. However put, a new approach of this kind requires a radical redesign of negotiations on conventional force reductions in Europe.

When these negotiations began, the political dividing line ran through the center of Germany, and Soviet ground forces were assumed to be vastly superior. Since then, the Communist regimes in Eastern Europe have collapsed; most of the new governments have asked the Soviet Union to withdraw its forces. For an interim period, symmetrical reduction of forces will provide a way for the Soviets to withdraw forces without losing face and without creating American obligations that go beyond what the budgetary process is likely to allow. But with every increment of withdrawal, the principle of symmetrical forces will become more firmly established. Arms control runs the risk of permitting more Soviet forces than the East European countries want. Alternatively, it could generate pressures on the United States to withdraw all its forces from Central Europe, thus jeopardizing NATO. This is why the present approach should be abandoned after the completion of the first stage of negotiations in favor of a scheme more in line with existing European political realities.

The design of a new security system for Europe and a new approach to arms control requires the closest consultation and coordination between Western Europe and the United States. In the foreseeable future, Soviet conventional forces will be needed at home. But its nuclear forces remain intact and are preponderant vis-à-vis Europe. Deterring nuclear blackmail requires a new strategy as well as a political relationship based on the premise that European and American destinies are inextricably linked.

European unity is rapidly advancing in the political field and will sooner or later encompass defense. Therefore, the existing institutions for transatlantic dialogue will grow increasingly fragile. At present, military issues are discussed within NATO; political issues will find their focal point in the European Community as Europe moves toward unity. The United States has sought to make German membership in NATO more palatable to the Soviets by hinting at a new political role for NATO. But aside from the difficulty of defining such a role, the proposal runs up against the old European suspicion that the United States is somehow manipulating NATO to undermine Europe's emerging political identity. For in NATO, the United States deals with the European countries individually; the European Community is not represented as an institution.

By the same token, the United States is for all practical purposes excluded from the political deliberations of the European Community. The standard procedure is for the Council of Ministers to convey its conclusions to the United States through a Chairman who rotates every six months. But that foreign minister is in effect an instructed messenger; he has no negotiating flexibility. The best he can do is to transmit the American views to colleagues understandably reluctant to hazard their hard-won consensus. Thus, security issues are relegated to a forum inimical to European identity while political issues are handled in a forum that excludes the United States from meaningful participation.

A solution must be found to permit the European Community to participate in NATO discussions, and for the United States to be heard within the European Community before deliberations harden into formal decisions. Perhaps a new comprehensive treaty between the United States and the European Community will be in order when European unity has sufficiently progressed.

The Soviets are entitled to a meaningful voice in European affairs. But their proposal for a European security system embracing North America, Europe and the Soviet Union to replace existing alliances is better designed to undermine the Atlantic alliance than to establish a forum for cooperation. If everybody agreed on everything, no structure would be necessary. And if they differ, the "system" could dissolve into competing national states. It would in fact come rather close to the map of Europe prior to World War I. Europe would disintegrate in the name of a "common European house."

There are, however, common objectives that unite rather than divide: the environment, worldwide economic growth, cultural exchange, human rights, and confidence-building measures on arms. All these are suitable for the kind of embracing institution Moscow has put forward.

These designs gain even greater relevance against the backdrop of the drama playing itself out inside the Soviet Union. In so fluid a situation, it is reckless to gear policy to one man; the only safe course is to put forward objectives and purposes to which any emerging Soviet leader could relate. The Western democracies will lose their bearings if they focus on personalities and equate amiability with harmony.

Though I am of the view that America has prevailed in the Cold War, I also believe that a new international order can emerge only if neither side claims victory and neither side feels defeated. And the best way to bring this about is to stop the debate about the issues of yesterday and redefine the questions that make up the agenda for the future.

East German Requiem

by Peter Marcuse

Peter Marcuse is professor of urban planning at Columbia
University. He originally wrote this piece for *The Nation,*
22 October 1990.

What remains after forty years of the German Democratic Republic? Three
things: some lessons, a few accomplishments and a different people.

The biggest lesson is what socialism isn't. Only conservatives now use the
word "socialism" to describe East Germany. Most of the left there have
stopped using it altogether; a few still speak of "socialism gone astray." For
those committed to the socialist tradition, it is now clear that state ownership
of the means of production is not a sufficient condition for socialism, though
it may be a necessary one. State ownership in any case is not social ownership.
For socialists, the word "democratic" can never again be uncoupled from the
word "socialist."

The lessons about state planning are more complex. Contrary to the widespread impression in the West, the economy of the G.D.R. was not a total
disaster. Its standard of living was comparable to that of some countries in
the European Economic Community, its recovery from the war and the burden
of reparations was remarkable, and its production of some goods was occasionally impressive. Food, clothing, and shelter were always at least minimally
adequate—and for all. There was no talk of an "underclass," no homeless,
no superrich; social integration was a fact of life (guest workers excepted)
and equality—perhaps too much—was largely achieved (the *nomenklatura* excepted).

In competition with West Germany, the G.D.R. lost. Today, within a unified
Germany, it is a comparative disaster; yesterday, it looked different. And it
avoided the inequalities, the internalized pressures, the unemployment and
economic insecurities that helped make the Federal Republic productive.
Perhaps productivity and its costs need to be re-examined to see where planning, if democratically undertaken, has advantages over a private, profit-driven
market—and where it does not. In some areas, the benefits of a market have
become clear; the concept of a market for choice, but not for the accumulation
of profit, was only beginning to be explored when unification overwhelmed
the discussion.

The accomplishments that formally survive the G.D.R.'s forty years are not
many. Women's rights, in particular to abortion and child care, are stronger

202

in the Federal Republic. Rights to housing, nonspeculative land ownership and public control of city development look very attractive to many Westerners. And the close connection between workplace and nonwork activities—recreation, health care, even shopping—provides some salutary examples for the future. The social net was in general indeed good, if at a level so much lower than that of West Germany that most East German residents would opt for Western benefits over their own. (Full pay in the East was often below unemployment benefits in the West. The East had unemployed, too, said the wags, but they kept their jobs.)

But the most important product of this history are people, people who have been through a different set of experiences, who have lived in a society proclaiming other goals, who have themselves pursued those goals, sometimes with, latterly more often against, the state. The "socialism" that was officially proclaimed was taken seriously by many, especially in the early years. Although many left in disillusionment and more withdrew, the rhetoric remained, and it survives as an articulation of goals. New experiences with the West may cause these goals to resurface in the future. In the West, private property is taken as the natural order of things; in the East, the starting point is public control, and, while its weaknesses have been made apparent, its advantages may seem more and more worth saving as time goes on.

For a brief period, some parties on the left attempted to call on a "national" loyalty of East German citizens. While the appeal touched a nerve, it was quickly overwhelmed by Pan-German nationalism. Yet there is undeniably a difference between residents of the two former states. Rosie Will, a professor of law at Humboldt University, perhaps expressed it best when she spoke of the "consciousness of living in a small country"; my own experience, living for a year in each, was that the self-assurance to the point of arrogance of many West Germans contrasted sharply, and unfavorably, with the self-awareness and skepticism, to the point of an underdog feeling, of most citizens of the G.D.R. Any photograph of West German Chancellor Helmut Kohl standing next to East German Prime Minister Lothar de Maizière illustrates the point. Perhaps one permanent contribution of the forty-year experience of East Germany is that at least 16 million Germans are not among those obsessed with power and dominance, not convinced of their own superiority and absolute rectitude.

Even consumerism, that psychological driving force of the Western economy, may yet play a different role in the East than in the West. True, once the wall was open, some visitors rushed back with six-packs of beer and stereos; the pent-up demand was huge. The trade-off between unlimited consumerism and public welfare, between incessant innovation and social stability, was not then apparent. But the first euphoria is wearing off, with rising unemployment, reduced services and more available but less affordable goods. Some rethinking of the trade-off may now take place.

The people of East Germany have learned the hard way some of the difficulties of central planning, undemocratic government and state ownership. Many in West Germany are aware of the shortcomings of the profit-oriented market, of parliamentary democracy, of private ownership. If a united left, in a united Germany, were willing to reconsider what each has learned, to look for alternatives that are neither real existing socialism nor real existing capitalism but that take something good from each, then the experience of the last forty years might yet leave a positive legacy. But neither blanket condemnation nor blanket defense of either experience is useful. The people of East Germany know better than most what the costs of a closed mind or a closed society can be.

The Attack on Christa Wolf

by Christine Schoefer

Christine Schoefer writes on German politics and culture.
This article first appeared in *The Nation* on 22 October
1990.

Christa Wolf, perhaps the most prominent woman writer in postwar Germany,
is today at the center of a literary and political storm. For more than twenty
years, the West German literary establishment lavished praise on her work
and brimmed with respect for the way she handled her role in authoritarian
East Germany. At the annual book fair in Frankfurt in October 1989 Wolf
was even rumored to be a finalist for the Nobel Prize in Literature.

Last summer, Wolf published a novella, *Was bleibt* ("What Remains"),
chronicling a period in her life when she was under surveillance by the East
German security police. Critics and writers who used to celebrate her work
are using *Was bleibt* to launch an attack on Wolf. They accuse her of cowardice
and opportunism because she had not risked publishing the manuscript, which
lay in her desk drawer for ten years, before the Communist government was
toppled. Their most damaging charge, however, relegates Wolf to the status
of a privileged state poet, a lap dog of the discredited East German regime.

This turnabout of the West German literary establishment, the vehemence
of the attack and the suspicious unity of voices in various media are perplexing,
until they are fit into the larger picture of post-wall German politics. Günter
Grass, the most illustrious of Wolf's few defenders, made this connection
when he cautioned, "We should not repeat in literature that which happens
daily in the political and especially the economic sphere; namely, the colonization of the G.D.R." This "literary" campaign reveals the hidden agenda
of the conservative model of German unification, which is intent not only on
doing away with the Communist East but on erasing the history of the G.D.R.
and the very idea of socialism itself. Wolf is a sacrificial lamb in a larger
project: the ideological shaping of unified Germany.

Why Christa Wolf? The fact that she is a woman may be coincidental. But
it goes without saying that if one of East Germany's most respected writers
is discredited, all East German writers who shared her vision will be silenced.

Wolf belonged to a group of East German writers who defied the Western
dichotomization of artists in Communist countries into "state poets" on the
one hand and "dissidents" on the other. Although she was a Communist Party
member, Wolf repeatedly criticized the policies and priorities of the East

German regime in her work. For years, she drew attention to the official neglect of the individual, criticized the facile treatment of German history, expressed concern about the situation of women and explored the subject of citizens' complicity and acquiescence. In *Cassandra,* she took up the themes of political corruption, intimidation and violence in the larger context of patriarchal power structures. In *Patterns of Childhood* she even suggested parallels between the Communist regime and National Socialism. After her first critical novel, *The Quest for Christa T.,* appeared in 1968, the East German authorities launched a campaign to discredit her as a writer. Wolf continued to publish in East Germany. But her work was printed in small editions, with most copies reportedly distributed directly by the state—to the shredders or to the army. Finding Wolf's books in East German bookstores was a virtual impossibility; more often than not one saw Western editions, which had already passed through many hands.

The difficulty of Wolf's work, which is characterized by a reminiscent and analytical style, limited her readership but not her following. For many East Germans, Wolf's was a voice of integrity, one that represented the vision of a socialism concerned with dignity, justice and tolerance, in opposition to the politics of the Communist Party. Her immense popularity, together with the respect and recognition she had gained in the West, was undoubtedly more important than her party membership in insulating Wolf from outright attacks by the regime. The fact that those circumstances did not prevent her surveillance and intimidation by the security police—as we find out in her latest novella—indicates that Wolf's ambivalent attitude toward the Communist Party was no secret. The charge of "state poet," therefore, deliberately misses the mark. But it strikes an extremely vulnerable spot. A campaign that identifies Wolf with the hated Communist regime is by far the easiest way to mobilize the anger of the East German population against her and destroy Wolf's status as a spokeswoman.

No doubt, Wolf's critical voice helped shape the process of political self-assertion in East Germany long before she began making moving statements to mass audiences at public rallies last autumn. But Wolf was among the first to criticize the unification fervor that so quickly captured the German imagination once authorities opened the wall. Shortly after the wall was opened, she and fellow writer Stefan Heym issued a public appeal to citizens of the G.D.R.: "We still have the chance . . . to develop a socialist alternative to the Federal Republic." Foreseeing the Western tidal wave that has since washed over the G.D.R., she insisted that a slower pace and a period of self-reflection were the only way for East Germans to find an authentic voice. She challenged the assumption that West Germany's political and social order would automatically provide solutions to the problems faced by East Germany. The fact that her great disappointment with the Communist regime did not lead her to abandon completely the idea of a more just social order makes Wolf a potentially strong voice in any opposition movement that may arise in a new united Germany, and must be counted among the reasons for the current campaign against her.

But anticipation of Wolf's critical voice in a united Germany could not alone have fueled a debate as heated as the one around *Was bleibt.* Wolf's refusal to participate in the current political, economic and cultural annexation of the G.D.R. has surely intensified the attack. By styling Wolf as a state poet, critics accomplish in the cultural realm what is already accepted in politics and economics: the facile splitting of East Germans into victims and perpetrators. This categorization distorts the reality of the G.D.R. It simply erases the hundreds of thousands of East Germans whose belief in the ideals of socialism led them to shape niches of freedom within the authoritarian social order, to criticize the regime and finally to revolt against it. Wolf is one of several authors whose work captures the complex reality, the living fabric, the burning questions of East German society. It preserves the German Democratic Republic—in literature. But after October 3, the G.D.R. is supposed to exist only as a nightmare that is best forgotten. Literary chroniclers like Wolf are perceived as a threat by those intent on presenting to the world once and for all a Germany healed not only of its division but of its National Socialist past.

The current effort to westernize East Germany in the process of unification constitutes yet another episode in the all-too-familiar repression of German history: The G.D.R. was, after all, an outcome of Hitler's popularly elected regime and World War II. Wolf's literary delving into the past might therefore uncover some Pan-German skeletons in the closet, jarring Germany's collective memory. A simple intellectual maneuver, however, heads off this possibility. Suddenly, people who never cared much for revealing traces of National Socialism in postwar Germany are finding Hitler's legacy well preserved—in all East German institutions and all Communists, and, by association, in anyone who refuses to abandon all aspects of what might be called an East German identity. "Only now," writes Ulrich Greiner in *Die Zeit,* "has the disaster that began in 1933 reached its final end." This collective psychological ploy projects all responsibility for the ills of German history onto the Communists. But East German Communism was not, no matter what parallels one can find, National Socialism. Political repression, corruption and intimidation in the context of the cold war do not add up to Auschwitz, a fact to which Wolf's work testifies eloquently.

The "literary" campaign against Christa Wolf has the simultaneous effect of discrediting her political message, of erasing facets of East German identity and history that Wolf and authors like her articulate, and of depriving critical East Germans of a potential voice in the united Germany. The near unanimity of Wolf's indictment is part of a larger truth: It is virtually impossible to find any reportage on East Germany that does not subscribe to the conservative agenda. This repression of social, political and historical reality represents a troublesome beginning for the "new" Germany. And in the fact that voices such as Wolf's might finally be silenced only after the Communists are gone, there is an inescapable irony.

Germany: Power and the Left

by Andrei S. Markovits

Andrei S. Markovits is Professor of Political Science at Boston University. This article is reprinted from *Dissent,* Summer 1991.

The momentous events of 1989 and the unification of Germany recast the long-standing debate about Germany's role in a changing Europe. Virtually all the English-language newsweeklies ran cover stories on the new "German question," and academic experts weighed in on the op-ed pages. At the risk of simplification, one can divide these commentaries into two categories: optimists, who viewed unification as a boon to Germany, Europe, and global peace, and pessimists, who were concerned that a strong Germany might repeat past mistakes. The optimists are the majority; but, for understandable reasons, both voices are preoccupied by the legacy of Auschwitz. The optimists have made it their mission to convince their audiences (perhaps even themselves?) that the ingredients that produced Auschwitz have been extirpated by "Modell Deutschland"—West Germany's exemplary democracy. Pessimists on the left worry that the Federal Republic's democratic foundations are not really democratic. Liberals fret that its institutions have never been truly tested in a crisis comparable to the depression of the early 1930s and are thus "fair weather" institutions at best. Conservatives, in turn, judge these structures irrelevant in a world ruled by renewed nationalism. Always cynical about the tenuous nature of the Federal Republic's "constitutional patriotism" (Jürgen Habermas's term), conservatives hope that nationalism will make a credible return as a new political force in a strong Germany, thereby challenging the anemic arrangements of the *Bundesrepublik.*

There is truth in both optimistic and pessimistic claims. Among the Federal Republic's greatest achievements is its eradication of most factors that might engender another Auschwitz. However, the optimists—and the vast majority of Germans—tend to see the future of Germany in Europe through rose-colored glasses, convinced that history—the Auschwitz trauma—now renders them essentially benevolent. Such assertions completely disregard the hegemonic power—resting on economics—already exercised by Germany in Europe. Its future extension is certain. Optimistic liberals and pessimistic conservatives, though from opposite vantage points, all see democratic institutions as mitigating power. But successful democracies, such as Germany's, are powerful because of the consensual nature of their politics and the high productive and distributive efficiency of their markets. Indeed, the adage that Deutsche marks will go much farther than Panzers seems compelling. It is encouraging that a substantial majority of Germans favor a low profile for their country in world affairs, and are, in the *Financial Times*'s words, "peacable, fearful—and Green." Yet, the power already exercised by a united Germany in Europe and beyond cannot be underestimated.

In virtually every aspect of economic life, the Federal Republic has a formidable lead over its nearest Western European competitors. The existence of the European Community (EC) seems to have benefited Germany more than any other country. West Germany's market share in terms of intra-EC exports has consistently grown since the 1970s, rising to nearly 28 percent by 1989. France, the runner-up, has 15.6 percent, and the United Kingdom 11.4 percent. Germany's share is nearly three times that of Italy. Using export prowess as an indicator, there can be little doubt that the Federal Republic in Europe and Japan in expanding parts of Asia have reached hegemonic status. Throughout the 1980s only West Germany had a positive balance of trade among Europe's "big four." Its $208.5 billion surplus for the decade contrasts sharply with the huge deficits incurred by Italy, France, and the United Kingdom. Data corroborate the view that the European Community— at least thus far—has constituted a zero-sum game between Germany and its major rivals. Germany wins what the other three lose.

As a consequence of its singularly advantageous position within the EC, Bonn has been the largest contributor to the community's budget. This makes Germany the major political player inside the EC. The Germans dominate the corridors of the EC headquarters in Brussels. German political prowess was attained quietly and "by doing"—hard committee work—rather than through constant posturing, which has been the French style, or the spoilsport negativism perfected by the British under Thatcher. Moves now under way to make German into the third official working language of the community (along with English and French) symbolize the political reality.

German influence in Eastern Europe is even more pronounced than in the West. In 1989 West Germany led all Western countries in export sales to Eastern Europe, and the figures are dramatic: $21.2 billion for West Germany, followed by Italy with $6.7 billion and $5.8 billion for the United States. In every category listed by the OECD (Organization for Economic Cooperation and Development), West Germany was the leading Western trading partner with Hungary, Poland, Czechoslovakia, Bulgaria, Romania, Yugoslavia, and the Soviet Union. And in each case Germany's trade was, at a minimum, double that of its nearest Western competitor. Germany firms have also taken the lead in forming joint ventures in Eastern Europe and the Soviet Union.

Culture and language are among the most decisive transmitters of economic and political influence. In East-Central Europe, German provided a common cultural bond and a *lingua franca* within the political and cultural elites at least until 1945. Despite its repression under communism, German has been reborn in postcommunist *Mitteleuropa*. This region wants to become European again—that is, Western, but in a commercial rather than cultural sense. East-Central Europeans are now learning German in order to converse with Siemens and Volkswagen, not to read Goethe and Schiller.

Precisely at this moment of national ascendance, the German left finds itself in one of its most serious crises since 1945. Although this malaise is in good part due to Germany's new power, it also stems from internecine battles that contributed to a certain loss of purpose and vision. The unique burden of Germany's past further exacerbates the left's malaise by complicating its relationship to such contemporary issues as nationalism.

December 2, 1990, witnesses the nadir of the German left. Its most important institutional representative, the Social Democratic party (SPD), lost the third national election in a row (1983, 1987, 1990). Its support in the western part of the country declined perilously close to 30 percent. True, the SPD won 23.6 percent in what was East Germany, a 3 percent gain over its March 1990 showing there (in the only democratic election ever held in the GDR—the German "Democratic" Republic). But East Germany was the SPD's cradle, and in such pre-1933 strongholds as Saxony and Thuringia voters gave the party only 15.1 percent and 17.5 percent, respectively. For the Greens, the left's other parliamentary representatives, December 2 ignominiously ended a decade of gains. Founded in 1980 as an "ecological, social, grass-roots democratic, nonviolent" movement, the Greens were arguably the New Left's most important political legacy in the advanced capitalist world. On December 2 they collapsed at the polls.

These setbacks reveal a deep identity crisis. The left is haunted by its memory of the 1950s, when the Christian Democrats were dominant and the SPD was politically "ghettoized" and excluded from power. In 1959 it responded with a dramatic change in direction: the SPD's Bad Godesberg Congress shed Marxism in favor of Keynesianism. Today, a new Bad Godesberg may be required, although perhaps not quite as dramatic.

Identity crises result, in part, from success. Social democracy's difficulties in Germany, indeed across Europe, come from its acceptance by much of the continent's political class. The fact that Helmut Kohl never attempted to pursue anything vaguely resembling Thatcherism or Reaganism has much to do with the successful integration of social democratic values into the mainstream of West German politics.

The SPD was caught between an Old Left insistence on growth and productivism and a New Left assertion of grass-roots democracy and anti-authoritarianism. In power in the 1970s, social democracy successfully expanded the state sector, introduced educational reforms, and spawned a general liberalization of West German public life. Ironically, this atmosphere helped to create the Greens just as much as did the SPD's failure to respond to the country's energy problems and demands for "new" politics.

The Greens also have a crisis of identity as a result of success. Polls convincingly demonstrate that in the course of the 1980s a majority of West Germans became "green" in attitude, though not "Green" at the ballot box. All three establishment parties (Christian, Free, and Social Democrats) developed strong proecology positions, became advocates of women's rights, and were defenders of disarmament and detente during the last few years. One of the Federal Republic's leading commentators aptly characterized the Greens as "soluble fertilizers on the fields of the classical parties."

One component of the left's identity crisis may be called the postnational consciousness of virtually all the Greens and much of the SPD. One by-product of the Federal Republic's westernization and bourgeoisification was the emergence of a broad milieu of intellectuals devoid of nationalist sentiments—people who are first and foremost "federal republican." Being a German nationalist—in any shape or form—simply became unacceptable for West German leftists, especially after the belated discovery of the Holocaust in the 1960s and the immense impact of the student revolt of the late 1960s, known in Germany as "1968." Indeed, it was at this time—and not immediately after World War II—that much of the West German left developed the notion that the country's permanent division was a just penalty for Auschwitz.

Oskar Lafontaine, the SPD candidate for chancellor last year, is a product of this milieu. Hence, he was simply no match for Helmut Kohl and Hans-Dietrich Genscher in an election that was dominated by the national question (even though it was surprisingly muted in nationalist fervor). It was obvious to all that the Social Democrats and the Greens were uncomfortable addressing the national dimension of German unity. Instead, they harped on its costs, which did not endear them to East Germans and provided insufficient appeal in the West. In short, the left's history rendered it unprepared to address unification on an equal footing with the right. To most West German leftists, the GDR—while certainly no model—had become at least acceptable, if not commendable.

It should come as no surprise that many West German leftists, including a substantial segment of the SPD's left wing, remain profoundly unsettled about the disappearance of the GDR. Their discomfort mixes anger, embarrassment, and nostalgia and seems explainable only through a larger, unhappy context. In the eyes of some in the West German left, the GDR was unequivocally the morally superior of the two German states: it was the first "socialist" experiment on German soil and embodied the only genuine break with the Nazi past. This lent a particular legitimacy to the GDR, a legitimacy bestowed by the left on few other countries, save in the Third World. The GDR's dictatorial ways and bureaucratic repression were criticized, but they paled beside the achievement of a truly antifascist society via the abolition of capitalism. Though poorer than the West and more repressive, the East was perceived to be an experiment worthy in principle if flawed in practice. After all, the GDR claimed the legacy of Marx, Engels, Liebknecht, Luxemburg, Thaelmann, and Brecht in a land where Hitler had ruled not long ago.

This perception of the GDR is linked to the political fate of the left inside the Federal Republic. Until the late 1960s, virtually all West German discourse was engulfed by an anticommunism that often bordered on outright hysteria. In no other European country did anticommunism serve to affirm the existing order as forcefully as in the Federal Republic of Germany. Much of the West German left—led by the Social Democratic party—shared this antipathy for everything communist throughout the 1950s and much of the 1960s.

The year 1968 changed this both "from above" and "from below." It marked the intellectual origins of social democracy's *Ostpolitik*—a policy that, in the long term, contributed decisively to Leninism's eventual collapse. One of *Ostpolitik*'s contradictions was best described by its political architect, Willy Brandt: "In order to shake up the status quo politically, we had to accept the status quo territorially." As for the changes "from below"—little in West German public and private life remained untouched by the challenges posed by the New Left. Concentrated in Berlin, Frankfurt, and a number of university towns, the '68ers created an extraparliamentary movement that confronted all German institutions, including social democracy. Initially operating against social democracy, the New Left was in good part transformed by social democracy's reforms during the 1970s, which led to an uneasy symbiosis between the New Left's successors—the new social movements—and an SPD that, in turn, had become radicalized by its contacts with these movements. The interaction between social democracy, the New Left, and its successors also changed the earlier adherence by the left—and by the general public—to traditional anticommunism. In the course of the 1970s the SPD and much of the West German left tempered its anticommunism and came to accept the GDR. The '68ers were much more critical of the GDR's communism than some of the Greens and a good portion of the SPD would be later. At the same time, they were equally opposed to the repressive aspects of Bonn's anticommunism. Whatever the rivalry between Social Democratic "reformism from above"—the SPD led the government from 1969 to 1982—and its extraparliamentary challengers "from below," both contributed to broad leftist milieu in which public criticism of the GDR became taboo. This "anti-anticommunism" was challenged only periodically by some daring Greens, but virtually never within the SPD, excepting some pockets of the party's right wing.

Unification upset the left's equilibrium. For a decade, the values of "old" and "new" politics had contended with each other. Just when the "new" priorities triumphed, enter the old GDR. Questions of feminism and ecology were again overwhelmed by bread-and-butter issues. Jobs, growth, energy, and investment all had to be debated again. In the united Germany of the 1990s, East Germany's 1950s-style materialism will undoubtedly challenge West Germany's 1980s-type postmaterialism as the left seeks a new identify.

Finally, a generational factor also helps explain the West German left's discomfort with unification. Surveys show that many young West Germans perceived the GDR as considerably more foreign than Holland, Austria, Switzerland, or even Italy. In other words, the division of Germany and Bonn's successful integration into Western Europe diluted identification with the GDR in favor of cultural empathy with other Western countries. In fact, the contemporary West German left is very much a creature of West Germany's successful integration into Europe. This has led, among other things, to an intellectual and experiential distancing of the left from Eastern Europe on a number of levels.

In recent decades the German left has been, by and large, uninterested in Eastern Europe's dissidents. The contrast with the French and Italian left could not have been more stark—at least in this area. The SPD and trade unions have an especially ignominious record. Mention of the Soviet invasion of Afghanistan—even in a "politically correct" combination with the U.S. involvement in Central America—was repeatedly shunned by one of the trade unions' main youth organizations. A leading activist (who was prominent in the leftist Media, Printers' and Writers' Union) condemned any union member who protested the dissolution of the Polish writers' union. The Polish union, he declared, was a "fifth column," which undermined "socialism." Some of his colleagues called KOR, the organization of Polish intellectuals associated with Solidarity, "a questionable organization which transforms Solidarity into a political resistance movement." Many unionists and Social Democrats railed against the "Catholic-reactionary" nature of Solidarity (in 1981, *not* 1991). One member of the media union went so far as to compare Polish unionists to Hitler's storm troopers.

Tacit approval of the communist status quo in Eastern Europe reached the highest echelons of the West German Social Democratic hierarchy in a bizarre—though telling—incident in December 1981. SPD Chancellor Helmut Schmidt spent a sequestered weekend consulting with GDR chief Erich Honecker—in the latter's country house—while General Jaruszelski's troops were imposing martial law in neighboring Poland. Schmidt was not sufficiently disturbed by the events to break off the meeting.* The neglect of Eastern

---

* Friends of mine who attended an anti-Jaruszelski demonstration that Sunday in Frankfurt were not surprised by the low turnout in a town known for the political activism of its sizable leftist subculture. Except for some anarchists and Trotskyists, most of the left stayed home. This would not have been the case had it involved comparable developments in Central America or other parts of the Third World, including Iraq, of course.

Europe by the German left led to an understandable mistrust by East Europeans of the German left. At the celebrations of Willy Brandt's seventy-sixth birthday in December 1989 in Berlin, Pavel Kohut declared that "you [Social Democrats] will yourselves have to analyze why you dropped us in the 1970s, and why you allied not with the beaten but with the beaters, or at best stayed neutral." The German left carries a heavy burden concerning Eastern Europe.

Looking West, we find problems of a somewhat different nature. One legacy of the "new" left is a tendency to frown on large-scale projects. Consequently, the German left has been rather uninterested in Europe '92. The Greens, in particular, exhibit substantial hostility toward the project. They have articulated the conventional (and largely correct) criticisms of the plans for a unified internal European market as a distant, overly bureaucratized, dehumanizing, and capitalist megamachine that will trample everything in its way. However, I have yet to see any comprehensive proposal from the German left that could even vaguely serve as a useful political strategy for these fundamentally new conditions. The unions seem completely preoccupied with defending the economic interests of their members and are fearful of a challenge to their position from the working classes of Europe's southern rim. Moreover, they have also been confronted with the onerous tasks of integrating the increasingly worried workers of the former GDR into a new union structure. This unexpected development demanded the unions' full attention and further diluted their lukewarm commitment to Europe '92. The extreme negativity of the Greens may render them peripheral to the entire debate on Europe's future. And the Social Democrats are once again caught between residues of their "old" left fixation on growth and their "new" left negation of growth and everything related to it. For too much of the German left, endless hearings in the committees of the Brussels-based Eurocracy—concerning issues like the standardization of measurements across the continent—seem boring and irrelevant to the "big picture." The German left is consequently largely absent from the trenches while European capitalism is dramatically reorganized. Its warnings that Europe '92 means a "Europe of capital" may become a self-fulfilling prophecy.

Finally, the German left harbors a fundamental mistrust of power and leadership as a consequence of the Nazi past. Although commendable in many ways, it can also lead to irresponsibility. This became evident in the process of unification, when many Social Democrats, and especially Greens, simply refused to accept a reality that contradicted their image of what should have been—and because this reality demanded forthright leadership from them. Had the Social Democrats recognized that unification—not a two-state solution—was the name of the game as of January 1990 and had they assumed a posture of leadership, German unity might not have become the exclusive preserve of the conservatives. The SPD and the Greens were reactive when they could and should have been active in shaping unity from the very beginning. A similar predicament pertains to Europe. Again the left seems resigned to accept the role of post hoc critic instead of vigorous creator. In fact, the German left has much to contribute in the formation of this new Europe. By virtue of Germany's hegemonic position its left has—despite itself—become Europe's most influential left. Its Social Democratic party, now led by the quiet but very capable Bjoern Engholm—a centrist—remains the dominant force in the Socialist International and on the European scene. Engholm is the SPD's fifth postwar leader (following Schumacher, Ollenhauer, Brandt, and Vogel) and gained national attention by leading the party to impressive successes in the state of Schleswig-Holstein. Although he belongs to the same "restless" generation inside the party as Oskar Lafontaine and Gerhard Schroeder, Engholm seems to be both temperamentally and strategically a conciliator. This is exactly what the party needs. Lafontaine's confrontational style and imperious personality were too divisive for a movement encumbered by serious identity problems. Engholm's quiet confidence will provide the party with fine leadership while at the same time offering it some respite from the frenzied conflicts of the recent past. Once the party is able to adjust to the fact that it operates in an enlarged Federal Republic in a completely new Europe, it will experience an electoral revival similar to the one that boosted it into power in the late 1960s. The absence of the West German Greens from the Bundestag during the following term should give the Social Democrats a much-needed breathing space. They can safely claim to be the sole parliamentary representatives of the left. Unlike in the 1980s, the Greens won't be able to upstage them. If the SPD's elites shed their unification phobia and develop a viable strategy for the new Europe (and, of course, the new Germany), Social Democrats could recapture power before the end of the century.

The Greens, too, can put their identity crisis to good use. Local and state contests after December's Bundestag election have demonstrated that the Greens will remain a permanent political force in Germany. Their disappearance from the federal level is a temporary phenomenon due mainly, though not solely, to the specific circumstances of unification. If the Greens can curtail the internecine battles that have disrupted them so often, they can re-enter the Bundestag in 1994. But both parties must recognize that German—and European—politics in the 1990s will differ dramatically from the previous four decades. Germany is no longer "merely" an economic giant and a political dwarf. It is a new and very powerful country in a new Europe no longer divided into East and West. True, many of the past markings that defined the identity of the German left still remain—relations vis-à-vis the Soviet Union, and the United States, the problems of capitalism and socialism. The surroundings, however, have changed significantly. It was one thing to be the progressive force in a smaller Federal Republic of Germany tied to the United States. It is entirely different to play this role in a united Germany within a transformed, and still changing, Europe. A new self-perception and a new strategic presence are required. *Ostpolitik,* to take one example, will no longer mean accommodation with a formidable communist foe for largely instrumental reasons and purposes of temporary detente. Instead, it will denote the projection of German power in an economically fragile and politically volatile part of an otherwise wealthy and stable continent. A new era in German politics has begun; the future of the German left will depend on its ability to adjust and innovate.

United Kingdom

Beware, the Reich Is Reviving

by Conor Cruise O'Brien

Conor Cruise O'Brien, born in 1917, is a writer, journalist, and politician. He was editor of the London *Observer* from 1978 to 1981, and in 1973–77 was minister for posts and telegraphs in the Republic of Ireland. This article appeared in the *Times* on 31 October 1989.

President Bush last week "reaffirmed" US support of Germany. Given the circumstances, it was more like a declaration than a reaffirmation. Until recently, US support for reunification has been vague and theoretical. In the days of Stalin, Khruschev and Brezhnev, German reunification was not on any serious political agenda, because pursuit of it was thought to risk precipitating a third world war.

But today, with the abandonment of Moscow's interventionist policy in Eastern Europe, German reunification is not only on the agenda but moving towards the top of it. Bush's "reaffirmation" was, in reality, a warning to Britain and France that the US would oppose efforts on their part to put obstacles in the way of reunification.

Understandably, made as it was in the week of Nigel Lawson's resignation, the statement attracted little interest here. But its significance should not be under-estimated. For it marks a stage in the two great interacting world-historical processes which will be seen to dominate the closing decades of our century: the dissolution of the Soviet empire and German reunification. The two together are likely to result in the advent of a German economic hegemony extending from the Aran islands off the west coast of Ireland to Vladivostok.

The British, the French and Europeans generally are right to feel deep disquiet at the prospect. Indeed, a report in the *International Herald Tribune* at the weekend, suggests that this disquiet is shared by some thoughtful Germans: "Mr. Bush's comments, publicly welcomed with enthusiasm in West Germany, got a mixed reception from some advisers of Mr. Kohl, who said they feared the Bush comments might fuel expectations of the unification on the far right in West Germany."

But neither West Europeans nor the more cautious among the Germans can avert reunification. The only people who *may* be able to do that are the rulers of the Soviet Union, who could prevent it by sending tanks into East Germany. That seems to be ruled out by the new non-interventionist policy. But is it really impossible? Might not the new policy be repealed once the Soviet people discover that it means reunification of Germany?

In these conditions of unexampled instability, one can only guess, and my own guess is that the Soviet Union will not intervene because it cannot. It is in the midst of an existential crisis which extends to every aspect of Soviet life, including the armed forces.

It now seems that more than half of the Soviet Union's citizens—almost all the non-Russians and large numbers of the Russians—don't want to be Soviet citizens at all. Moscow has its hands full trying to hold the Soviet Union together, and so had perforce to keep those hands off Eastern Europe. By publicly allowing the countries of Eastern Europe to go their own ways, it is only making a virtue of necessity.

If this view of the Soviet Union is correct, then German reunification is now inevitable. We are on the road to the Fourth Reich: a pan-German entity, commanding the full allegiance of German nationalists, and constituting a focus for national pride.

The First Reich was that founded in AD 800 by Karl der Grosse, known to the West as Charlemagne. It was dissolved in 1806, at the behest of Napoleon. Germany then remained a state in dissolution until the advent of the Second Reich, that of the Hohenzollerns, in 1871. The Second Reich was destroyed in 1918, and the Weimar Republic was substituted for it, by the victorious foreigners. And when the Third Reich was destroyed in 1945, new political institutions were once more imposed on the Germans by victorious foreigners.

This is history from a German nationalist point of view, and we are sure to hear a lot more of it before long. Reunification will be celebrated with an explosion of nationalist enthusiasm, and a rejection of everything thought to have been imposed on Germany: the Democratic Republic along with West Germany; NATO along with the Warsaw Pact. Once Germany is reunited, by agreement between the governments of the two existing German republics, it will demand the termination of the state of occupation and the evacuation of all remaining foreign troops. These demands will be met. Berlin will become the capital of a united Germany.

In the new, proud, united Germany, the nationalists will proclaim the Fourth Reich, for while the term *Reich* is associated with victory and periods of German ascendancy, *Republik* is associated with defeat and the ascendancy of alien values. I would expect a revived German to bring back the black-white-red flag of the Hohenzollerns, and possibly a Hohenzollern Kaiser to go with it. Before the Fourth Reich can formally be proclaimed, however, there will have to be some cleansing of the image of the Third Reich. Nationalist intellectuals will set about that task with a will. It will require the rehabilitation of National Socialism and of Adolf Hitler, but so much the better from a German nationalist point of view: Germans have spent too long grovelling to foreigners about all that; now Germany will get off its knees.

The main front for the counter-attack will be "racial science." Books by eminent German geneticists will pour from the presses, aiming to show that racial science is truly scientific, that efforts to discredit it are a Jewish trick, and that the racial policies of the Nazis—up to and including the Holocaust— were correct and far-sighted. With the Holocaust, we will be told, that great man Adolf Hitler left the German nation its most precious heritage, racial purity.

Nationalist intellectuals will explain that true Germans should feel not guilt but pride about the Holocaust, that great courageous and salutary act. The self-awarded "not guilty" verdict will be welcomed by the German public, and I can see some of the consequences: expulsion of Jews, breaking off of relations with Israel; a military mission to the PLO; a statue of Hitler in every town . . .

What else might follow. I don't know. But I fear that the Fourth Reich, if it comes, will have a natural tendency to resemble its predecessor.

Two Germanys Don't Add Up

by Harold James

Harold James, born in 1956, is the author of *A German Identity* (1989) and one of the editors of this volume. These articles appeared in the *Sunday Telegraph* on 3 December 1989 and 11 February 1990.

The unification of the two Germanys is now an historical inevitability. This is not just a matter of superpower logic: of the interest President Gorbachev has in a dramatic political gamble that might destroy NATO and detach an economically powerful Europe from the United States and bring it closer to the Soviet Union. There is also a compelling economic logic to the unification process. The fact is that the current situation—with complete freedom of movement across the frontier—cannot remain for very long. The Germans just cannot go on meeting like this.

Already many East Germans are looking for jobs in border areas, and especially in West Berlin, while continuing to live in subsidised rental accommodation in the East. This may be less humiliating to Egon Krenz and his colleagues than a large-scale relocation of people, but the results are equally devastating. The already severe labour shortage will become much more acute. Raising wages in the East, and perhaps even paying them in Western currency, will be the only solution. But most East German factories will not be able to do this because they operate at low productivity levels on out-dated equipment. Only a handful of prestige enterprises, such as Zeiss at Jena or the Meissen porcelain works, will be able to make the readjustment without substantial infusions of new Western technology.

Most East German factories are less like Zeiss and more like the sad example of the steel-mills at Eisenhüttenstadt, which use imported Polish coal and Soviet ore, and exist only for the ideological reason that a workers' state cannot be without a heavy industrial sector. Or the television factory that makes sets as heavy as possible because plants were once rewarded on the basis of the weight of their output.

When plants like these fail to raise additional sums to pay the new wages, and close down, the result will be a sudden surge in unemployment, which will appear terrifying in a society that has always prided itself on avoiding the insecurity that characterised capitalist regimes. This is a recipe for political collapse. The only possible way out would be to attract large numbers of Western firms to establish new and modern plants in the East. There is certainly a substantial business potential, and the new airline flights between Leipzig and West German cities testify to the curiosity of Western business-men. Several companies, including Thyssen and Volkswagen, have expressed an interest, but are not prepared to act in the uncertainty of present conditions. Politics would have to become much more stable for the foundations of a second German economic miracle to be laid.

This situation should not be surprising to anyone with a memory of the past. It was a similar dilemma in 1961 that led Ulbricht to put up the Wall in the first place. The only difference twenty-eight years later is that the two economies have moved yet further apart, and the technology gap between the two has become even more painfully obvious. The Democratic Republic is often said to be the centre of East bloc electronics and information technology, but the majority of computer systems are fifteen years behind those used in Western Europe.

However, the East now no longer has the 1961 option of sealing itself off with a wall. November 9, 1989, represents a genuinely irreversible act. But without the Wall, East Germany's economy will simply collapse and bring down any regime—not just a communist one—associated with it. Liberals or social democrats could not make the old-fashioned factories competitive; and even Ludwig Erhard could not run the GDR's economy right now.

The same instant bankruptcy would arise in Poland if, say, it were located next to the United States and people could flow freely every day across the border. The proximity of Poland to the free market in West Berlin is already enough to impose a major strain on Polish policy-makers and to make liberalisation much harder.

If the East cannot resurrect the Wall, then the imminent economic collapse of the GDR will compel the West German Government to take some very drastic measures. Offering more generous credits to the East, which for most of the 1980s was how West Germany propped up the GDR, will no longer be sufficient. The West would have to tackle the labour question: stop the free flow of people, forbid employment to East Germans, and end the availability of social security and medical services to those coming from the GDR. In short, Bonn would have to end the automatic right to West German citizenship for Easterns.

There is no doubt that such measures would be illegal and unconstitutional. They violate the Preamble of the West German Basic Law, which declares that West Germany is only a provisional state pending the free self-determination of all Germans. Even if all parties agreed on revising a Basic Law, the process of building a judicial wall against the East would take much longer than building a physical wall; and in practice no one could afford to erect the equivalent of the Wall that Eastern politicians have just agreed to demolish. And without the Wall, the economic self-destruction of any political entity in East Germany is an inevitability.

At present the West German parties are not being realistic about the catastrophe that is hitting East Germany. Even Chancellor Kohl's ten-point plan for German unification via confederation is much too cumbersome and not nearly fast enough. It simply does not recognise the way in which a socialist command economy is blown apart by the winds of the market.

German parties and politicians have a responsibility that arises out of the collapse of their neighbour. Although some West Germans may wish otherwise, their country cannot legally deny citizenship to the mass of East Germans who will continue to move west as long as Germany remains divided. Their only response can be unification: not for grand international or European reasons, not because of the possibility of a superpower trade-off or because of the yearnings of the German soul, but because unification is an economic necessity.

West Germany's Green Imperialism

by Harold James

The international order is now extraordinarily uncertain and unstable. Since most newspaper headlines deal with events that one year ago would have seemed like flights of fancy, there is an open field for the propagation of political dreams and utopian fantasies. There are a great many patent solutions around.

Ours is apparently the end of the age of empire: the end of the communist empire and at the same time the end of the Russian empire. Russia was the only one of the great multinational empires to survive the First World War, and it survived because the old regime was taken over by a new imperial ideology, Marxism-Leninism.

In the Potsdam-Yalta world, small nation states that had been the fulfilment of nineteenth-century dreams disappeared into the imperial security calculations of Soviet power. Now they are back again, and nations are the focus of political activity. In making the East European revolutions, national symbols played a central part. There was the Black Madonna of Czestochowa, the Crown of St Stephen, even Empress Zita's funeral, Wenceslas Square and the Brandenburg Gate. National heroes from the past—such as a Masaryk or a Pilsudski—come into modern debates. The Lithuanian Communist Party now treats Mr Gorbachev as a distinguished foreign visitor.

This world of nations is comforting, because nations are a much more appropriate forum for political activity, and can engage loyalties and allegiance even in a period of tremendous upheaval and distress. And we can be certain that the transition from state-controlled, centrally planned economies to decentralised liberal markets will bring just such traumatic disturbance.

Those worried about the political future, however, should contemplate the possibility of a revival of imperial thoughts and longings that might interfere with the vision of what General de Gaulle saw as a *Europe des patries.*

Empires are created not just out of power political motives, out of a lust for sheer expansion, but because powerful ideas seem to hold out ways of improving the general human lot. In the minds of classical 19th-century liberal imperialists, education and moral uplift for the rest of the world were human imperatives. In the early 20th century the Bolsheviks believed that they would improve the condition of workers everywhere. The modern idea that captures the mind of well-thinking people everywhere is environmental protection.

It is also an idea that played a part in the East European trauma. There was a national awakening in the aftermath of the Pope's first Polish visit of 1979; but there was also a great environmental stirring in the aftermath of Chernobyl in 1986.

In East Europe, ecological collapse is quite close; in the denuded forests of northern Czechoslovakia and southern Poland, in the blackened crumbling buildings of Cracow, the acid rain from the chimneys of Nowa Huta. For years in the early 1980s, the most sensitive hard information that dissidents in Hungary and Poland could reveal related to the environment and its human cost. In Poland, Dr Marek Okulski produced alarming data showing how the age-specific mortality figures revealed increases in cancers and fatal circulatory disease that followed from industrial pollution.

In the GDR today the most immediate and pressing of the multitude of apparently insuperable economic problems is the electricity supply. The brown coal-burning plants are spectacularly polluting; while the major nuclear reactor near Greifswald is unsafe and has in the past (in 1976) come close to blowing up. The consequence is that East Germany will need to be dependent on West German electricity.

Now air and water pollution are obviously international and not national problems. When it comes to European conservationism, the Germans are self-consciously progressive. They also suffer from Eastern pollution: West Berlin has Eastern smog, and the Bavarian Forest dying trees. In consequence, Germans will try to impose higher standards on the rest of Europe, and particularly on their East European neighbours.

In the short term, the costs of such an operation would be astronomical. They will add considerably to the expense of the transition from central planing to free market, because even the usable industrial plant will be condemned as unsafe. East European industry will be condemned as unsafe, and its workers will be unemployed.

For West Europeans, the choice will be between living in relative harmony with a polluting Eastern Europe at least for the time being; or imposing Western standards. The environment in this picture will play the role that in the past was taken by disputes about the mistreatment of national minorities: it will become the major pretext or cause for the intervention of one nation in the affairs of another.

Some people have been worried to the point of hysteria about the possibility of the resurgence of German militarism. That is an unlikely proposition. But it is not at all impossible that conscientious Germans in white coats and with test tubes will take the paths once trod by the jackboots, and that this will waken old national hatreds.

Particularly should the ecologically minded Social Democrat Oskar Lafontaine become German Chancellor, Germany will take a much sterner line on the international environment. It will demand the closure of unsafe and polluting factories, and make the flow of much-needed investment dependent on progress in the quality of air and water.

This may not be bad for the world, any more than is heavy-handed US insistence on the preservation of Brazilian tropical rain forests. But it will create great resentments in those countries in Eastern Europe with closed factories unable to live up to Western norms.

The Eastern Europeans will feel that they are being made to pay the price for a world problem, suffering for the ecological sins of the communists and the ecological obsessions of the capitalists. The national and democratic revolutions will come into conflict with an international ecological movement, which in its high-mindedness threatens to become a new imperialism demanding the sacrifice to its cause of every other value.

Germans Lack the Key to Their National Identity

by Ralf Dahrendorf

Sir Ralf Dahrendorf was born in Germany in 1929, and took British nationality in 1988. He is the author of *Class and Class Conflict* (1959), *Society and Democracy in Germany* (1966), and is currently warden of St. Antony's College, Oxford. This essay was published in the *Independent* on 13 April 1990.

The German problem of 1990 has to do with money and with identity, both shrouded in dreams and delusions. Perhaps the East Germans will rise up again, once they discover that instead of voting for unity on 18 March they have elected a government bent on recreating their non-existent state and on engaging in endless national and international negotiations. (In fact, East Germans do not need to rise—they can simply pack up and leave, as 5,000 are still doing each week.) West Germans, on the other hand, seem more worried than pleased about the prospect of unity. They are worried about the value of the Deutschmark, jobs and housing. Oskar Lafontaine, the Social Democrat candidate for Chancellor in this year's elections, is unlikely to win, but he has caught the mood of many with his insistence that social achievements in both Germanys must not be jeopardised.

There are also some in West Germany, many of them intellectuals, who do not like the whole idea of unification. In part, they mirror international concern about a possible revival of a greater German nationalism, but they also fear a "return of the 1950s"—in the sense of an extended rule by centre-right governments hell-bent on economic growth and hostile to matters of the mind. Some fear both. The social scientist, Jürgen Habermas, recently wrote, for example, about the threat of "D-Mark nationalism."

Two conclusions are drawn from these concerns. Some want to use unification to make the changes that they have been unable to bring about at home. They want the East Germans to demand the "right to work," an environmental commitment and certain social guarantees as a part of the package. Others stress the need to keep the process of German unification "firmly embedded" in the process of European unification.

Dreams and delusions, indeed. The historian Harold James has pointed out that German unity was always driven either by economic interest or by cloudy

230

visions. Between the two, the key to national identity fell into a deep black hole.

In other nations, institutions fill this hole. When Americans talk about their country, they talk about the Constitution—however much they may like their wealth and the more sentimental symbolism of the flag and the American dream. In Britain, the country is of course about hope and glory, but it is the sovereignty of the Queen in Parliament that matters.

Germans who think about their nation almost never consider its institutions. There were rare exceptions. In 1848, national liberalism combined the desire to create a nation with that to create a constitution. But today there is little pride in the Basic Law, which has served the Federal Republic so well for the last 41 years.

What is wrong about economic interest, or indeed about the desire to feel at home? Are they not motives for joining forces with "significant others" that deserve as much support as any? Perhaps, but questions remain. Economic success comes and goes. It is a shaky ground on which to build a (German) nation, or a (European) community for that matter. Life may be nice as long as it is a positive-sum game from which everyone benefits. However, if our countries are just fine-weather communities, we are in for trouble. After all, institutions are supposed to protect us when the weather turns bad. The great depression of 1929–1932 was the test of Western democratic constitutions, and very few countries passed it.

The question of "identity" is even more vexing. Do we have to feel at home in our country? The Lithuanians believe that they must, and who would criticise them for it? However, identity without a clear sense of institutions brings problems. It may lead usurpers to claim that they represent what everyone feels. It may even turn whole countries into usurpers who define themselves by making demands on others. Those who are lucky enough to be able to define their identity clearly—usually with the help of geography or history, or both—probably do not realise what it means to be a German, or a Pole, or even a Russian who realises that he or she is not just a Soviet. People who are worried about their identity are also worrying. They tend to become aggressive or protectionist, sometimes both.

In a sense, all this is a comment on the European Community as well as on Germany. Margaret Thatcher is often criticised for her hesitant approach towards Europe. Her critics are right if their concern is that Britain may miss the "tide of history", as Michael Heseltine put it in his *Challenge of Europe,* which "has carried us close to Europe's shore." He adds: "We should accept that destiny; the wind will never be more favourable."

Mrs. Thatcher is right in insisting, however, that Britain's record in accepting decisions by the EC as binding is good. Precisely because this country has a sense of institutional commitment, it is a better European in a sense than those countries that love beautiful phrases but quickly turn their backs on ideals when vested interests are at stake. Did Helmut Kohl think of Europe, when he presented his ten-point programme on German unity to the West German Parliament on 28 November 1989, or when he campaigned in East Germany before the elections of 18 March?

Many conclusions follow from such considerations, but two are pre-eminent. One is that the course of German unity leaves room for concern, because it will come about for the wrong reasons. Once again, the motivation will not be constitutional but economic and ideological. The result is more instability than anyone would want.

The second conclusion is that we must ensure the EC proceeds in the right manner. It is all very well to seek common policies that are economically useful and to praise the European idea. But the reality of Europe will be institutional, or it will not be at all. In retrospect I regret my doubts of the plans Altiero Spinelli, former European Commissioner for Industry, had for a European Constitution. He may not have chosen the right moment, but his idea was right.

What the PM Learnt About the Germans

by Charles Powell

Charles Powell, born in 1941, was in the British diplomatic service and in the Foreign Office from 1963 to 1984,
when he became private secretary to the Prime Minister
(Mrs. Margaret Thatcher). He attended a meeting at
Chequers, the Prime Minister's country residence, on 24
March 1990 with Mrs. Thatcher and six leading authorities on German politics and history: Timothy Garton Ash
(author of *The Polish Revolution: Solidarity 1980–82,* as well
as a book on the GDR, and a prolific newspaper and
journal writer), Professor Gordon Craig (author of *The
Germans*), Lord Dacre (the historian Hugh Trevor-Roper,
author of *The Last Days of Hitler*), Professor Fritz Stern
(author of *Dreams and Delusions*), Professor Norman Stone
(author of a biography of *Hitler*), and George Urban (a
writer and former director of Radio Free Europe). This
memorandum provided a record of the discussion, but it
was not sent to the academic participants. It was leaked
to *The Independent on Sunday* and to *Der Spiegel* in the
wake of a dispute about Mrs. Thatcher's attitude to Europe and to Germany occasioned by an unusually frankly
anti-German interview given by her Secretary of State for
Industry, Nicholas Ridley, who was obliged to resign as
a consequence of the "Ridley Affair."

Introduction

The Prime Minister said that Europe had come to the end of the postwar
period. Important decisions and choices about its future lay ahead. She herself
had a number of crucial meetings in the weeks ahead, with President Bush,
President Gorbachev, and Chancellor Kohl, as well as an informal EC Summit.
In all of these, German unification would be the main issue. We needed to
reach an assessment of what a united Germany would be like. History was a
guide, but one could not just extrapolate. We also had to devise a framework
for Europe's future, taking account of German unification and the sweeping
changes in the Soviet Union and Eastern Europe. It was important to get the

balance right between the lessons of the past and the opportunities of the future. She would welcome the wisdom and advice of those present.

Who are the Germans?

We started by talking about the Germans themselves and their characteristics. Like other nations, they had certain characteristics, which you could identify from the past and expect to find in the future. It was easier—and more pertinent to the present discussion—to think of the less happy ones: their insensitivity to the feelings of others (most noticeable in their behaviour over the Polish border), their obsession with themselves, a strong inclination to self-pity, and a longing to be liked. Some even less flattering attributes were also mentioned as an abiding part of the German character: in alphabetical order, *angst,* aggressiveness, assertiveness, bullying, egotism, inferiority complex, sentimentality. Two further aspects of the German character were cited as reasons for concern about the future. First, a capacity for excess, to overdo things, to kick over the traces. Second, a tendency to over-estimate their own strength and capabilities. An example of that, which had influenced much of Germany's subsequent history, was the conviction that their victory over France in 1870 stemmed from a deep moral and cultural superiority rather than—as in fact—a modest advance in military technology.

Have the Germans Changed?

It was as well to be aware of all these characteristics. But there was a strong school of thought among those present that today's Germans were very different from their predecessors. It was argued that our basic perception of Germans related to a period of German history running from Bismarck until 1945. This was the phase of imperial Germany, characterised by neurotic self-assertiveness, a high birth-rate, a closed economy, a chauvinist culture. It had not been greatly affected by defeat in 1918, which had been regarded in Germany as unfair. German attitudes, German teaching, German historiography all continued virtually unchanged after 1918, together with a sense of Germany's historic mission (which was why the German aristocracy had supported Hitler, even while regarding him as a vulgarian). But 1945 was quite different and marked a sea-change. There was no longer a sense of historic mission, no ambitions for physical conquest, no more militarism. Education and the writing of history had changed. There was an innocence of and about the past on the part of the new generation of Germans. We should have no real worries about them.

This view was not accepted by everyone. It still had to be asked how a cultured and cultivated nation had allowed itself to be brain-washed into barbarism. If it had happened once, could it not happen again? Apprehension about Germany did not relate just to the Nazi period but to the whole post-Bismarckian era, and inevitably caused deep distrust. The way in which the Germans currently used their elbows and threw their weight about in the European Community suggested that a lot had still not changed. While we all admired and indeed envied what the Germans had achieved in the last 45 years, the fact was that their institutions had not yet been seriously tested by adversity such as a major economic calamity. We could not tell how Germans would react in such circumstances. In sum, no one had serious misgivings about the present leaders or political élite of Germany. But what about 10, 15 or 20 years from now? Could some of the unhappy characteristics of the past re-emerge with just as destructive consequences?

What will be the Consequences of Reunification?

We looked more closely at two particular aspects of the future: the consequences of unification and Germany's role in Eastern Europe.

Even those most disposed to look on the bright side admitted to some qualms about what unification would mean for German behaviour in Europe. We could not expect a united Germany to think and act in exactly the same way as the Federal Republic which we had known for the last 45 years—and this would be true even though a united Germany would almost certainly inherit the FRG's institutions. The Germans would not necessarily think more dangerously, but they would think differently. There was already evident a kind of triumphalism in German thinking and attitudes which would be uncomfortable for the rest of us. Reference was also made to Günter Grass's comment: in the end reunification will get everyone against us, and we all know what happens when people are against us.

Then, too, there were reasons to worry about the effects on the character of a united Germany of bringing in 17 million predominantly Protestant north Germans brought up under a mendacious orthodoxy. How would this alter the basically Catholic Rhineland basis of the post-war FRG, with its political and economic centre of gravity increasingly in the south and west? We could not assume that a united Germany would fit quite so comfortably into Western Europe as the FRG. There would be a growing inclination to resurrect the concept of *Mittel-Europa*, with Germany's role being that of broker between East and West. It was noticeable that Chancellor Kohl now spoke of Germany's partners in East *and* West.

That tendency could be strengthened by the effect of unification on Germany's party system. The vote for the conservative alliance in East Germany could be seen as a vote for quick unification rather than for the values and policies of the West German CDU. There was a strong pacifist, neutralist, anti-nuclear constituency in East Germany, which could have a considerable effect on the views of a united Germany. That effect could be to make a united Germany both less "Western" and less politically stable than the FRG. At worst, the extremes at both ends of the political spectrum could grow in influence, leading to a return to Weimar politics (although no one argued this with any great conviction.)

Will a United Germany Aspire to Dominate Eastern Europe?

This led on naturally enough to debate about a united Germany's likely role and ambitions in Eastern Europe. It was widely agreed that Chancellor Kohl's handling of the Polish border issue, in particular his reference to the need to protect the German minority in Silesia, had given the wrong signals. Historic fears about Germany's "mission" in Eastern and Central Europe had been revived. Some of President von Weizsäcker's comments had contributed to this.

But the facts were more reassuring. The German minorities in Eastern Europe were much reduced in number, and the ambition of most of them was to move within the borders of Germany rather than have the borders of Germany come to them. The Germans' own interest lay in keeping the minorities where they were rather than in encouraging their return. They thus had an incentive to give substantial aid to Eastern Europe.

There was no evidence that Germany was likely to make further territorial claims, at least for the foreseeable future. To the extent that border problems might arise, it would be as a result of comparatively wealthy Germans buying land and property in poorer Poland and Czechoslovakia (bearing in mind that the Polish border would be only 40 minutes' drive from the assumed capital of a united Germany).

More widely, it was likely that Germany would indeed dominate Eastern and Central Europe economically. But that did not necessarily equate to subjugation. Nor did it mean that a united Germany would achieve by economic means what Hitler had failed to achieve militarily. There were undoubtedly still some who believed that Germany had a "civilising mission" to the east. But the fact was, the pressure for a German economic presence came as much from the East Europeans themselves as from the Germans. They wanted and needed German help and German investment; indeed it was probably the only way to restore and revive Eastern Europe ("There is only one thing worse than being exploited, and that is not being exploited"). It might indeed be ironic that after 1945 Eastern Europe had set out to avoid ever again being dependent on Germany, but after 45 years of communism was more dependent than ever. But it was nonetheless a fact. The East Europeans might prefer a British or French presence. But neither was prepared to commit adequate resources.

What Sort of Framework Should We Build for the Future?

Given that a much larger and more powerful Germany would soon be upon us, we had to consider what sort of European framework would be most likely to encourage the benign effects and diminish the adverse consequences.

The East/West aspects roused the greatest concern. There was a tendency on the part of the Germans to take the credit for unification themselves. In fact the real credit should go to the people of Eastern Europe and to Mr. Gorbachev. *They* were the ones who created the conditions in which unification could happen. Whatever solutions we adopted—whether in relation to Germany or to the current problems in Lithuania—must take account of their interests, and above all, of Mr. Gorbachev's position. That would affect in particular the security arrangements made for the territory of the former GDR in a united Germany. We could not just shove the Russian troops out.

To an extent Soviet and East European interests paralleled those of Western Europe. We wanted Germany to be constrained within a security framework which had the best chance of avoiding a resurgence of German militarism. We wanted a continuing American military presence in Europe as a balance to Germany's power. We would want to see limits, preferably self-imposed through a further CFE [Conventional Forces in Europe] agreement, on the size of Germany's armed forces. We would want a renewed self-denying ordinance on acquisition by Germany of nuclear and chemical weapons. We would want to involve the Soviet Union institutionally in discussions of Europe's future security through the CSCE [Conference on Security and Cooperation in Europe], not least because in the long term (and assuming continued development in the direction of democracy) the Soviet Union would be the only European power capable of balancing Germany.

All that would suggest that an accommodation could be found which would enable a united Germany to remain in NATO, with transitional arrangements to permit the Soviet Union to help keep forces in East Germany. It would also favour building up the CSCE (and possibly giving it a directorate based on the Five). The idea that a united Germany might be a member both of NATO and the Warsaw Pact simultaneously was also canvassed, but given short shrift.

But there were real risks that the situation could develop differently. One was that Gorbachev would be manoeuvred into using force in Lithuania or in some analogous situation; or that his failure to do so would lead to his replacement by a much less moderate leadership. That risk was one reason why it was so important to hold on to the existing structure of NATO: the fact that things had gone the West's way for the last year or so did not absolve us from continuing to guard against something worse.

Another and possibly more likely danger was that the Soviet Union would exploit discussion in the Four Plus Two group [Britain, the US, the Soviet Union and France plus the Germanies] of a united Germany's membership of NATO and the presence of nuclear weapons in Germany, so that they became issues in the West German election campaign. German public opinion was seen as vulnerable on both points, but particularly on the nuclear issue.

The worst fear was that NATO could unravel on the election hustings of Germany. The more positive view argued that this danger only underlined the importance of settling the question of a united Germany's membership of NATO as rapidly and decisively as possible.

Looking longer-term, the aim of building up the CSCE seemed sensible to everyone, not least as a way of managing and conciliating disputes between national minorities in Eastern and Central Europe.

The European Community was surprisingly not much mentioned. German behaviour in the EC—"we pay so we must have our way"—was seen by some as the harbinger of Germany's economic dominance over Western Europe.

There were differing views over how genuine the Germans were in saying they wanted a more integrated Europe in parallel with unification. Was it just a tactic to reassure others? Or a genuine desire to subsume the latent nationalist drive of a united Germany into something broader? The latter was not wholly convincing, given that the structure of the EC tended to favour German dominance, particularly in the monetary area. Against this, it was pointed out that the more assertive Germany became, the easier it ought to become to construct alliances against Germany on specific issues in the Community.

Conclusions

Where did this leave us? No formal conclusions were drawn. The weight of the evidence and the argument favoured those who were optimistic about life with a united Germany. We were reminded that in 1945 our aim had been a united Germany shorn of its eastern provinces but under democratic and non-communist government, with the states of Eastern Europe free to choose their own governments. We had failed to get that in 1945, but had won it now. Far from being agitated, we ought to be pleased. We were also reminded that Anglo-German antagonisms since the fall of Bismarck had been injurious to Europe as a whole and must not be allowed to revive once more. When it came to failings and unhelpful characteristics, the Germans had their share and perhaps more, but in contrast to the past, they were much readier to recognise and admit this themselves.

The overall message was unmistakable: we should be nice to the Germans. But even the optimists had some unease, not for the present and the immediate future, but for what might lie further down the road than we can yet see.

Fawlty Logic

by Donald Sassoon

Donald Sassoon was a regular contributor to the British journal *Marxism Today*, which was affiliated with the British Communist Party, and which ceased publication in 1991. This article appeared in the August 1990 issue.

The Ridley affair and the leaked Chequers memorandum on the German national character have revealed the existence of a Fawlty Towers tendency within the cabinet, so called after the episode in the tv series in which John Cleese/Basil Fawlty compulsively reminds his perfectly well-behaved German customers about the last war. Basil Fawlty represents a particular national type: the stiff, crass, middle-class Englishman without whom Thatcherism would find it difficult to exist.

Fawlty compensates for his inferiority complex by "aggressiveness, bullying, egotism, a capacity to excess, a strong inclination to self-pity, a longing to be liked and chronic insensitivity for the feelings of others," to list but a few of the German national traits so brilliantly highlighted by the distinguished gin-and-tonic ('easy on the tonic') academics who took part in the Chequers seminar.

But could Fawlty and the Tory who hates Germany have a point? Germany is big, rich, powerful—soon to be bigger, richer and even more powerful. And if the Germans can only behave "like Germans," which, presumably, means like jackbooted stormtroopers itching to rape Czechoslovakia, is it not proper to worry about it?

It took particular historical conditions to make the Germans "behave like the Germans." Prior to 1914 the world appeared to Germany as a hostile place dominated by two imperial powers, France and Britain, which had effectively carved up the world. After defeat in the first world war, a humiliated Germany lost its status as a major power and was devastated, first by inflation, then by unemployment. Its new democratic political system had few supporters. This was the background to Hitler and Nazism.

And now? Germany enjoys unparalleled prosperity. Its democratic institutions are strong and supported by all political parties in both Germanys. Reunification, the dream of German nationalism, is being achieved peacefully and democratically with the blessing of both superpowers. And contrary to present nationalist trends in eastern Europe, Germany wants more integration into the EC. This means accepting the loss of national sovereignty which goes with further integration. Not much to worry about then. And if it is German economic preponderance within the EC that one fears, then this can be checked more effectively by a democratic, integrated Community than by a free-market Europe. Today's Germans, unlike Adolf Hitler, can hardly be discontented with what they have achieved. German success may cause envy, but self-satisfied fat cats do not usually go to war.

If we are uneasy about European stability and peace it is further east than Berlin that we must look. If the USSR, though one should say Russia, having failed to achieve economic recovery within a democratic framework, is isolated and cut off from Europe, its empire disintegrated, its national dignity in tatters, then the road will be open for the emergence of an authoritarian Russian populism with no stake in the present international order. This is understood in Paris and Bonn where the wait-and-see attitude of the British is rejected in favour of a more concrete support for Gorbachev.

Great Britain, though one should say England, lags far behind, worrying about its past and its future, its foreign policy in disarray, its special relationship with the USA a music-hall joke, its European policy non-existent. In the western part of Europe, it approximates more than any other to the conditions which, in the past, led the Germans to behave like Germans; a diseased economy, a semi-democratic political system (a hereditary and appointed upper chamber, a ridiculous electoral system, a pathetically secretive governing class) and a longing for a long-lost empire.

The Chequers Affair

by Timothy Garton Ash

Timothy Garton Ash is the author of *The Polish Revolution:
Solidarity 1980–1982* (1983), *The Uses of Adversity* (1989),
and *The Magic Lantern* (1990). He is currently a fellow
of St. Antony's College, Oxford. This essay was published
in the *New York Review of Books* of 27 September 1990.

In July this year, in the midst of far, far more important developments, such
as NATO's London Declaration, the 28th Congress of the Communist Party
of the Soviet Union, and the Stavropol accord giving Soviet approval to the
full sovereignty of a united Germany, Anglo-German relations suffered a little
shake. The first part of this little shake was an interview given to *The Spectator*
by Britain's then secretary for trade and industry, Nicholas Ridley, in which,
after lunch, but just one glass of wine, Mr. Ridley talked about the proposed
European Monetary Union as "a German racket designed to take over the
whole of Europe," and declared that if you were prepared to give up sovereignty to the Commission of the European Communities, "you might just as
well give it to Adolf Hitler, frankly." Saltily written up by the new editor of
The Spectator, Dominic Lawson, son of former Chancellor of the Exchequer
Nigel Lawson, and adorned with a characteristically vivid cartoon by Nicholas
Garland showing a schoolboy-like Mr. Ridley daubing a poster of Chancellor
Kohl with a Hitler moustache, this "outbreak of the Euro-hooligan Ridley,"
as the normally restrained *Frankfurter Allgemeine Zeitung* described it, caused
a political storm and the resignation of Mr. Ridley.

The second part of this little shake was the publication in *The Independent
on Sunday* and *Der Spiegel* of a leaked, highly confidential memorandum of a
meeting between Mrs. Thatcher and a small group of historians held at Chequers, the prime minister's country residence, on March 24, to discuss Germany.[1] The memorandum, which I had not seen until its publication, although
I participated in the Chequers meeting, was written by Mrs. Thatcher's influential private secretary for foreign affairs, Charles Powell. "Ver-bloody-
batim" was how one British minister reportedly described this singular document. But ver-bloody-batim is precisely what it was not. Rather it was a
report, with no views attributed specifically to anyone, but some by implication

---

[1] Edited extracts were subsequently published, and somewhat misleadingly presented, in *The
New York Times* of July 20.

to all. And like all good Whitehall *rapporteurs,* Mr. Powell managed to flavor this rich cream soup with a little of his own particular spice.

One sentence was especially rich:

> Some even less flattering attributes were also mentioned [at the meeting] as an abiding part of the German character: in alphabetical order, angst, aggressiveness, assertiveness, bullying, egotism, inferiority complex, sentimentality.[sic]

Well, perhaps in the course of a long discussion those attributes were mentioned by some participants, along with many more positive ones. But plainly they were never listed like that by anyone, nor, indeed, was there anything like a collective view of "the German character"—if such a thing exists. Still, as one might expect, this was the sentence that made the headlines, whether in London, Paris, or Frankfurt.

What really happened was this. Mrs. Thatcher invited six independent experts on Germany to give their views. Besides two leading American historians of Germany, Fritz Stern of Columbia University and Gordon Craig of Stanford, there were four British historians and commentators, Lord Dacre (Hugh Trevor-Roper), Norman Stone, George Urban, and myself. This was no ideological cabal. The guests had different views on Germany, and different views on Europe. Thus, for example, Norman Stone is a member of the Bruges Group, named after Mrs. Thatcher's Bruges speech, and opposing further steps of federal integration in the European Community, while I have repeatedly criticized Mrs. Thatcher for not going further in that direction. Fritz Stern is well-known to readers of *The New York Review* not only as an outstanding authority on German history but also as an outspoken defender of the "L word." All spoke their own minds. Fritz Stern said nothing that he has not said already in his published work,[2] I said nothing that I have not said in mine.

Yet the most remarkable feature of this quite diverse group was the degree of unanimity that emerged in answering the central questions of whether and how Germany has changed, and what we might expect from the new, united Germany. As the main body of Mr. Powell's memorandum fairly indicated, the weight of the argument was overwhelmingly positive. We explained why 1945 was a great caesura in German history. We described how, self-consciously, but increasingly self-confidently, the democratic West Germany dif-

---

[2] Fritz Stern gave his comment on the controversy surrounding the Chequers meeting in an article in *The Washington Post* of July 29. He concluded with the striking thought that "This century ends as it began, with a Germany in ascendancy, based on its economy, its technology and its human capabilities," and so it has a "second chance" to use its strength for the good.

fered from its predecessors; and how the unification of Germany in one democratic state, bordering on East Central European states that were also choosing their own governments, was a development heartily to be welcomed. And, we argued that it should be, precisely, welcomed.

Of course concerns were also expressed about this new Germany. Historians will always find continuities as well as discontinuities. But almost every doubt or question that was raised by the guests around the Chequers table could also have been heard in Bonn, from distinguished German historians, commentators, and, indeed, leading politicians. For as several participants pointed out, one of the signal strengths of West Germany has been its capacity for constant, relentless, sometimes almost masochistic self-examination and self-criticism, soundly based on a strong, free press and an exemplary critical historiography. Neither Japan nor Italy, nor indeed Austria, could match this. Thus I think it is fair to say that if Chancellor Kohl himself had sat in on that meeting, he would have agreed with, or, at the very least, accepted as fair comment, 90 percent of what was said around the Chequers table.

For a private, no-holds-barred, brainstorming session, that is not a bad percentage. After all, everyone, but everyone, speaks slightly differently *about* his neighbors than he does *to* them. Auden says somewhere that if men knew what women said about them in private, the human race would cease to exist. The same might almost be said about the nations of Europe, and the European community. (Men as much as women, of course.) If we had a completely frank account of, say, President Mitterrand's discussions with some French intellectuals on this issue, would the score even be as high? Or, for that matter, of a comparably frank discussion between Chancellor Kohl and some German specialists about Britain?

The remaining 10 percent was as much a matter of style as of content, of tone rather than analysis. This was, of course, the problem *a fortiori* with Nicholas Ridley's remarks, as presented in *The Spectator*. As it happens, Mr. Ridley's analysis was wrong. (If there is a danger, it is not Germany's commitment to further West European integration but rather a weakening of that commitment as a result of the new possibilities opening to the east.) But even if he were right, he would have been wrong for the way he said it. I have thought a good idea about this particular British tone and style in discussing Germany and Europe, a tone and style reflected outrageously in Mr. Ridley's remarks, somewhat also in *The Spectator*'s presentation of them (the *Boy's Own* cartoon of Kohl daubed as Hitler, the almost light-hearted spirit of the interview), but also, to a much more limited degree, and in a more defensible way, in the personal spice of Mr. Powell's memorandum.

I am told this is a matter of age and personal experience, and no doubt it is easier for someone of my generation, born after the war, to come to like and admire present-day Germany, and to make friendships unburdened by the past. Yet the generation gap does not quite account for this peculiar British tone, a unique mixture of resentment and frivolity. This may, I think, partly be explained by geography and history. America is far enough away, and still big and powerful enough, to be relaxed about the reemergence of Germany as a great power in Central Europe. France (let alone Poland) is too small, and relatively too weak, to be anything but deadly serious about it. But Britain is somewhere in between: close enough to be worried, and weak enough to be resentful ("Who won the war anyway?"), yet also far enough away, and still self-confident enough, to be outspoken and outrageous.

This slightly resentful insouciance is, like so many national weaknesses, the flip side of a strength. With a few notable exceptions, most German political speeches and commentaries are still so earnest, learned, scrupulous, and responsible that they are better than any sleeping pill. British political speeches and commentaries, by contrast, are still often amusing, original, and uninhibited—to a fault. But the fault in this case was a very serious one.

It is not just that it is profoundly offensive to the leaders and people of a democratic Germany to paint Hitler on the wall (or on the remnants of the Wall). It is also consummately counterproductive. Such sauce does not make the meat of substantive criticism more interesting. It means that the whole dish is pushed away. It does not mean that Britain's voice is listened to more attentively in the counsels of Europe. It means that it is listened to even less.

In a sense, the July crisis was just another chapter in a much longer story: the story of how numerous responsible British policy makers, including successive foreign secretaries, have worked extraordinarily hard to produce a positive yet still distinctive British contribution to the development of Europe, and how this work has again and again been frustrated. There are many reasons for this frustration, in the EC itself, in the legacy of past mistakes, in the Labour party as well as the Conservative party, but some of the responsibility must plainly lie with Mrs. Thatcher. The buck stops there. A large part of this most persistent problem lies in that 10 percent region of tone and style: in the failure to find a distinctive language of British Europeanism, a language in which criticisms do not automatically become accusations and praise does not sound like blame.

The very fact that Mrs. Thatcher invited six independent experts for a day's seminar, and listened, shows a genuine wish to come to a serious, informed judgment of these extraordinary developments in the center of Europe, and hence to find an appropriate response to them. There are those, including some in Bonn, who say that her interventions on these issues were more obviously measured, informed, and helpful in the second quarter of 1990 than perhaps they were in the first. Yet the effect of the leaked Powell memo, coming on top of the Ridley affair, was to set things back once again.

Chancellor Kohl took it all very sportingly, saying that Mr. Ridley was not the only person to have made tactless remarks, and recalling his own gaffe a few years ago, when he compared Gorbachev to Goebbels. In Britain, an investigation was ordered into the source of the leak. Few thought the culprit would ever be found. Questions were asked in the House of Commons. The prime minister defended Mr. Powell. The foreign secretary invited Hans-Dietrich Genscher, the German foreign minister, to the Glyndebourne Opera. Then the Germans went on uniting and the British went on holiday.

Finding a New Weak Link

by Martin Gilbert

Martin Gilbert, born in 1937, is a British historian and the author of numerous works, including *The Final Journey: The Fate of the Jews of Nazi Europe* and *Auschwitz and the Allies*. The piece was first published in the *New York Times* on 27 September 1990.

I always thought the division of Germany after 1945 was unnatural. The wartime allies, at Teheran and Yalta, were clearly thinking of Germany as a whole, even while demilitarizing and deindustrializing it to make sure that it could not start another war. In a sense, what is happening on October 3 is what might have happened shortly after the war, if the United States and the Soviet Union had not been at odds.

I was always taught to look for the weak link in the chain, the cause of potential trouble in the apparently stable order of things. As it looks now, potential trouble lies not in a united Germany, but in a disintegrating Soviet Union. The phase of history that is opening with the unification of Germany is, in a sense, the reversal of processes that began in 1918 with the overly severe Versailles Treaty terms against Germany.

One must assume and hope that for most Germans, Germany will be complete once its two parts are united; that it will have no more unresolved territorial claims. The problem in the future will not then be the eastern border of Germany, it will be the western border of Russia. The issues to be resolved are not those between Germans and their eastern neighbors; they are between Russians and Ukrainians, Poles, Hungarians, Lithuanians, and their other western neighbors, and they stem from the way Stalin created the western border of the Soviet Union in 1940.

In the next decade, a united Germany could be a lifesaver, a source of economic strength and political stability for all the countries of central Europe, and it could continue to be the driving force for the unification of Europe.

Now that the Germans have acknowledged and paid for their war crimes, they can put behind them the last great question from their past. But the Russians are still agonizing over their past, and living uncomfortably through its still-emerging consequences. The questions the Russians are asking are things like, "Father, what were you doing during Katyn?" And, "Uncle, how can we justify and legitimize the annexation of the Baltic states, of East Prussia, and the Polish-Russian border?"

The New Germany

by Lord Weidenfeld

Lord Weidenfeld, born in 1919, is a publisher and has
been chairman of Weidenfeld and Nicolson since 1948.
He made this statement during a conference on "The
German Question" in Berlin and Potsdam in June 1991.

I feel like the pianist who has prepared an intermezzo for the entr'acte and
suddenly finds that the curtain falls and he has to play to jolly the audience
out of the theatre. But I would like to take the cue from Michael Stürmer's
earlier remarks on German foreign policy, relations with the Middle East and
Israel, and I want to both widen and narrow them and strike a global note,
speaking as a European Jew who is a partisan of Israel and who hopes at the
same time not to have too jaundiced a view.

I would like to submit that world Jewry and the state of Israel might well
find that they have in a united Germany which, as Timothy Garton Ash said
is the primus inter pares in Europe—any Europe, be it confederated, a Europe
des nations, Europe to the Oder or Europe to Brest-Litovsk—its most important friend alongside the United States. And because of the importance
of these two friends one must admit to a certain preference for an atlanticist
Europe rather than a narrow Europe for the following reasons, some of which
are obvious, some of which may not be so obvious.

Not enough has been said about the lessons of the Gulf War and particularly
the prelude to the Gulf War. The real trauma for Jews and for Israel was not
so much the Scud missile attacks, though of course they were a tremendous
shock, but the diplomatic and psychological prelude to the war, and in particular the nuances in the attitudes of the various European nations. As Henry
Kissinger said earlier—and I hope I am not misquoting him—if the French
had had their way, or rather if Saddam Hussein had been a more subtle
statesman, they would have met him half way. It could be said that perhaps
the Belgians and the Italians would have met him three fifths of the way and
as for the Greeks, they might have paid him a premium. But the fact is, that
it was America, aided by Great Britain and the stout and valiant Dutch who
reacted intuitively. They knew exactly where they stood and in the end the
whole of Europe rallied around. I don't wish to excuse the Germans but they
really had a good alibi, the constitutional alibi, and a tremendous preoccupation with priorities—the unification of Germany, and a side glance at the
Baltic revolt, and in the end they made it up in a different way.

This political prelude was a great trauma for Israel. It also gave a foretaste of what Europe could be. Had the decision been left to a majority vote, Europe would have caved in. It's all very well to speak of the Europe that could be, or should be, but there was a case in point.

One looks to Germany for friendship and hopes that even in an integrated and federal Europe it will intercede and, through lobbying, arguing and presenting one's case, lean on others. It goes without saying that German leaning is more important than Luxembourg leaning. The other reason why this relationship with Germany could be so important is because Germany will have the clout in Eastern Europe, and if any country can play a really decisive part in the building of an infrastructure of whatever the Soviet Union or Russia will be, it is Germany. This does not mean that it could not share the burden through consortial cooperation with Japan or other Europeans, but, as Keynes said, in the end it will be German bodies and souls sitting in that Soviet or other Russia and doing their job. One is reminded of Mussorgsky's opera *Khovanshchina* that is set mainly in the German quarter of Moscow where the craftsmen, skilled workers and foremen lived. That is the foretaste of things to come at the end of the century. I mean this extremely benignly and not in any neocolonial way. On the contrary.

This Germany already is, but will increasingly be an influence with clout on whatever government will be in power in those countries in Eastern Europe which still harbour the last large reservoir of Jewish manpower. However many or few Russian Jews emigrate to Israel there will still be millions there, and we never know what twists and turns the internal events in those countries will impose on that minority. In this context German influence is very important.

I will venture to speculate on events that might come to pass next century. After all, we have to think of the eternal road of historical development in decades, if not centuries. The day may well come when Siberian oil will flow and gas will flow so that the bargaining power—I use my words cautiously—of the Arab oil producers will no longer have the same weight as it does now. That is another reason why there is a kind of empathy, a commonality between Germany and the Jews. It is extraordinary that in two days no-one has mentioned fundamentalism! A billion Muslims: millions of Muslims in Europe. South of the Caucasus whoever has a role to play in that part of the world which is now called the USSR, will be faced with that great problem.

I would like to establish that there is a commonality of interest, certainly on the part of the Jews. The question is, how does it fit with the national interest of Germany. The reason why I have this muted optimism is that I really believe in the course of pragmatic humanism of this German people from Adenauer to Weizsäcker. These leaders as well as Chancellors Schmidt, Brandt and Kohl and the much maligned Franz Josef Strauβ were and are remarkable people in their own way and consistent in their pragmatic humanism.

There is a genuine change in attitude which I perceive as a professional man who has to study the catalogues of general publishers, specialised publishers, libraries, etc., who all show an extraordinary interest, I would almost say preoccupation with Judaica of every sort. There is Rachel Salamander's Jewish bookshop in Munich, for example, which is always full, and the clientele is entirely non-Jewish. Bearded young students browse and buy books of Gershom Scholem, the Kabbala, mysticism—the kind of books no British publisher could afford to publish as they would never find the buyers, and the American Jewish foundations wouldn't back such projects as they wouldn't even know what these works were. So you find it only in Germany. I believe that the attitude towards the Jews of the younger generation has changed from that sense of genocidal guilt to the responsibility of a benign uncle or cousin. I have seen enough German students in kibbutzim or processions to commemorate some event and there wasn't that sickly sense of guilt. There was a genuine feeling of solidarity. Therefore I finish on this wildly optimistic note and apologise for the pianist's last chords but there are some *Leitmotivs* in what I have played that are relevant to the meetings of yesterday and today.

France

Toward a Confederal System

by Roland Dumas

Roland Dumas, born in 1922, is a lawyer, journalist, and politician. From 1984 to 1986, and since 1988, he has been France's minister for foreign affairs. This article appeared in the *New York Times* on 13 March 1990.

It is time to build a greater Europe. The desire for liberty and democracy has overthrown outdated ideologies. Everywhere we hear the same demands: a society based upon democratic values, separation of powers to protect against arbitrary acts, multiparty systems that safeguard the will of the people, an end to suffocating bureaucracy.

The German question lies at the heart of the challenge of building this new Europe.

I always believed that the arbitrary division of Germany was senseless. Since no one can permanently divide a nation, a people, a country, German unity will put an end to one of history's anomalies. And it is up to the Germans themselves to determine the pace and internal conditions of this unification. But the situation inherited from the war cannot be improved without the participation of countries other than the two Germanys.

With this in mind, six countries will meet before the end of this month: both Germanys and the four victorious powers, France, Britain, the U.S. and the Soviet Union. Together, we will decide what new international agreements may be needed. Together, we will discuss borders, peace settlement, the status of Berlin, security and other subjects of common interest.

German unification can be achieved only if it is accepted by all European countries. For Germany's neighbors, and most of all for Poland, it must be absolutely clear that borders cannot be altered. This must be recognized in and of itself.

Everything revolves around a simple idea: German unification must be accompanied by a strengthening of European stability, and the opportunity lends itself to this. The reduction of East-West tensions favors disarmament, even if considerable arsenals still exist. Agreements will be signed in 1990, and further negotiations should then follow.

But will the structures of security be both strong and flexible enough to withstand the shock of German unity? Should we not review our old alliances and establish new bonds that take into account Europe's changing balance of power?

The existing alliances were born of confrontation between East and West.

253

In the coming months, serious reconsideration will undoubtedly be given to their structure, role and doctrines.

The Atlantic alliance reflects common values and the sense of belonging to the same sphere of security. This is why I hope a unified Germany becomes part of the alliance. This is its natural place. I welcome statements by West Germany's leaders rejecting neutrality.

NATO should, of course, adapt to the changes resulting from German unification and from progress toward disarmament. Yet, trans-Atlantic ties and the American presence in Europe must continue to be recognized as key elements in the future stability of our continent.

Another important element of security is the distinctive friendship between my country and Germany. Common elements in the area of defense are already in place.

Together, we must discuss all aspects regarding the future of Europe. The Conference on Security and Cooperation in Europe is the ideal forum for this. It is within the Helsinki framework that we have made significant progress on human rights. It is within this framework that we shall reach an agreement on reducing military forces and develop new forms of cooperation.

This is why France immediately supported the idea of holding a major summit of the heads of the C.S.C.E.'s 35 member nations before the end of this year. Everyone now agrees to this. The summit meeting will take place, and Paris, need I add, is willing to host it.

However, the Helsinki framework is not a political model for Europe. Western Europe has been built around the European Community, and the community's success has certainly influenced events in the East. France has always expressed its commitment to progress toward European union in all its aspects, including political union based on new institutions. A unified Germany will have to be part of this strengthening of the community.

Beyond this, France's President, François Mitterrand, wishes to promote another approach, one embracing all aspects of relations between our countries: the European Confederation.

Confederation is the most flexible form of association between countries that want to come together on what is most important. It is within this framework that we, together, can build a future of peace and prosperity for Europe.

Police Logic Often Prevails Over Common Sense and Political Reason

by Luc Rosenzweig

Armin Riecker, born in 1944, was the East German ambassador to France. This interview, conducted by Luc Ro-
senzweig, first appeared in *Le Monde* on 21 February 1990
under the title *"La logique policière l'emportait souvent sur
le bon sens et la raison politique."*

On December 1, 1989, forty-six year old Armin Riecker left the East German
Communist party. Since last August, he has been trying to persuade his
comrades to open up to reality and set out on the path toward reform. The
wave of immigration had begun, and his position as head of domestic affairs
services in the Leipzig district enabled him to perceive the extent of the crisis
that was upsetting his country.

In September he spent a two-week vacation with his family in Hungary,
where he was in for a surprise: "Watching East German citizens flee across
the newly opened border, I realized that I was the servant of a power rejected
by the people. I saw only one way out remaining: that the GDR undertake
a radical reform of the Socialist system, the kind that Gorbachev was trying
to put into operation in the USSR."

Back in Leipzig, Armin Riecker was an eyewitness of the peaceful revolution that caused the fall of Erich Honecker on October 18, 1989. The
accession of Egon Krenz as head of the SED and of the State has stirred up
his hopes for a renewal: a member of the party for twenty-one years, Armin
still hopes that the ideals to which he has devoted his life have some chance
of surviving the Stalinist debacle.

Only a Total Democratic Process

His hopes would seem to be short-lived. Egon Krenz was in a position to
effect only minor reforms. Meanwhile, the Stalinist apparatus has not been
dismantled and clings to power, to its privileges, and to its positions. On
November 30, in the Leipzig sections of the SED, a move was made to elect
a delegate to the party's extraordinary congress. His program of reforms was
rejected, and he was forced to conclude that a Stalinist party like the SED

was incapable of radical reform despite the good will and honesty of leaders like Gregor Gysi.

The acceleration of the decay of the Party and the State and the risk of deepening political and social conflict convinced Armin Riecker that only a total democratic process, one that would expose every cog of the former system's machinery, is likely to guarantee the future of a Germany on the path towards unity.

Before becoming head of territorial administration, Armin Riecker served for nineteen years in the popular national army and in the East German diplomatic service. After obtaining degrees in foreign languages and in political science, he was recruited in 1967 by the Ministry of Defense to take charge of the army's foreign relations, which of course included "intelligence."

In 1975 these duties brought him to the Paris Embassy of the GDR. Officially, he occupied the position of First Secretary at the Embassy, but in actuality he was there as commander of the popular national army, in this way averting the suspicions of the French who would not accept the presence of a military attache from the GDR, an enemy power during the Second World War.

"Today, to describe some of the mechanisms placed in the service of a mistaken security policy is not an act of treason, but rather the duty of anyone who feels that it is his responsibility to prevent a return to such practices. Whereas the likes of a Schalck-Golodkowski might deliver his secrets to the East German secret service, I have chosen to address myself to the public by using the media.

"Two aspects of this past era must be brought to light: the all-powerfulness of the state security (*Stasi*), and the activities of the Party that escaped democratic control. This holds true not only within the territory of the GDR, where each day brings its harvest of scandals, but also for foreign diplomatic missions, that up to now have been spared democratic criticisms. I don't want a manhunt, but I do want the destruction of those structures in which I participated during my stay in Paris."

Armin Riecker noticed how diplomatic positions were reserved for figures of the *Stasi*, more or less competent. "For example, when an ambassador plenipotentiary and a real diplomat like Gunter Buering, number two at the embassy in the late Seventies, refuses to carry out the orders of the head of the *Stasi* at the embassy, Waldemar Zoerner, who theoretically was his inferior within the hierarchy, the conflict resulted in the premature departure of Buering. Police logic usually prevailed over common sense and political reason."

This domination of the security apparatus must come to an end, according to Armin Riecker. He hopes that the East German Minister of Foreign Affairs, Oaker Fischer, one of the few survivors of the former government, makes a formal declaration announcing that the structure and the influence of the *Stasi* in embassies have been eliminated. "This concerns first and foremost France and the other countries of the EEC, for it makes no sense to pursue intelligence operations in a community of which one will soon be a member."

Money for the French Communist Party

The defects of the fallen system are brought to light slowly; this also characterizes the foreign activity of the SED. On the fifth of last February, the Party's central organ, *Neues Deutschland,* published the accounts of the organization for the first time ever. One expense item in particular caught Armin Riecker's attention. It was labled "Aid in solidarity with progressive movements the world over," and its total came to more than three-fourths of the SED's expenditure in hard currency. A considerable sum, to which must be added the importation of foreign Communist publications, actually subsidies granted to these organizations which amount to 10.8 percent of total expenses.

Armin Riecker thinks that it would be "necessary to know in detail who benefited from this aid." During his Paris stay, he was able to verify that this "aid in solidarity" was not only tagged for the support of clandestine or poorly funded revolutionary movements, but also served to finance prosperous and respected parties, like the French Communist party.

"When I speak about this, in no way do I want to offend those sincere militant Communists whom I met in France. I have as much regard for them as for those who fought in the Resistance against the Nazi occupying forces. But today it doesn't make any sense to carry on with these conspiracies in interparty relations. That's why I now regret having carried a suitcase stuffed with money to Gaston Plissonier's secretary, 'comrade Ghislaine,' in the beginning of 1979. While she had another comrade count the notes, I spoke to Gaston Plissonier about the political situation in France.

"At the time, I was proud to accomplish such a task in the name of the Party; today I am ashamed of it. I expect Georges Marchais also to say that he is ashamed today of having been a good friend of Erich Honecker, of having spent pleasant vacations in the luxurious homes of the East German *nomenklatura,* and of being the General Secretary of a party that accepted money— the hard-earned money of the East German people, or money obtained by unscrupulous means."

It has indeed turned out to be true that the currency generously distributed to "friendly movements" came from state-owned enterprises, like Genex for example, a commercial firm that allowed foreigners or East Germans who had hard currency to purchase goods unavailable in the country. In this way West Germans could give an automobile to their East German families as a present, while unwittingly financing the SED's foreign activities.

The links between a few heads of the French Communist Party and German Communists like Hermann Axen were forged during the Resistance, when they fought together on French soil. Others met during the Spanish Civil War. "Back then, and later during the Cold War, these methods had their reason. That they were perpetuated in order to assure the conservation of a Stalinist apparatus seems to me to be thoroughly immoral."

Armin Riecker could have kept quiet and done like so many of his compatriots, taking his chances in the West. But, he says, "life won't be easy, in one way or another. Some will call me a traitor, others see in me a culprit from the former regime. I'll stay in Leipzig, to try to participate in the democratic reform of my reunited country. I'll take up whatever position the new democratic results of the next elections entrust me with." ·

Despite a disappointing first experience, he intends to make known his point of view and his discoveries in his country. In fact he has already addressed one of those "citizens' committees" that thrived during the November revolution, and that was entrusted with investigating the activities of the internal security forces. A few weeks thereafter, it turned out that the president of this citizens' committee was in the service of the *Stasi*.

A New Row Between an Old Couple

by Joseph Rovan and George Suffert

Joseph Rovan, born in 1918, is a journalist and academic. Since 1968 he has been professor of German literature at the University of Paris-Vincennes. He is the author of *Allemagne* (1955).

Georges Suffert, born in 1927, is a writer and journalist. He was editor of the news weekly *Le Point* from 1972 to 1985, and since 1986 has been editor of the social problems section of *Figaro Magazine*.

Their essay appeared in *Figaro* on 18 March 1990 under the title *"Nouvel orage sur un vieux couple."*

Between François Mitterrand and Helmut Kohl, it's neither pouting nor bickering. At best, it's a cool politeness; at worst, an almost uncontrollable exasperation. Yet both these men are hoping for Europe; they know that the next version will come about only if France and Germany retain close ties.

How did Paris and Bonn manage in the course of a few months to shatter a forty year friendship that was the wonder of all the world? Who is to blame? The character and the mood of men? Economic difficulties? Or is it the eternal long nose that lady geography, that tranquil old lady, gives to lady history, that inconstant flirt who always changes her corsage? All three, of course.

First, the protagonists. The misunderstanding began a little over a year ago. Mitterrand and Kohl knew each other well. They met on a regular basis. The French President was somewhat awed by this giant arisen out of the woods beyond the Rhine. But he was wary, for two reasons. First because he is wary of everybody. Secondly because something about this Christian-Democrat doesn't ring true; he plays the fool too well.

On Kohl's side, there seemed to be fewer misgivings. No doubt that the first years of Mitterrand's septennate shocked him; but since then, things have fallen back into place. For Kohl, Mitterrand is primarily a clever politician. Not the sort of stuff to scare a chancellor; as far as ruses are concerned, he shows, when the cards are down, that he is a first-class player.

Meanwhile back in Paris, the German's impatience regarding the East is causing much astonishment. What's the rush? One must wait and see what happens, buy time with time. In this matter, Mitterrand has missed the mark by far. He doesn't see anything coming, and, when the event stares him in the eye, he still shuffles.

Yet he also grumbles about his partner in Bonn. Paris is of the opinion that the German monetary authorities, disoriented by their fear of inflation, are hampering the French economy. The theme will return again and again. Another complaint: the disagreements between Kohl and Genscher, which make it seem as though there were two German foreign policies.

Seen from Paris, the compromises made between the Chancellery and the Ministery of Foreign Relations, appear confused. The list of points of contention between these two countries goes on and on.

It is in this worsening atmosphere that the Wall has come down. Its fall has taken the two capitals by surprise. In Paris, nobody would believe it. They had always been favorable toward German unity so long as it appeared far away. And so the collapse of the East German communist state has caused them to panic.

The government adopted a policy that sought to slow down the process, and hence François Mitterrand's ill-fortuned trip to the GDR. Kohl can't put up with him. There had been an earlier attempt to revive the Franco-Russian agreement, in order to curb any surprises from the Germans. A few weeks after the meeting in Kiev, Mikhail Gorbachev followed his own rationale: instead of trying to beat the inevitable, he went ahead and joined it.

And so in early 1989 Kohl sent his closest advisors to Paris. The message was relatively simple, but it was reiterated at least three times before summer. Here is the gist: "Warning! Something is happening in the East! Hungary and Poland are knocking at our door. It isn't Brandt's *Ostpolitik*. It is almost the opposite. These two countries want to detach themselves progressively from the East. Germany can't help them unaided. Economically she can, but politically she can't take part in this without France. What do you suggest?"

Paris offered no answer to this direct question. That was the first mistake, and the price will be high for both countries. Kohl cannot fathom the silence; he gets angry, and confides his anger in his closest aides. When the time comes, he will remember.

Moreover, recent events come to his mind; he recalls the phrase spoken by—or attributed to—Giscard D'Estaing: "If Schmidt wants to go to Moscow, I, Giscard, I'll beat him there." In other words, when the time comes, France just might beat out Germany by a hair in the race toward rapprochement with the East. Quite an error in calculation. For the USSR, Germany will always be an end, and France but a means to achieve that end.

The Myth of Rapallo

The other thorn in the Chancellor's side is the myth of Rapallo. Each term, French politicians vie with each other to be the first to pull this one out of their hat: Marchais, Debré, and even Alain Minc. Bonn can't take half a step toward the East (and the East is at its border) without being confronted by the bugbear of overthrown alliances. What mania.

More recently, the tactical weapons affair. During the winter of 1988–89 Helmut Kohl insisted on a renunciation of short-range missiles which, in the event of a conflict, would first fall on Germany. He hoped for the support of Paris in this affair: on the banks of the Seine, silence. Paris does not want to get involved.

Occasionally the Chancellor asserts others intentions—those of all the others, and especially of the French. Germany remains under suspicion no matter what she does. For a long time it was because of the Nazis, and today, is it not because of its wealth and power?

A Ten-Point Plan

In the GDR, public opinion has it that France is letting go of her favorite ally. Kohl speaks for his fellow citizens in this matter. Even in France, though no one is saying much, the idea of a new Great Germany sets nerves on edge— even though it would constitute only a second-rate power in a world filled with beasts like the United States, Russia, and China, or even India. While the course of history is rapidly accelerating in Germany, in Paris there reigns a concerned silence. They're counting the pin-pricks.

Then falls Chancellor Kohl's real blow, the ten points of his reunification plan. Paris protests vehemently, the French were not forewarned (not that Kohl had forewarned his Minister of Foreign Affairs, who nonetheless found himself instructed to "sell" the ten points). As a result, François Mitterrand selected the date of his visit to the GDR without letting Mr. Kohl know.

The disagreement worsened. At last December's Strasbourg summit of the twelve member-nations, Kohl revealed the date for the Conference on Monetary Union only under much pressure. He didn't want it to fall before the Bundestag elections set for December 1990. But is it in France's interest that Mr. Schoenhuber, Le Pen's German friend, cross the 5 percent barrier and join the Bundestag, making it impossible to maintain a moderate coalition?

France would like to see German unity accelerate European unification. But in Bonn, no concrete proposition for political union has been forthcoming. Over there they are preoccupied by the arrival of March 18. The Franco-German alliance is practically frozen. Helmut Kohl could have given partial satisfaction now and again to his friend, François. He didn't do it.

The European Defense Community and the Saar

François Mitterrand has made a collection of political mistakes and judgment errors that have made the German Chancellor more willing and alone than ever. Even concerning the Oder-Neisse border question, Paris knows very well that Bonn is holding itself strictly to the letter of the text signed by Willy Brandt and Helmut Schmidt in 1970 and 1975.

And so the distance that separates the two countries has grown. As if forty years of privileged relations disappeared in a flash; as if history and geography had joined forces to combat the dream of the 1950s.

The situation is worrisome. And still, the actual events of the past must not be forgotten, which have little to do with the past as it is imagined. The exceptional Franco-German alliance has always been threatened by crises that now seem to have been forgotten. Here are a few of them.

- Just after the war, the French government, dazed by the possible rebirth of the German party, opposed the formation of central German administrations which the three other powers desired. And so, each victor ruled in his own zone. Curiously, it is that very decision that accelerated the birth of two Germanys—the same one that prevented Stalin from extending his tentacles too far into Germany.

- Second crisis: The Saar. France wanted to keep it, to prevent the area's coal from falling back into German hands. Relations between Adenauer and Schuman were strained. Only the plebescite accepted by Mendès and realized by Pinay (1956) could rid them of both the German Saar and of the unwanted coal. And yet, it had only been six years since the "petite Europe" had sprung up from the ground.

- Third crisis: France rejected the European Defense Community. Communists and Gaulists alike sent it toppling to the ground. In Germany, there was much consternation: was Europe dead?

- Fourth crisis (and one of the strangest yet): de Gaulle rejected the very European renewal that he had helped to design, Fouchet's plan. In one night the General modified a good number of articles in the treaty without taking German views into consideration. The next day, Germany said no. And then how France protested that it was Bonn that had just refused Europe. From that time on, we have been swimming in misunderstanding.

Hence, though probably the most serious since the end of the war, the current crisis is not insurmountable. Perhaps public opinion will have to get involved. We've come a long way since the time of Monnet, de Gaulle, and Adenauer. Kohl and Mitterrand aren't made of the same stuff. If a rupture between France and Germany is to be avoided, between those two countries upon whom hinges the balance of Europe's future, then France will have to open up to Germany, and Mitterrand will have to develop a keener appreciation of the stakes. After all, if these two men can overcome this crisis, they have a good chance of entering the ranks of history. If not, they'll be swept away by time like so many others before them.

After 45 Years, the War Is Over

by Simone Veil

Simone Veil, born in 1927, is a former French Minister of Health and former president of the European Parliament. This article originally appeared in the *New York Times* on 27 September 1990.

The date of German unification is a very great date, a historic date. La guerre est finie. The war is over. It is an emotional thing not only for the Germans but for everyone. I think young people understand that the war is finally over 45 years afterward. In my view, it has ended on a vision of hope because it is based on agreement by two worlds that used to clash with each other. Yalta was division and today we have reconciliation.

German unification gives us a feeling of joy. We're seeing people who are tasting freedom. It's a big victory for Europe because East Germany has chosen very clearly to integrate itself into Europe. There were once big fears that previous attempts at German unification would be made under unacceptable terms, that a united Germany would be neutral. This has been avoided due to the firmness of the West, and I think this is a big victory.

I have been involved in building Europe because I believe in the possibility of a reconciliation between France and Germany. Most of all, I thought that was the only solution. If there wasn't a reconciliation, we would be obliged to confront a conflict-laden, more difficult situation. There could have been a desire for revenge that would have been very difficult to live with. We felt that our priority should be to encourage democracy and to arrange matters so that what happened would never again be possible.

Of course I could be wrong in all this. If I'm wrong, well then this has represented everything that I have done for 45 years, everything that I believe in. Everything I have hoped for would be put into question. If I am wrong then there is no hope, and the evolution of history was not what we thought. But we will have done our best.

None of what I am saying is blind confidence. We must not give in on certain conditions. For example, we have to be very tough on the Oder-Neisse [the German-Polish border]. We should also not yield on remilitarization. There are certain actions we must take with a desire to succeed and without any afterthought of revenge.

My last point is that we must never forget. And that means that we must be very vigilant, very demanding that we never forget.

Mitterrand Sees Threat to His "Grand Design"

by Jacques Amalric

Jacques Amalric is a French journalist who writes for *Le Monde*. This article is reprinted from the *Manchester Guardian Weekly*, 3 December 1989. It originally appeared in *Le Monde*.

President Mitterrand usually likes to appear serene, but today he is worried. What is bothering him, but which is also a cause for satisfaction, is the break-up of the order established at the end of World War II which had the advantage of being stable. Destabilised by communism's "unqualified failure" and people's aspiration for liberty, this longstanding old equilibrium is threatening to collapse before an alternative solution can even be imagined. "History can today swing one way or another, and we're unable to say which," he told the *Wall Street Journal* recently.

It is in an interview he gave Paris *Match* and in the report of the conversation he had with Stephan Denis of the *Quotidien de Paris* that the President's fears come through more clearly than in his public addresses. They may be summed up as follows: history is moving too fast; it threatens to spin out of control and drag us back to the 19th century rather than propel us into the 21st. It is therefore urgent to make sure that the wild horses of liberty do not stampede and tip the coach into the ditch.

In Mitterrand's view, there are only two cards left to play. They are the European Community and Mikhail Gorbachev. The French President's argument about the need to strengthen the Europe of Twelve is known, not just by Margaret Thatcher, and it will be at the center of the European Council's deliberations in Strasbourg on December 8 and 9.

His analysis of a "communist Europe that is unravelling" under Gorbachev's wise leadership is less well known. To Mitterrand's mind, it is in fact clear today that it is worth posing the possibility of Gorbachev falling down on his job, given the many serious difficulties that the Soviet leader is encountering. "It can only get worse," says Mitterrand.

The West must therefore help him, with economic assistance of course, but above all by not causing him any additional problem over Germany. "I personally have no ideological or political objections to [German] reunification," he says, but "the Russians have very real strategic, geopolitical and historical interests" which prevent this from being considered at present.

On the other hand, Mitterrand is convinced Gorbachev would be toppled by a military coup if he gave in on this point. He hinted at it in his interview with the *Wall Street Journal,* and told Stephane Denis that Gorbachev had confided to him: "The very day that German reunification is announced, a two-line communique will report that a marshal has taken my place."

The new government, says Mitterrand, could even be non-communist, but it would always be "a great danger." That is why the President is opposed to any Soviet-American deal on the neutralisation of Germany in return for the withdrawal of Soviet and American troops. "We cannot forget that Soviet military power is still very considerable," he says.

He also fears German reunification producing a knock-on effect and intensifying old quarrels which are already being exhumed again all over Europe.

Consequently, only a solid European pole stands any chance of transcending these old enmities through the power of its attraction. Such is the European community's "grand mission." This is also in its interest, for by winning in the East it could become an unquestioned world power. So here are responsibilities Margaret Thatcher cannot avoid. Mitterrand had this in mind when addressing the Strasbourg parliament on November 22 he said: "Nothing will be done if in a few days' time in Strasbourg we fail to conclude fundamental projects that will enable our Europe to provide itself with the instruments of an economic, monetary and social policy, an environmental policy and put the finishing touches to the internal market in keeping with the pace and the initiatives already agreed."

Is Mitterrand deliberately making things look worse the better to promote his views on the construction of Europe and appear, at the end of his six months' tenure of the Commission presidency, not only as the man who formerly succeeded in persuading Ronald Reagan to change his policy towards the Soviet Union, but also as the architect of a new Europe still emerging from the mists, and the alter ego of Bush and Gorbachev, whom he will be meeting in December?

As for the pessimistic scenario, without commenting on the "Bonapartist" themes that Kremlinologists have long been quarrelling over, it may be asked whether the worst dangers threatening Gorbachev are not to be found more in the USSR than in Berlin. And could not this man, whom Mitterrand tells us is "clear-headed," "courageous" and driven by a "formidable conviction" and "genuine intuition," but who also happens to be an extraordinary politician skilled in coming up with dramatic initiatives to conceal every situation of inferiority—could not this man, at least as far his own country is concerned, do an about-turn and himself suspend the liberalism he is displaying today?

Germany in the Singular

by Jacques Delors

Jacques Delors, born in 1925, is president of the European
Commission. This interview was conducted by Jacques
Amalric and Jean-Pierre Langellier and first appeared in
Le Monde on 12 October 1990 under the title *"L'Allemagne
au singulier."*

We shall conclude our "Germany in the Singular" series by an interview with
the president of the European Commission.

What is your assessment of the price of German unification?
For the European Community, from a political point of view as well as from
the point of view of the economic reinforcement of that Community, the price
of unification is small. We have hastened our efforts to prepare the entry of
seventeen million East Germans into the European Community. We have
perhaps underestimated certain aspects, but all in all the governments have
been satisfied with the way in which we have acted.

What advantages are to be expected from unification?
A mortgage has been dissolved. If the Community had had to pursue its
internal development with the unknown factor of support for the GDR, we
would have been doubly handicapped. First of all, the Germans were hoping
for that unification, and they could have been led to believe that as long as
that unification went unaccomplished, the development of a communal Europe
would constitute an obstacle. Moreover, the lack of unification would have
obstructed clearer vision of a Greater Europe. As a result, unification is a
globally positive phenomenon.

And its political costs?
What do we call political costs? No doubt there exists an embryonic tendency
toward economic expansion. But at the present time it is in the service of the
Community. If the EEC happened to slow down the pace of integration, then
we could legitimately start asking questions.

**Two arguments concerning the risks of unification are making them-
selves heard. According to the first, it's awful, we are heading towards
a German Europe. According to the second, it's frightening, the Germans are no longer concerned with Europe, they're thinking only of
bilateral treaties, especially with the Soviet Union. What do you think
of these two arguments?**
These two arguments are worth bringing up. It is evident that the European
Community unites peoples, but also it associates nations. It is realistic and

266

not at all out of place to judge each nation carefully, to scrutinize its thoughts and its hidden motives. From this point of view, it is true that Germany wields influence in European organizations; but you'll perhaps be surprised to hear me say that Luxembourg counts too, because such is the nature of the marriage that weds us. I'll say it again, we are bringing together peoples, but at the same time we are associating nation-states.

As for the second argument, let me say that, having attended the unification ceremonies, while there were no instructions given, while there were none to give, I was surprised to see that all of the Germans that we met, officials and people in the streets, were celebrating this event with sobriety and reserve, as if they felt deep down inside that they shouldn't get carried away. Will this go on? I can't say. But for the moment Germany's commitment to building up Europe can't sincerely be doubted by anyone.

Does it worry you that Germany hastened to sign the German-Soviet pact, article three of which has been judged ambiguous by several French officials?
We took part in elaborating the section of the agreement that concerns the Community and we found nothing that conflicts with the obligations that Germany has assumed towards the Community. Of course, the Community is an imperfect construct. It has a trading policy, I would even say a common foreign policy, but there are always national policies, and one would have to be truly naive or a hypocrite to take issue with the fact that each nation still makes use of its own interests. That's the way Europe is built. In my position, I have to take these things into account, realistically, with the hope of arriving at a greater level of cohesion and integration. There is nothing in this treaty that warrants taking up proceedings against Germany.

Then what is to be made of the worries expressed by the French and the Italians, those that you judge unfounded?
I once tried to find out something about the interim destiny of Germany. I did this because I was of course one of the first to approve the Germans' desire to unify, which I did for both moral and practical reasons. Moral, because one only had to refer to the FRG 1949 constitution to realize that we were all committed. Practical, because I don't see how we could have opposed it. Anyway, bolstered by this authority, I took the liberty of questioning some members of the public about the destiny of Germany, and its capacity to honor its commitment to the construction of Europe in spite of the temptations stemming from its economic might and its geopolitical position.

Is it possible to envisage a series of collective treaties between the Community and other states or groups of states—USSR, Japan, the United States, etc.?
We live in a system where commercial agreements between the Community as such and different states, including the Soviet Union, exist side by side

with treaties signed by two states. This situation is not altogether satisfactory, but the two steps are complementary. I am well aware of the risk that they may become antagonistic or contradictory. For the time being, that's the way we live; no one can deny that Europe has made progress over the last five years. I don't see why it can't make another qualitative leap forward—toward a political union and an economic and monetary union—taking into account the formal agreements made by Chancellor Kohl and Mr. Genscher.

Many observers estimate that, by speeding things up, Mr. Kohl has in the end underestimated the economic cost of unification for West Germany.
Did he underestimate it, or did he think there was no course other than the rapid one? I am inclined to agree with the second hypothesis. From the very beginning I had thought that the sums proposed for the cost of financing the operation were less than they would turn out to be. This has shown itself to be true, since the East German economy literally collapsed when it came into contact with the West German economy—even in areas like agriculture where it had some advantages. From an economic point of view, unification is first of all a test of the West Germans. Will they lucidly and collectively take upon themselves the solidarity required of them?

But the chief difficulty is of a psychological nature. Of these 17 million East Germans, many were born and raised knowing only communism. Even if today almost all of them agree that this regime was intolerable, it has nonetheless shaped who they are. The most serious challenge that faces both Germanys is thus to accept themselves, to recognize themselves as members of the same nation, with the same values and the same notions of life. This concerns us to the extent that we can facilitate the solution of this difficult problem, or on the other hand complicate it by our indifference and our reservations.

The European Choice

Do you fear that this mutual agreement will take time?
Yes. The confrontation between Germans on both sides, between two cultures, between two educational heritages, this will take time. It will take time for the new Germany to find its identity. Will this Germany, conscious of its economic might and of the psychological and cultural complications involved in integration, find itself a political consciousness, a national consciousness that will arouse its citizens and be acceptable to those of other nations? I wouldn't be speaking the truth were I to say that one can't ask such a question. It is at the heart of Germany's destiny.

Yet, this generation to which you allude has been open for some time now to the outside world.

Their situation, as well as that of all West European peoples, supposes a more fundamental question: what are the East German motivations? Is it "everything right away," which is to say freedom plus the life-style of their Western neighbors? Or is it more than this, which is to say that profound internal satisfaction that comes from recognizing that, at last, the family is reunited, and that from now on the collective adventure will be a personal matter for all?

These are two different things. Taking into account the forcefulness of their demand for "everything right away," it was difficult for Mr. Kohl not to accelerate. At the same time, this must not depend on a misunderstanding. It will take time for the conditions and levels of life, for the systems of social protection, for the values and for the cultures of East and West to exist in harmony. Although this poses quite a few financial problems, the coexistence of the sixteen Länder might facilitate coexistence in the midst of diversity. That's the great advantage of a federal structure. Yet in the end the Germans have decided to take this risk, for in their eyes the greatness of their nation, of their ideal, is at stake. Unlike others, I feel sympathy for them, because of this awesome challenge that awaits them.

Essentially, the question is whether East Germans have their own specificity, for one doesn't spend forty years under a regime and yet remain unaffected by it.

You've hit the nail on the head. Of course, everything that is said outside of Germany is considered suspect, but will it be permitted for a long-standing friend of all Germans to say that this is a real problem? And not just a question brought up by Günter Grass on the one hand, East German intellectuals on the other.

In your opinion, how intense is the desire to become European among citizens of the former GDR?

Like West Germans, East Germans must decide between European integration, which implies sharing sovereignty, and another geopolitical situation in which they would become the economic, and tomorrow perhaps the political, lodestone of all Europe. It is their choice to make. Nothing is decided yet. It is by measuring the extent of this question that each of us will come to understand the importance of the pro-European choice for Germany as well as for its partners, like France.

Should unification translate into an increase in the number of German functionaries within the Commission?

Let's discuss German participation in all the institutions. It would be advisable for this country, with its population of 80 million, not to demand more electoral participation in assemblies and in institutions than the FRG currently enjoys with its population of 63 million.

Has there been any talk of making such a request?
Not on the part of government.

Would it be wise for the East German leaders to yield to Soviet wishes and demand a permanent seat in the Security Council?
This is not the right time to bring up such questions. The four victorious powers of the war have most generously agreed to give in to the course of history. They have left with discretion. Though the honor was theirs, they did not enjoy much respect in official pronouncements. They have behaved in an exemplary fashion. Please, let's not say anything more.

How far has economic and monetary unification come?
History creates itself too, it isn't just the product of men's will. Today, fixing a date for entry into the second phase of economic and monetary union—an esoteric question if ever there was one—has become a test of the confirmation of German desire for unification. That's how it is. As a result, in the months that come, we expect Germany to confirm its desire in favor of building Europe. It can't be avoided. I have to take this into account, not as a disservice to the Germans, but because that is the nature of life and because I must consider the worries, fears, and questions of other member countries.

More and more officials seemed resigned to the fact that January 1, 1993 will not occur on January 1, 1993.
There is a way of doubting Europe's will that *a priori* ends up preventing that from happening. I, however, am not of that school. Risks must be taken.

Won't the accumulated weight of Germany incite the Community to stabilize itself by drawing closer to Great Britain?
Since the affair in the Gulf, the British Prime Minister [Margaret Thatcher] has been manifesting her difference with enthusiasm and energy. She hopes to reinforce her special relation with the United States; she tells the Czechs, the Hungarians, and the Swiss that they can join the Community because it has a limited goal: to create a greater market. Finally, she gives a categorical warning about the German risk.

How do the British view the future role of nation and Community? The question is worth asking. I am alarmed by the return to stances that I thought long since abandoned. I feel as patriotic as the anti-Europeans: I want to remain French and think that my country has a role to play in the world. Can it play that role alone, or in harmony and in cooperation with other countries within a vast conglomerate? In other words, what is sovereignty today? My response is already made. The operational limits of a nation-state in Europe are such that we cannot realize our basic objectives unless we work together.

As for the pace, as for the modalities—nothing has been decided yet. But there's the rub. Listening to the British Prime Minister, I have the impression that she thinks that only at the national level can the progress be realized towards which tends all political action. That's why I'm delighted by the full participation of the pound in the EMS, because political union implies the reinforcement of the twelve-member community, a common foreign policy as well as the exercise in common of sovereignty.

Did the Gulf crisis advance the elaboration of a political Europe and the idea of a European defense policy?
The need to realize political union is even stronger today that it was before the Gulf crisis. True, the Community did do what the provisions of the treaty allowed it to do. By August 2 it condemned Iraq's invasion of Kuwait, and it decreed an embargo. Next it rallied behind the flag of the United Nations. In fact it did more than this, considering that the post-crisis was as important as was the resolution of the crisis. But public opinion didn't see things that way, and hence, a certain feeling of frustration.

Yet the need for political cooperation has made itself known. It has even become the fulcrum of European renewal. As far as security goes, the West European Union has played its part.

If I were under thirty, I would ask myself three questions. First, are the European nations conscious of having essential interests in common, and if so, are they prepared to defend them together, because in that way they will be more efficient? Second question, where does their political ambition stand? Is it to seclude themselves in their prosperity, taking care of their own internal problems, or is it to be present on the scene of world events, through realism, idealism, or through both?

Under these circumstances, are they able to explain to their peoples what this represents, from the perspective of the opening up of their markets, of financial solidarity with countries to the south, of international monetary reform, of the valorization of international rights?

Third, are these countries thinking in the same way about guaranteeing their security in common? According to the response of European officials, I could tell you whether the European venture is worth the trouble or not. And I hope, to use the expression of François Mitterrand, that the sum of our audacity will amount to more than the sum of our prudence.

To Build a Confederation

As far as defense goes, the Twelve would be wrong to put the institutional question before more fundamental questions. Institutions are the consequence, but also the bond, of political choices. As a result, if the Twelve have essential interests to defend together, they'll find the institutional apparatuses that they need. One of the dangers of the intergovernmental conference of December on political union, is that the institutional discussion precede the discussion of motivations. The institutional "Mecano'" is important, but it can be resolved only in the light of larger political choices, clearly made.

That is the way to avoid a new "*Hernani* quarrel" amongst federalists, confederationists, and intergovernmentalists. It is my concern to act in such a way that the new institutional schema perform as well as the old one—a product of the genius of the fathers of the Rome treaty, and that has shown its effectiveness over the last five years. If we disrobe Peter to clothe Paul, I'll have to say no.

The European project aims too much at elitists and technocrats. Too make it more democratic, we must begin by reflecting on the rights and responsibilities of citizens in such a way that they feel that they are participating in a collective venture. The great danger that threatens us democrats is the weakening of a sense of belonging. For me, national character and communal character are compatible, and not antagonistic. It would be far more serious to start off with weak democracies, whose peoples are no longer capable of acting together and of forging their own destiny. The real struggle is between those who take note of the actual situation and adapt to it and those, including myself, who believe that democracy is founded upon institutions that are ever opening up discussion between officials and public opinion.

But doesn't the problem of the two types of legitimacy remain?
Yes. Each time that we change treaties, national sovereignties must ratify the new treaty. Next, it is the turn of each country's government to bring its legislative body into the decision-making process, with regard to the application of treaties. That's why the idea of creating a second Assembly comprising national parliaments seems a silly one to me. What will that bring about? It will further weaken the European parliament, that on the contrary needs to be strengthened. And I'm not the one who would recommend today a complete switch to a federalist system in which the Commission would become an entirely separate government. People are not prepared for this, although it is advisable to hold on to the possibility of such an evolution for the future.

And the Confederation?
President Mitterrand's message concerning the Confederation was the clearest, the most important given to Eastern European countries. Since then, other politicians have complicated matters. This Confederation must be constructed gradually, by drawing together ever-tighter political, economic, and cultural ties with other European countries. Action is what the Community directs, so as to bestow character and action upon all these countries.

Italy

Germany and History Have Taken a Leap

by Giuliano Ferrara

Giuliano Ferrara, born in 1952, is a journalist and member of the European Parliament. He is a frequent contributor to *Corriere della sera*. This piece is reprinted from *Corriere della sera*, 27 December 1989 and originally appeared under the title, *"Germania e la storia ha fatto un salto."*

In Europe, there is a new party: the fear of Germany. Perhaps anti-German feelings, worthy of consideration like all authentic emotions, concerns primarily the chancelleries, the ruling classes, the intellectuals, the journalists, the historians, the churches and other mediators of the public conscience. Perhaps, the fear of Germany produces more fear than Germany does in actuality—like ghosts, like all things which one evokes out of the obscurity of symbolic memory, out from under a covering thickened by the passing of time.

During the press conference in Milan, like everyone else, I listened attentively to Gorbachev's response to the colleague from *Messagero* who asked him what he thought of German reunification. The most stupefying thing was that the Soviet leader, always so long-winded and tortuous in his responses and smiles, seemed truly embarrassed, reticent, almost unable to formulate an answer.

The only device which seemed available to him was to invite History to the microphone and to give History the job of answering the question. This verbal appeal to History is now dragged in with unprecedented impertinence as a powerful and irrefutable force in the pace of events. With this [excuse], it is difficult to find a political phenomenon which frightens, which is beyond the grasp of instant intellectual understanding and the static and obvious categories forged during decades of equilibrium without change in European and world relations.

Gorbachev's embarrassment is not the only example of this. The parliament in Strasbourg, for example, met a few weeks ago and had a discussion of great interest regarding the November events—the Berlin Wall, changes in the [European] Community schedule set off by the new and overwhelming events in Eastern Europe. Special guests included French President Mitterrand and Federal Chancellor Kohl.

But, at the moment of action, of voting on a resolution, the Parliament found itself discussing self-determination or self-decision, with terminological variations according to the diverse strands of thought (translated into the various languages), which seemed to parallel the most abstract and quibbling disputes of Byzantine theology.

There was a truly comic moment in which each group claimed the right to vote on the resolution in their preferred language, in order to avoid misunderstandings between *déterminer* and *décider*, *bestimmen* and *entscheiden*, *decidere* and *determinare*.

In the interest of mental health one would have to confess every morning and rattle off a litany of things that we all know: that the division of Germany and Berlin has already lasted an historically significant amount of time and an infinite political time; that the opening of the frontiers has *ipso facto* created an inter-German situation open only to the one option of national unity within a federal framework; that around this new political center turns the future of the EC and the easing of East-West tensions.

In order to have coherent and firm values, in which this part of the world believes or should believe, one must add to the morning prayer of the good European that this chain of inevitable facts is also a chain of hoped for eventualities, conforming to the final Helsinki Accords and a shared liberal-democratic sensibility.

Today, as never before, instead of feeding the fear of Germany, the task should be to lay down the historical-political conditions for the removal of obstacles so that German unity can freely take place in the shortest possible time.

By worrying about the Oder-Neisse line and the legal tidiness with which Germany must regain her tragic, but unavoidable European political centrality, the continental chancelleries, the people and the culture classes are competing to fan the flames of the mistrust, suspicion, and questioning of German intentions.

On French television, I watched with horror a documentary, more than two hours long, on Nazism from its origins to the Lager. After watching the painful pictures of Auschwitz and Treblinka, I was dumbstruck by the debate which followed on the historical responsibility for Nazism and the future of Germany, which mixed politics and memory [in a way that] confused reason and emotion in a blend too heated to accept.

And while the experts discuss the Lager and reunification, the Second World War and the power of the German mark, I thought, "what have they to decide?" Whether or not there is a continuity between the Third Reich and the Federal Republic, History has taken a leap and one must finally face it.

Changes in the European Equilibrium

Massimo Salvadori interviewed by Antonio Landolfi

Massimo Salvadori is professor of history and political philosophy at the University of Turin. The interview, originally titled, *"In Europa cambiano tutti gli equilibri,"* was conducted by Antonio Landolfi, who is a commentator for *Avanti*. This article originally appeared in *Avanti* on 3 October 1990.

What will the future of "Greater Germany" be? What influence will the new nation have on the European and international scene? What will be the political, economic and cultural ramifications of the fusion of the GDR with the Federal Republic? Professor Antonio Landolfi interviewed Professor Massimo Salvadori, Professor of History and Politics at the University of Turin, on this subject.

Do you think that the European and Italian left's historic fear of German unification has ended?

I have the sense that this distrust of German unification has not completely abated. But, I do not believe that this in and of itself is a prevailing characteristic of the left, but forms part of a heritage which has some roots in all the political parties. It seems to me, for example, that just yesterday, in an article published in *Avanti*, Günter Grass expressed in an eloquent and representative way a position which exists to a certain extent in all political and cultural movements, independently of a left or nonleft orientation. Naturally, one must discuss the foundations [of such fears].

Can we say that by now it represents a minority position?

It is difficult to say whether or not [such fears] represent a minority position. I certainly believe that these positions are not diffused enough to deserve too much consideration. It is clear that, rejecting a deterministic and racist interpretation of history, one cannot assert that the Germans have within themselves a determining negative characteristic, because German history clearly reveals many and varied tendencies. Germany has a body of history which is broken down into components, even if it is important to understand why in Germany at a certain point authoritarian, reactionary and antimodern ideas coalesced and became dominant and then culminated in Nazism. But we must realize, and one must insist on this, that today's Germany is economically prosperous, even if East Germany poses serious problems which I believe will be resolved quite rapidly within a few years. This is an economically prosperous and democratic Germany and it must certainly offer reassurances, which can only come from this direction. United Germany is a country which will have an enormous influence on the continent. In France and England, fears of a strong Germany were raised from the point of view of old ideas of state sovereignty. These [reactions] in reality reflected fears tied to the growing weakness of England, on the one side, and France, on the other, when confronted with German economic might. Without a doubt, we have to deal with a changed European horizon in which German influence will be great. We will have to see how the other Western European partners establish a fruitful relationship with the German presence on the continent, which will be an undeniable fact.

Like many other commentators, you emphasize German economic productivity, but at the same time this Germany, by now strongly bound to democratic values, offers as well a political system and an electoral system among the best existing in Europe.
Yes, it is worth the trouble to fill out the picture. Up until last year, until very recent times, we were unprepared for radical change and we were used to a divided Germany of relatively little importance in international politics, even if one cannot underestimate the growing role of the Federal Republic. In short, calculations were made with a divided Germany in mind, an economically strong Federal Republic with political influence far inferior to its economic power. With a territorally and demographically united Germany, we will have to deal, in the near future, with a Germany which will have, on the whole, a greater weight in economic affairs and, therefore, in politics as well. As far as one can surmise, I am convinced that Germany does not pose any foreseeable problems for democratic development. Germany does pose a problem in its economic and political influence; [this] poses a problem for the European Economic Community, for Eastern Europe, for the Soviet Union and for the United States. This is an objective fact which must be faced.

Naturally I would be afraid of a Germany analogous to ones from the past or if we were faced with a destabilized, impoverished Germany, an internally or internationally dissatisfied Germany. We have, instead, a Germany that will count for much and will continually count for more. This forces a reconsideration of past equilibriums which no longer exist and therefore we can say that German reunification is the end of past balances of power, and this presents important problems for all. We cannot think of remaining in the old gardens of European politics because German unification has radically altered the outlines of the picture. Let's not forget, [these are] radical changes which, beyond Germany, affect Eastern Europe and the Soviet Union.

German unification, in this sense, is the decisive pole of international shifts with respect to Europe. Germany will be the strongest pole of a Western-

Central Europe which will face a "soft underbelly," in the shape of Eastern Europe and the Soviet Union in the throes of structural crisis. In this situation, all factors indicate that the role of Germany is destined to become one of the important factors of international politics.

I don't think it worthwhile to express dread or to celebrate. These are the objective givens, and the thing to do is face them realistically.

A Christian Democratic majority and a victory by Kohl are foreseen in the upcoming election. But, . . . couldn't something similar happen to that which took place in Great Britain in which Churchill won the war and unexpectedly lost the first [postwar] elections?

I think this recalling of and reference to the case of Churchill is useful and stimulating, but it is impossible to forecast since electoral predictions are often proven wrong. However, they do present some issues for consideration. I don't know if we will have a "Kohl effect" or a "Churchill effect." It is worth saying that Churchill won the war, but was then dismissed by the English people who were then primarily preoccupied by social questions. One will have to see whether or not united Germany prizes the achievement, of which Kohl was the primary protagonist, which produced national unification or whether in some way the sense of the difficulty created by the economic integration of East Germany becomes stronger. In the second case, it could be that all those worried about the economic costs of unification, above all those in a precarious economic situation, push for a defense of, or return to the welfare state or the protective state. If this tendency prevails, we could be surprised. It is very difficult to decode beforehand the strongest tendency within the German people. History does not let us decode things *a priori;* we still have to see which feelings and aspects of rational reflection are introduced into the debate and how the two [political] parties respond.

I Do Not Fear German Nationalism

by Umberto Eco

Umberto Eco, born in 1932, is professor of semiotics at the University of Bologna and is author of *The Name of the Rose* and *Foucault's Pendulum*. This piece is reprinted from the *New York Times*, 27 September 1990.

It is an unavoidable process because a country with one tradition and one language has the right to find unity for itself. Nothing can stop such a natural trend. We have to respect this natural urge, this tendency to be a single nation.

Germany has a similar history to Italy's. In the last century both tried to establish themselves as separate countries. I understand the worries of other European countries. But I don't have that typical concern–the fear of a new pan-Germany, the fear of a new Nazism—because the younger generation is different from the previous one and democracy has produced a profound change.

When I meet German people of my generation I find people who have a sense of their historical responsibility for what Nazism had been. They have a profound sense of what their duty should be. I do not fear German nationalism.

If you look at the historical background of Germany you see almost a neurotic split personality. On one side there is a nationalistic, imperialistic Prussian drive. On the other hand, there is a part of German culture that is constantly critical of itself, much like Italians are. The Italian national sport is self-criticism. There is a struggle between the two sides of the German soul. But there are two of them.

I cannot say that a country or a culture is condemned to behave always in the same way. To think that is another form of racism.

Three Cartoons From *L'Unità*

"There are no longer East Germans and West Germans . . . After tonight they are all clients of the same Mercedes." *L'Unità*, 2 October 1990.

"Once upon a time, there was a Germany of the East and one of the West. . . .
Then at midnight Cinderella was taken over by the ball." *L'Unità*, 3 October
1990.

"Will we succeed in forgetting Germany's past? . . . Perhaps, with a few million marks." *L'Unità*, 4 October 1990.

Israel

The Grand Appeasement

by Arye Dayan

Arye Dayan, born in 1950, emigrated to Israel from Argentina in 1969 and is a journalist. This piece is reprinted from *Ha'aretz*, 7 September 1990.

For Zalman Shazar, the third president of Israel, the night of the 19th of August 1965 was sleepless. His spokesman did not hide this fact from the numerous reporters from around the world who congregated in his quarters in Jerusalem the following morning. They came to witness a diplomatic ceremony, which was sombre, charged and awkward.

Three people were seated in the center of the lounge, underneath Israel's emblem, obviously uneasy and tense. To the right of the president was the Israeli foreign minister, Mrs. Golda Meir; to his left, Dr. Rolf Pauls, who was now to be confirmed as Germany's first ambassador to Israel. According to newspaper reports, the three had passed more than two full minutes in strained silence, before the German finally dared to break the ice.

Now, twenty five years after that momentous ceremony, Israel is found to be practically a supporter of German unification, her newly appointed foreign minister chose Bonn for his first formal visit to a foreign country, and Israeli public opinion is indifferent, not even protesting against demanding compensation-payments from East Germany, which is about to become defunct.

Then, in 1965, all hell broke loose; the heightened tension during the confirmation ceremony in the presidential quarters was but a faint echo of the far-reaching furor throughout Israel. In the week between Pauls's arrival in Israel and the ceremony, there were daily demonstrations and vigils against establishing normal diplomatic relations with Germany. The organization of the survivors of the concentration camp Treblinka led protest meetings in cemeteries across the country. When the future ambassador visited Yad Vashem, the museum of the Holocaust, one of the museum's staff burst at him, cursing and crying in German, "Pauls go home." Members of Israeli Kibbutzim painted anti-German slogans at major road intersections. Leftist parties organized a big demonstration in one part of Tel Aviv, the right organized a march in another. Tens of thousands heard Menachem Begin, then the leader of the minority right (and later Israel's prime minister), declare that "Israel will never have proper relations with the murderers"; another member of parliament urged the police orchestra to defy their orders and refuse "to play Hitler's anthem in Jerusalem." The press delved into the past of the new diplomatic mission. The ambassador Pauls, it turned out, had been

287

an officer in the wehrmacht during the war. His major aide was found to have served in the Hungarian Embassy in Germany during the time that it was a channel for conveying instructions for extermination of the Jews from Berlin to Budapest. Near the hotel in Tel Aviv where Pauls and his aide were staying, the Israeli police arrested a man who was spying on it with military binoculars.

While the ceremony in the president's house was taking place, thousands of demonstrators congregated in the narrow streets around it, many wearing concentration camp uniforms. They had been standing since dawn along Pauls's route from his hotel, holding anti-German banners ("Pauls Go Home," "No Nazis in Israel," "Six Million Times No"). When the ceremony began, the atmosphere heated up. While the police orchestra was playing the German national anthem, their colleagues outside, wearing helmets and swinging clubs, found it increasingly difficult to prevent the crowd from storming in. By the time Pauls was reviewing the honor guard (the soldiers' weapons were previously checked, to make sure they were not loaded), the first demonstrators managed to break through the police lines. Stones were thrown, one of which hit the president's car. The police, failing to disperse the angry crowd with their hands and clubs, were forced to stampede into it on horseback. Some demonstrators retaliated by showing their worn invalid cards; others denounced the policemen as "murderers," or even "Nazis." All in all, ten people, of the crowd and the police, ended up in the hospital.

The extent of the transformation which the Israeli public has undergone since those days is astonishing, and its rapidity is no less startling. Its full power and implications are becoming evident now, as Germany moves toward complete reunification. In the German left, some yet-too-weak voices are expressing concern about the possible consequences of a rise in German nationalist feelings following the reunification. The Polish Government wanted to make sure that the unified Germany will not attempt to modify their joint borders, which were determined at the end of the war. A British minister was heard criticizing the unification sharply. Official concern has been expressed in both Norway and the Netherlands, countries which have both shared in the suffering of Nazi occupation.

In Israel, the Jewish state, none of this can be found. Prime Minister Shamir declared that Israel had no intention of meddling in the process of German reunification, or in any other issue regarding internal European borders. He furthermore chose to make this announcement in a special meeting of the Israeli Knesset on the occasion of a special session commemorating the forty-fifth anniversary of the Nazi defeat. Things had been different in the first few days after the Berlin Wall had fallen, when Shamir had said on American television that Israel remembers the deeds of a unified Germany, and is apprehensive about what it will do if it ever became strong again. The poignancy of this first statement had even required the foreign minister, Moshe Arens, to visit Bonn unexpectedly with some conciliatory explanations, saying that Germany needs only to reaffirm its historical commitment toward Israel in order to assuage any possible Israeli apprehension. Since then, official reservations about German reunification were never heard again.

It seems that Israel's formal position on this issue accords with general public opinion. A quarter of a century after the German ambassador had to be appointed under police protection, an opinion poll taken by Moshe Zimmerman, Professor of German History at the Hebrew University, has found that only 21 percent of Israeli Jews think their government ought to oppose German reunification, while 27 percent believe Israel's position should be one of approval. More interestingly, his survey shows that 41 percent of Israeli Jews maintain that German reunification is none of Israel's business, and that the Israeli government should not declare any stance on this issue. An additional 10 percent had no opinion on the subject at all. Obviously, most of the Jewish citizens of the state of Israel are indifferent to the question of the reunification of Germany.

Recent years, argues Zimmerman, have witnessed a process of "diminishing actuality of the Holocaust with regard to relationships with Germany," which has two apparently contradictory manifestations. On the one hand, the young generation in Israel is deepening its historical understanding of the Holocaust; on the other hand, a distinct political frame of reference emerges with regard to present-day Germany and to Israel's relationship with it. The Holocaust is seen as a historical phenomenon, while German-Israeli relationships are perceived to be a political one. Already in 1979, when Zimmerman had asked students to classify the "West German people" and the "East German people" with other nationalities, most students classified them by their present political relationship with Israel: the West German next to the Dutch, the East German next to the Russian.

The Israeli public, on the whole, has few reservations about relationships with Germany. While it is true that many Israelis would not buy a German car, one importing agency was found a couple of years ago to mislead the consumers that a Belgian-made car was in fact German-made: it helped sales, explained the importers. Although some Israelis will never visit Germany, there are more Israeli charter flights to German cities on weekends than to any other destination. And even if some Israelis refrain from watching German films or plays, the overall cultural exchange with Germany is quite remarkable. In the domain of culture, nevertheless, several taboos remain: Wagner and Strauss are as yet forbidden. Israeli television does not broadcast German-speaking films, unless they are related to the Holocaust, though this prohibition seems to be weakening.

According to the journalist Tom Segev, who is now completing a book on the Israelis and the Holocaust, the dominant process between Germans and Israelis since 1952 has been one of "appeasement." Its roots go back to David Ben-Gurion's decision to accept reparations: "once Israelis accepted compensation money, it became very difficult to resist other things." The opposition to the reparations agreement was not only political; many had strong honest reservations, both emotional and ideological. However, Segev claims that the opposition to establishing diplomatic relations in 1965 was, by contrast, overwhelmingly political. Furthermore, between these two events occurred the famous trial of Adolf Eichmann: "the Israeli press," says Segev, "followed closely the reactions to the trial in Germany, and they seemed all right. Thus, paradoxically, the trial ameliorated the reaction of many Israelis to Germany."

German-Israeli relations are closer than those with any other European country. "The intensity of these relations is exceptional," says Mordechai Levi, of the department in the foreign ministry dealing with the EEC. "They are considerably more intense than the Israeli relations with France or England, and this in spite of the support for such relations by a strong Jewish community, as in France, for example." Asher Ben-Nathan, Israel's first ambassador to Germany, describes Israeli-German relations as "intimate." They permeate most domains: economy, tourism, culture, youth exchanges, and defense. In its contribution to Israel in almost all of these, Germany is secondary in importance only to the United States.

More than sixty towns in Israel have a twin-city agreement with German cities—more than double than with any other country. Functionaries mostly go from Israel to Germany; money tends to flow in the other direction. In virtually all these sixty Israeli towns, there is a German-financed park, jungle gym or nursery, carrying the name of the twin German town. These small-scale investments are dwarfed by the much larger sums of money channelled to Israel through a variety of public and private foundations. Israel receives annual aid of 140 million marks, on favorable terms, as if it were a developing country—though for many years Israel has not met the criteria for inclusion in this category. Some of the biggest projects in Israel in recent years, like the major Tel Aviv-Jerusalem highway, have been funded with German aid. Each of the three largest political parties in Germany has a special fund for international contacts; as far as we can tell, Israel is the only country in the world where all three funds are represented simultaneously.

All academic institutions in Israel use German research funds, and regularly exchange scholars with German institutions. Israeli science receives both private and public German funding; the Volkswagen foundation, one of the most active German funds in Israel, has allocated in the past year alone a million and a half marks for physical and chemical research in the Hebrew University of Jerusalem and the Technion at Haifa.

German financial support of Israel is matched by a cordial diplomatic relationship. Two years after these relations had been established, both the German government and German public opinion voiced support for Israel's position in the period preceding the Six Day War. During the 1973 war,

Germany proved to be more flexible in allowing the United States to use its bases there for aiding Israel than other European countries.

This pattern was reversed only twice, when in 1981 Germany wished to sell Leopard tanks to Saudi Arabia, and when Chancellor Helmut Schmidt remarked in an interview on the German commitment to solving the Palestinian problem. Menachem Begin, then Israel's prime minister, responded immediately: "this is arrogance motivated by greed," he said, "Mr. Schmidt is ignoring the past." The conflict led to the cancellation of Schmidt's planned visit to Israel.

Yohanan Meroz, Israel's ambassador in Bonn from 1974 to 1981, claims that "for the last twenty-five years Germany's behavior toward Israel was more fair and honest than other West European countries," among which he mentions France, Britain, Italy and Spain. The Israeli interest, he further argues, demands to preserve those ties with Germany. Yet, he also thinks that on the declarative level, Israel could have acted differently, stressing more the lessons of the past and the German commitment to the Jewish people. But practically, he does not think Israel should object to the reunification. "Until recently, East German attitudes toward Israel were humiliating and antagonistic, more than other countries in the Soviet bloc. They never responded to demands for compensation, they opposed us in every international arena, they supplied arms to all our enemies. When such a state becomes amalgamated with another, much more favorable toward us—Israel can hardly lose. Had these been two equal countries, I would have been more skeptical; but since one is three times bigger than the other, our apprehensions—while not obliterated—should be considerably diminished."

"In Israeli-German relations," says Ben-Nathan, Israel's first ambassador to Bonn, "emotion and reason have always contradicted each other. Reason dictated investing in relations which the heart found disturbing. Similarly, the present argument that a divided Germany is the price that the German people have to pay for past crimes is an emotional argument. Israel does not need to support German reunification, but simply to learn to live with reality. German reunification is inevitable and cannot be reversed; we can worry, but we cannot change it."

Chayka Grossman, former partisan during World War II and former member of the Knesset, denies that the opposition to reunification is only an emotional response. She thinks that those who see the end of the Berlin Wall and German reunification as a victory of liberalism and freedom, now conquering Eastern Europe, are deeply mistaken. "Dividing Germany," she has written recently, "was decided upon in order to balance its ability to resurrect its infamous nationalism." According to Grossman, this danger is not yet over. She points to the fact that Germany's declared expenditure on defense is proportionally much higher than that of countries such as Canada, the Netherlands, Belgium, Spain or Greece. In spite of internationally sanctioned limitations, Germany continues to distribute banned arms, both directly and indirectly. "In my opinion," she concludes, "Germany has not yet undergone a genuine process of de-Nazification. The partial de-Nazification through the Nüremberg trials was imposed upon her by the allies."

Grossman is very disappointed by the official position of the Israeli government, as well as by that of her own party on the left (Mapam). Israel's attitude is as if the country involved is not Germany, but some nation out-of-space. If Grossman could have it her way, she would impose certain preconditions on German reunification: for instance, a demand for Germans' explicit acknowledgement of their past crimes against humanity and against the Jewish people, rather than sufficing, in Adenauer's formula, that crimes were committed "in the name of" the German people; drastic restrictions on Germany's rearmament; and introducing explicit recognition of Germany's historical and moral responsibility for Nazi crimes into German school textbooks.

Another disappointed politician is the head of the Knesset's defence and foreign affairs committee, Eliyahu Ben-Elissar of the Likud. "Our prime minister says that German reunification will enhance peace and democracy. What can I say? The Herut movement [the major political movement on the right, the central pillar of the Likud party] has changed significantly. Obviously Israel cannot prevent German reunification. But are we not permitted to admonish? To point to the dangers? Not only do I eat pork, I also have to show to the world that I am enjoying it?!"

"When the Austrians elected a president with previous Nazi associations," says the Knesset member of the Labour Party Shevach Weiss, "Israel came close to severing all diplomatic relations, in spite of his reputation as a friend of Israel. With regard to the reunification of Germany, Israel could make any formal declaration, without risking any harm to its interests."

Chayka Grossman of Mapam, Eliyahu Ben-Elissar of the Likud, and Shevach Weiss of the Labour party, have perhaps only one thing in common, hidden in their biographies: all three were born in Poland, all three survived the Holocaust.

Unholy Trinity

by Shevach Weiss

Shevach Weiss, born in 1935, is a Labour party member
of the Israeli Knesset and professor of political science at
Haifa University. This article is reprinted from *Al Ha'mishmar*, 15 October 1990.

The reunification of Germany became irreversible once the democratic revolution in East Germany had occurred. One could not imagine a force which
could have prevented the Germans from exercising their right to self-determination. The collapsing Soviet empire could not subvert reunification, while
the United States did not want to. In such circumstances, France as well could
not pose any obstacles.

With reunification at the door, all the symbols of the Reich reappeared—
the symbols of a previous Germany: Berlin as capital, the Brandenburg Gate,
the Reichstag building—symbols which evoke particular memories. The memories are not of Beethoven, but of Wagner; not of Goethe or Schiller, but of
Streicher; not of Immanuel Kant, but of Goebbels. Hence, not only the reunification was inevitable, but concommitantly melancholy, apprehension, and
more than a tinge of real fear. Ambivalence toward a great Germany is not
restricted only to the victims of Nazism. A great powerful Germany conjures
up in the minds of those who remember an image of an unholy trinity. Once
again, emotion and reason do not necessarily move along parallel tracks.

Evaluating the reunification from a political, social, and economic point of
view, may lead to a conclusion that there is no real danger lurking behind it.
After all, West Germany is a strong bastion of democracy; its economy is
stronger and more stable than ever before; it is embedded in the western
European network of alliances, and deeply committed to the common European home. Many Germans have also learned to what extent the Nazi
tyranny hurt them, and imprinted an eternal stigma on the Germans collectively.

From a moral point of view, it is difficult to attribute collective guilt to
those who were born after Hitler, and to those who were only children during
the Second World War. All Germans under the age of 55, and perhaps under
the age of 60, were not personally implicated in the Nazi war and extermination machine. And after all, we refuse to accept the racist Nuremberg
formula, by which the rotten germs are passed from one generation to another.

We see racial theories as alien and detestable. Therefore, apparently, we should not indict the sons' generation for the sins of their fathers, nor attribute to them some quasi-deterministic hereditary potential for inhumanity. Nevertheless, the heart refuses to accept, and the eye refuses to watch, the ecstasy of reunification, the reinstitution of power, in the shadow of the Brandenburg Gate.

It is not only size which is worrisome in the reunification, since West Germany, with sixty million Germans, was not weaker than a unified Germany with seventy-seven million. Rather, it is in particular the social components of East Germany which are terrifying. Those had replaced a brown tyranny with despotism, and have undergone forty years of nationalism—perhaps implicit, but quite strong.

If the Germans and their political, spiritual, and social leaders will persevere in the inculcation of democracy, will emphasize humanist education, and will continually remind their people of their ancestors' deeds during the Nazi hell; and if Europe and the enlightened world will constantly keep them under close scrutiny, it is of course very plausible that what had happened before will not happen again. Yet we, surviving smoky embers from the hellish furnace fire which had burned us, cannot participate in the celebrations of the victory of reunification.

I have recently participated as the Israeli delegate to the European Council in Strasburg, together with over two hundred parliamentary delegates from all the democracies of Europe. The atmosphere in the Council was not one of elation. All participants were polite and correct, and some even took part in the reception organized by the Germans on the occasion of the reunification ceremony, but one could feel the overhanging sadness which accompanied the event. As we said, a unified Germany upsets the European balances as they had been established after the Second World War. Many Germans are aware of this, and it is in their hands to try to calm these fears.

Europe is still a frozen lake of blood, and as the poets of the late 1940s said, after Auschwitz it is difficult to write poetry.

Now We Shall be Reduced to Our Due Place Within German Priorities

Yaron London interviewing Saul Friedlander

Saul Friedlander, born in 1932, is professor of history at the University of California at Los Angeles and Tel Aviv University. This interview is reprinted from *Yediot Aharonot*, 3 October 1990.

Before presenting you with questions about the future of Germany and of post-reunification Europe, can you describe the German political entity as it was formed after the defeat of the Third Reich; what did we have up until now?

Indeed, we will do better to understand the starting point before getting into speculations. West Germany, as it was created at the end of the Second World War, was completely democratic, and has internalized the prevalent western democratic norms. Furthermore, it can be said that the Germans were particularly keen on establishing those norms, in order to prove their acceptability into the society of nations. Otherwise, they would have remained lepers, as it were. They even invented a term, wholly misleading in a historical perspective: "the zero hour," which is 1945, when the new German society was allegedly reborn, liberated from its past. They have repeatedly attempted to prove this, in any possible way.

What were the elements in German society and culture which made this process possible?

This is debatable. First, we must not forget the effort on the part of the Americans and the other Allies of re-education. Although this effort is commonly seen as a failure which entailed not inconsiderable harmful effects, I am not sure how bad this purported failure really was. I do believe that it left some imprint on German society. Secondly, the Federal Republic was led by politicians who had experienced Weimar democracy themselves, and hence understood well that in order to re-establish their state and introduce it as an equal into the family of nations, they had to maintain an exemplary democracy and to suppress any manifestation of nationalistic recklessness. This understanding was shared by German politicians regardless of their political camps: Christian-Democrats like Konrad Adenauer, FRG's first chancellor, and Socialists, like his rival Schumacher.

Following the events of the last two years, can one say that the Americans are the greatest educators of the twentieth century, having shaped the Germans, the Japanese, and now Eastern Europe?
Indeed they have succeeded in Germany and Japan, and they may very well succeed in the Soviet Union as well; but these successes have not been the fruits of deliberate efforts. While capitalist liberal democracy proved its resilience, the two competing ideologies, fascism in its various manifestations and communism, collapsed. What has survived? Only the aspiration to live in a more-or-less democratic and more-or-less liberal system, attempting to minimize social inequality. These aspirations have been internalized by humankind in our times at least among the inhabitants of the industrialized parts of the world.

How can we explain such a drastic transformation in the realm of national culture? Have German and Japanese societies really been able to suddenly internalize values, which had previously been alien to their history? In this question I wish to express a common concern, that behind the superficial democratic makeup, recently assumed, lurks a more fundamental tenet of German culture, or even of the authoritarian German family structure, which will ultimately prevail.
I do not accept such claims, and neither do most scholars nowadays. I believe that the penetration of democracy depends on a coincidental constellation of factors, and later perhaps on gradual education. Here, the coincidence was the success of the German and Japanese markets; had they failed, this political process would have been aborted. Instead, the opposite occurred: Germany witnessed the famous economic miracle, which had begun already in 1947 with the reform of the mark; and Japan similarly went through an amazing recovery, with American help, several years after her defeat. Both these peoples were presented with economic success as proof of the merits of the new political regime. It is economic prosperity which convinces people; only later is it supplemented by values such as freedom of speech.

So how did the United States succeed in surviving the depression of the 1930s, without falling back on a totalitarian regime?
The United States survived only with many difficulties. Other societies failed, for instance the French: Vichy was a belated consequence of the economic crisis. Apparently the political culture of the Anglo-Saxon countries is more resilient, in comparison with French society, which had been fragmented even before the crisis. However, to return to Germany, it is a fact that following the war it has had a social system, which when aided by economic success, imbued the nation with democratic consciousness.

And where were the national aspirations relegated to?
This is a very important point. The Federal Republic was a social system which functioned extremely well, but the Germans never equated it with a

realization of their emotional or national identity. No German said, "I see Federal Germany as my 'Heimat'." West Germans identified themselves only with the social and economic success, which some of them then turned into an ideology. For instance, Jürgen Habermas, the Frankfurt philosopher, who said that in such identification the Germans have preceded others. Because of the disasters which we had brought on ourselves and on others, he argues, we have shed off traditional nationalism, replacing it with an identification with our liberal constitution and with our links to European society and its values. He calls this "constitutional patriotism." However, most people cannot identify with such abstract notions, and have lately begun to search for an anchor in a new national identity. This had begun even before the events leading to reunification, and led to the renowned debate among German historians, since coping with the twelve years of the Third Reich was a prerequisite for establishing a new German identity.

And now, does reunification create a new situation within German national consciousness?
People like Habermas or the famous author Günter Grass are apprehensive about the possible consequences. In *Der Spiegel*, a young German author has expressed concern for the values on which the Federal Republic has been founded.

But in fact all that is happening is a certain expansion in Germany's size: why is it so significant?
Here we enter the domain of speculation. It can be said, that indeed the change is not very significant, and that already before reunification Germany has been a mighty power, to which the addition of further territory and population is not of considerable importance. Others, however, point to symptoms which they see as the re-emergence of the old German nationalism. For these, even the rock concert by the Berlin Wall, or Germany's winning the world cup, are signs of worse to come. It goes without saying, that if the Belgians had won the cup, and would have gone berserk with ecstasy, nobody would have objected. As I said, these are only speculations.

What, then, are the changes that are certainly true?
It is certain that a mighty superpower has been created, unparalleled in Europe, which can exercise its will far and wide.

Was Germany ever as powerful as now?
I do not think so. It seems to me that Germany has never been so powerful in its whole history. It lacks military power, but in our times real power lies in the checkbook.

One other thing can be said with certainty: with this unified Germany, it is easy now for a German to identify emotionally. The Federal Republic wished to be sterile; the unified Germany cannot be sterile. The unification reunites the Germans not only with the eastern parts of their country, but with their past, with their national myths.

Is this already apparent?

I cannot yet perceive any conspicuous expressions of nationalistic mysticism, and I do not think we will see dramatic ones in the near future. However, apprehensions do exist, not only among Germany's neighbors, but among the Germans themselves. The generation for which the Federal Republic came to be seen as a guarantee of democracy, has mixed feelings. A young author, Patrik Süsskind, who wrote the famous novel *The Perfume*, has expressed his expectations and fears in *Der Spiegel*. His bottom line is not fear, but hesitation. In the Federal Republic he felt comfortable, he says. While the Eastern regions—like Mecklenburg or Silesia—were foreign lands to him, he felt at home in Florence, Paris, or London. He definitely perceived Germany as part of western Europe. Now he is abruptly confronted with the lost provinces: Dresden, Leipzig, Königsberg—which now goes still by the name of Kaliningrad, but to be sure not for long—and, like everyone, this leaves him wondering.

What are the consequences for Germany within Europe?

A year or two ago, all this was inconceivable. The pretensions of Sovietologists and political scientists crumbled like a house of cards. We were all wrong, so we need to speak now with particular humility.

Two years ago, and even last year, the first phase of German development was supposed to have been its firm integration within Europe; the next step was supposed to have been European unification, and the last one involved some growing influence in Eastern Europe. Now it has all turned upside-down, and consequently the nature of the unification of Europe in 1992 cannot be foreseen. Germany's immediate preoccupation is to put its eastern part back on its feet, while new venues toward the east are opening up—toward Poland, Czechoslovakia, Hungary, and the Soviet Union.

Is this a world Germany would want to deal with on her own, independently of her western European partners?

This process cannot be fully determined by deliberate political intentions. Germany has the necessary power, the financial resources, and I dare say even the experience—though the latter statement does invoke some macabre overtones. When the Germans bought the Soviet rights in East Germany for several tens of millions of dollars, it was a striking demonstration of the supremacy of economic power over military power; and we have not seen it all yet.

We were talking before about the constellation of factors around the economic prosperity of 1947, which had allowed Germany to become democratic. We are now witnessing a similar conjuncture: an enormous national state, opening avenues eastward, admittedly with certain economic difficulties due to rising oil prices and the cost of reunification, but within a broader historical perspective these are but minor impediments. Germany has gained access to a vast market, which can be developed and expanded for the next hundred years, and thus add power to power.

Will this engender German neo-colonialism?
Such terms are irrelevant, since the East wishes this to happen. I saw this myself in Czechoslovakia, and heard from others who had visited Poland and the Soviet Union. It is well known there, that without Germany these states would simply collapse.

Nevertheless, will this not re-enact the familiar colonial scenario, whereby the developed country gains cheap labor and raw materials, and then sells expensive finished products?
Every developed economy needs markets. Even Israel is seeking marketing options in the East, and obviously its importance for the Germans is much greater, with their mechanical, chemical, and car industries. The problem will be to get paid, since the Russians have no dollars; so the Germans will need to give them long-term loans, in order to rehabilitate their economies and then repay the loans. These are obvious questions, about which I cannot enlighten you much further, since I am not an economist.

So let me pose a question related directly to your line of expertise, the relationship between politics and culture. What will be the cultural implications of the German momentum?
Certain aspects of this question have not been given proper consideration. After the war, two million Germans were expelled from the Sudeten region of Czechoslovakia, and other millions were driven out of the German provinces which became part of Poland. These people will now commence procedures to get back the property that they had lost. This, by the way, also will be the case with Jews, who are already beginning to express interest in their lost property. Although the demands for property compensation are expressed by organizations of German emigrés, on an apolitical private basis, they may still create extremely complex cultural, political, and humanitarian problems. Beyond the wish to liberate property, these demands express obvious aspirations and longing for regions which had belonged to the German cultural sphere.

More than anyone, we Israelis should be able to understand these demands. If one thinks about the analogy with Israel, we are demanding to retain the rights of prayer and of ownership of land in Nablus, regardless of the political future solution found for the occupied territories. So what is wrong with the Germans wishing that Königsberg, the city where Kant was born, will regain its original name, rather than the name given to it by the Soviets in honor of their president Kalinin. After all, we are dealing with a German culture which has a long lineage, which prevails throughout the intermediate regions between eastern and western Europe, as well as in islands of German presence deep within Russia. To my mind, therefore, we shall see a reinvigorated expansion of German culture, both officially—for instance, through cultural agreements—and unofficially.

Would you describe this development as threatening?
Nobody can predict whether this development will be perceived in Germany itself as merely functional, or whether it will trigger feelings of omnipotence, which will then form the basis for renewed nationalistic sentiments.

What will be the consequences of the emergence of such a powerful state for western Europe?
One can only wonder. You see, we have here a tree, one of whose branches turns out to be heavier than the whole; so it is questionable whether this European tree, which two years ago seemed in excellent condition, buttressed by economic and political unity and by the gradual obliteration of internal borders, will now be able to preserve its balance.

Would you say that some of the other European partners will now refuse to remain part of this tree?
So far, all indications for such a development are only on the level of emotional reactions. If you visit the Netherlands or Norway, those small countries known for their anti-German feelings, you encounter not only fear, but also hostility. The French quote De Gaulle's famous dictum, that he loves Germany so much, that he is glad to have not merely one but several; while in Britain Mrs. Thatcher expresses typical conservative British nationalism. But these reactions are superficial, and will not upset the economic processes.

Regarding future developments, when one is faced with the power of the D-mark as the dominant currency, around which all the other European currencies have to line up; when one witnesses how the German economy is purchasing chunks of other Western economies; when one sees an interminable influx of German tourists buying houses along the Mediterranean coast, one begins to wonder, whether all this will not provoke stronger reactions in the days to come.

With your permission, let us move now to the Jewish perspective.
Let us begin with some evaluation of the facts. I have just returned from Germany, where a biochemist friend from Frankfurt has said some things to me which are typical of prevalent trends. He admitted that indeed one can hear unpleasant nationalist and anti-Semitic expressions coming from East Germany. This is explained, he said, by the fact that these people were never forced to struggle with their national past, since the heavy Marxist presence muted every argument, and confined German history only to its official interpretation. Now that their world has collapsed, some unpleasant sounds can be heard, but they are dwarfed by the momentous historical events, and will disappear once the liberal tendencies strengthen their grip. I believe my friend

was justified in saying that such voices have so far not proved to be anything more than marginal.

How will the relations between Germany and Israel, and between Germans and Jews, change?

These relationships will undergo only minor changes. After all, since the reparation agreement (of 1952) we are living, whether officially or non-officially, in a political and economic symbiosis with the Germans. Although not necessarily too meaningful, it is worth noting that the favored second foreign language in our universities is not French, but German. On the one hand, relations will continue to improve. On the other hand, those special German investments induced by a particular German commitment toward us, for instance in Israeli universities, may be diminished. Now we shall be reduced to our due place within German priorities.

In his most recent declaration, the Chancellor Kohl addressed the Jewish community, and promised, naturally, that Germany will never forget what had happened to the Jewish people. But every now and then the Germans talk about the "finish line," beyond which the Germans would have no further particular commitments toward the Jewish people. They tried to fix this line in the affair of the Waffen-S.S. cemetery in Bitburg, but this provoked a strong reaction among Jews and among the German left; yet eventually this moment will come.

And for us this will hurt, as we wish the world to remember our scars forever . . .

I would like to disagree. I am not sure that all of us see it that way. Israel has an intermediate generation, now aged 40 or 50, born in Israel, mostly indeed of German Jewish extraction, which would like some distance from the historical past, and prefer a healthy German identity, as opposed to the Jewish or Israeli-Jewish wish to continually commemorate the past, either emotional or for more practical reasons. It is true, though, that many others, even of the young generation that had not experienced the Holocaust, manifest extraordinary interest in it.

And yourself, being a Holocaust survivor, what is your emotional reaction to the latest developments in Germany and in Europe?

In my work, I had tried to distance myself from personal sentiments, until I came to realize that the historian's attempt to dissociate himself from his feelings creates only an illusion of objectivity. Hence, it is better to articulate explicitly this emotional stance, in order to be able to control it, and to allow a well-defined angle for others to review his findings. This approach has been advocated also by some formidable colleagues. I can say that I am attempting now to deal in an objective manner with my subjectivity.

What is your current interest in your historical work?
I am thinking about the ways in which the Nazi period is represented in art and in historical writing. That is to say, how events are reflected through the distorting mirror of private and collective consciousness. Incidentally, this seems also to have been the subject of our conversation.

East Germany, Why Hast Thou Forsaken Us?

by Nahum Barne'a

Nahum Barne'a, born in 1944, is a prominent Israeli journalist. This article is reprinted from *Yediot Aharonot*, 9
October 1990.

Now that East Germany has been engulfed by the womb of the Great Germany, now that one member of the Likud wears sacks while his colleagues
are on their way for a tour of fun and money-raising in the unified Germany,
now is the last opportunity to say a few longing words in the memory of East
Berlin.

I visited there twice, on journalistic missions, each time only for a few
hours, coming over from West Berlin. Passing from one side to the other gave
me great satisfaction, perhaps the only real satisfaction I could ever feel in
Germany. Only then was it conspicuously apparent, in a clear and tangible
way, that the Germans had been defeated in the Second World War, and were
duly punished for it.

I loved the wall that tore this city in half. I loved the observation turrets
and the soldiers of the Russian Occupation Army which strolled along it as
if it were their own. I loved the partially demolished Potsdam station, the
railway cars which were left as they had been in the forties. The rudeness of
the uniformed personnel toward civilians who wished to cross over through
Check Point Charlie. Their behavior reinforced all my stereotypes of Germany: and this had a tranquilizing effect.

My eyes could not have enough of reviewing again and again the ruins of
the bastions of power of the Nazi regime: the isolated Reichstag building, the
blocked Brandenburg Gate, the ruined buildings—indeed, whole streets—on
the Eastern side. I enjoyed strolling in the Unter den Linden, in front of the
eternal flame commemorating the dead of the Red army. The Russian soldiers,
marching heavily back and forth, were a proper reminder of the chaos.

I loved the poverty of people's clothes, of the facades of their houses; the
long queues, the cold emptiness of Alexanderplatz, the pitiful shelves in
impoverished stores. A visit to the East entailed a joy of revenge, which was
particularly wonderful for being easily within reach, harmless. The process is
inevitable, they said, and there is no point in trying to prevent it. It entails
dangers—Germany has proven in the past that success and power cause her

to lose her mind—but also positive potential. A hungry Germany was much more of a danger to the world in the past than a content Germany.

On the whole, it seems that more than the mind revolting against reunification, it is the heart that feels the pain: as if the outcome of the Second World War was appealed to the supreme court of history, who declared Germany victorious.

I heard Elie Wiesel protesting on Israeli television against German reunification, and I was with him. Then he complained that "world Jewry" was not consulted (not in order to prevent, but to prove that consultations take place) and he lost me completely. It is possible to protest against reunification, and it is possible not to. But what is the point of protesting that your stamp of approval was not requested?

Since the reparation agreements between Israel and Germany, Israel and the Jewish establishment work under the assumption that we have established a permanent stronghold in the realm of the German conscience. This belief, understandable and authentic as it may be, is of lesser consideration to the German establishment today than in the past. For the Germans, the relationship with Israel is not a precondition nor a guarantee for Germany's normalcy. What they want is to extend eastward the foundations which allowed West Germany to be a democratic, stable, successful state.

The horrible failure of the Nazi adventure forced the Germans to assume an air of humility. No more Germany over all. Now they shall be tested for their ability to preserve, within their great victory, something of their previous lesson. This will not be easy.

I watch the triumphant celebration in Germany and like many other Jews grit my teeth. But we should not try to forcefully extract from the Germans a gesture of sadness, in remembrance of the Holocaust. They do not deserve this favor. We do not deserve this beggary.

The Unification of the Germanys—
A World Disaster

by Yonah Cohen

Yonah Cohen, born in 1920, is a journalist. This article
first appeared in *Ha'Zofeh*, which is aligned with the National Religious Party, on 17 November 1989.

There is little doubt that this week's events in East Germany are a historical
moment, whose consequences will become apparent to the world only in the
years to come.

Initially, the free world welcomes the transformation of East Germany from
a communist regime to a democratic one, along Western norms. But in a
deeper vision, the world remembers well the catastrophes brought about by
a unified Germany, which had caused two world wars. Dividing Germany into
two separate states, and stationing foreign troops there, were but a minimal
punishment and a grave warning against even the shadow of a possibility of
a third world war, a muzzle forced upon the uncontrollable German lust for
power.

Already the first four words of the German anthem, the anthem of the
millions of cruel murderers, "Germany, Germany over all," express clearly
the evil and arrogant aspiration to be "over all." German democracy is also
different from that of other enlightened nations. In a "democratic" process,
in "free" elections, was that man, the arch-murderer, brought to power. With
little difficulty he mobilized so many, so many of his people into his cruel
murderous machine, destroying millions of Jews: many teachers and educators,
doctors and musicians, professors and scientists, as well as plain Germans and
Poles.

The command we have been given by the death of the holy and pure
millions, of the millions of men and women, children and infants, was, "remember and do never forget." It is our duty, as the Jewish people, to lead
the determined opposition to this idea of the reunification of the two Germanys. The separation of the wicked is what they deserve and what the world
deserves.

A unified Germany, a bloc of eighty million people, can bring a disaster
upon the world. Gradually she will attain supremacy over the economy of
Europe. Soon a unified Germany will achieve independent nuclear armament
and further expansion of military power; these, in turn, will fuel the aspiration
and lust for domination. While seeking power, accompanied by a reinforced

national—and nationalist—pride, they will not hesitate to trample upon every human and moral value. Her army will immediately be prepared to submit the European states, striving to satisfy this unquenchable thirst for universal domination, following their anthem: Germany, Germany over all.

The United States and Europe, motivated by honest concern for their safety and security, will need to keep the happenings in Germany under close scrutiny, to maintain foreign troops in East Germany, and to impose limitations on the expansion of the military power of the Germanys. Albeit such an imposition did supply the Nazis with a poignant propagandistic weapon against the United States during the Second World War.

The effort to prevent the reunification of Germany is the concern and duty of all of the free world, and the Jewish people must have a crucial role in this determined and relentless resistance.

Czechoslovakia

Speech on 15 February 1990 on the occasion of the visit of President Richard von Weizsäcker to Prague

by Vaclav Havel

Vaclav Havel, born in 1936, is a playwright and the president of Czechoslovakia. He was imprisoned for his dissident activities under the Czech communist government.

On 15 March 1939 a madman in jackboots ended our first attempt at building a democratic state when he entered this castle and announced that force had triumphed over freedom and human dignity.

He came here as the herald of war. The herald of violence. The herald of lies. The herald of pride and evil, of injustice and cruelty. A mass murderer came here, a perpetrator of genocide.

Who let this man in here? Who allowed him to desecrate these ancient halls?

Above all it was a group of his fellow countrymen, who succumbed to his primitive appeal to malice, to archetypal visions and national and social yearnings.

Furthermore it was the limitless short-sightedness of the governments of France and England at that time, who believed that they could rescue peace by opening the door to this herald of war.

And finally it was the fear of our own political leadership to rise up against a predominant power and risk great sacrifices. It was a fear perhaps sustained by a sense of a shared responsibility for the supercilious conduct of our then state towards the rights of national minorities, the result of which was that many Czechoslovak citizens of German nationality allied themselves with that madman against their own state.

Today, standing at the beginning of our second experiment in democracy and remembering what happened fifty-one years ago, we welcome another guest in our castle.

A representative of German democracy. A herald of peace. A herald of decency. A herald of truth. A herald of humanity. A bearer of the message that force must not triumph over freedom, lies over truth and evil over human life. A man who has said that nothing must be forgotten, because memory is the source of hope in salvation.

Fifty-one years ago the enemy came here uninvited. Now at our invitation a friend is here.

The visit then brought death to prewar democracy. The visit today is a greeting to our new democracy.

The visit then was the beginning of the misfortune of our century. The visit today coincides with the end of that misfortune.

Our guest then led us to oppression. Our guest today congratulates us on our new won freedom.

I believe that we are experiencing an important day, important for many reasons.

Above all it could be a beginning of a new act in the thousand year Czech-German drama, in which tension, conflict and struggle are inexorably bound up with fruitful cooperation and a deep mutual influence. In this new act, after the bitter experiences of recent history, the second group of themes can at last predominate over the first.

The time is ripe to clasp each other's hand with a friendly smile and the certainty that we do not need to fear each other, because we are united by a common and heavily paid respect for human life, human rights, citizens' rights and general peace.

This common point of departure offers great horizons of possible cooperation. We can together work for a democratic Europe, for Europe as unity in plurality, for Europe with no more war but rather tolerance, for Europe continuing her best cultural traditions, for Europe no longer polluted by poisonous smoke and deadly water.

We agree that the fundamental precondition for the true friendship of our peoples is truth. However hard it is, the truth must be told.

Our guest has for his nation said many hard truths about the suffering that many Germans have inflicted on the world in general and us in particular. Or to put it more accurately: the ancestors of many present Germans.

Have we too succeeded in saying on our side what should be said? I am not sure of it.

Six years of Nazi rage sufficed to infect us with the bacillus of evil, so that we denounced each other during the war and after, and so that we took up in just but also exaggerated outrage the principle of collective guilt. Instead of trying in a proper fashion those who had betrayed their state, we chased them out of our country and imposed on them a penalty unknown to our laws.

That was no punishment but revenge. And in addition we chased out many not on the basis of proved guilt but because they belonged to a specific nation. Thus in the assumption that we were smoothing the path of historic justice, we inflicted suffering on many innocents, chiefly women and children.

And, as it seems to be usual in the course of history, we inflicted suffering not only on them, but also on ourselves. Our reckoning with totalitarianism brought its germ into our own actions and our own soul, and we were soon repaid with the inability to confront another totalitarianism, imported from somewhere else. Yes, there was even more: many of us actively helped this totalitarianism.

In another way our decision then was repaid. By devastating a substantial area of our country, we let devastation into our own country.

The sacrifices required in reparation will also be in part the price for the errors and sins of our fathers.

We cannot undo history, and so apart from a free investigation of truth we are left only with one option: of always greeting in friendship those who come in peace to bow at the graves of their ancestors and see what remains of the villages in which they were born.

The relationship of Germany to the family of European peoples and the relationship of that family to Germany is by tradition—simply because of its size, power and central position—the most important element in European stability.

That is also true today. All of Europe must thank the Germans for beginning to tear down the Wall that divided them, because they also tore down the Wall that separated Europe. But despite that, many Europeans still fear a united Germany.

I believe that this gives Germans a great historic opportunity. It is their responsibility to drive fear away from Europe. If they for instance succeed in confirming unambiguously their frontiers, including that with Poland, and in dealing with those who still flirt today with Nazi ideology, they will reduce European fears and Europe will not oppose their unification.

It is also up to Germans whether their unity is a welcome motor to drive for European unity, or a brake. In their own interest they should bring to this project their well known love of order. If it is conducted hastily or chaotically, as a chance product of electoral speculation, this cannot increase the trust-worthiness of Germany.

If on the other hand everything is conducted sensibly, we will soon live the day for which Europe has long waited: the day on which the Second World War is ended and all its terrible consequences overcome, including the division of Europe and the existence of huge pyramids of weapons in the two halves of the continent.

If everything runs rationally and in an atmosphere of mutual trust, this day might come already in the year after next and it will certainly be happier than the peace settlement that ended the First World War. Then Europe can embark on its long wished for dream: a friendly union of free peoples and democratic states based on common respect for human rights.

The forty-five years since the end of the fighting are a sufficient distance to make a truly wise treaty, unmoved by any anger, however comprehensible that might be.

It is clear that the future of all depends today again above all on German developments.

In this situation who can be surprised that the newly born democratic Czechoslovakia is interested in the events in both German states?

Who can be surprised at me for visiting both German states just three days after my election?

Who can be surprised at us for receiving so gladly in Prague's Hradcany castle a guest who for us embodies the best spiritual traditions of Germany?

Who can be surprised that we accord to today such importance, as two peoples long separated by suspicion join hands?

I have spoken of the historic duties facing Germany today. I should also say what we should do.

Here too after all that has happened there is still much fear of Germans and a big Germany. People are still alive who have experienced the war, lost loved ones, suffered in concentration camps and hidden from the Gestapo. Their suspicion is understandable, and it is natural that others share it. From this comes our task of overcoming this fear.

We must at last understand that it was not the German people that injured us, but specific human beings. Evil will, blind obedience, lack of concern for the neighbor—all these are characteristics of individuals, not of peoples.

Or did we not have enough bad Czechs and Slovaks? Were there not in our midst enough informers for the Gestapo and later the secret police? Was there not our own indifference and egoism, which allowed us to devastate our land over decades and to be silent, in order not to endanger our bonuses and our peace in front of the television set?

In addition, it was the Nazis who insidiously managed to identify their cause with that of Germany. We should not follow them! If we make their lie our own, we will only carry on further their destructive madness.

Occasionally peoples disliked men who spoke another language, especially if it was the language of a tyrant. But the language cannot be responsible for the tyrant who spoke it. To judge someone by language, skin color, descent or shape of the nose is to be consciously or unconsciously a racist.

To condemn Germans as such, or Vietnamese, or the members of any other people, or to fear them, is to be the same as an anti-Semite.

In other words: to accept the thought of collective guilt means directly and unavoidable to weaken individual responsibility and guilt. And that is something very dangerous.

If we only think how many of us were still recently deprived of our individual responsibility by the observation that we were willy nilly Czechs and could not change. This sort of consideration is the beginning of moral nihilism.

Of course there are things which distinguish us as Czechs and Slovaks from each other and from others. We have different preferences, different tastes, different memories and experiences. But we are not good or bad simply because we are Czechs or Slovaks or Germans or Vietnamese or Jews.

Blaming the German people for the guilt of individual Germans means removing the individuals' guilt and plunging them into the anonymity of a pessimistic fatalism. And depriving ourselves of every hope. It would be the same if someone said we were a people of Stalinists.

Suffering obliges us to be just, not unjust. Those who have really suffered usually know this.

In addition forgiveness—and with it one's own freedom from anger—can only come from justice.

Today seems to me to be important for another reason.

I do not know whether in the future multi-polar world Germany will be called a Great Power or not. But she has long been a potential Great Power: as a pillar of European spirituality that, if she wishes, can help us all to defy the dangerous pressure of technological civilization with the stupefying dictatorship of consumerism and a ubiquitous commercialization, leading to precisely that alienation analyzed by German philosophers.

After Germany has definitely constituted its statehood, long the goal of the practical occupation of her systematically ordering spirit, she will be able to use her creative potentials without reservation for a renewal of global human responsibility, this only possible salvation for the world of today, and one for which the spirit of the German philosophic tradition is particularly suited.

If today is a small step towards understanding in Europe, it may also be a small step in the awakening out of the narcosis induced by the daily effects of an ethical materialism without conscience, whose symptoms include the feeling that after us will come devastation.

Honored friends, I believe the visit today by President Richard von Weizsäcker to be the true opposite of that painful visit of the past which we remember today. If that visit was a sign of the terror to come and of a growing desperation, today's visit brings hope to us all.

It is the hope for a world whose center is the individual human being, whose questioning vision lifts up to the heavens in order to draw from there that mysterious power which alone is capable of bringing moral order to our souls. It is that which today constitutes the main guarantee of a meaningful future for humanity.

Poland

Both Partners and Competitors

by Jerzy Eysymontt

Jerzy Eysymontt became minister for the Central Planning Office in the administration of Kryzystof Bielecki in 1991, and developed into a critic of immediate economic liberalization. This article was published in *Tygodnik Solidarnosc* on 19 January 1990.

Our state enters the year 1990 in a changed form—as the Polish Commonwealth with a crowned eagle, without the leading role of the Polish United Workers' Party, but instead, with a convertible currency even though it is far from the stability of the Polish interwar currency which also bore the crowned eagle. We also enter this year in the context of a transformed international environment. In almost all those countries which only a few months ago had been ruled by communist monoparties and had been members of the seemingly stable and united so-called socialist camp, the system of government crumbled in a matter of days. Czechoslovakia, East Germany, Rumania and also, though less dramatically so, Bulgaria, all became countries making great strides toward the goal of becoming multiparty democracies on the Western model.

It is inevitable that all those countries will make radical changes in their economic systems toward the creation of market economies. As a result, Poland will cease to preoccupy Western public opinion, and we will cease to be an exceptional phenomenon. Even though we started first, today the interest of the West is directed toward others. Certainly we are glad that other nations have achieved political freedom because this process insured the irreversibility of changes in the region. We cease to be an island in a sea of hostility. At the same time, however, the Polish economy encounters new challenges.

Above and beyond everything else, numerous competitors for Western credits and various kinds of economic assistance have emerged. Poland is the largest debtor country in the Eastern Bloc, which by itself puts us in a disadvantageous position. Creditors are more willing to lend to someone who is not already deeply in debt. This, however, is not our only disadvantage.

Despite their different political systems, there are strong and old economic ties between the East German Democratic Republic and West Germany. In the context of current changes, independently of the pace and form of the unification, the interest and attention of the government of West Germany and West German businessmen will be directed immediately across their eastern border.

317

Czechoslovakia, especially the Czechs, have traditionally strong economic links with Germany. The economies of both East Germany and Czechoslovakia, although technologically lagging behind the developed Western countries, are nevertheless more robust than the Polish one. The Hungarian economy has also enjoyed a better reputation in the West than the Polish one. And as far as the emotional and moral justification for aid is concerned, Rumania is at this point more entitled to it than we are.

Irrespective of the current political situation, political sympathies and antipathies, there are some more general factors that need to be considered. For several decades the Eastern Bloc has been separated from the world by the proverbial iron curtain and with an entirely real Berlin Wall. We were not able to take advantage of many civilizational breakthroughs that took place in the West, while at the same time our business firms were protected from competition in quality with the outside world. We made some technological progress, but it was never integrated with progress in Western developed nations. On the other hand, economic relations between states in the Eastern Bloc were artificial; administrative "coordination of plans" and narrow specialization displaced authentic trade and competition.

When today the Berlin Wall crumbles and the curtain has rusted through, we face an entirely new situation. Our economy, by means of, for example, making currency convertible, must open to the world.

The relations within the countries of the Council for Mutual Economic Assistance (CMEA = Comecon) must undergo radical transformation. The effort to catch up with Western civilization will take place in the context of competition. Our industry must compete not only with those of West Germany, France, or Britain, but also with Czechoslovakia, Hungary, East Germany, and perhaps Rumania and Bulgaria. These developments will be ruled not by sentiments but by sound economic calculations. Only the effective and the innovative, and therefore competitive producers, will be attractive partners to cooperation.

This new context creates not only chances but also challenges. For businessmen, workers, engineers, farmers, and scientists. For everyone. We start from low levels of productivity, great needs for energy and an uneconomic use of materials in production, and equipped with only few technologies that stand up to Western standards.

If the businesses of our neighbors, now free from bureaucratic constraints, get ahead of us, we will find ourselves in an even more difficult situation. They—like us—will soon open their economies in an attempt to take the best possible position on world markets. Polish television sets and farm products must be better and cheaper than the foreign ones. We should not protect our producers from competition in an artificial way, because in this way the Polish consumer would suffer losses. These are banal truths, generally accepted, but unfortunately only generally, and when the issue becomes more concrete, takes the form of a concrete situation in a concrete area of our economy, concrete factory, one immediately hears argument about the need for state protection in this and that "exceptional case," protection also from competition from abroad.

These difficulties, however, should not prevent us from seeing the opportunities. Poland has a chance to become an attractive economic partner. We are a nation of forty millions in the middle of Europe, and we are no more lazy and no less talented than others. A Pole abroad works efficiently, and so do Poles working in the newly created private firms. We have some valuable raw materials which our neighbors need. Poland may soon become a bridge which will connect the West and the East, with much benefit to ourselves.

Not Only for Ourselves

by Maciej Zalewski

Maciej Zalewski contributed to the Solidarity newspaper
Tygodnik Solidarnosc, which is associated with the Democratic Center. This article was in the 9 March 1990 issue.

Who needs Poland? Kisiel in the ninth issue of *Tygodnik Powszechny* writes in
a way that explicitly challenges our fears concerning the future of Poland. He
writes about Russia and Gorbachev with anxiety and also says: "Why in the
process of reconstructing our economy should we not seek help from a wealthy
and unified Germany, even at a price of concessions concerning the (what he
calls) 'unimportant' areas of Western Pomerania or the port of Szczecin?"
Now that the 'internationale' no longer constrains, everything goes.

About Germans Kisiel writes: "They are reliable, honest, hard-working,
humanist, democratic, loyal, loving, etc. However, when someone convinces
them that they should be angry, then their anger knows no boundaries!"

About our situation he writes: "I fear this periodical, unconscious fanaticism
of Germans as well as I fear the age-old, slave to ideology fanaticism of
Russians."

Kisiel spells out ideas which shock us. They are age-old and brutal, but
they do help one get rid of self-delusions. The time of nationalisms in Europe
is not over yet, the play between Great Powers is not finished, we need to
make efforts to maintain Poland on the surface. The Yalta order is over but
we still cannot feel secure or comfortable.

Kisiel does not give an answer to the question of who needs Poland (except,
of course, for Poland itself). As a result, his analysis, like all analyses which
explore only domestic factors, fails to account for the really important issues.

It is important that Poland should have a strong economy and a well-
developed political structure, and that it be self-governed by social groups.
Unfortunately these elements of domestic politics still remain in the sphere
of wishful thinking.

But what is Poland's international position today when the new balance of
power is being created in Europe? It is the strength of that position that will
dictate our politics toward our immediate neighbors and toward Europe.

Today, we do not need to fear the possibility of a dramatic reenactment of
the interwar history. Then Poland was strong in that it was sovereign, but,
more importantly, it was weak because Europe was unstable and its neighbors
had great power at their disposal while Poland was torn internally by problems
associated with the interaction of various minority groups.

Today Europe is different, and a different kind of expansionism characterizes our neighbors. Europe moves (or at least we would like to believe so) towards integration. Its integration does not rely on ideology, but stems from the requirements of civilizational progress. When the pivot of the world, the center of most movement and changes moves away from the Atlantic Basin to an extensive and exotic area of the Pacific, the only chance of the old Europe to preserve its power is integration. Integration, in turn, determines the degree of expansionism of our neighbors.

Germans face a gigantic task of the conquest of their Eastern territories. Up to the Oder. The border on the Oder is demarcated not only by military force. This border is also dictated, at least at the time being, by the economic capacities of West Germany. To conquer East Germany implies the need to assimilate it with the European market and that has a price tag attached to it (we are talking here about several hundred billion marks).

Poland in this situation gains in terms of time, but loses in terms of German capital interested in investing in the East.

Russians look at us yet differently. We are not, or at least we soon will not, be their launching pad for tanks going westward. We have become an economic basketcase for them and created doubts concerning the value of an alliance with us, an alliance whose value could increase only when accounts between us are settled clearly and honestly.

Who needs us then? Germans do. What we can offer them is consent to the form of unification. Moreover, Poland, a nation of forty million which enjoys Western sympathy, a nation that is undergoing the normalization of its relations with Russia, potentially constitutes a barrier to German eastern expansion. Poland could play that role at times when German politics is incoherent or aggressive. However, our cry "nothing about us without us" must not be too hysterical.

Russia also needs us. If we formulate the conditions for an alliance which might take into consideration the differences that divide us. If we prove that we are successful in moving away from communism by means of economic success and internal stability. Kisiel concludes that our new eastern policy has the chance for a successful start.

Attention—An Ambush!

by Ryszard Wojna

Ryszard Wojna was born in 1920 and became a journalist and political commentator immediately after the Second World War. He was a deputy member of the Central Committee of the Polish United Workers' party (Communist party) from 1971 to 1976, and a full member from 1976 to 1981. He holds many prizes, including the Order of the Banner of Labor, first and second class. This article was published in *Polityka* on 10 March 1990.

The events that are currently taking place in our country and around us in Europe will determine the course of international politics for a long time. Therefore, with great care and responsibility we should be able to separate the short-term elements in our foreign policy from what may have epochal meaning. Our diplomacy should be devoted to the differentiation between short- and long-term trends and to the creation of conditions for taking advantage of opportunities brought by the long-term tendencies.

However, as it is, our diplomacy moves away from the long-term view. The tactics of Chancellor Kohl have drawn us into a situation in which our past fears and hurt feelings are being reactivated. To put it simply, we are witnessing the awakening of an anti-German bias.

Is it an ambush designed to trap our future? Are we already caught in it? Now, against our will, are we supporting those in Germany who affirm their nationalism with a desire to perpetuate German-Polish antagonisms? Even though we encounter similar nationalistic phenomena in our recently freed democratic political life?

The essence of this ambush is that by activating the discussions about the Polish-German border, which in fact is not likely to be altered, we create a bad start to the process of forging good neighborly relations with the unified Germany. And these relations will to a large extent determine the shape of our Polish future, our chances to catch up with Western civilization.

Rightly so, we call for support concerning the legal guarantees of our German border upon our friends in France, Great Britain, and in the United States, and we do receive their sincere support. However, these are not the states who will have a decisive influence on our future just as they have not had it until now (well, perhaps except in Yalta . . .).

From the beginning of the eighteenth century, the Polish fate has been

322

played out between Germany and Russia. And there is nothing new that might indicate that this may change. Our future depends above and beyond everything else on our relations with these two neighbors.

The truth is that we will not catch up with the civilizational progress that characterizes the West without direct help from Germany. This is a new factor in Polish history. The road West leads through Germany and with Germany. We cannot circumvent it. We must establish our relations with them. But what we are doing instead is falling back into old ways of thinking, opening old sores, anxieties, and traumas.

Unless we speedily transform the unfortunate old doctrine of two enemies into a doctrine of two friends, we will not build a Poland that would fulfill our dreams and our needs.

This essay was already at the editor when Chancellor Kohl set forth two preconditions for the confirmation of the border. I ask myself whether it is a game calculated to save face in front of the nationalist right or whether it is calculated to create a leverage with the help of which the right will be able to maintain its influence on the climate of German relations with Poland.

The area of freedom within which people of good will on both sides can act is shrinking rapidly. Kohl pushes us into the past!

Dignified Partnership

by Anna Wolf-Poweska

Anna Wolf-Poweska is a professor in the Western Institute
of the University of Poznan, Poland. This article appeared
in *Polityka* on 24 March 1990.

Never before in postwar history have Poles faced such difficult tests in political maturity. We keep talking again and again about the return to Europe— through Germany. We keep reminding ourselves about the key role of a reconciliation with Germany in a process of building a new balance of power. However, how should we go about cooperating with a partner whom we fear and distrust? How to break away from this vicious circle?

The sick century which has given birth to fascism and communism is nearing its end. The liberation of European societies from totalitarian systems constitutes an optimistic starting point to a new century. An explosion of nationalistic feelings in the two German states and the unification taking place in front of our eyes are logical consequences of the processes started by Solidarity in Poland. We are now facing the inevitability of the process to whose creation we contributed. Therefore, instead of trying to turn the current of the river with a stick, we should rather think about ways of building a dignified partnership with a unified Germany.

Our society is learning today how to live in freedom. In order to achieve a full sense of security, we need to master one more task, namely living free from fears and anxieties concerning Germans.

In the difficult process of overcoming the traumas and apprehensions toward Germans much will depend on ourselves, our political maturity, tolerance, and the ability to judge critically our own attitudes. The celebratory gestures of reconciliation which accompanied Chancellor Kohl's visit to Poland are already behind us. Now on an everyday basis we have to fulfill the commitments and agreements that have been signed. Do we fully realize the difficulties we will encounter in this process?

The fully recognized German minority in Poland is an open card. What role is it going to play in our society? For both sides, the dialogue is going to be difficult.

The accumulated anger, still painful traumas, and mistrust of the Germans who live in western Poland sometimes explode in fits of aversion towards Polish neighbors. For those inhabitants of Gogolin who think of themselves as Germans and who were interviewed by West German magazine *Stern*, Poles represent the opposite of everything that is honest, pure, orderly, and Polish economic administration is a ruin which requires international supervision. The Silesian villages inhabited by Germans are given as a model that Poles, it is claimed, will never achieve. Likewise, German families are presented to Poles as models of communities in which men are hard working, women are faithful, and children well behaved.

For Poles the idea of a German minority inevitably implies the Fifth Column and the entire historical ballast attached to it. The different political conditions that we live in now force us to look at this problem in its complexity. However, this process of giving meaning to our everyday coexistence requires good will and willingness to make efforts on both sides. It may become a practical lesson of a dialogue between different cultures and a process of working out new forms of coexistence.

A danger of an economic *Drang nach Osten* [expansionism in the East] on the part of the German power is another cause of anxiety. It originates in the awareness that for Poland the process of distancing itself from political dependence on the Soviet Union is accompanied by economic dependence on the West, and in particular the West German Republic.

However, no one is going to help us in overcoming this anxiety. Whether we are going to be treated with benevolent forgiveness or with respect and understanding depends on our talents, our entrepreneurship, and good administration. The vision of German firms and joint ventures on Polish soil will not cause us nightmares only if we treat them not as an omen of an invasion but as a challenge to competition and mobilization.

The reconciliation with Germans cannot be limited only to intellectual elites of the two societies.

Recent years have brought an unquestionable progress in forging mutual contacts between various social groups, professional and age groups. More and more agreements are being implemented which will bring an invigoration of Polish-German cooperation in many areas. If we want the young people who work in those cooperative programs to be good ambassadors of Polishness, we have to instill in them an objective image of a German. There is an unquestionable need to introduce corrections in our school textbooks and to expand our knowledge about our German neighbors. In doing so we must follow the principle of intellectual honesty.

Many emotions are aroused by the tide of anti-Polish moods in the German Democratic Republic.

After years of artificial uniformization, when political thinking was free from extremisms of either rightist or leftist kind, freedom of speech has been introduced to our western neighbors. The unfulfilled national aspirations of Germans, subordinated for forty years to the imperial interests of the Soviet Union, have taken a form of a sudden eruption of nationalism. This is a price that the liberated societies pay for democracy and freedom. East Germans,

326 / When the Wall Came Down

just like Poles, Hungarians, Czechs, Bulgarians, and Rumanians are now in the process of forming civil societies. We shall trust that the main tone of political discussion in East Germany will be dictated by the forces interested in good neighborly relations with Poland and the forces that we associate with Prussian arrogance will be marginalized. The moods of the last couple of months have brought a realization both to Poles and to East Germans that a mutual friendship, expressed in decrees signed by ruling parties on both sides has established only a theoretical formula which we will need to fill with a concrete matter. Everything indicates that the main pivot in the process of normalization of relations with Germany will be East Germany. Notwithstanding the form of unification, there will be the same people living between the Oder and the Elbe [i.e. in the former territory of the GDR] and we will have to cooperate with them. And we must keep in mind that the dismantling of the Berlin Wall does not imply an automatic eradication of the differences between East and West. We still have ahead of us the task of abolishing the wall of distrust, apprehension, and sometimes even hostility that has grown between Poland and East Germany.

The German issue is for Poles a test in political realism. It is extremely difficult because it is taken against the historical experience and resentments.

However, the present and the future require us to undergo such a test. Our nation, which will forever remain a neighbor of Germany, needs a profound reevaluation of its perceptions of Germans. This does not imply a total oblivion of the past, the ignorance of extremisms and a lack of criticism toward different political options. I believe that the following thought expressed by Emmanuel Mounier in 1947 provides a good guideline for dealing with our current task: "We trust that Germans will withstand the temptations of the past, the return of which everyone wants to prevent in their own country; let the chain of alert guards and Europeans united in brotherhood bring light to our dark times." The "Brotherhood of Europeans" can be a guarantee that the situation from fifty years ago will not repeat itself.

Opportunity Rather Than a Threat

by Adam Michnik

Adam Michnik, born in 1945, is a Polish historian. He is editor-in-chief of Warsaw's daily *Gazeta Wyborcza*, and is a deputy to the Polish parliament. He was a leading dissident during the Communist regime in Poland and organized the KOR (Committee for the Defense of the Workers). His publications include *Letters from Prison and Other Essays*. This article was translated for the *New York Times* of 27 September 1990.

I view German reunification as the realization of the just aspirations of the German nation to live within its own state.

Looking back at the collapse of the Berlin wall, I would like to affirm that miracles can occur in our unsettled century, and that those who are directed by justice are right, and not those who follow pure political realism.

It was impossible to maintain the division of Germany, since East Germany was an artificial creation of Soviet policy. To paraphrase the well-known words of Mirabeau, I would affirm that East Germany was not a state having Soviet bases within it, but a Soviet base with a state within it.

A new and powerful German state is arising in Europe today. The history of the last hundred years taught Europeans to distrust a powerful Germany. This efficient, highly skilled and disciplined nation once succumbed to the temptations of nationalism and expansionism. For many, the memory of this continues to be the source of fear.

I do not share this fear, but rather I see in a united Germany an opportunity rather than a threat. An opportunity, because a German state written into the concert of European nations and states can only strengthen democratic Europe and democratic tendencies on the continent.

Nevertheless, I also perceive a threat. The nature of such a threat lies in our unclear picture of the psychology of the Germans from the east. These are the Germans who did not live through the process of de-Nazification. They are the Germans who never felt the guilt of Nazi crimes. And finally, they are the Germans who are now doomed to uncritical searching into the collective national memory and to frustrations related to the process of economic transformation.

It is extremely difficult to say today what effect these Germans will have on an all-German community and on the European Community. And yet this is a fundamental question, for what Europe will be depends to a large extent on what Germany wants. A democratic Germany will foster democratic tendencies. A Germany ruled by nationalist vanity will further the development of nationalist tendencies in post-Communist Europe.

This Is One Party I Think I'll Miss

by Marek Edelman

Marek Edelman is the only surviving leader of the Warsaw Ghetto uprising against the Nazis of 1943. He was a critic of the Polish Communist regime. This letter was sent to the German Ambassador to Poland, Guenter Knackstedt, on 1 October 1990. It was first reprinted in the *New York Times* on 15 October 1990.

Dear Mr. Ambassador,

Thank you very much for your kind invitation to a reception celebrating German unification. Unfortunately, I will not be able to take part in these celebrations.

The division of Germany was not a punishment for the war lost by Germany or the inhuman crimes of the Nazi regime. It was a result of the military and political situation at the end of the war. Similarly, the unification of Germany is not a result of the Germans' struggle for unity, but an effect of the political, economic and military power relations in the world today. It is a gift from the victorious United States and the collapsing regime of the Soviet Union.

I am very far from accusing the whole German nation of the Nazi crimes. I know that many Germans opposed the Nazi regime, although I have never met one of them during the course of my life; as a matter of fact, I have not encountered even those who simply refrained from doing evil and remained inactive. But this was probably an accident.

A few months ago, I asked Chancellor Kohl for his help on behalf of the Solidarity Health Foundation in its fight against cancer in Poland. The Chancellor responded that his budget was so tight that he could not help us. As we could see a few months later, much greater sums could be found to help other people when, I am sorry to say, German interests were at stake.

In addition, the recent attitude of the Chancellor's government toward Polish citizens does not—to say the least—evoke my enthusiasm. In my modest opinion, it is a sign of a narrowness of vision, if not xenophobia.

I hope you will excuse me, Mr. Ambassador, if I do not drink champagne with you this time.

Soviet Union

Political Diary: Germany, Victory or Defeat?

by Aleksandr Bovin

Aleksandr Bovin is a political commentator in the (former) Soviet Union. This piece was originally published in *Izvestiya* on 14 November 1990.

The documents regulating cooperation between the Soviet Union and Germany, which were signed Friday [9 November], open a new stage in the development of Soviet-German relations. Instead of GDR Germans and FRG Germans, our partners will again be "simply" Germans—the inhabitants of Germany.

The first time Germany was united by Bismarck, after he conquered France. The second time, 120 years later, by Gorbachev, after he conquered himself. . . .

Judging by the letters which I receive, many Soviet people are alarmed by what is happening. They write that the passiveness of our foreign policy has led to the loss of East Europe and the swallowing up of the GDR by the Federal Republic and NATO; they write that the breakup of the Warsaw Pact and CMEA has impaired the international position of the USSR and weakened its security. It is possible, of course, and frequently even necessary, to put on a brave face if things are going badly, but there is no denying that, having allowed the FRG to seize the GDR and having allowed the West to incorporate GDR territory in NATO, we have suffered a political defeat. This is what many people write.

And I understand them. I respect their feelings. But after all, politics do not boil down to feelings. Is it a victory or a defeat? Psychologically, it is possible to pose this question. But the answer to it can be provided only by logic, by a logical analysis of the given political processes and phenomena. Let us consider this together.

Let us begin with what is most important. Did we fight for the division of Germany? No. This is not at all what we wanted. We wanted something else. We wanted Germany to cease being the source of the threat of war, of aggression.

The existence of two German states, the preservation of the rights of the victor-powers, and the general balance of forces in the world between East and West did, of course, remove the German threat as such. It was possible to pretend that the German question had been resolved. But it was impossible

333

to ignore that the division of a single nation and the dissatisfaction with this situation in both parts of Germany were creating an alarming uncertainty at the very center of Europe.

The prevailing status quo could, obviously, have been maintained for a relatively long time. However, the people and history decided otherwise. The breaching of the Berlin Wall set off a chain reaction of changes which led to the unification of Germany less than one year later.

Now let us ask ourselves the following question: What specific changes of a military-strategic nature does the unification of Germany entail? The territory controlled by NATO will increase by approximately 10,000 square kilometers. The human potential of NATO will increase by 17 million persons. In a few years' time the last Soviet soldier will quit the territory of what used to be the GDR. And that is all. If we take into consideration that we are not living in 1941 but half-a-century later, that the emergence of nuclear weapons has fundamentally changed the notion of security, and that the changes which are taking place in no way disrupt or impair the general balance of forces, then any talk about deterioration of the USSR's military-strategic position loses all real substance.

- Especially since the FRG will become an active participant in the future deep cuts in Armed Forces and armaments in Europe.
- Especially since the FRG has renounced the possession of chemical, biological, and nuclear weapons.
- Especially since the FRG has signed all conceivable legal guarantees preventing the militarization of its foreign policy.

I foresee the following objections: Guarantees are merely words, documents, signatures. New generations of Germans, of German politicians will rise, and they will use different words and want to sign different documents. Theoretically, this is correct. History does not contain any absolutes, and that includes absolute guarantees. But it is important to understand that true guarantees are not words or letters, but real interests. For the present (and within the foreseeable historical future) no German interests require war. Germans do not need war. It will give them nothing, but may destroy everything (and this applies not only to the Germans). These are the real and reliable guarantees of peace in Europe. And if the development of Europe follows the Helsinki track—and so far it is difficult to imagine anything else— then the said guarantees will strengthen rather than weaken.

And another point: Could the Soviet Union have prevented the unification of Germany, could it have "not ceded" the GDR to West Germany? In abstract terms, it is impossible to deny that it probably could have done so. It could have done so, had it resorted to the use of military force to preserve the Berlin Wall and to build new walls wherever necessary. And then what? Even if it had been possible to prevent a third world war and a nuclear missile clash, we would have blown up detente and torn it into shreds, we would have again turned Washington from a partner into a foe, we would have resuscitated the worst kind of "cold war," and, undoubtedly, unleashed another spiral of the arms race. In my opinion, the game is not worth the candle.

But what matters is not only, or even primarily, this relatively primitive calculation. What matters is something else. In the second half of the eighties, we finally managed—with much delay but managed it nonetheless—to perceive the world around us such as it is. We managed to cast off anodyne illusions and grasp that the people and peoples whom the Soviet Army had liberated from fascism do not accept the Stalinist and neo-Stalinist models of "regimented socialism," that they do not want to occupy the position of junior partners, and that they condemn our armed interference in their affairs.

Realizing this was the first step. The second step was bringing our policy in line with this realization, and granting the "fraternal" countries freedom of choice. And finally, the third step was accepting this choice even that did not suit us. Within a very short time we traversed this path and, having won a victory over ourselves and our past, we brought our policy in line with the principles which we ourselves have proclaimed. This was the beginning of the healing of the division of Europe which was logically and politically completed with the unification of Germany.

Yes, we have lost. We have lost a world that we ourselves had created and that therefore suited us, where people obeyed us, and where we felt to be the most important and the smartest. The world which we acquired instead, in which we find ourselves, is more complex and contradictory. In it it is impossible to issue orders, it is necessary to negotiate. It is impossible to demand respect for yourself if you do not respect others.

Time will pass and the sense of loss and defeat, which stems from the fact that we are judging current events by yesterday's criteria, will become less painful and will disappear altogether. And that which we have gained—cooperation instead of enmity, disarmament instead of arms race, free circulation of ideas and people instead of visible and invisible walls—will become more obvious, significant, and tangible.

In conclusion, I will reiterate what I have said and written many times before. No one is threatening us. No one is getting ready to attack us. Both because "they" do not need war, and because we are sufficiently strong to be left in peace. Against this backdrop the new treaty with the new Germany is a major step forward in the creation of the new Europe. And consequently it is also a step forward in the consolidation of our international position and our security.

Germany and the 'Soviet Issue'

by Andrei Kortunov

Andrei Kortunov is a political scientist in the (former) Soviet Union. This piece first appeared in the *Moscow News Weekly*, No. 46, 1990.

The recent visit of the Soviet President to the Federal Republic of Germany was bound to be successful. Problems involved in the issue of the united Germany's future niche in Europe's structures, its membership in NATO, the status of Soviet troops stationed on German soil, and prospects of trade and other economic ties between the USSR and the FRG, were solved mainly before the visit, so that the two leaders had only to symbolically proclaim the agreements as "historic." Both participants in the Bonn meeting needed success for Helmut Kohl, that meant important advantage in the intra-party contest before the first all-German elections; for Mikhail Gorbachev, that meant further establishment of the USSR presidency and a boost in personal popularity, even given the background of deepening economic crisis and disintegration of political structures in the Soviet Union.

Perhaps, this explains both sides' grandiloquent speeches, mutual compliments and references to history, as well as some vague wording in the documents signed. Undoubtedly, both Mikhail Gorbachev and Helmut Kohl can consider the results of the visit a major victory: it built a political and legal basis for new Soviet-German relations, for the transition period as well as for a more distant future. The "German issue" as a factor of European and international politics has become as good as decided.

However, the solution of the "German issue" also means that the "Soviet issue" gets promoted to the forefront in European as well as world politics. The general outline of Germany's future is quite definite, while the future of the Soviet Union remains a controversial subject open to speculation. Today, even a dyed-in-the-wool German-hater would find it impossible to believe in a German threat to the world community. But the worldwide aftershock as a result of chaos and anarchy in the USSR is evident.

At present, the "Soviet threat" is assuming a new and unexpected aspect: even if we exclude the possibility of a militarist and anti-Western regime coming to power in Moscow, the political instability, ecological disasters, right-wing and left-wing extremism, millions of refugees could easily spill over the Soviet national borders and become an ever-present headache for Western leaders.

All other issues with which Europe is concerned today—NATO's future, development of the Helsinki process, West European integration, and the Vienna talks—would seem child's play compared with that issue. If the "Soviet issue" is not solved, then the building of the "common European home" would become senseless, but once the solution is found, the realization of the project will be purely a technical task.

Germany bears special responsibility for the solution of the "Soviet issue." For it, the stakes are particularly high, considering the specifics of her geographical position, the traditional links with Russia throughout history, and the FRG's economic potential. Should the USSR collapse, it would have greater repercussions on Germany than on the USA, watching the drama of *perestroika* from overseas. Should the Soviet reforms misfire, Germany would have to play the unenviable role of buffer between an agonized, impoverished and divided nation of 300,000,000 radicals, and an affluent, pragmatic, and democratic West. If Soviet *perestroika* succeeds, Germany will be the first country to enjoy the fruits of it and strengthen its own position on the continent.

However, it would be a mistake fraught with potentially dangerous consequences to indulge in the delusion that the FRG can play the role of an engine pulling our economy out of its slump. Germany's resources are limited, like the resources of any country. It will be spending a lot of its resources on economic and social integration of the former GDR. Poland, Czechoslovakia, and other East European countries are counting on German aid too.

Moscow's ability to really benefit from the German credits and to digest vast German capital investments remains a moot point. Certain presidential decrees and recent ministerial orders hamstringing Soviet enterprises in matters concerning their independence in making contracts, operating on foreign markets, in fact dampen the Bonn agreements from the point of view of practical business matters. Thus, Gorbachev the administrator nullifies the gains of Gorbachev the diplomat. The same is true of the issue of Soviet Germans: Germany is prepared to help them establish themselves in the Soviet Union, but the Soviet authorities haven't even solved the question of German autonomy and thus are encouraging their emigration.

Illusory hopes for a "generous German uncle" quickly evaporate in the face of strict laws governing free market operation. It will be regretful if our benevolent attitude towards Germans vanishes into thin air along with our hopes.

Avoiding a transformation of *perestroika*-related social problems into anti-German sentiments and xenophobia in general is a singularly important task which will partially determine the success of *perestroika*. The solution of the task, as well as the solution of other aspects of the "Soviet issue," depend on the Soviet administration to an infinitely greater extent than on the Soviet partners in world politics.

At the USSR Supreme Soviet

by Aleksandr Sergeyevich Dzasokhov

Aleksandr Sergeyevich Dzasokhov was chairman of the
Supreme Soviet International Affairs Committee. He gave
this speech at the Supreme Soviet in Moscow on 4 March
1991.

Esteemed members of the Supreme Soviet: Commencing the examination of
the treaties concerning the German settlement, I would say that in the process
of their ratification, the Soviet parliament is facing an exceptionally important
and responsible task—namely to strengthen the hope of the peoples of the
Soviet Union, the whole of Europe, and also of the whole world that it is only
peace that will from now on emanate from the German soil. This moral legal
norm, enshrined in the documents under examination, should become an
imperative for the present and future Germany. Such is the will of the wartime
and postwar generations of the Soviet people and mankind as a whole. Our
country, the Soviet people, have a moral right to be exacting regarding the
content of the treaty on the final settlement with respect to Germany and all
the Soviet-German documents. It is understandable, it is easily explained,
and it is timely to recall this. This summer we shall mark the 50th anniversary
of the start of the Great Fatherland War and Hitlerite Germany's attack on
the Soviet Union. Our country sustained sacrifices which cannot be compared
with anyone's or anything, in the name of our state's independence and the
liberation of the peoples of Europe. In connection with this, I would like to
recall, supplementing Deputy Kvitsinskiy's very thorough report, that the
Soviet Union did not set as its goal to divide Germany. It is the Western
allies, not the Soviet Union, that strove for Germany to be split. It is precisely
the West that advocated setting up the FRG. Right up until the end of the
fifties, the Soviet Union advocated unification of Germany.

Only after the leadership of the German Democratic Republic put forward
a concept of two German nations did the USSR change its position. It is also
important to state that the division of Germany was a consequence of the
cold war which divided the whole world and all Europe into two camps. The
end of the cold war made the overcoming of this division inevitable. The
postwar period could not go on forever, of course. The stay of our troops on
the territory of another country, for more than 41 years, is really unprecedented in the history of our state. But analyzing retrospectively our activities
and initiatives, I must say that we, of course, should have prepared earlier
for the end of this stay.

338

The following notion has taken shape: Documents which are being examined today are of special interest in a ratification process undertaken by the Supreme Soviet. This is also proven by the fact that the International Affairs Committee, the sittings of which were extensively attended by a large group of people's deputies, gathered three times and spent quite a number of hours with the participation of experts, international affairs specialists, economists, and political scientists representing large scientific centers dealing with international affairs. Discussions, without any exceptions, were always involved and were always open to questions. Following a deepened and all-around analysis, it was recognized that the package submitted has met the interests of the USSR in its consolidated results. A common opinion expressed advocated the ratification of the package of treaties and agreements concerning German settlement. Treaties and agreements submitted to ratification as well as other documents connected with them represent an interconnected system of international juridical obligations which basically create a new legal regime in relations between the USSR and the FRG, a normative frame for a future political structure in Europe.

This represented a distinguishing feature of the elaboration of these documents, because it took place against the backdrop of a vigorous European process, and it was important to normalize these two natural processes. The treaties and agreements submitted for ratification finally draw a line under the results of the Second World War, signifying the end of an entire period of military and political confrontation on the European continent. Naturally, each and every time and, particularly, when looking back at the past, the peoples of the Soviet Union, just as the peaceloving peoples of the planet, would like to believe in the letter and spirit of the treaties that are being adopted. At the same time, it is necessary to set oneself the goal of ensuring their full implementation. The settlement with respect to Germany was not accomplished by itself, but in the context of a different political atmosphere in Europe, a course aimed at creating new security structures within the framework of the continent. The central goal here is to set up a pan-European security system.

Adopting a decision to recommend the USSR Supreme Soviet to ratify the package of these international treaties and agreements, we also proceeded from the fact that they do not just have a political, economic, and military dimension, but that they also have a moral and psychological dimension: the emergent new atmosphere of mutual trust. All this was reflected in the course, nature, and results of the examination, because one had to take account of the most widely differing positions and viewpoints, expressed by the USSR people's deputies.

I will not now dwell upon the fundamental tenets, the outline of which is beginning to emerge thanks to the military and political aspects and bilateral relations as a result of the talks. Let me merely draw your attention to those questions which gave rise to particularly sharp discussions, namely, in the first place: As those that took part in the discussion pointed out, the documents under consideration today must not be superimposed upon the old conceptual model or the old political map of Europe. It is essential to project them onto a Europe where a fundamentally new reality is taking shape, which has come a long way from the ideas of the cold war era. The discussion of the documents in the International Affairs Committee and also the repeated discussions in the Defense and State Security Committee focused particular attention on aspects such as the state of the USSR's national security in the conditions of the altered balance of forces on the European continent and in the world as a whole, with the preservation, at this present stage, of the NATO bloc, the breakup of the Warsaw Pact and the rise in economic potential and political role of the unified Germany. All of these components provoked particularly substantial discussions.

The issue of the permanence and unchanging nature of the current European borders—very many views were also expressed on this issue, proposing an attentive attitude to the progress of implementing the points in the treaty, and to the working-out of our bilateral relations with the Eastern European states. There was also the issue of reparations and the prospects for the USSR's trade and economic relations with the lands which, prior to unification, were part of the German Democratic Republic. Talk was of finding ways of preserving and restoring the well-established trade and economic relations, including those at the level of one enterprise with another.

Further, the material and financial conditions of our group of forces' presence in Germany and the agenda and timescale for the withdrawal of the Western Group of Forces from the Federal Republic of Germany. Some very productive ideas were expressed on this matter about the necessity of setting up a special state program, with the Supreme Soviet playing the role of initiator. Compensation for people who were forcibly driven from the USSR to Germany during the war, and who were made to do forced labor, were also discussed. I must note that as regards the agenda for implementing the wishes of the deputies, the Ministry of Foreign Affairs, as Comrade Kvitsinskiy's recent visit to the FRG shows, has undertaken a number of measures to see that these issues move toward practical realization.

At the same time, the speed at which the process of German settlement proceeded, a truly cosmic speed, has led, unfortunately, to lack of necessary parliamentary monitoring of the progress in the talks and in preparing the documents. Deputies devoted their justified attention to this during the examination of the documents which had been submitted.

At the same time, we came to a firm conclusion and conviction that the package of treaties and agreements on German settlement meets the state interests of the Soviet Union. In terms of prospects, they open an opportunity to significantly step up cooperation with the united Germany, including cooperation in science, technology, trade, and economy, and to develop this cooperation on a constructive basis of international law.

I must note that the entire period since the documents on Soviet-German interaction which were submitted for our consideration were signed shows the disposition of the leadership of the Federal Republic of Germany to strictly follow the provisions of the treaties signed, and to confirm the course for political and economic cooperation with our country. This was illustrated in a very convincing way during the Persian Gulf crisis.

Finally, I must inform the Supreme Soviet that in the near future the FRG foreign minister is expected to visit the Soviet Union to turn to the content of the documents which have been mentioned again and again and to examine the prospects for their implementation in the spirit of benevolence. The International Affairs Committee has received hundreds of letters from war veterans, Soviet public figures, representatives of mass public organizations, which invariably express interest in the treaties on German settlement which are under examination. I think that we could confirm the course of the Soviet Union toward building new inter-state relations on the European continent by our attitude to ratification of these treaties.

At the same time, it would be advisable to adopt, on behalf of the Supreme Soviet, a political statement which reflects the will and aspirations of the Soviet people, prior to the adoption of such responsible decisions connected with the ratification of the treaties on a German settlement.

Japan

A New Rendezvous with Destiny

This unsigned editorial appeared in the *Japan Times* on 6 July 1990.

This week the two Germanys are struggling vigorously with the challenges and consequences of the formal economic union that went into effect on Sunday. Thus far, the process has met few snags. Except, that is, among non-German commentators.

Amid the flood of print about the impact of a united Germany—and that, in effect, is what has been achieved in all but name this week—there has been a conspicuous failure to look the new reality of German power in the eye and not flinch. This appears to be true particularly among pundits and analysts from the four principal victors of World War II, the United States, the Soviet Union, Great Britain, and France.

Even the administration of President George Bush, which has welcomed the prospect of German unification with a realism unmatched in London, Paris, or Moscow, still sees the problem as one of "anchoring" the new Germany in a variety of international bodies, the North Atlantic Treaty Organization (NATO) and others, that will keep things more or less as they were before 1989. This is a dangerous illusion because it implicitly neglects the power question.

Our point, in essence, is this: German power means that all its neighbors will have to learn to live with the reality of its growing influence. The eclipse of Soviet power in Eastern Europe therefore will not result in a new era in which small states will no longer be shadowed by larger ones.

This point appears not to have been lost on West German Chancellor Helmut Kohl, who is now on course to become the first head of a reunited Germany. In the recent furor over the German border with Poland, Mr. Kohl gave Europe a crucial first taste of what life almost certainly will be like under the new German dispensation that will take shape during the 1990s.

Where the four great Allied powers of 1945 have seemed to miss the point of the arm wrestling over the Oder-Neisse Line, the Poles mastered the lesson at once. The press of four decades of Soviet power on Polish affairs is not now going to yield to a never-never land of power considerations, but rather to a new diplomatic dynamic in which German influence will increasingly crowd European affairs as the Kremlin recalls its foreign legions.

Nature is said to abhor a vacuum. German power will ensure that there will be none. So the question is less one of anchoring Germany than of conceding the head seat at the table to the German government that shortly will re-establish Berlin as Europe's most important capital. This means that the formal economic union proclaimed this week, and the complete unification of Germany that should follow, perhaps before the end of the year, is the revolution that counts in the dramatic changes we have witnessed since last summer.

The fact that the Germans have forgotten their inflationary fears to make this revolution happen, the fact that Mr. Kohl has humbled even the *Bundesbank* to achieve it, should confuse no one about how events this week mark the end of the postwar era, and the beginning of something previously unexperienced in modern European affairs: German domination without war or barbarism.

German power, like Japanese power, is based not on arms or superpower pretensions, but on the economic discipline and social creativity of an entire society. This kind of power lends itself poorly to Red Square-style displays of military muscle. It therefore is frequently underrated. That can be a good thing. It makes the drive to build a borderless economy—call it internationalization or globalization—that much easier. Both Germany and Japan are committed to the goal.

For both the Tokyo of today and the Berlin of tomorrow, this power means enormous responsibilities. We are convinced that the burdens will be met, in both Eastern Europe and East Asia, wherever German and Japanese wealth and energy can be of use to human society.

But for the sake of the sane management of power relations among states in a complex world, such quiet strength must not be ignored. By virtue of their hard work, their commercial and manufacturing prowess, and now the approaching unification of their country, nearly 80 million Germans have earned the right to a larger say in world affairs. It must be given to them.

Germany's New Start and Japan

This unsigned editorial was published in the *Japan Times* on 3 October 1990.

Today Germany becomes one again. This is a momentous occasion, both for Europe and the world. It is certainly the most important consequence to date of the 1989 revolution against Communist rule and Soviet domination in Eastern Europe. The German Democratic Republic (East Germany)—Joseph Stalin's creation and the supreme symbol of the Soviet victory over Adolf Hitler's armies in 1945—is, as of this morning, no more.

The local implications of the unification of Germany will be lost on few Japanese. However divided this nation has been on the meaning of its defeat in 1945, on the balance sheet of losses and gains from the Allied Powers' occupation of 1945–52, or even on the pros and cons of our postwar Constitution, the Japanese public has been united in the perception that this country was lucky to have survived the war without being dismembered. This has without question been the chief lesson of the postwar German experience for the Japanese people.

Observing Germany's trauma has made us determined that the Northern Territories, which have been under Soviet occupation since 1945, be very soon once again part of the nation. The fate of these four islands, however small they appear on the map, should remind us that if history during crucial months of 1945–46 had taken even a slightly altered turn, we might be celebrating the demise of a "People's Republic of Hokkaido" this autumn. Our narrow escape from Soviet occupation should keep us mindful of the German tragedy that is just now ending.

The spectacle of German unification has other lessons to teach us. The birth of the "new Germany" has an undeniable feeling of a fresh start precisely because the German break with the past has been so thorough. Despite the evidence of a revival of German right-wing extremism and anti-Semitism, the German people have gone a long way toward mastering what German philosopher Theodor Adorno called his country's "unmastered past."

If the Germans have mastered their unhappy past, then the question, on this birthday of the new Germany, must be: "Have we mastered ours?" Our sanitized history textbooks, the intolerable racial slurs of our politicians, and indeed our curious ambivalence toward our global responsibilities all suggest that we still have much to learn from the postwar experience of our former Axis ally.

Postwar West Germany has also demonstrated, certainly to our critics abroad, that a new economic superpower can compete in world markets without needing to be "contained." The complaint that this nation pursues "adversarial trade" has pivoted on the perception that Germany, unlike Japan, not only practices fair trade but also can boast a genuinely open economy.

Senior West German businessmen who know Japan well have long argued that certain Japanese export tactics are unworkable in their country. They insist that Germany is too well integrated into the world economy and possesses too wide and diverse a manufacturing base to be able to indulge in the successful targeting of overseas markets in massive export drives. This Japanese skill may have to be unlearned.

In the current crisis in the Gulf, the difficulties of the new Germany illuminate with unique force some of the key dilemmas of Japanese foreign and defense policymaking. The postures of both Tokyo and Bonn have been severely criticized for their failing to rally either to the defense of international world order or of Western oil interests.

Despite the great economic power of Japan and Germany, it is Britain and France that have acted with vigor and purpose in the Gulf. Constitutional restraints aside, these old imperial powers retain a sense of global responsibility and of "national will" that Germany and Japan have lost since the war. Glib talk in some Japanese media about handing over the permanent seats of the United Nations Security Council now held by France and Britain to Japan and Germany is clearly out of step with the demands of world policing.

We are nevertheless convinced that by learning from each other, Germany and Japan can transcend their weakness and contribute in powerful ways to world peace and prosperity as the postwar era finally closes and a new century approaches. The world community will accept nothing else.

Permissions Acknowledgments

Grateful acknowledgment is made to the following for permission to reprint previously published material:

Al Ha'mishmar: "Unholy Trinity" by Shevach Weiss, 15 October 1990. Reprinted by permission of *Al Ha'mishmar.*

Avanti: "In Europa cambiano tutti gli equilibri" interview with Massimo Salvadori by Antonio Landolfi, 3 October 1990. Reprinted by permission of *Avanti.*

Corriere della sera: "Germania e la storia hanno fatto un salto" by Giuliano Ferrara, 27 December 1989. Reprinted by permission of *Corriere della sera.*

Dissent: "Germany: Power and the Left" by Andrei Markovits, Summer 1991. Reprinted by permission of *Dissent.*

Hans Magnus Enzensberger: "Rigamarole" by Hans Magnus Enzensberger from the 9 July 1990 issue of *Time* magazine. Reprinted by permission of Hans Magnus Enzensberger.

Le Figaro: "Nouvel orage sur un vieux couple" by Joseph Rovan and Georges Suffert, 18 March 1990. Reprinted by permission of *Le Figaro.*

Saul Friedlander: "Now We Shall Be Reduced to Our Due Place Within German Priorities," Saul Friedlander, interview in *Yediot Aharonot,* 3 October 1990. Reprinted by permission of Saul Friedlander and *Yediot Aharonot.*

Ha'aretz: "The Great Appeasement" by Arye Dayan, 7 September 1990. Reprinted by permission of *Ha'aretz.*

The Independent: "Germans Lack the Key to Their National Identity" by Ralf Dahrendorf, 13 April 1990. Reprinted by permission of *The Independent.*

Harold James: "Two Germany's Don't Add Up" by Harold James from the 3 December 1989 issue of *The Sunday Telegraph;* "West Germany's Green Imperialism" by Harold James from the 11 February 1990 issue of *The Sunday Telegraph.* Reprinted by permission of Harold James.

Henry Kissinger: "A Plan for Europe" by Henry Kissinger from the 18 June